DNS and BIND

DNS and BIND

Third Edition

Paul Albitz and Cricket Liu

O'REILLY®

Beijing · Cambridge · Farnham · Köln · Paris · Sebastopol · Taipei · Tokyo

DNS and BIND, Third Edition

by Paul Albitz and Cricket Liu

Copyright © 1998, 1997, 1992 O'Reilly & Associates, Inc. All rights reserved.
Printed in the United States of America.

Published by O'Reilly & Associates, Inc., 101 Morris Street, Sebastopol, CA 95472.

Editor: Mike Loukides

Production Editor: Ellie Fountain Maden

Printing History:

October 1992:	First Edition.
January 1997:	Second Edition.
September 1998:	Third Edition.

This book is printed on acid-free paper with 85% recycled content, 15% post-consumer waste. O'Reilly & Associates is committed to using paper with the highest recycled content available consistent with high quality.

ISBN: 1-56592-512-2 [5/99]

Table of Contents

Preface

You may not know much about the Domain Name System—yet—but whenever you use the Internet, you use DNS. Every time you send electronic mail or surf the World Wide Web, you rely on the Domain Name System.

You see, while you, as a human being, prefer to remember the *names* of computers, computers like to address each other by number. On an internet, that number is 32 bits long, or between zero and four billion or so.* That's easy for a computer to remember, because computers have lots of memory ideal for storing numbers, but it isn't nearly as easy for us humans. Pick ten phone numbers out of the phone book at random, and then try to remember them. Not easy? Now flip to the front of the book and attach random area codes to the phone numbers. That's about how difficult it would be to remember ten arbitrary internet addresses.

This is part of the reason we need the Domain Name System. DNS handles mapping between host names, which we humans find convenient, and internet addresses, which computers deal with. In fact, DNS is the standard mechanism on the Internet for advertising and accessing all kinds of information about hosts, not just addresses. And DNS is used by virtually all internetworking software, including electronic mail, remote terminal programs such as *telnet*, file transfer programs such as *ftp*, and web browsers such as Netscape Navigator and Microsoft Internet Explorer.

Another important feature of DNS is that it makes host information available *all over* the Internet. Keeping information about hosts in a formatted file on a single computer only helps users on that computer. DNS provides a means of retrieving information remotely, from anywhere on the network.

---

* And, with IP version 6, it's soon to be a whopping 128 bits long, or between zero and a decimal number with 39 digits.

More than that, DNS lets you distribute the management of host information among many sites and organizations. You don't need to submit your data to some central site or periodically retrieve copies of the "master" database. You simply make sure your section, called a *zone*, is up to date on your *name servers*. Your name servers make your zone's data available to all the other name servers on the network.

Because the database is distributed, the system also needs the ability to locate the data you're looking for by searching a number of possible locations. The Domain Name System gives name servers the intelligence to navigate through the database and find data in any zone.

Of course, DNS does have a few problems. For example, the system allows more than one name server to store data about a zone, for redundancy's sake. But inconsistencies can crop up between copies of the zone data.

But the *worst* problem with DNS is that despite its widespread use on the Internet, there's really very little documentation about managing and maintaining it. Most administrators on the Internet make do with the documentation their vendors see fit to provide, and with whatever they can glean from following the Internet mailing lists and Usenet newsgroups on the subject.

This lack of documentation means that the understanding of an enormously important internet service—one of the linchpins of today's Internet—is either handed down from administrator to administrator like a closely-guarded family recipe, or relearned repeatedly by isolated programmers and engineers. New administrators of domains suffer through the same mistakes made by countless others.

Our aim with this book is to help remedy this situation. We realize that not all of you have the time or the desire to become DNS experts. Most of you, after all, have plenty to do besides managing a domain or a name server: system administration, network engineering, or software development. It takes an awfully big institution to devote a whole person to DNS. We'll try to give you enough information to allow you to do what you need to do, whether that's running a small domain or managing a multinational monstrosity, tending a single name server or shepherding a hundred of them. Read as much as you need to know now, and come back later if you need to know more.

DNS is a big topic—big enough to require two authors, anyway—but we've tried to present it as sensibly and understandably as possible. The first two chapters give you a good theoretical overview and enough practical information to get by, and later chapters fill in the nitty-gritty details. We provide a roadmap up front, to suggest a path through the book appropriate for your job or interest.

When we talk about actual DNS software, we'll concentrate almost exclusively on BIND, the Berkeley Internet Name Domain software, which is the most popular implementation of the DNS specs (and the one we know best). We've tried to distill our experience in managing and maintaining a domain with BIND into this book— a domain, incidentally, that is one of the largest on the Internet. (We don't mean to brag, but we can use the credibility.) Where possible, we've included the real programs that we use in administration, many of them rewritten into Perl for speed and efficiency.

We hope that this book will help you get acquainted with DNS and BIND if you're just starting out, let you refine your understanding if you're already familiar with them, and provide valuable insight and experience even if you know 'em like the back of your hand.

Versions

This book deals with the new 8.1.2 version of BIND as well as the older 4.9 versions. While 8.1.2 is the most recent version as of this writing, it hasn't made its way into many vendors' versions of UNIX yet, partly because 8.1.2 has only recently been released, and many vendors are wary of using such new software. We will also occasionally mention other versions of BIND, especially 4.8.3, because many vendors continue to ship code based on this older software as part of their UNIX products. Whenever a feature is available only in the 4.8.3, 4.9, or 8.1.2 version, or there is a difference in the behavior of the versions, we try to point out which version does what.

We use *nslookup*, a name server utility program, a great deal in our examples. The version of *nslookup* we use is the one shipped with the 8.1.2 BIND code. Older versions of *nslookup* provide much, but not quite all, of the functionality in the 8.1.2 *nslookup*. We have tried to use commands common to most *nslookup*s in our examples; when this was not possible, we tried to note it.

Organization

This book is organized, more or less, to follow the evolution of a domain and a domain administrator. Chapters 1 and 2 discuss Domain Name System theory. Chapters 3 through 6 help you to decide whether to set up your own domain, then describe how to go about it, should you choose to. The middle chapters, 7, 8, 9, and 10, describe how to maintain your domain, how to configure hosts to use your name server, how to plan for the growth of your domain, and how to create subdomains. The last chapters, 11 through 15, deal with troubleshooting tools and problems, and the lost art of programming with the resolver library routines.

Here's a more detailed, chapter-by-chapter breakdown:

- Chapter 1, *Background*, provides a little historical perspective and discusses the problems that motivated the development of DNS, then presents an overview of DNS theory.

- Chapter 2, *How Does DNS Work?*, goes over DNS theory in more detail, including how the DNS name space is organized, domains, and name servers. We also introduce important concepts like name resolution and caching.

- Chapter 3, *Where Do I Start?*, covers how to get the BIND software, if you don't already have it, and what to do with it once you've got it: how to figure out what your domain name should be, and how to contact the organization that can delegate your domain to you.

- Chapter 4, *Setting Up BIND*, details how to set up your first two BIND name servers, including creating your name server database, starting up your name servers, and checking their operation.

- Chapter 5, *DNS and Electronic Mail*, deals with DNS's MX record, which allows administrators to specify alternate hosts to handle a given destination's mail. The chapter covers mail routing strategies for a wide variety of networks and hosts, including networks with security firewalls and hosts without direct Internet connectivity.

- Chapter 6, *Configuring Hosts*, explains how to configure a BIND resolver. We also include notes on the idiosyncrasies of many major UNIX vendors' resolver implementations, as well as the Windows 95 and NT resolvers.

- Chapter 7, *Maintaining BIND*, describes the periodic maintenance administrators need to perform to keep their domains running smoothly, like checking name server health and authority.

- Chapter 8, *Growing Your Domain*, covers how to plan for the growth and evolution of your domain, including how to get big, and how to plan for moves and outages.

- Chapter 9, *Parenting*, explores the joys of becoming a parent domain. We explain when to become a parent (create subdomains), what to call your children, how to create them (!), and how to watch over them.

- Chapter 10, *Advanced Features and Security*, goes over less-often-used name server configuration options that can help you tune your name server's operation, secure your name server, and ease administration.

- Chapter 11, *nslookup*, shows the ins and outs of the most popular tool for doing DNS debugging, including techniques for digging obscure information out of remote name servers.

- Chapter 12, *Reading BIND Debugging Output*, is the Rosetta Stone of BIND's debugging information. This chapter should help you make sense of the cryptic debugging information that BIND emits, which in turn will help you understand your name server better.

- Chapter 13, *Troubleshooting DNS and BIND*, covers many common DNS and BIND problems and their solutions, then describes a number of less common, harder-to-diagnose scenarios.

- Chapter 14, *Programming with the Resolver and Name Server Library Routines*, demonstrates how to use BIND's resolver routines to query name servers and retrieve data from within a C program. We include a useful (we hope!) program to check the health and authority of your name servers.

- Chapter 15, *Miscellaneous*, ties up all the loose ends. We cover DNS wildcarding, special configurations for networks that have Internet connectivity through firewalls, hosts and networks with intermittent Internet connectivity via dialup, network name encoding, and new, experimental record types.

- Appendix A, *DNS Message Format and Resource Records*, contains a byte-by-byte breakdown of the formats used in DNS queries and responses, as well as a comprehensive list of the currently-defined resource record types.

- Appendix B, *Compiling and Installing* BIND *on a Sun*, contains step-by-step instructions on how to compile the 8.1.2 version of BIND on Solaris 2.X.

- Appendix C, *Top-Level Domains*, lists the current top-level domains in the Internet's domain name space.

- Appendix D, *Domain Registration Form*, is the current form for requesting the establishment of a subdomain of an InterNIC-run domain.

- Appendix E, *in-addr.arpa Registration Form*, is the American Registry for Internet Numbers' current form for requesting the establishment of a subdomain of the *in-addr.arpa* domain.

- Appendix F, BIND *Name Server and Resolver Statements*, summarizes the syntax and semantics of each of the parameters available for configuring name servers and resolvers.

Audience

This book is intended primarily for system administrators who manage a domain and one or more name servers, but it also includes material for network engineers, postmasters, and others. Not all of the book's chapters will be equally interesting to a diverse audience, though, and you don't want to wade through fifteen chapters to find the information pertinent to your job. We hope this roadmap will help you plot your way through the book.

System administrators setting up their first domain should read Chapters 1 and 2 for DNS theory, Chapter 3 for information on getting started and selecting a good domain name, then Chapters 4 and 5 to learn how to set up a domain for the first time. Chapter 6 explains how to configure hosts to use the new name servers. Soon after, they should read Chapter 7, which explains how to "flesh out" their domain implementation by setting up additional name servers and adding additional data. Then, Chapters 11, 12, and 13 describe troubleshooting tools and techniques.

Experienced administrators could benefit from reading Chapter 6 to learn how to configure DNS resolvers on different hosts, and Chapter 7 for information on maintaining their domains. Chapter 8 contains instructions on how to plan for a domain's growth and evolution, which should be especially valuable to administrators of large domains. Chapter 9 explains parenting—creating subdomains—which is *de rigueur* reading for those considering the big move. Chapter 10 covers security features of the new BIND 8.1.2 name server, many of which may be very useful for experienced administrators. Chapters 11 through 13 describe tools and techniques for troubleshooting, which even advanced administrators may find worth reading.

System administrators on networks without full Internet connectivity should read Chapter 5 to learn how to configure mail on such networks, and Chapter 15 to learn how to set up an independent DNS infrastructure.

Programmers can read Chapters 1 and 2 for DNS theory, then Chapter 14 for detailed coverage of how to program with the BIND resolver library routines.

Network administrators not directly responsible for a domain should still read Chapters 1 and 2 for DNS theory, then Chapter 11 to learn how to use *nslookup*, plus Chapter 13 for troubleshooting tactics.

Postmasters should read Chapters 1 and 2 for DNS theory, then Chapter 5 to find out how DNS and electronic mail coexist. Chapter 11, which describes *nslookup*, will also help postmasters dig mail routing information out of the domain name space.

Interested users can read Chapters 1 and 2 for DNS theory, and then whatever else they like!

Note that we assume you're familiar with basic UNIX system administration, TCP/IP networking, and programming using simple shell scripts and Perl. We don't assume you have any other specialized knowledge, though. When we introduce a new term or concept, we'll do our best to define or explain it. Whenever possible, we'll use analogies from UNIX (and from the real world) to help you understand.

Obtaining the Example Programs

The example programs in this book are available electronically via *ftp* from these URLs:

> *ftp://ftp.uu.net/published/oreilly/nutshell/dnsbind/dns.tar.Z*
> *ftp://ftp.ora.com/published/oreilly/nutshell/dnsbind/dns.tar.Z*

In either case, extract the files from the archive by typing:

```
% zcat dns.tar.Z | tar xf -
```

System V systems require the following *tar* command instead:

```
% zcat dns.tar.Z | tar xof -
```

If *zcat* is not available on your system, use separate *uncompress* and *tar* commands.

If you cannot get the examples directly over the Internet, but can send and receive email, you can use *ftpmail* to get them. For help using *ftpmail*, send email to *ftpmail@online.oreilly.com* with no subject and the single word "help" in the body.

Conventions Used in This Book

We use the following font and format conventions for UNIX commands, utilities, and system calls:

- Excerpts from scripts or configuration files are shown in a constant width font:

```
if test -x /etc/named -a -f /etc/named.conf
then
      /etc/named
fi
```

- Sample interactive sessions, showing command-line input and corresponding output, will be shown in a constant width font, with user-supplied input in bold:

```
% cat /etc/named.pid
78
```

- If the command must be typed by the superuser (root), we use the sharp or pound sign (#):

```
# /etc/named
```

- Command lines, when they appear exactly as a user would type them, are printed in italic when they appear in the body of a paragraph. For example: run *ls* to list the files in a directory.

- Domain names are also printed in italic when they appear within a paragraph.

- UNIX commands (when mentioned in passing, and not as part of a command line) and UNIX manual pages mentioned in the body of a paragraph appear italicized. For example: to find more information on *named*, a user could consult the *named* (1m) manpage.

- Filenames are printed in italic; for example: the BIND name server's conf file is usually */etc/named.conf.*

Quotations

The Lewis Carroll quotations that begin each chapter are from the Millennium Fulcrum Edition 2.9 of the Project Gutenberg electronic text of *Alice's Adventures in Wonderland* and *Through the Looking-Glass.* Quotations in Chapters 1, 2, 5, 6, 8, and 13 come from *Alice's Adventures in Wonderland,* and those in Chapters 3, 4, 7, 9, 11, 12, and 15 come from *Through the Looking-Glass.*

Acknowledgments

The authors would like to thank Ken Stone, Jerry McCollom, Peter Jeffe, Christopher Durham, Hal Stern, Bill Wisner, Dave Curry, Jeff Okamoto, Brad Knowles, K. Robert Elz, and Paul Vixie for their invaluable contributions to this book. We'd also like to thank our reviewers, Eric Pearce, Jack Repenning, Andrew Cherenson, Dan Trinkle, Bill LeFebvre, and John Sechrest for their criticism and suggestions. Without their help, this book would not be what it is (it'd be much shorter!).

For the second edition, the authors would like to add their thanks to their sterling review team: Dave Barr, Nigel Campbell, Bill LeFebvre, Mike Milligan, and Dan Trinkle.

For the third edition, the authors salute their technical review Dream Team: Bob Halley, Barry Margolin and Paul Vixie.

Cricket would particularly like to thank his former manager, Rick Nordensten, who is the very model of a modern HP manager, on whose watch the first version of this book was written; his neighbors, who bore his occasional crabbiness for many months; and of course his wife, Paige, for her unflagging support and for putting up with his tap-tap-tapping during her nap-nap-napping. For the second edition, Cricket would like to add a thank you to his former managers, Regina Kershner and Paul Klouda, for their support of Cricket's work with the Internet. For the third edition, Cricket acknowledges a debt of gratitude to his partner, Matt Larson, for his co-development of the Acme Razor.

Paul would like to thank his wife Katherine for her patience, for many review sessions, and for proving that she could make a quilt in her spare time more quickly than her spouse could write his half of a book.

We would also like to thank the folks at O'Reilly & Associates for their hard work and patience. Credit is especially due our editor, Mike Loukides; our production editor for the second edition, Nancy Kotary; Ellie Fountain Maden (third edition), Robert Romano (third edition), Steven Abrams (third edition); our production copy editor, Kismet McDonough-Chan; our indexers, Seth Maislin (second and third editions) and Ellie Cutler (first edition); our production tools specialists, Mike Sierra and Lenny Muellner; and our illustrator, Chris Reilley (second edition). Thanks besides to Jerry Peek, for all sorts of miscellaneous help, and to Tim O'Reilly, for inspiring us to put it all in print.

And thanks, Edie, for the cricket on the cover!

1

Background

> *The White Rabbit put on his spectacles. "Where shall I begin, please your Majesty?" he asked.*
>
> *"Begin at the beginning," the King said, very gravely, "and go on till you come to the end: then stop."*

It's important to know a little ARPAnet history to understand the Domain Name System (DNS). DNS was developed to address particular problems on the ARPAnet, and the Internet—a descendant of the ARPAnet—remains its main user.

If you've been using the Internet for years, you can probably skip this chapter. If you haven't, we hope it'll give you enough background to understand what motivated the development of DNS.

A (Very) Brief History of the Internet

In the late 1960s, the U.S. Department of Defense's Advanced Research Projects Agency, ARPA (later DARPA), began funding an experimental wide area computer network that connected important research organizations in the U.S., called the *ARPAnet*. The original goal of the ARPAnet was to allow government contractors to share expensive or scarce computing resources. From the beginning, however, users of the ARPAnet also used the network for collaboration. This collaboration ranged from sharing files and software and exchanging electronic mail—now commonplace—to joint development and research using shared remote computers.

The TCP/IP (Transmission Control Protocol/Internet Protocol) protocol suite was developed in the early 1980s, and quickly became the standard host-networking protocol on the ARPAnet. The inclusion of the protocol suite in the University of California at Berkeley's popular BSD UNIX operating system was instrumental in democratizing internetworking. BSD UNIX was virtually free to universities. This meant that internetworking—and ARPAnet connectivity—were suddenly available cheaply to many more organizations than were previously attached to the ARPAnet. Many of the computers being connected to the ARPAnet were being connected to local networks, too, and very shortly the other computers on the local networks were communicating via the ARPAnet as well.

The network grew from a handful of hosts to a network of tens of thousands of hosts. The original ARPAnet became the backbone of a confederation of local and regional networks based on TCP/IP, called the *Internet*.

In 1988, however, DARPA decided the experiment was over. The Department of Defense began dismantling the ARPAnet. Another network, funded by the National Science Foundation and called the NSFNET, replaced the ARPAnet as the backbone of the Internet.

Even more recently, in the spring of 1995, the Internet made a transition from using the publicly-funded NSFNET as a backbone to using multiple commercial backbones, run by long-distance carriers like MCI and Sprint, and long-time commercial internetworking players like PSINet and UUNET.

Today, the Internet connects millions of hosts around the world. In fact, a significant proportion of the non-PC computers in the world are connected to the Internet. Some of the new commercial backbones can carry a volume of 622 megabits per second, over ten thousand times the bandwidth of the original ARPAnet. Tens of millions of people use the network for communication and collaboration daily.

On the Internet and internets

A word on "the Internet," and on "internets" in general, is in order. In print, the difference between the two seems slight: one is always capitalized, one isn't. The distinction between their meanings, however, *is* significant. The Internet, with a capital "I," refers to the network that began its life as the ARPAnet and continues today as, roughly, the confederation of all TCP/IP networks directly or indirectly connected to commercial U.S. backbones. Seen close up, it's actually quite a few different networks—commercial TCP/IP backbones, regional TCP/IP networks, corporate and U.S. government TCP/IP networks, and TCP/IP networks in other countries—interconnected by high-speed digital circuits.

A lowercase internet, on the other hand, is simply any network made up of multiple smaller networks using the same internetworking protocols. An internet (little "i") isn't necessarily connected to the Internet (big "I"), nor does it necessarily use TCP/IP as its internetworking protocol. There are isolated corporate internets, and there are Xerox XNS-based internets and DECnet-based internets.

The new term "intranet" is really just a marketing term for a TCP/IP-based "little i" internet, used to emphasize the use of technologies developed and introduced on the Internet within a company's internal corporate network. An "extranet," on the other hand, is an internet that connects partner companies, or a company to its distributors, suppliers, and customers.

The History of the Domain Name System

Through the 1970s, the ARPAnet was a small, friendly community of a few hundred hosts. A single file, *HOSTS.TXT*, contained all the information you needed to know about those hosts: it held a name-to-address mapping for every host connected to the ARPAnet. The familiar UNIX host table, */etc/hosts*, was compiled from *HOSTS.TXT* (mostly by deleting fields that UNIX didn't use).

HOSTS.TXT was maintained by SRI's *Network Information Center* (dubbed "the NIC") and distributed from a single host, SRI-NIC.* ARPAnet administrators typically emailed their changes to the NIC, and periodically *ftp*ed to SRI-NIC and grabbed the current *HOSTS.TXT*. Their changes were compiled into a new *HOSTS.TXT* once or twice a week. As the ARPAnet grew, however, this scheme became unworkable. The size of *HOSTS.TXT* grew in proportion to the growth in the number of ARPAnet hosts. Moreover, the traffic generated by the update process increased even faster: every additional host meant not only another line in *HOSTS.TXT*, but potentially another host updating from SRI-NIC.

And when the ARPAnet moved to the TCP/IP protocols, the population of the network exploded. Now there was a host of problems with *HOSTS.TXT*:

Traffic and load
> The toll on SRI-NIC, in terms of the network traffic and processor load involved in distributing the file, was becoming unbearable.

Name collisions
> No two hosts in *HOSTS.TXT* could have the same name. However, while the NIC could assign addresses in a way that guaranteed uniqueness, it had no authority over host names. There was nothing to prevent someone from adding a host with a conflicting name and breaking the whole scheme. Someone adding a host with the same name as a major mail hub, for example, could disrupt mail service to much of the ARPAnet.

Consistency
> Maintaining consistency of the file across an expanding network became harder and harder. By the time a new *HOSTS.TXT* could reach the farthest shores of the

---

* SRI is the Stanford Research Institute in Menlo Park, California. SRI conducts research into many different areas, including computer networking.

enlarged ARPAnet, a host across the network had changed addresses, or a new host had sprung up that users wanted to reach.

The essential problem was that the *HOSTS.TXT* mechanism didn't scale well. Ironically, the success of the ARPAnet as an experiment led to the failure and obsolescence of *HOSTS.TXT.*

The ARPAnet's governing bodies chartered an investigation into a successor for *HOSTS.TXT.* Their goal was to create a system that solved the problems inherent in a unified host table system. The new system should allow local administration of data, yet make that data globally available. The decentralization of administration would eliminate the single-host bottleneck and relieve the traffic problem. And local management would make the task of keeping data up-to-date much easier. It should use a hierarchical name space to name hosts. This would ensure the uniqueness of names.

Paul Mockapetris, then of USC's Information Sciences Institute, was responsible for designing the architecture of the new system. In 1984, he released RFCs 882 and 883, which describe the Domain Name System. These RFCs were superseded by RFCs 1034 and 1035, the current specifications of the Domain Name System.* RFCs 1034 and 1035 have now been augmented by many other RFCs, which describe potential DNS security problems, implementation problems, administrative gotchas, mechanisms for dynamically updating name servers and for securing domain data, and more.

The Domain Name System, in a Nutshell

The Domain Name System is a distributed database. This allows local control of the segments of the overall database, yet data in each segment are available across the entire network through a client-server scheme. Robustness and adequate performance are achieved through replication and caching.

Programs called *name servers* constitute the server half of DNS's client-server mechanism. Name servers contain information about some segment of the database and make it available to clients, called *resolvers.* Resolvers are often just library routines that create queries and send them across a network to a name server.

The structure of the DNS database, shown in Figure 1-1, is very similar to the structure of the UNIX filesystem. The whole database (or filesystem) is pictured as an inverted tree, with the root node at the top. Each node in the tree has a text label, which identifies the node relative to its parent. This is roughly analogous to a

---

* RFCs are Request for Comments documents, part of the relatively informal procedure for introducing new technology on the Internet. RFCs are usually freely distributed and contain fairly technical descriptions of the technology, often intended for implementors.

"relative pathname" in a filesystem, like *bin*. One label—the null label, or ""—is reserved for the root node. In text, the root node is written as a single dot ("."). In the UNIX filesystem, the root is written as a slash ("/").

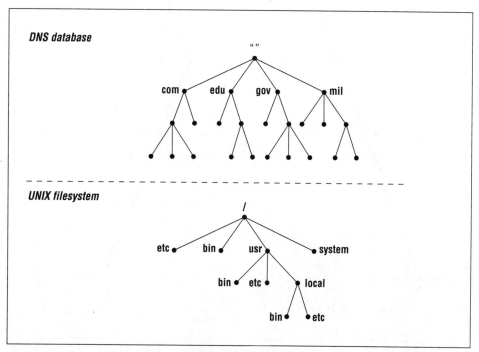

Figure 1-1. The DNS database versus a UNIX filesystem

Each node is also the root of a new subtree of the overall tree. Each of these subtrees represents a partition of the overall database—a "directory" in the UNIX filesystem, or a *domain* in the Domain Name System. Each domain or directory can be further divided into additional partitions, called *subdomains* in DNS, like a filesystem's "subdirectories." Subdomains, like subdirectories, are drawn as children of their parent domains.

Every domain has a unique name, like every directory. A domain's *domain name* identifies its position in the database, much as a directory's "absolute pathname" specifies its place in the filesystem. In DNS, the domain name is the sequence of labels from the node at the root of the domain to the root of the whole tree, with "." separating the labels. In the UNIX filesystem, a directory's absolute pathname is the list of relative names read from root to leaf (the opposite direction to DNS, as shown in Figure 1-2), using a slash to separate the names.

In DNS, each domain can be administered by a different organization. Each organization can then break its domain into a number of subdomains and dole out

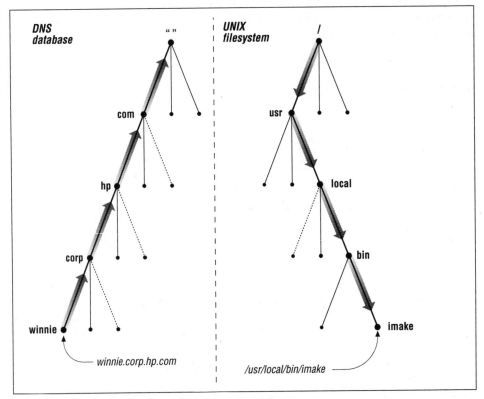

Figure 1-2. Reading names in DNS and in a UNIX filesystem

responsibility for those subdomains to other organizations. For example, the InterNIC runs the *edu* (educational) domain, but assigns U.C. Berkeley authority over the *berkeley.edu* subdomain (Figure 1-3). This is something like remotely mounting a filesystem: certain directories in a filesystem may actually be filesystems on other hosts, mounted from a remote host. The administrator on host *winken*, for example (again, Figure 1-3), is responsible for the filesystem that appears on the local host as the directory */usr/nfs/winken*.

Domain names are used as indexes into the DNS database. You might think of data in DNS as "attached" to a domain name. In a filesystem, directories contain files and subdirectories. Likewise, domains can contain both hosts and subdomains. A domain contains those hosts and subdomains whose domain names are within the domain.

Each host on a network has a domain name, which points to information about the host (see Figure 1-4). This information may include IP addresses, information about mail routing, etc. Hosts may also have one or more *domain name aliases*, which are simply pointers from one domain name (the alias) to another (the official or

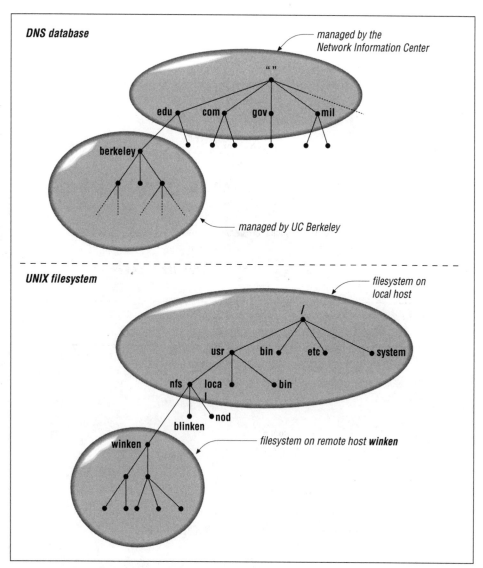

Figure 1-3. Remote management of subdomains and of filesystems

canonical domain name). In the figure, *mailhub.nv...* is an alias for the canonical name *rincon.ba.ca....*

Why all the complicated structure? To solve the problems that *HOSTS.TXT* had. For example, making domain names hierarchical eliminates the pitfall of name collisions. Each domain has a unique domain name, so the organization that runs the domain is free to name hosts and subdomains within its domain. Whatever name they choose for a host or subdomain, it won't conflict with other organizations' domain

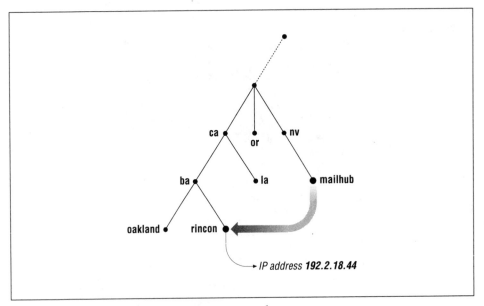

Figure 1-4. An alias in DNS pointing to a canonical name

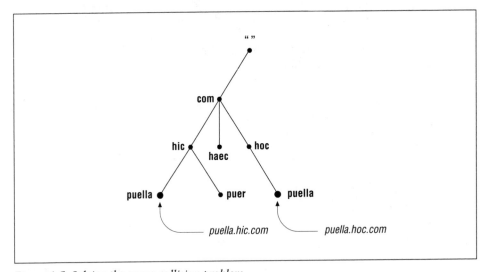

Figure 1-5. Solving the name collision problem

names, since it will end in their unique domain name. For example, the organization that runs *hic.com* can name a host *puella* (as shown in Figure 1-5), since it knows that the domain host's domain name will end in *hic.com*, a unique domain name.

The History of BIND

The first implementation of the Domain Name System was called *JEEVES*, written by Paul Mockapetris himself. A later implementation was *BIND*, written for Berkeley's 4.3BSD UNIX operating system by Kevin Dunlap. BIND is now maintained by the Internet Software Consortium.*

Berkeley Internet Name Domain (BIND) is the implementation we'll concentrate on in this book. BIND is by far the most popular implementation of DNS today. It has been ported to most flavors of UNIX, and is shipped as a standard part of most vendors' UNIX offerings. BIND has even been ported to Microsoft's Windows NT.

Must I Use DNS?

Despite the usefulness of the Domain Name System, there are still some situations in which it doesn't pay to use it. There are other name resolution mechanisms besides DNS, some of which may be standard with your operating system. Sometimes the overhead involved in managing a domain and its name servers outweighs the benefits. On the other hand, there are circumstances in which you have no other choice but to set up and manage a domain. Here are some guidelines to help you make that decision:

If you're connected to the Internet...

...DNS is a must. Think of DNS as the *lingua franca* of the Internet: nearly all of the Internet's network services use DNS. That includes the World Wide Web, electronic mail, remote terminal access, and file transfer.

On the other hand, this doesn't necessarily mean that you have to set up and run a domain *by* yourself *for* yourself. If you've only got a handful of hosts, you may be able to find an existing domain to become part of (see Chapter 3, *Where Do I Start?*). Or you may be able to find someone else to run a domain for you. If you pay an Internet service provider for your Internet connectivity, ask if they'll manage a domain for you, too. Even if you aren't already a customer, there are companies who will help out, for a price.

If you have a little more than a handful of hosts, or a lot more, then you'll probably want your own domain. And if you want direct control over your domain and your name servers, then you'll want to manage it yourself. Buy this book and read on!

---

* For more information on the Internet Software Consortium and its work on BIND, see *http://www.isc.org/bind.html.*

If you have a UUCP connection to a host on the Internet...

...it's a good idea to set up a domain. *user@domain*-style addressing has become standard on the Internet. Once you've set up a domain, your correspondents on the Internet will be able to send you mail using these simpler addresses. You'll also be prepared if you decide later to get a connection to the Internet.

It's a common misconception that you actually need to be connected to the Internet to set up a domain and use *user@domain* addresses. You'll need hosts on the Internet to act as name servers for your domain, but they don't have to be *your* hosts. You'd be surprised how many people are willing to "host" your domain gratis: the Internet is still a fairly neighborly place. (And even if you can't find anyone willing, there are companies who will do it for you for cheap.)

If you have your own TCP/IP-based internet...

...you probably want DNS. By an internet, we don't mean just a single Ethernet of workstations using TCP/IP (see the next section if you thought that was what we meant); we mean a fairly complex "network of networks." Maybe you have a forest of Appletalk nets and a handful of Apollo token rings.

If your internet is basically homogeneous and your hosts don't need DNS (say you have a big DECnet or OSI internet), then you may be able to do without it. But if you've got a variety of hosts, especially if some of those run some variety of UNIX, you'll want DNS. It'll simplify the distribution of host information and rid you of any kludgy host table distribution schemes you may have cooked up.

If you have your own local area network or site network...

...and that network isn't connected to a larger network, you can probably get away without using DNS. You might consider using Microsoft's Windows Internet Name Service (WINS), host tables, or Sun's Network Information Service (NIS) product.

But if you need distributed administration or have trouble maintaining the consistency of data on your network, DNS may be for you. And if your network is likely to be connected to another network soon, like your corporate internet or the Internet, it'd be wise to start up a domain now.

2

How Does DNS Work?

> *"... and what is the use of a book,"* thought Alice,
> *"without pictures or conversations?"*

The Domain Name System is basically a database of host information. Admittedly, you get a lot with that: funny dotted names, networked name servers, a shadowy "name space." But keep in mind that, in the end, the service DNS provides is information about internet hosts.

We've already covered some important aspects of DNS, including its client-server architecture and the structure of the DNS database. However, we haven't gone into much detail, and we haven't explained the nuts and bolts of DNS's operation.

In this chapter, we'll explain and illustrate the mechanisms that make DNS work. We'll also introduce the terms you'll need to know to read the rest of the book (and to converse intelligently with your fellow domain administrators).

First, though, let's take a more detailed look at concepts introduced in the previous chapter. We'll try to add enough detail to spice it up a little.

The Domain Name Space

DNS's distributed database is indexed by domain names. Each domain name is essentially just a path in a large inverted tree, called the *domain name space*. The tree's hierarchical structure, shown in Figure 2-1, is similar to the structure of the UNIX filesystem. The tree has a single root at the top.[*] In the UNIX filesystem, this is called the root directory, represented by a slash ("/"). DNS simply calls it "the root." Like a filesystem, DNS's tree can branch any number of ways at each intersection

---

[*] Clearly this is a computer scientist's tree, not a botanist's.

point, called a node. The depth of the tree is limited to 127 levels (a limit you're not likely to reach).

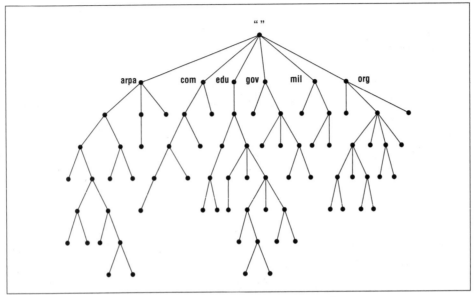

Figure 2-1. The structure of the DNS name space

Domain Names

Each node in the tree has a text label (without dots) that can be up to 63 characters long. A null (zero-length) label is reserved for the root. The full *domain name* of any node in the tree is the sequence of labels on the path from that node to the root. Domain names are always read from the node toward the root ("up" the tree), and with dots separating the names in the path.

If the root node's label actually appears in a node's domain name, the name looks as though it ends in a dot, as in "www.oreilly.com.". (It actually ends with a dot—the separator—and the root's null label.) When the root node's label appears by itself, it is written as a single dot, ".", for convenience. Consequently, some software interprets a trailing dot in a domain name to indicate that the domain name is *absolute*. An absolute domain name is written relative to the root, and unambiguously specifies a node's location in the hierarchy. An absolute domain name is also referred to as a *fully qualified domain name*, often abbreviated FQDN. Names without trailing dots are sometimes interpreted as relative to some domain other than the root, just as directory names without a leading slash are often interpreted as relative to the current directory.

DNS requires that sibling nodes—nodes that are children of the same parent—have different labels. This restriction guarantees that a domain name uniquely identifies a single node in the tree. The restriction really isn't a limitation, because the labels only need to be unique among the children, not among all the nodes in the tree. The same restriction applies to the UNIX filesystem: You can't give two sibling directories the same name. Just as you can't have two *hobbes.pa.ca.us* nodes in the name space, you can't have two */usr/bin* directories (Figure 2-2). You can, however, have both a *hobbes.pa.ca.us* node and a *hobbes.lg.ca.us*, as you can have both a */bin* directory and a */usr/bin* directory.

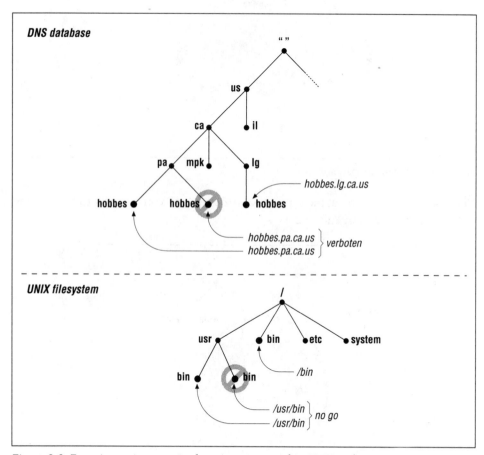

Figure 2-2. Ensuring uniqueness in domain names and in UNIX pathnames

Domains

A *domain* is simply a subtree of the domain name space. The domain name of a domain is the same as the domain name of the node at the very top of the domain.

So, for example, the top of the *purdue.edu* domain is a node named *purdue.edu*, as shown in Figure 2-3.

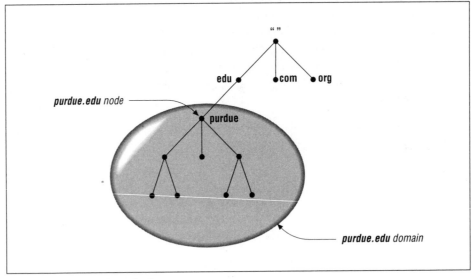

Figure 2-3. The purdue.edu domain

Likewise, in a filesystem, at the top of the */usr* directory, you'd expect to find a node called */usr*, as shown in Figure 2-4.

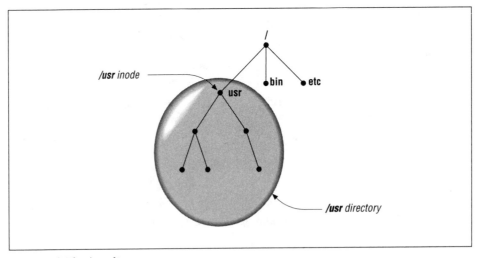

Figure 2-4. The /usr directory

Any domain name in the subtree is considered a part of the domain. Because a domain name can be in many subtrees, a domain name can also be in many domains. For example, the domain name *pa.ca.us* is part of the *ca.us* domain and also part of the *us* domain, as shown in Figure 2-5.

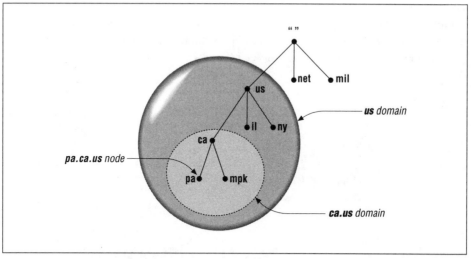

Figure 2-5. A node in multiple domains

So in the abstract, a domain is just a subtree of the domain name space. But if a domain is simply made up of domain names and other domains, where are all the hosts? Domains are groups of hosts, right?

The hosts are there, represented by domain names. Remember, domain names are just indexes into the DNS database. The "hosts" are the domain names that point to information about individual hosts. And a domain contains all the hosts whose domain names are within the domain. The hosts are related *logically*, often by geography or organizational affiliation, and not necessarily by network or address or hardware type. You might have ten different hosts, each of them on a different network and each one perhaps even in a different country, all in the same domain.[*]

Domain names at the leaves of the tree generally represent individual hosts, and they may point to network addresses, hardware information, and mail routing information. Domain names in the interior of the tree can name a host *and* can point to information about the domain. Interior domain names aren't restricted to one or the other. They can represent both the domain they correspond to and a particular

---

[*] One note of caution: Don't confuse domains in the Domain Name System with domains in Sun's Network Information Service (NIS). Though an NIS domain also refers to a group of hosts, and both types of domains have similarly structured names, the concepts are quite different. NIS uses hierarchical names, but the hierarchy ends there: hosts in the same NIS domain share certain data about hosts and users, but they can't navigate the NIS name space to find data in other NIS domains. NT domains, which provide account management and security services, also don't have any relationship to DNS domains.

host on the network. For example, *hp.com* is both the name of the Hewlett-Packard Company's domain and the domain name of a host that runs HP's main web server.

The type of information retrieved when you use a domain name depends on the context in which you use it. Sending mail to someone at *hp.com* would return mail routing information, while *telnet*ing to the domain name would look up the host information (in Figure 2-6, for example, *hp.com*'s IP address).[*]

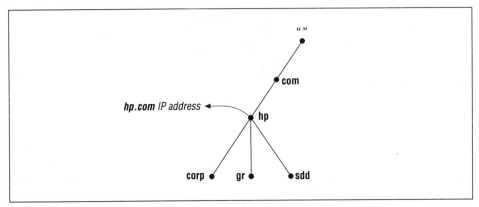

Figure 2-6. An interior node with both host and structural data

A simple way of deciding whether a domain is a subdomain of another domain is to compare their domain names. A subdomain's domain name ends with the domain name of its parent domain. For example, the domain *la.tyrell.com* must be a subdomain of *tyrell.com* because *la.tyrell.com* ends with *tyrell.com*. Similarly, it's a subdomain of *com*, as is *tyrell.com*.

Besides being referred to in relative terms, as subdomains of other domains, domains are often referred to by *level*. On mailing lists and in Usenet newsgroups, you may see the terms *top-level domain* or *second-level domain* bandied about. These terms simply refer to a domain's position in the domain name space:

• A top-level domain is a child of the root.

• A first-level domain is a child of the root (a top-level domain).

• A second-level domain is a child of a first-level domain, and so on.

---

[*] The terms *domain* and *subdomain* are often used interchangeably, or nearly so, in DNS and BIND documentation. Here, we use *subdomain* only as a relative term: a domain is a subdomain of another domain if the root of the subdomain is within the domain.

Resource Records

The data associated with domain names are contained in *resource records*, or RRs. Records are divided into classes, each of which pertains to a type of network or software. Currently, there are classes for internets (any TCP/IP-based internet), networks based on the Chaosnet protocols, and networks that use Hesiod software. (Chaosnet is an old network of largely historic significance.)

The internet class is by far the most popular. (We're not really sure if anyone still uses the Chaosnet class, and use of the Hesiod class is mostly confined to MIT.) We concentrate here on the internet class.

Within a class, records also come in several types, which correspond to the different varieties of data that may be stored in the domain name space. Different classes may define different record types, though some types may be common to more than one class. For example, almost every class defines an *address* type. Each record type in a given class defines a particular record syntax, which all resource records of that class and type must adhere to. (For details on all internet resource record types and their syntaxes, see Appendix A, *DNS Message Format and Resource Records.*)

If this information seems sketchy, don't worry—we'll cover the records in the internet class in more detail later. The common records are described in Chapter 4, *Setting Up BIND*, and a comprehensive list is included as part of Appendix A.

The Internet Domain Name Space

So far, we've talked about the theoretical structure of the domain name space and what sorts of data are stored in it, and we've even hinted at the types of names you might find in it with our (sometimes fictional) examples. But this won't help you decode the domain names you see on a daily basis on the Internet.

The Domain Name System doesn't impose many rules on the labels in domain names, and it doesn't attach any *particular* meaning to the labels at a particular level. When you manage a part of the domain name space, you can decide on your own semantics for your domain names. Heck, you could name your subdomains A through Z and no one would stop you (though they might strongly recommend against it).

The existing Internet domain name space, however, has some self-imposed structure to it. Especially in the upper-level domains, the domain names follow certain traditions (not rules, really, as they can be and have been broken.) These traditions help domain names from appearing totally chaotic. Understanding these traditions is an enormous asset if you're trying to decipher a domain name.

Top-Level Domains

The original top-level domains divided the Internet domain name space organizationally into seven domains:

com

> Commercial organizations, such as Hewlett-Packard (*hp.com*), Sun Microsystems (*sun.com*), and IBM (*ibm.com*)

edu

> Educational organizations, such as U.C. Berkeley (*berkeley.edu*) and Purdue University (*purdue.edu*)

gov

> Government organizations, such as NASA (*nasa.gov*) and the National Science Foundation (*nsf.gov*)

mil

> Military organizations, such as the U.S. Army (*army.mil*) and Navy (*navy.mil*)

net

> Networking organizations, such as NSFNET (*nsf.net*)

org

> Noncommercial organizations, such as the Electronic Frontier Foundation (*eff.org*)

int

> International organizations, such as NATO (*nato.int*)

Another top-level domain called *arpa* was originally used during the ARPAnet's transition from host tables to DNS. All ARPAnet hosts originally had host names under *arpa*, so they were easy to find. Later, they moved into various subdomains of the organizational top-level domains. However, the *arpa* domain remains in use in a way you'll read about later.

You may notice a certain nationalistic prejudice in the examples: all are primarily U.S. organizations. That's easier to understand—and forgive—when you remember that the Internet began as the ARPAnet, a U.S.-funded research project. No one anticipated the success of the ARPAnet, or that it would eventually become as international as the Internet is today.

Today, these original domains are called *generic top-level domains*, or gTLDs. By the time you read this, we may have quite a few more of these, such as *firm, shop, web,* and *nom,* to accommodate the rapid expansion of the Internet and the need for more domain name "space." For more information on a proposal to create new gTLDs, see *http://www.gtld-mou.org/*.

To accommodate the internationalization of the Internet, the implementers of the Internet name space compromised. Instead of insisting that all top-level domains describe organizational affiliation, they decided to allow geographical designations, too. New top-level domains were reserved (but not necessarily created) to correspond to individual countries. Their domain names followed an existing international standard called ISO 3166.[*] ISO 3166 establishes official, two-letter abbreviations for every country in the world. We've included the current list of top-level domains as Appendix C, *Top-Level Domains*, of this book.

Further Down

Within these top-level domains, the traditions and the extent to which they are followed vary. Some of the ISO 3166 top-level domains closely follow the U.S.'s original organizational scheme. For example, Australia's top-level domain, *au*, has subdomains such as *edu.au* and *com.au*. Some other ISO 3166 top-level domains follow the *uk* domain's lead and have subdomains such as *co.uk* for corporations and *ac.uk* for the academic community. In most cases, however, even these geographically-oriented top-level domains are divided up organizationally.

That's not true of the *us* top-level domain, however. The *us* domain has fifty subdomains that correspond to—guess what?—the fifty U.S. states.[†] Each is named according to the standard two-letter abbreviation for the state—the same abbreviation standardized by the U.S. Postal Service. Within each state's domain, the organization is still largely geographical: most subdomains correspond to individual cities. Beneath the cities, the subdomains usually correspond to individual hosts.

Reading Domain Names

Now that you know what most top-level domains represent and how their name spaces are structured, you'll probably find it much easier to make sense of most domain names. Let's dissect a few for practice:

lithium.cchem.berkeley.edu
> You've got a head start on this one, as we've already told you that *berkeley.edu* is U.C. Berkeley's domain. (Even if you didn't already know that, though, you could have inferred that the name probably belongs to a U.S. university because it's in the top-level *edu* domain.) *cchem* is the College of Chemistry's subdomain of *berkeley.edu*. Finally, *lithium* is the name of a particular host in the domain— and probably one of about a hundred or so, if they've got one for every element.

---

[*] Except for Great Britain. According to ISO 3166 and Internet tradition, Great Britain's top-level domain name should be *gb*. Instead, most organizations in Great Britain and Northern Ireland (i.e., the United Kingdom) use the top-level domain name *uk*. They drive on the wrong side of the road, too.

[†] Actually, there are a few more domains under *us*: one for Washington, D.C., one for Guam, and so on.

winnie.corp.hp.com

This example is a bit harder, but not much. The *hp.com* domain in all likelihood belongs to the Hewlett-Packard Company (in fact, we gave you this earlier, too). Their *corp* subdomain is undoubtedly their corporate headquarters. And *winnie* is probably just some silly name someone thought up for a host.

fernwood.mpk.ca.us

Here you'll need to use your understanding of the *us* domain. *ca.us* is obviously California's domain, but *mpk* is anybody's guess. In this case, it would be hard to know that it's Menlo Park's domain unless you knew your San Francisco Bay Area geography. (And no, it's not the same Menlo Park that Edison lived in—that one's in New Jersey.)

daphne.ch.apollo.hp.com

We've included this example just so you don't start thinking that all domain names have only four labels. *apollo.hp.com* is the former Apollo Computer subdomain of the *hp.com* domain. (When HP acquired Apollo, it also acquired Apollo's Internet domain, *apollo.com*, which became *apollo.hp.com*.) *ch.apollo. hp.com* is Apollo's Chelmsford, Massachusetts, site. And *daphne* is a host at Chelmsford.

Delegation

Remember that one of the main goals of the design of the Domain Name System was to decentralize administration? This is achieved through *delegation*. Delegating domains works a lot like delegating tasks at work. A manager may break up a large project into smaller tasks and delegate responsibility for each of these tasks to different employees.

Likewise, an organization administering a domain can divide it into subdomains. Each of those subdomains can be *delegated* to other organizations. This means that an organization becomes responsible for maintaining all the data in that subdomain. It can freely change the data and even divide its subdomain up into more subdomains and delegate those. The parent domain contains only pointers to sources of the subdomain's data so that it can refer queriers there. The domain *stanford.edu*, for example, is delegated to the folks at Stanford who run the university's networks (Figure 2-7).

Not all organizations delegate away their whole domain, just as not all managers delegate all their work. A domain may have several subdomains and also contain hosts that don't belong in the subdomains. For example, the Acme Corporation (it supplies a certain coyote with most of his gadgets), which has a division in Rockaway and its headquarters in Kalamazoo, might have a *rockaway.acme.com* subdomain and a *kalamazoo.acme.com* subdomain. However, the few hosts in the

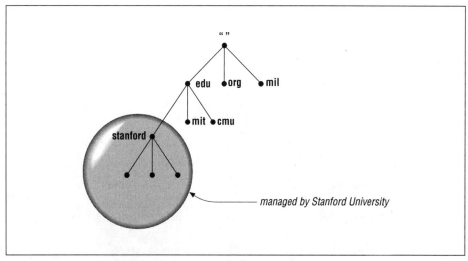

Figure 2-7. stanford.edu is delegated to Stanford University

Acme sales offices scattered throughout the U.S. would fit better under *acme.com* than under either subdomain.

We'll explain how to create and delegate subdomains later. For now, it's only important that you understand that the term *delegation* refers to assigning responsibility for a subdomain to another organization.

Name Servers and Zones

The programs that store information about the domain name space are called *name servers*. Name servers generally have complete information about some part of the domain name space, called a *zone*, which they load from a file or from another name server. The name server is then said to have *authority* for that zone. Name servers can be authoritative for multiple zones, too.

The difference between a zone and a domain is important, but subtle. All top-level domains, and many domains at the second level and lower, like *berkeley.edu* and *hp.com*, are broken into smaller, more manageable units by delegation. These units are called zones. The *edu* domain, shown in Figure 2-8, is divided into many zones, including the *berkeley.edu* zone, the *purdue.edu* zone, and the *nwu.edu* zone. At the top of the domain, there's also an *edu* zone. It's natural that the folks who run *edu* would break up the *edu* domain: otherwise, they'd have to manage the *berkeley.edu* subdomain themselves. It makes much more sense to delegate *berkeley.edu* to Berkeley. What's left for the folks who run *edu*? The *edu* zone, which would contain mostly delegation information to subdomains of *edu*.

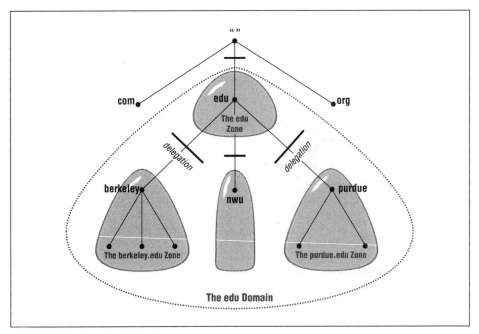

Figure 2-8. The edu domain broken into zones

The *berkeley.edu* subdomain is, in turn, broken up into multiple zones by delegation, as shown in Figure 2-9. There are delegated subdomains called *cc, cs, ce, me,* and more. Each of these subdomains is delegated to a set of name servers, some of which are also authoritative for *berkeley.edu.* However, the zones are still separate, and may have a totally different group of authoritative name servers.

A zone contains the domain names that the domain with the same domain name contains, except for domain names in delegated subdomains. For example, the top-level domain *ca* (for Canada) may have the subdomains *ab.ca, on.ca,* and *qc.ca,* for the provinces Alberta, Ontario, and Quebec. Authority for the *ab.ca, on.ca,* and *qc.ca* domains may be delegated to name servers in each of the provinces. The *domain ca* contains all the data in *ca* plus all the data in *ab.ca, on.ca,* and *qc.ca.* But the *zone ca* contains only the data in *ca* (see Figure 2-10), which is probably mostly pointers to the delegated subdomains.

If a subdomain of the domain isn't delegated away, however, the zone contains the domain names and data in the subdomain. So the *bc.ca* and *sk.ca* (British Columbia and Saskatchewan) subdomains of the *ca* domain may exist, but might not be delegated. (Perhaps the provincial authorities in B.C. and Saskatchewan aren't yet ready to manage their subdomains, but the authorities running the top-level *ca* domain want to preserve the consistency of the name space and implement subdomains for all the Canadian provinces right away.) In this case, the zone *ca* has

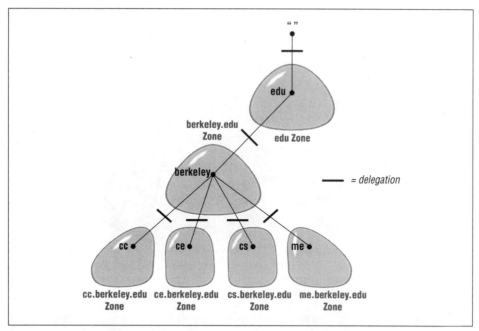

Figure 2-9. The berkeley.edu domain broken into zones

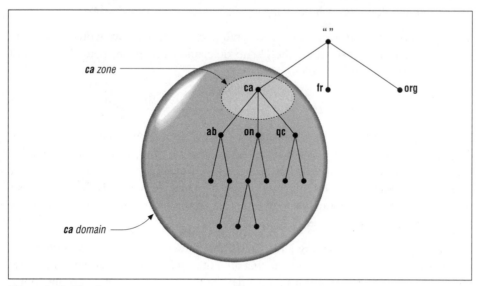

Figure 2-10. The domain ca...

a ragged bottom edge, containing *bc.ca* and *sk.ca*, but not the other *ca* subdomains, as shown in Figure 2-11.

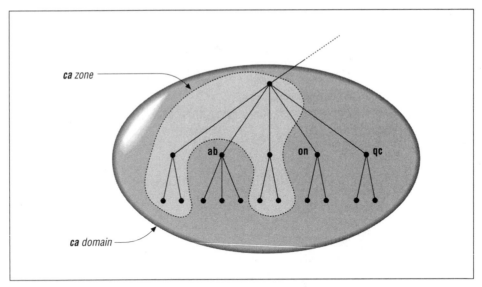

Figure 2-11. ...versus the zone ca

Now it's clear why name servers load zones instead of domains: a domain might contain more information than the name server would need.[*] A domain could contain data delegated to other name servers. Since a zone is bounded by delegation, it will never include delegated data.

If you're just starting out, however, your domain probably won't have any subdomains. In this case, since there's no delegation going on, your domain and your zone contain the same data.

Delegating Domains

Even though you may not need to delegate parts of your domain just yet, it's helpful to understand a little more about how the process of delegating a domain works. Delegation, in the abstract, involves assigning responsibility for some part of your domain to another organization. What really happens, however, is the assignment of authority for your subdomains to different name servers. (Note that we said "name servers," not just "name server.")

Your data, instead of containing information about the subdomain you've delegated, includes pointers to the name servers that are authoritative for that subdomain. Now if one of your name servers is asked for data in the subdomain, it can reply with a list of the right name servers to talk to.

---

[*] Imagine if a root name server loaded the root domain instead of the root zone: it would be loading the entire name space!

Types of Name Servers

The DNS specs define two types of name servers: *primary masters* and *secondary masters*. A *primary master* name server for a zone reads the data for the zone from a file on its host. A *secondary master* name server for a zone gets the zone data from another name server that is authoritative for the zone, called its master server. Quite often, the master server is the zone's primary master, but that's not required: a secondary master can load zone data from another secondary. When a secondary starts up, it contacts its master name server and, if necessary, pulls the zone data over. This is referred to as a *zone transfer*. Nowadays, the preferred term for a secondary master name server is a *slave,* though many people (and much software, including Microsoft's DNS Manager) still call them secondaries.

Both the primary master and slave name servers for a zone are authoritative for that zone. Despite the somewhat disparaging name, slaves aren't second-class name servers. DNS provides these two types of name servers to make administration easier. Once you've created the data for your zone and set up a primary master name server, you don't need to fool with copying that data from host to host to create new name servers for the zone. You simply set up slave name servers that load their data from the primary master for the zone., Once they're set up, the slaves will transfer new zone data when necessary.

Slave name servers are important because it's a good idea to set up more than one name server for any given zone. You'll want more than one for redundancy, to spread the load around, and to make sure that all the hosts in the zone have a name server close by. Using slave name servers makes this administratively workable.

Calling a *particular* name server a primary master name server or a slave name server is a little imprecise, though. We mentioned earlier that a name server can be authoritative for more than one zone. Similarly, a name server can be a primary master for one zone and a slave for another. Most name servers, however, are either primary for most of the zones they load or slave for most of the zones they load. So if we call a particular name server a primary or a slave, we mean that it's the primary master or a slave for *most* of the zones it loads.

Data Files

The files from which primary master name servers load their zone data are called, simply enough, zone data files or just data files. We often refer to them as *db files*, short for *database files*. Slave name servers can also load their zone data from data files. Slaves are usually configured to back up the zone data they transfer from a master name server to data files. If the slave is later killed and restarted, it will read the backup data files first, then check to see whether the data are current. This both obviates the need to transfer the zone data if it hasn't changed and provides a source of the data if the master is down.

The data files contain resource records that describe the zone. The resource records describe all the hosts in the zone and mark any delegation of subdomains. BIND also allows special directives to include the contents of other data files in a data file, much like the *#include* statement in C programming.

Resolvers

Resolvers are the clients that access name servers. Programs running on a host that need information from the domain name space use the resolver. The resolver handles:

- Querying a name server
- Interpreting responses (which may be resource records or an error)
- Returning the information to the programs that requested it

In BIND, the resolver is just a set of library routines that is linked into programs such as *telnet* and *ftp*. It's not even a separate process. It has the smarts to put together a query, to send it and wait for an answer, and to resend the query if it isn't answered, but that's about all. Most of the burden of finding an answer to the query is placed on the name server. The DNS specs call this kind of resolver a *stub resolver*.

Other implementations of DNS have had smarter resolvers, which can do more sophisticated things such as build up a cache of information already retrieved from name servers.[*] But these aren't nearly as common as the stub resolver implemented in BIND.

Resolution

Name servers are adept at retrieving data from the domain name space. They have to be, given the limited intelligence of some resolvers. Not only can they give you data about zones for which they're authoritative, they can also search through the domain name space to find data for which they're not authoritative. This process is called *name resolution* or simply *resolution*.

Because the name space is structured as an inverted tree, a name server needs only one piece of information to find its way to any point in the tree: the domain names and addresses of the root name servers (is that more than one piece?). A name server

---

[*] Rob Austein's CHIVES resolver for TOPS-20 could cache, for example.

can issue a query to a root name server for any name in the domain name space, and the root name server will start the name server on its way.

Root Name Servers

The root name servers know where there are authoritative name servers for each of the top-level domains. (In fact, most of the root name servers *are* authoritative for the generic top-level domains.) Given a query about any domain name, the root name servers can at least provide the names and addresses of the name servers that are authoritative for the top-level domain that the domain name is in. And the top-level name servers can provide the list of name servers that are authoritative for the second-level domain that the domain name is in. Each name server queried gives the querier information about how to get "closer" to the answer it's seeking, or it provides the answer itself.

The root name servers are clearly important to resolution. Because they're so important, DNS provides mechanisms—such as caching, which we'll discuss a little later—to help offload the root name servers. But in the absence of other information, resolution has to start at the root name servers. This makes the root name servers crucial to the operation of DNS; if all the Internet root name servers were unreachable for an extended period, all resolution on the Internet would fail. To protect against this, the Internet has thirteen root name servers (as of this writing) spread across different parts of the network. Two are on the MILNET, the U.S. military's portion of the Internet; one is on SPAN, NASA's internet; two are in Europe; and one is in Japan.

Being the focal point for so many queries keeps the roots busy; even with thirteen, the traffic to each root name server is very high. A recent informal poll of root name server administrators showed some roots receiving thousands of queries per second.

Despite the load placed on root name servers, resolution on the Internet works quite well. Figure 2-12 shows the resolution process for the address of a real host in a real domain, including how the process corresponds to traversing the domain name space tree.

The local name server queries a root name server for the address of *girigiri. gbrmpa.gov.au* and is referred to the *au* name servers. The local name server asks an *au* name server the same question, and is referred to the *gov.au* name servers. The *gov.au* name server refers the local name server to the *gbrmpa.gov.au* name servers. Finally, the local name server asks a *gbrmpa.gov.au* name server for the address and gets the answer.

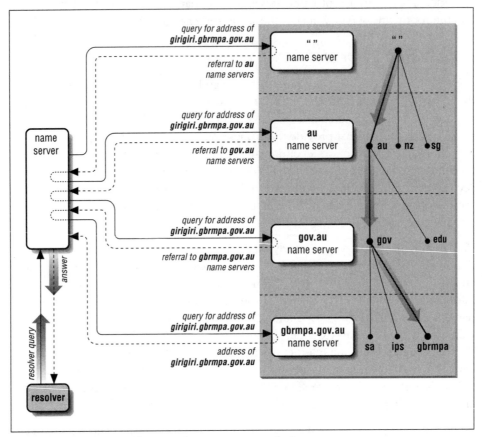

Figure 2-12. Resolution of girigiri.gbrmpa.gov.au on the Internet

Recursion

You may have noticed a big difference in the amount of work done by the name servers in the previous example. Four of the name servers simply returned the best answer they already had—mostly referrals to other name servers—to the queries they received. They didn't have to send their own queries to find the data requested. But one name server—the one queried by the resolver—had to follow successive referrals until it received an answer.

Why couldn't the local name server simply have referred the resolver to another name server? Because a stub resolver wouldn't have had the intelligence to follow a referral. And how did the name server know not to answer with a referral? Because the resolver issued a *recursive* query.

Queries come in two flavors, *recursive* and *iterative*, also called *nonrecursive*. Recursive queries place most of the burden of resolution on a single name server.

Recursion, or *recursive resolution,* is just a name for the resolution process used by a name server when it receives recursive queries.

Iteration, or *iterative resolution,* on the other hand, refers to the resolution process used by a name server when it receives iterative queries.

In recursion a resolver sends a recursive query to a name server for information about a particular domain name. The queried name server is then obliged to respond with the requested data or with an error stating that data of the requested type don't exist or that the domain name specified doesn't exist.[*] The name server can't just refer the querier to a different name server, because the query was recursive.

If the queried name server isn't authoritative for the data requested, it will have to query other name servers to find the answer. It could send recursive queries to those name servers, thereby obliging them to find the answer and return it (and passing the buck). Or it could send iterative queries and possibly be referred to other name servers "closer" to the domain name it's looking for. Current implementations are polite and do the latter, following the referrals until an answer is found.[†]

A name server that receives a recursive query that it can't answer itself will query the "closest known" name servers. The closest known name servers are the servers authoritative for the zone closest to the domain name being looked up. For example, if the name server receives a recursive query for the address of the domain name *girigiri.gbrmpa.gov.au,* it will first check whether it knows the name servers for *girigiri.gbrmpa.gov.au.* If it does, it will send the query to one of them. If not, it will check whether it knows the name servers for *gbrmpa.gov.au,* and after that *gov.au,* and then *au.* The default, where the check is guaranteed to stop, is the root zone, since every name server knows the domain names and addresses of the root name servers.

Using the closest known name servers ensures that the resolution process is as short as possible. A *berkeley.edu* name server receiving a recursive query for the address of *waxwing.ce.berkeley.edu* shouldn't have to consult the root name servers; it can simply follow delegation information directly to the *ce.berkeley.edu* name servers. Likewise, a name server that has just looked up a domain name in *ce.berkeley.edu* shouldn't have to start resolution at the roots to look up another *ce.berkeley.edu* (or *berkeley.edu*) domain name; we'll show how this works in the upcoming section on caching.

---

[*] The BIND 8 name server can be configured to refuse recursive queries; see Chapter 10, *Advanced Features and Security,* for how and why you'd want to do this.

[†] The exception is a name server configured to forward all unresolved queries to a designated name server, called a *forwarder.* See Chapter 10 for more information on using forwarders.

The name server that receives the recursive query always sends the same query that the resolver sends it, for example, for the address of *waxwing.ce.berkeley.edu*. It never sends explicit queries for the name servers for *ce.berkeley.edu* or *berkeley.edu*, though this information is also stored in the name space. Sending explicit queries could cause problems: There may be no *ce.berkeley.edu* name servers (that is, *ce.berkeley.edu* may be part of the *berkeley.edu* zone). Also, it's always possible that an *edu* or *berkeley.edu* name server would know *waxwing.ce.berkeley.edu*'s address. An explicit query for the *berkeley.edu* or *ce.berkeley.edu* name servers would miss this information.

Iteration

Iterative resolution, on the other hand, doesn't require nearly as much work on the part of the queried name server. In iterative resolution, a name server simply gives the best answer *it already knows* back to the querier. No additional querying is required. The queried name server consults its local data (including its cache, which we're about to talk about), looking for the data requested. If it doesn't find the data there, it makes its best attempt to give the querier data that will help it continue the resolution process. Usually these are the domain names and addresses of the closest known name servers.

What this amounts to is a resolution process that, taken as a whole, looks like Figure 2-13.

A resolver queries a local name server, which then queries a number of other name servers in pursuit of an answer for the resolver. Each name server it queries refers it to another name server that is authoritative for a zone further down in the name space and closer to the domain name sought. Finally, the local name server queries the authoritative name server, which returns an answer.

Mapping Addresses to Names

One major piece of functionality missing from the resolution process as explained so far is how addresses get mapped back to names. Address-to-name mapping is used to produce output that is easier for humans to read and interpret (in log files, for instance). It's also used in some authorization checks. UNIX hosts map addresses to domain names to compare against entries in *.rhosts* and *hosts.equiv* files, for example. When using host tables, address-to-name mapping is trivial. It requires a straightforward sequential search through the host table for an address. The search returns the official host name listed. In DNS, however, address-to-name mapping isn't so simple. Data, including addresses, in the domain name space are indexed by name. Given a domain name, finding an address is relatively easy. But finding the

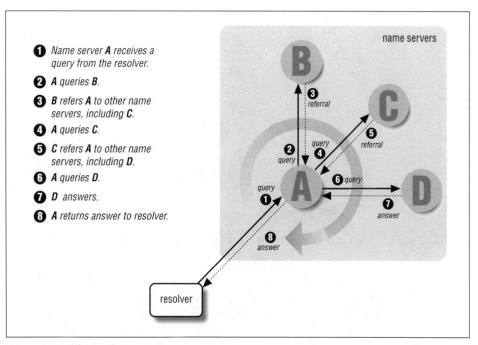

❶ Name server **A** receives a query from the resolver.

❷ **A** queries **B**.

❸ **B** refers **A** to other name servers, including **C**.

❹ **A** queries **C**.

❺ **C** refers **A** to other name servers, including **D**.

❻ **A** queries **D**.

❼ **D** answers.

❽ **A** returns answer to resolver.

Figure 2-13. The resolution process

domain name that maps to a given address would seem to require an exhaustive search of the data attached to every domain name in the tree.

Actually, there's a better solution that's both clever and effective. Because it's easy to find data once you're given the domain name that indexes that data, why not create a part of the domain name space that uses addresses as labels? In the Internet's domain name space, this portion of the name space is the *in-addr.arpa* domain.

Nodes in the *in-addr.arpa* domain are labelled after the numbers in the dotted-octet representation of IP addresses. (Dotted-octet representation refers to the common method of expressing 32-bit IP addresses as four numbers in the range 0 to 255, separated by dots.) The *in-addr.arpa* domain, for example, could have up to 256 subdomains, one corresponding to each possible value in the first octet of an IP address. Each of these subdomains could have up to 256 subdomains of its own, corresponding to the possible values of the second octet. Finally, at the fourth level down, there are resource records attached to the final octet giving the full domain name of the host or network at that IP address. That makes for an awfully big domain: *in-addr.arpa*, shown in Figure 2-14, is roomy enough for every IP address on the Internet.

Note that when read in a domain name, the IP address appears backward because the name is read from leaf to root. For example, if *winnie.corp.hp.com*'s IP address

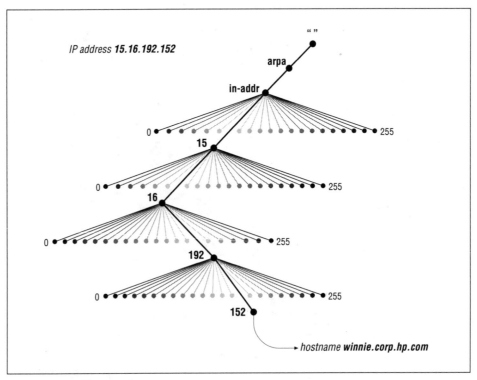

Figure 2-14. addr.arpa domain

is 15.16.192.152, the corresponding *in-addr.arpa* subdomain is *152.192.16.15.in-addr.arpa*, which maps back to the domain name *winnie.corp.hp.com*.

IP addresses could have been represented the opposite way in the name space, with the first octet of the IP address at the bottom of the *in-addr.arpa* domain. That way, the IP address would have read correctly (forward) in the domain name.

IP addresses are hierarchical, however, just like domain names. Network numbers are doled out much as domain names are, and administrators can then subnet their address space and further delegate numbering. The difference is that IP addresses get more specific from left to right, while domain names get less specific from left to right. Figure 2-15 shows what we mean.

Making the first octets in the IP address appear highest in the tree gives administrators the ability to delegate authority for *in-addr.arpa* domains along network lines. For example, the *15.in-addr.arpa* domain, which contains the reverse mapping information for all hosts whose IP addresses start with 15, can be delegated to the administrators of network 15.0.0.0. This would be impossible if the octets appeared in the opposite order. If the IP addresses were represented the other way

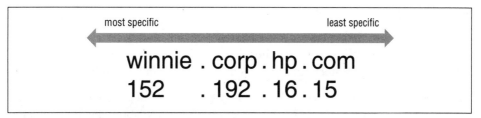

Figure 2-15. Hierarchical names and addresses

around, *15.in-addr.arpa* would consist of every host whose IP address *ended* with 15—not a practical domain to try to delegate.

Inverse Queries

The *in-addr.arpa* name space is clearly only useful for IP address-to-domain name mapping. Searching for a domain name that indexes an *arbitrary* piece of data— something besides an address—in the domain name space would require another specialized name space like *in-addr.arpa* or an exhaustive search.

That exhaustive search is to some extent possible, and it's called an *inverse query*. An inverse query is a search for the domain name that indexes a given datum. It's processed solely by the name server receiving the query. That name server searches all of its local data for the item sought and returns the domain name that indexes it, if possible. If it can't find the data, it gives up. No attempt is made to forward the query to another name server.

Because any one name server only knows about part of the overall domain name space, an inverse query is never guaranteed to return an answer. For example, if a name server receives an inverse query for an IP address it knows nothing about, it can't return an answer, but it also doesn't know that the IP address doesn't exist, because it only holds part of the DNS database. What's more, the implementation of inverse queries is optional according to the DNS specification; BIND 4.9.7 still contains the code that implements inverse queries, but it's commented out by default. BIND 8 no longer includes that code at all, though it does recognize inverse queries and can make up fake responses to them.[*] That's fine with us, because very little software (such as archaic versions of *nslookup*) actually still uses inverse queries.

---

[*] For details on this functionality, see "Query Refused," in Chapter 11, *nslookup*.

Caching

The whole resolution process may seem awfully convoluted and cumbersome to someone accustomed to simple searches through the host table. Actually, it's usually quite fast. One of the features that speeds it up considerably is *caching*.

A name server processing a recursive query may have to send out quite a few queries to find an answer. However, it discovers a lot of information about the domain name space as it does so. Each time it's referred to another list of name servers, it learns that those name servers are authoritative for some zone, and it learns the addresses of those servers. And, at the end of the resolution process, when it finally finds the data the original querier sought, it can store that data for future reference, too. With version 4.9 and all version 8 BINDs, name servers even implement *negative caching*: if an authoritative name server responds to a query with an answer that says the domain name or data type in the query doesn't exist, the local name server will temporarily cache that information, too. Name servers cache all of this data to help speed up successive queries. The next time a resolver queries the name server for data about a domain name the name server knows something about, the process is shortened quite a bit. The name server may have cached the answer, positive or negative, in which case it simply returns the answer to the resolver. Even if it doesn't have the answer cached, it may have learned the identities of the name servers that are authoritative for the zone the domain name is in and be able to query them directly.

For example, say our name server has already looked up the address of *eecs.berkeley.edu*. In the process, it cached the names and addresses of the *eecs.berkeley.edu* and *berkeley.edu* name servers (plus *eecs.berkeley.edu*'s IP address). Now if a resolver were to query our name server for the address of *baobab.cs.berkeley.edu*, our name server could skip querying the root name servers. Recognizing that *berkeley.edu* is the closest ancestor of *baobab.cs.berkeley.edu* that it knows about, our name server would start by querying a *berkeley.edu* name server, as shown in Figure 2-16. On the other hand, if our name server had discovered that there was no address for *eecs.berkeley.edu*, the next time it received a query for the address, it could simply have responded appropriately from its cache.

In addition to speeding up resolution, caching prevents us from having to query the root name servers again. This means that we're not as dependent on the roots, and they won't suffer as much from all our queries.

Time to Live

Name servers can't cache data forever, of course. If they did, changes to that data on the authoritative name servers would never reach the rest of the network. Remote name servers would just continue to use cached data. Consequently, the

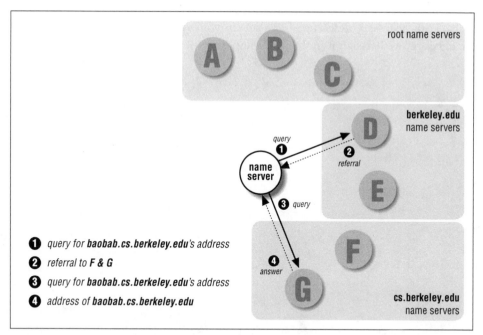

Figure 2-16. Resolving baobab.cs.berkeley.edu

administrator of the zone that contains the data decides on a *time to live*, or TTL, for the data. The time to live is the amount of time that any name server is allowed to cache the data. After the time to live expires, the name server must discard the cached data and get new data from the authoritative name servers. This also applies to negatively cached data; a name server must time out a negative answer after a period, too, in case new data has been added on the authoritative name servers. However, the time to live for negatively cached data isn't tunable by the domain administrator; it's hardcoded to ten minutes.

Deciding on a time to live for your data is essentially deciding on a trade-off between performance and consistency. A small TTL will help ensure that data about your domain is consistent across the network, because remote name servers will time it out more quickly and be forced to query your authoritative name servers more often for new data. On the other hand, this will increase the load on your name servers and lengthen resolution time for information in your domain, on the average.

A large TTL will shorten the average time it takes to resolve information in your domain because the data can be cached longer. The drawback is that your information will be inconsistent for a longer time if you make changes to your data on your name servers.

Enough of this theory—I'll bet you're antsy to get on with this. There's some homework necessary before you can set up your domain and your name servers, though, and we'll assign it in the next chapter.

3

Where Do I Start?

> *"What do you call yourself?" the Fawn said at last.*
> *Such a soft sweet voice it had!*
>
> *"I wish I knew!" thought poor Alice. She answered,*
> *rather sadly, "Nothing, just now."*
>
> *"Think again," it said: "that won't do."*
>
> *Alice thought, but nothing came of it. "Please,*
> *would you tell me what you call yourself?" she said*
> *timidly. "I think that might help a little."*
>
> *"I'll tell you, if you come a little further on," the*
> *Fawn said. "I can't remember here."*

Now that you understand the theory behind the Domain Name System, we can attend to more practical matters. Before you set up a domain, you may need to get the BIND software. Usually, it's included as a standard part of most UNIX-based operating systems. Occasionally, however, you'll need to seek out a version for a more obscure operating system, or you'll want the current version with all the latest functionality.

Once you've got BIND, you need to decide on a domain name—which may not be quite as easy as it sounds, because it entails finding an appropriate parent domain in the Internet name space. That decided, you need to contact the administrators of the parent domain of the domain name you've chosen.

One thing at a time, though. Let's talk about where to get BIND.

Getting BIND

If you plan to set up your own domain and run name servers for it, you'll need the BIND software first. Even if you're planning on having someone else run your domain, it's helpful to have the software around. For example, you can use your local name server to test your data files before giving them to your remote domain administrator.

Most commercial UNIX vendors ship BIND with the rest of their standard TCP/IP networking software. And, quite often, the networking software is included with the operating system, so you get BIND free. Even if the networking software is priced separately, you've probably already bought it, since you clearly do enough networking to need DNS, right?

If you don't have a version of BIND for your flavor of UNIX, though, or if you want the latest, greatest version, you can always get the source code. As luck would have it, it's freely distributed. The most up-to-date BIND source, as of this writing (the BIND 8.1.2 release), is available on the web at the Internet Software Consortium's web site, *http://www.isc.org/*, or via anonymous *ftp* from *ftp.isc.org* in */isc/bind/src/ cur/bind-8/bind-src.tar.gz*. Compiling it on most common UNIX platforms should be relatively straightforward. The ISC includes sample definitions in the top-level *Makefile* for most common versions of UNIX, including HP-UX, Irix, AIX, Solaris, and SunOS. We include instructions on compiling BIND 8.1.2 on Solaris 2.x as Appendix B, *Compiling and Installing* BIND *on a Sun.*

Some of you may already have a version of BIND that comes with your operating system, but you're wondering whether you really need the latest, greatest version of BIND. What does it have to offer that earlier versions of BIND don't? Here's an overview:

Security patches

> Arguably the most important reason to run the newest BIND is that only the most recent version is patched against most name server attacks, some of them widely known. BIND 8.1.2 is resistant to a variety of these attacks, while BIND 4.9.7 can withstand an important subset of them. Earlier versions of BIND have many well-known vulnerabilities. If you're running a name server on the Internet, we strongly recommend you run BIND 8.1.2 or at least BIND 4.9.7, or whatever the current released version is as you read this.

Security features

> BIND 8.1.2 supports access lists on queries, zone transfers, and dynamic updates. BIND 4.9 servers supported access lists on queries and zone transfers. Earlier versions of BIND didn't support access lists at all. Certain name servers, particularly those running on bastion hosts or other security-critical hosts, may require these features.
>
> We cover these features in Chapter 10, *Advanced Features and Security.*

DNS UPDATE

> BIND 8.1.2 supports the Dynamic Update standard described in RFC 2136. This allows authorized agents to update zone data by sending special update

messages to add or delete resource records. BIND 4 servers don't support Dynamic Update.

We cover Dynamic Update in Chapter 10.

DNS NOTIFY

BIND 8.1.2 supports zone change notification, which allows the primary master name server for a zone to notify the zone's slaves when the serial number has incremented. BIND 4 servers don't support NOTIFY.

We describe NOTIFY in Chapter 10.

Configuration syntax

BIND 8's configuration syntax is completely different from BIND 4's. While the new configuration syntax is more flexible and more powerful, it will also require learning a brand-new system for configuring BIND. But then, you have this book to help you through that.

We introduce the BIND 8 configuration syntax in Chapter 4, *Setting Up BIND*, and describe it throughout the rest of the book.

If, after reading through this list, you're convinced you need BIND 8's features, and a BIND 8 server doesn't come with your operating system, download the source code and build your own.

Handy Mailing Lists and Usenet Newsgroups

Instructions on how to port BIND to every other version of UNIX could consume another book this size, so we'll have to refer you to the BIND users mailing list, *bind-users@vix.com*, or the corresponding Usenet newsgroup, *comp.protocols.dns.bind*, for further help.[*] The bind-workers mailing list, *bind-workers@vix.com*, used by folks testing the new versions of BIND 8 code, is also an excellent place to turn. The folks who read and contribute to the BIND lists can be enormously helpful in your porting efforts. Be sure to ask whether the port you're after has already been done—you may be pleasantly surprised. Also, take a look at the BIND 8 errata page at *http://www.isc.org/bind8/errata/* for notes specific to your operating system, and check Andras Salamon's DNS Resource Directory for pre-compiled BIND software. The directory currently has a short list of pre-compiled binaries at *http://www.dns.net/dnsrd/bind.html*.

---

[*] To ask a question on an Internet mailing list, all you need to do is send a message to the mailing list's address. If you'd like to join the list, however, you have to send a message to the list's maintainer first, requesting him or her to add your electronic mail address to the list. Don't send this request to the list itself—that's considered rude. The Internet convention is that you can reach the maintainer of a mailing list by sending mail to *list-request@domain*, where *list@domain* is the address of the mailing list. So, for example, you can reach the BIND workers mailing list's administrator by sending mail to *bind-workers-request@vix.com*.

Another mailing list you might be interested in is the *namedroppers* list. Folks on the *namedroppers* mailing list usually discuss DNS issues, rather than BIND-specific problems. For example, a discussion of extensions to the DNS protocol or proposed DNS record types would probably take place on *namedroppers* instead of the BIND mailing list. Avoid sending the same message to more than one of these mailing lists; many people are on more than one.

The address for the *namedroppers* mailing list is *namedroppers@internic.net*, and it is gatewayed into the Internet newsgroup *comp.protocols.tcp-ip.domains*. To join the *namedroppers* mailing list, send mail to *majordomo@internic.net* with the text "subscribe namedroppers" as the body of the message. The InterNIC also provides a web-based front end for subscribing at *http://rs.internic.net/cgi-bin/lwgate/NAMEDROPPERS/*.

Finding IP Addresses

You'll notice we gave you a number of domain names of hosts that have *ftp*able software, and the mailing lists we mentioned include domain names. That should underscore the importance of DNS: see what valuable software and advice you can get with the help of DNS? Unfortunately, it's also something of a chicken-and-egg problem. You can't send email to an address with a domain name in it unless you've got DNS set up, so how can you ask someone on the list how to set DNS up?

Well, we could give you the IP addresses for all the hosts we mentioned, but since IP addresses change often (in publishing timescales, anyway), we'll show you how you can *temporarily* use someone else's name server to find the information instead. As long as your host has Internet connectivity and the *nslookup* program, you can retrieve information from the Internet name space. To look up the IP address for *ftp.isc.org*, for example, you could use:

```
% nslookup ftp.isc.org. 207.69.188.185
```

This instructs *nslookup* to query the name server running on the host at IP address 207.69.188.185 to find the IP address for *ftp.isc.org*, and should produce output like:

```
Server:  ns1.mindspring.com
Address:  207.69.188.185

Name:    pub1.pa.vix.com
Address: 204.152.184.33
Aliases: ftp.isc.org
```

Now you can *ftp* to *ftp.isc.org*'s IP address, 204.152.184.33.

How did we know that the host at IP address 207.69.188.185 runs a name server? Our ISP, Mindspring, told us—it's one of their name servers. If your ISP provides name servers for its customers' use (and most do), use one of them. If your ISP doesn't provide name servers (shame on them!), you can *temporarily* use one of the name servers listed in this book. As long as you only use it to look up a few IP addresses or other data, the administrators probably won't mind. It's considered very rude, however, to point your resolver or query tool at someone else's name server permanently.

Of course, if you already have access to a host with Internet connectivity *and* DNS configured, you can use it to *ftp* the stuff you need.

Once you've got a working version of BIND, you're ready to start thinking about your domain name.

Choosing a Domain Name

Choosing a domain name is more involved than it may sound, because it entails both choosing a name *and* finding a parent. In other words, you need to find out where you fit in the Internet domain name space, and decide what you'd like to call your particular corner of that name space.

The first step in picking a domain name is finding where in the existing domain name space you belong. It's easiest to start at the top and work your way down: decide which top-level domain you belong in, then which of that top-level domain's subdomains you fit into.

Note that in order to find out what the Internet domain name space looks like (beyond what we've already told you), you'll need access to the Internet. You don't need access to a host that already has Domain Name Service configured, but it would help a little. If you don't have access to a host with DNS configured, you'll have to "borrow" name service from other name servers (as in our previous *ftp.isc.org* example) to get you going.

Where in the World Do I Fit?

If your organization is attached to the Internet outside of the United States, you first need to decide whether you'd rather request a domain under the generic top-level domains, like *com* and *edu*, or under your country's top-level domain. The generic top-level domains, even though some are used largely *by* U.S. organizations, aren't exclusively *for* U.S. organizations. If your company is a multi- or transnational company, you may wish to join a generic top-level domain, or if you'd simply prefer a generic top-level to your country's top-level domain, you're welcome to ask to join one. If you choose this route, skip to the section "The generic top-level domains" later in this chapter.

If you opt for a subdomain under your country's top level, you should check whether your country's top-level domain is registered, and if it is, what kind of structure it has. Consult our list of the current top-level domains (Appendix C, *Top-Level Domains*) if you're not sure what the name of your country's top-level domain would be.

Some countries' top-level domains, like New Zealand's *nz*, Australia's *au*, and the United Kingdom's *uk*, are divided organizationally into second-level domains. The names of their second-level domains, like *co* or *com* for commercial entities, reflect organizational affiliation. Others, like France's *fr* domain, and Canada's *ca* domain, are divided into a multitude of subdomains managed by individual universities and companies, like the University of St. Etienne's domain, *univ-st-etienne.fr* and Bell Northern Research's *bnr.ca*. You'll have to use a tool like *nslookup* to grope around and discover your top-level domain's structure if it isn't well-known. (If you're uncomfortable with our rushing headlong into *nslookup* without giving it a proper introduction, you might skim Chapter 11, *nslookup*.) For example, here's how you could list the *au* domain's subdomains using *nslookup*:

```
% nslookup - 207.69.188.185     —Use the name server at 207.69.188.185
Default Server: ns1.mindspring.com
Address:  207.69.188.185

> set type=ns                   —Find the name servers (ns)
> au.                           —for the au domain
Server:  ns1.mindspring.com
Address: 207.69.188.185

au      nameserver = MUNNARI.OZ.AU
au      nameserver = MULGA.CS.MU.OZ.AU
au      nameserver = JATZ.AARNET.EDU.AU
au      nameserver = NS.UU.NET
au      nameserver = NS.EU.NET
au      nameserver = NS1.BERKELEY.EDU
au      nameserver = NS2.BERKELEY.EDU
au      nameserver = VANGOGH.CS.BERKELEY.EDU
MUNNARI.OZ.AU      internet address = 128.250.1.21
MUNNARI.OZ.AU      internet address = 128.250.22.2
MULGA.CS.MU.OZ.AU       internet address = 128.250.1.22
MULGA.CS.MU.OZ.AU       internet address = 128.250.37.150
JATZ.AARNET.EDU.AU      internet address = 139.130.204.4
NS.UU.NET       internet address = 137.39.1.3
NS.EU.NET       internet address = 192.16.202.11
NS1.BERKELEY.EDU  internet address = 128.32.136.9
NS1.BERKELEY.EDU  internet address = 128.32.206.9
NS2.BERKELEY.EDU        internet address = 128.32.136.12
NS2.BERKELEY.EDU        internet address = 128.32.206.12

> server ns1.berkeley.edu.       —Now query one of these name servers—preferably a close one!
Default Server:  ns1.berkeley.edu
Addresses:  128.32.136.9, 128.32.206.9

> ls au.  —List the au zone
            —the zone's NS records mark delegation to
```

—subdomains and will give
—you the names of the subdomains
—Note that not all name servers will allow you to list zones, for security reasons.

```
[ns1.berkeley.edu]
            3D IN SOA      munnari.OZ hostmaster.munnari.OZ (
                  1998051400      ; serial
                  6H              ; refresh
                  1H              ; retry
                  23w5d16h        ; expire
                      3D )        ; minimum


                 3D IN NS              munnari.OZ
                 3D IN NS              mulga.cs.mu.OZ
                 3D IN NS              vangogh.CS.Berkeley.EDU.
                 3D IN NS              ns1.Berkeley.EDU.
                 3D IN NS              ns2.Berkeley.EDU.
                 3D IN NS              ns.UU.NET.
                 3D IN NS              ns.eu.NET.
ORG              1D IN NS              yalumba.connect.COM
yalumba.connect.COM      1D IN A      203.8.183.1
ORG              1D IN NS              mulga.cs.mu.OZ
mulga.cs.mu.OZ           1D IN A      128.250.1.22
                 1D IN A              128.250.37.150
ORG              1D IN NS              rip.psg.COM.
                 1D IN NS              munnari.OZ
munnari.OZ               1D IN A      128.250.1.21
                 1D IN A              128.250.22.2
info             1D IN NS             ns.telstra.net.
                 1D IN NS             ns1.telstra.net.
                 1D IN NS             munnari.oz
munnari.oz               1D IN A      128.250.1.21
                 1D IN A              128.250.22.2
info             1D IN NS             svc01.apnic.net.
a                3D IN A              139.130.23.2
otc              4H IN NS             ns.telstra.com
ns.telstra.com           4H IN A      192.148.160.10
otc              4H IN NS             ns2.telstra.com
ns2.telstra.com          4H IN A      192.148.160.11
otc              4H IN NS             munnari.oz
munnari.oz               1D IN A      128.250.1.21
                 1D IN A              128.250.22.2
CSIRO            1D IN NS             steps.its.CSIRO
steps.its.CSIRO          1D IN A      152.83.8.3
CSIRO            1D IN NS             munnari.OZ
munnari.OZ               1D IN A      128.250.1.21
                 1D IN A              128.250.22.2
CSIRO            1D IN NS             manta.vic.cmis.CSIRO
manta.vic.cmis.CSIRO     1D IN A      144.110.16.100
CSIRO            1D IN NS             dmssyd.nsw.cmis.CSIRO
dmssyd.nsw.cmis.CSIRO    1D IN A      130.155.16.1
CSIRO            1D IN NS             zoiks.per.its.CSIRO
zoiks.per.its.CSIRO      1D IN A      192.245.210.1
[]

> ^D
```

The basic technique we used is straightforward: look up the list of authoritative name servers for the top-level domain—because they're the only ones with complete information about the corresponding zone—then connect to one of those name servers, and list the name servers for the second-level domains.

If you can't tell from the names of the subdomains which one you belong in, you can look up the contact information for the corresponding zone and send email to the technical contact asking, politely, for advice. Similarly, if you think you should be part of an existing subdomain but aren't sure, you can always ask the folks who administer that subdomain to double-check.

To find out who to ask about a subdomain, you'll have to look up the corresponding zone's SOA record. In each zone's start of authority (SOA) record, there's a field that contains the electronic mail address of the zone's technical contact.* (The other fields in the start of authority record provide general information about a zone—we'll discuss them in more detail later.) You can look up the zone's SOA record with *nslookup*, too.

If you're curious about the purpose of the *csiro* subdomain, you can find out who runs it by looking up *csiro.au*'s SOA record:

```
% nslookup - 207.69.188.185
Default Server:  ns1.mindspring.com
Address:  207.69.188.185

> set type=soa      —Look for start of authority data
> csiro.au.         —for csiro.au
Server:  ns1.mindspring.com
Address: 207.69.188.185

csiro.au
        origin = steps.its.csiro.au
        mail addr = hostmaster.csiro.au
        serial = 1997122201
        refresh = 10800 (3 hours)
        retry  = 3600 (1 hour)
        expire = 3600000 (41 days 16 hours)
        minimum ttl = 86400 (1 day)
```

The mail addr field is the Internet address of *csiro.au*'s contact. To use the address with most UNIX mailers, you'll need to change the first "." in the address to a "@". So *hostmaster.csiro.au* becomes *hostmaster@csiro.au*.[†]

---

* The subdomain and the zone have the same domain name, but the SOA record really belongs to the zone, not the subdomain. The person at the zone's technical contact email address may not manage the whole subdomain (there may be additional delegated subdomains beneath), but he should certainly know what the purpose of the subdomain is.

† This form of Internet mail address is a vestige of two former DNS records, MB and MG. MB (mailbox) and MG (mail group) were to be DNS records specifying Internet mailboxes and mail groups (mailing lists) as subdomains of the appropriate domain. MB and MG never took off, but the address format they would have dictated is used in the SOA record, maybe for sentimental reasons.

whois

The *whois* service can also help you figure out what a given domain is for. Many vendors ship a simple *whois* client that queries a database on a host at the InterNIC (or on another host that you specify) for information about domains, networks, and the people that run them. For example:

```
% whois bob
```

will turn up every match for *bob* in the database, including people, networks and domains. To restrict the search to domains or networks, you can use the keywords *dom* or *net*, respectively:

```
% whois dom foo  # print information on all domains that match foo
% whois -h whois.arin.net. net 17  # print information on network 17
```

If your copy of *whois* is outdated, it'll probably try to query the InterNIC's database on an old host, like *sri-nic.arpa* or *nic.ddn.mil*. That'll produce either a pleasant message from the InterNIC staff or a gruff error like this:

```
sri-nic.arpa: Unknown host
```

If this happens and you have access to the source code and a compiler, just recompile *whois* to query *whois.internic.net*. If you don't have the source, you can still direct *whois* to use *whois.internic.net* from the command line with the *-h* option, as in:

```
% whois -h whois.internic.net dom au
```

If you don't have a *whois* client, or would prefer a friendlier interface, you can use the InterNIC's *whois* web page, at *http://rs.internic.net/cgi-bin/whois/*. This gives you an HTML forms-based interface for querying the InterNIC's database.

Unfortunately, the InterNIC's *whois* database only lists contacts for top-level country domains and subdomains of generic top-level domains, so you won't find *csiro.au*. Still, you can use it to find the administrative contact for *au*.

Click on search, and you'll see a screen like Figure 3-1.[*]

If we scroll down a little, we find "Australia top-level domain," which is what we're after. If you click on the hypertext link labeled "AU-DOM" on that line, you'll see a screen like Figure 3-2, which tells us to talk to Robert Elz about the top-level *au* domain.

To get *csiro.au* contact information on the web, you'd need to query the Australian NIC. Is there such a thing? You can check *http://www.allwhois.com/*, shown in Figure 3-3 to find out. Click on "Australia" in the left-hand frame, and you'll see a screen like the one shown in Figure 3-4.

---

[*] Believe it or not, when we did this for the first edition of this book, there was only one match.

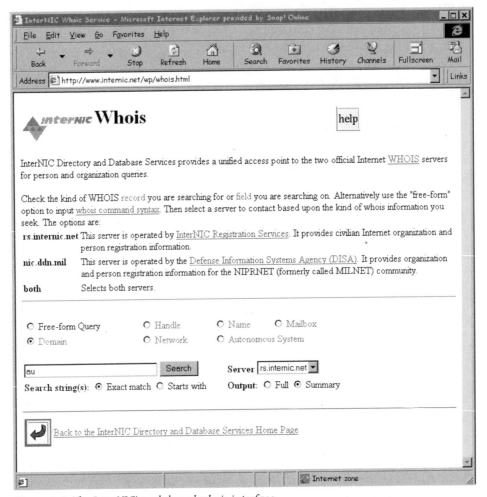

Figure 3-1. The InterNIC's web-based whois interface

Click on "Whois" to take you to a forms front-end that will let you query the AUNIC's (Australian NIC's) database.

Obviously, this is a very useful web site if you're looking for the contact for a domain outside of the U.S.

Elsewhere in the World

In true cosmopolitan spirit, we covered international domains first. But what if you're from the good ol' U.S. of A.?

If you're in the U.S., where you belong depends mainly upon how many hosts you have. If you only have one or two, or maybe a handful of hosts you'd like registered

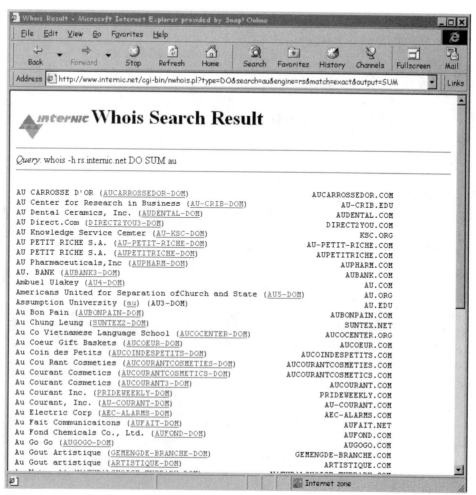

Figure 3-2. Results of an InterNIC whois search

in the Internet's domain name space, you can join the *us* domain. The *us* domain registers individual hosts under third-level domains largely named after cities; the second-level domains correspond to the appropriate U.S. Postal Service two-letter state abbreviation (recall our discussion in the section called "The Internet Domain Name Space" in Chapter 2, *How Does DNS Work?*). So, for example, if all you need is to register the two internetworked hosts in your basement in Colorado Springs, Colorado, you can just have them added to the *colospgs.co.us* domain.

You can even get your own domain to manage, thanks to a change in policy by the administrators of the *us* domain. Originally, the *us* domain was purely geographical. The *us* domain administrators added address and mail handling information for your host(s) (more on this in the next two chapters—be patient), but not name server

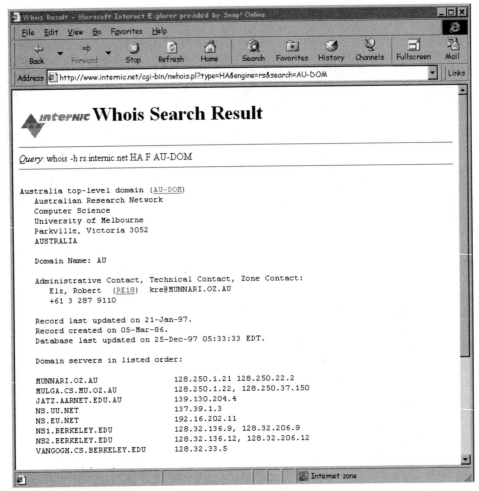

Figure 3-3. Detailed results of an InterNIC whois search

information. In other words, they wouldn't delegate a portion of their domain to you. Nowadays, they encourage U.S. schools, governments, and companies to join the *us* domain. If you're interested in the details, check out RFC 1480, available from *ftp:// ftp.ds.internic.net/rfc/rfc1480.txt*, or see the information on the *us* domain on ISI's web site, at *http://www.isi.edu/in-notes/usdnr/*.

You can also ask for a subdomain of one of the generic top-level domains, like *edu* and *com*. As long as you don't ask for an overly long subdomain name (the InterNIC recommends 12 letters or fewer), or one that's already taken, you should get the one you ask for. We'll cover membership under the generic top-levels later in this chapter.

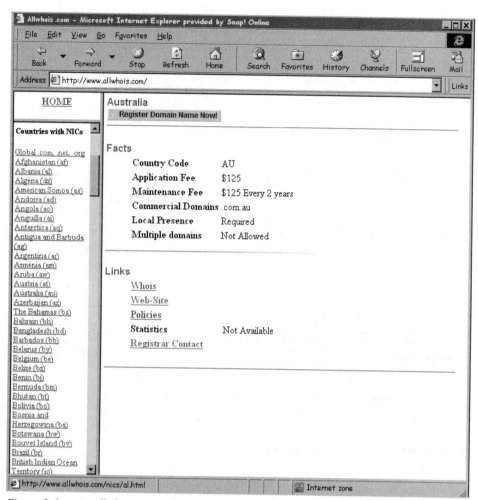

Figure 3-4. www.allwhois.com

The us domain

Let's go through an example to give you an idea of how to comb the *us* domain name space for the perfect domain name. Say you live in Rockville, Maryland, and you want to register the UNIX workstation you just bought out of the back of a truck (hey, it could happen). You're not directly connected to the Internet, but you do have a UUCP connection to UMD in College Park.

Since you only need to have a single host registered, you really don't need your own domain to manage. You just need to have your host registered in the Internet domain name space somewhere. The *us* top-level domain is the one for you. Letting someone else take care of the name server and domain administration will save you a lot of administrative effort.

Using an account you still have on a host at UMD (from your undergrad days), you can check to see whether a domain for Maryland exists. (If you didn't have an account there, but you did have Internet connectivity, you could still use *nslookup* to query a well-known name server.)

```
% nslookup
Default Server:  noc.umd.edu
Address: 128.8.5.2

> set type=ns             —Look up the name servers
> md.us.                  —for md.us
Server:  noc.umd.edu
Address:  128.8.5.2


md.us    nameserver = NS.UU.NET
md.us    nameserver = ADMII.ARL.MIL
md.us    nameserver = EXCALIBUR.USC.EDU
md.us    nameserver = VGR.ARL.MIL
md.us    nameserver = TRANTOR.UMD.EDU
md.us    nameserver = MX.NSI.NASA.GOV
md.us    nameserver = VENERA.ISI.EDU
md.us    nameserver = NS.ISI.EDU
md.us    nameserver = RS0.INTERNIC.NET
```

Sure enough, there's a domain for Maryland. Now change servers to a *md.us* name server, say *venera.isi.edu*, and check to see if there are any subdomains (you haven't exited out of *nslookup* yet):

```
> server venera.isi.edu.    —Change server to venera.isi.edu
Default Server:  venera.isi.edu
Address:  128.9.0.32

> ls md.us.       —List the md.us zone to look for NS record
[venera.isi.edu]
          1D IN SOA      VENERA.ISI.EDU. us-domain.ISI.EDU. (
                 980112          ; serial
                 12H             ; refresh
                 1H              ; retry
                 2W              ; expire
                 1D )            ; minimum


          1W IN NS      RS0.INTERNIC.NET.
          1W IN NS      NS.UU.NET.
          1W IN NS      ADMII.ARL.MIL.
          1W IN NS      EXCALIBUR.USC.EDU.
          1W IN NS      VGR.ARL.MIL.
          1W IN NS      TRANTOR.UMD.EDU.
          1W IN NS      MX.NSI.NASA.GOV.
          1W IN NS      VENERA.ISI.EDU.
          1W IN N       NS.ISI.EDU.
 north-laurel.md.us.    1D IN NS      top2.domainregistry.net.
          1D IN NS      top.domainregistry.net.
          1D IN NS      primary.southern-domains.com.
```

```
fruitland.md.us.        1D IN NS      top2.domainregistry.net.
            1D IN NS       top.domainregistry.net.
            1D IN NS       primary.southern-domains.com.
frostburg.md.us.        1D IN NS      winnt.i-theta.com.
            1D IN NS       ns2.us-domains.com.
            1D IN NS       ns.manchester.mo.us.
creativedesign.college.md.us.   1W IN NS       ns.webindonesia.com.
            1W IN NS       ns2.webindonesia.com.
carroll.md.us.          1W IN NS      auth00.ns.uu.net.
            1W IN NS       auth50.ns.uu.net.
oxon-hill.md.us.        1D IN NS      winnt.i-theta.com.
            1D IN NS       ns2.us-domains.com.
            1D IN NS       ns.manchester.mo.us.
    [...]
```

Aha! So there *is* life in Maryland! There are subdomains called *aa, adelphi, al, allegany,* and many others. But there doesn't seem to be a domain for Rockville. No matter—you may be the first host in Rockville to want to register under the *md.us* domain. Or perhaps this naming scheme is based on county names, and Rockville would fit under its county name. Either way, the administrators of *md.us* can find a home for you. Since your domain name will just be part of the *md.us* zone, it won't require very much work for them—there's no need to set up separate servers.

What to call the new subdomain, if you need a new one? *rockville.md.us? rock.md.us?* Turns out there's a convention in the *us* domain that city-level domains be named after the appropriate Western Union "City Mnemonic." (Don't worry: the *us* administrators have a copy.) The alternative is to use the full name of the city.

Actually, with any parent domain, it's possible that the administrators of the domain will have strong feelings about the names of their child domains (just as your parents probably had strong feelings about naming you). They may want to preserve the consistency of their name space. We think it's polite to defer to your parent if they feel strongly about naming—after all, they could simply refuse to let you join the domain. You still get to choose the name of your host, after all.

How do you find out how to contact your parent domain's administrator? You can try *whois,* but since *md.us* isn't a top-level country domain or part of a generic top-level domain, you probably won't find much. Your best bet is probably to use *nslookup* to find the SOA record for the *md.us* zone, just as you did to find out whom to ask about *csiro.au.* Though the person or persons who read mail sent to the address in the SOA record may not handle registration themselves (technical and administrative functions for the zone may be divided), it's a good bet they know the folks who do and can direct you to them.

Here's how you'd use *nslookup* to dig up the SOA record for *md.us:*

```
% nslookup
Default Server: noc.umd.edu
Address: 128.8.5.2
```

```
> set type=soa      —Look up SOA record
> md.us.            —for md.us
Server:  noc.umd.edu
Address:  128.8.5.2

md.us
        origin = VENERA.ISI.EDU
        mail addr = us-domain.ISI.EDU
        serial = 971109
        refresh = 43200 (12 hours)
        retry   = 3600 (1 hour)
        expire  = 1209600 (14 days)
        minimum ttl = 86400 (1 day)
```

As in the *csiro.au* example, you need to swap the first "." in the mail addr field for
an "@" before you use it. Thus, *us-domain.ISI.EDU* becomes *us-domain@ISI.EDU*.

The generic top-level domains

As we said, there are many reasons that you might want to ask for a subdomain of
one of the generic top-level domains, like *com, edu,* and *org*: you work for a multi-
or transnational company, you like the fact that they're better-known, or you just like
the sound of your domain name better with "com" on the end. Let's go through a
short example of choosing a domain name under a gTLD.

Imagine you're the student administrator of a small university network in Hopkins,
Minnesota. You've just gotten a grant for Internet connectivity, and are about to be
connected to your regional network, MRNet. Your university has never had so much
as a UUCP link, so you're not currently registered in the Internet name space.

Since you're in the United States, you have the choice of joining either *us* or *edu*.
You've already got over a dozen computers on your local network, though, and you
expect more, so *us* wouldn't be a good choice. A subdomain of *edu* would be best.

Your university is known as The Gizmonics Institute, so you decide *gizmo.edu* might
be an appropriate domain name. Now you've got to check if the name *gizmo.edu*
has been taken by anyone, so you use an account you have at UMN:

```
% nslookup
Default Server:  ns.unet.umn.edu
Address:  128.101.101.101

> set type=any      —Look for any records
> gizmo.edu.        —for gizmo.edu
Server:  ns.unet.umn.edu
Address:  128.101.101.101

*** ns.unet.umn.edu can't find gizmo.edu.: Non-existent domain
```

Looks like there's no *gizmo.edu* yet (hardly surprising), so you can go on to the next step: finding out who runs your intended parent domain. You use *whois*:

```
% whois dom edu
Education top-level domain (EDU-DOM)
   Network Solutions, Inc.
   505 Huntmar Park Dr.
   Herndon, VA  22070

   Domain Name: EDU

   Administrative Contact, Technical Contact, Zone Contact:
      Network Solutions, Inc.  (HOSTMASTER)  HOSTMASTER@INTERNIC.NET
      (703) 742-4777 (FAX) (703) 742-9552

   Record last updated on 17-Jan-97.
    Record created on 01-Jan-85.
    Database last updated on 25-Dec-97 05:33:33 EDT.



   Domain servers in listed order:

   [...]
```

Checking That Your Network Is Registered

Before proceeding, you should check whether or not your IP network or networks are registered. Many parent domains won't delegate a subdomain to name servers on unregistered networks, and registries won't delegate an *in-addr.arpa* subdomain that corresponds to an unregistered network.

An IP network defines a range of IP addresses. For example, the network 15/8 is made up of all IP addresses in the range 15.0.0.0 to 15.255.255.255. The network 199.10.25/24 starts at 199.10.25.0 and ends at 199.10.25.255.

The InterNIC was once the official source of all IP networks; they assigned all IP networks to Internet-connected networks and made sure no two ranges overlapped. Nowadays, the InterNIC's old role has been largely assumed by Internet Service Providers (ISPs), who allocate space from their own networks for customers to use. If you know your network came from your ISP, the larger network from which your network was carved is probably registered (to your ISP). You may still want to double-check that your ISP took care of registering their network, but you don't (and probably can't) do anything yourself, except nag your ISP if they didn't register their network. Once you've verified their registration, you can skip the rest of this section and move on.

If, however, your network was assigned by the InterNIC, way back when, or you *are* an ISP, you should check to see whether your network is registered. Where do

A Sidebar on CIDR

Once upon a time, when we wrote the first edition of this book, the Internet's 32-bit address space was divided up into three main classes of networks: class A, class B, and class C. Class A networks were networks in which the first octet (first eight bits) of the IP address identified the network, and the remaining bits were used by the organization assigned the network to differentiate hosts on the network. Most organizations with class A networks also subdivided their networks into subnetworks, or subnets, adding another level of hierarchy to the addressing scheme. Class B networks devoted two octets to the network identifier and two to the host; class C networks gave three octets to the network identifier and one to the host.

Unfortunately, this small/medium/large system of networks didn't work well for everyone. Many organizations were large enough to require several class C networks, which could accommodate at most 254 hosts, but too small to warrant a full class B network, which could serve 65534 hosts. Many of these organizations were allocated class B networks, anyway. Consequently, class B networks quickly became scarce.

To help solve this problem, and create networks that were just the right size for all sorts of organizations, Classless Inter-Domain Routing, or CIDR (pronounced "cider") was developed. As the name implies, CIDR does away with the old class A, class B, and class C network designations. Instead of allocating either one, two, or three octets to the network identifier, the allocator could allocate any number of contiguous bits of the IP address to the network identifier. So, for example, if an organization needed an address space roughly four times as large as a class B network, the powers-that-be could assign it a network identifier of 14 bits, leaving 18 bits (four class Bs' worth) of space to use.

Naturally, the advent of CIDR made the "classful" terminology outdated— although it's still used a good deal in casual conversation. Now, to designate a particular CIDR network, we specify the particular high-order bit value assigned to an organization, expressed in dotted octet notation, and how many bits identify the network. The two terms are separated by a slash. So 15/8 is the old, class A-sized network that begins with the bit pattern 00001111. The old, class B-sized network 128.32.0.0 is now 128.32/16. And the network 192.168.0.128/25 consists of the 128 IP addresses from 192.168.0.128 to 192.168.0.255.

you go to check whether your network is registered? Why, to the same organizations that register networks, of course. These organizations, called (what else?) registries, each handle network registration in some part of the world. In the Western

Hemisphere, ARIN, the American Registry of Internet Numbers, at *http://www.arin.net/*, hands out IP address space and registers networks. In Asia and the Pacific, APNIC, the Asia Pacific Network Information Center, at *http://www.apnic.net/*, serves the same function. In Europe, it's the RIPE Network Coordination Centre, at *http://www.ripe.net/*. Each registry may also delegate registration authority for a region; for example, ARIN delegates registration authority for Mexico and for Brazil to registries in each country. Be sure to check for a registry local to your country.

If you're not sure your network is registered, the best way to find it is to use the *whois* service provided by the various registries and look for your network. Here are the URLs for each registry's *whois* page:

ARIN

> *http://www.arin.net/whois/arinwhois.html*

APNIC

> *http://www.apnic.net/reg.html*

RIPE

> *http://www.ripe.net/db/whois.html*

If you find out your network isn't registered, you'll need to get it registered before setting up your *in-addr.arpa* zones. Each registry has a different process for registering networks, but most involve money changing hands (from your hands to theirs, unfortunately).

You may find out that your network is already assigned to your ISP. If this is the case, you don't need to register independently with the registry.

Once all your Internet-connected hosts are on registered networks, you can give your parent domain a call.

Registering with Your Parent

Different domains have different registration policies. We've included the InterNIC's current registration form for second-level domains as Appendix D, *Domain Registration Form*. The form is only valid for registration under the InterNIC-run generic top-level domains like *com* and *edu*. (In other words, don't submit it to the administrators of the *au* or *fr* domain and expect them to honor it.) It should, however, give you an idea of what to expect in a registration form (especially if you're registering under one of the InterNIC's domains). Other domains often have more informal registration processes. Sometimes simply sending the "registrar" the necessary information in an email message will do.

Since the forms will undoubtedly become obsolete before we update this book again, you should check out the InterNIC's online, HTML forms-based registration process at *http://www.rs.internic.net/rs-internic.html*. Although this process doesn't actually submit the form yet, it does automate the process of creating a properly-formatted request that you can then email to the InterNIC. Or you can just retrieve the current forms and print them, then fill them out by hand.

The basic information that your parent needs is the names and addresses of your domain name servers. If you're not connected to the Internet, give them the addresses of the Internet hosts that will act as your name servers. Some parent domains also require that you already have operational name servers for your domain. (The InterNIC doesn't, but they ask for an estimate of when the domain will be fully operational.) If that's the case with your parent, skip ahead to Chapter 4, and set up your name servers. Then contact your parent with the requisite information.

If the InterNIC runs your parent domain, they'll also ask for some information about your organization, and for an administrative contact and a technical contact for your domain (which can be the same person). If your contacts aren't already registered in the InterNIC's *whois* database, you'll also need to provide information to register them in *whois*. This includes their names, surface mail addresses, phone numbers, and electronic mail addresses. If they are already registered in *whois*, just specify their InterNIC *whois* "handle" (a unique alphanumeric ID) in the registration.

There's one more aspect of registering a new domain with the InterNIC that we should mention: cost. Network Solutions, Inc. (NSI), the contractor that manages the InterNIC, has begun charging to register new top-level domains and domains under the generic top-level domains *com*, *net*, and *org*. The startup fee is $70 (U.S.). NSI has also instituted an ongoing, annual charge of U.S. $35 for each domain. If you already have a subdomain under *com*, *net*, or *org* and haven't received a bill from NSI recently, it'd be a good idea to check your contact information with *whois* to make sure they've got a current address and phone number for you. For more information on the billing policy and the current scoop on the InterNIC registration process, see *http://www.rs.internic.net/rs-internic.html*.

If you're directly connected to the Internet, you should also have the *in-addr.arpa* domains corresponding to your IP networks delegated to you. For example, if your company was allocated the network 192.201.44/24, you should manage the *44.201.192.in-addr.arpa* domain. This will let you control the IP address-to-name mappings for hosts on your network. Chapter 4 also explains how to set up your *in-addr.arpa* domains.

In the last section, "Checking That Your Network Is Registered," we asked you to find the answers to several questions: is your network a slice of an ISP's network? Is your network, or the ISP's network that your network is part of, registered? In which registry? You'll need these answers to have your *in-addr.arpa* domains delegated to you.

If your network is part of a larger network registered to an ISP, you should contact the ISP to have the appropriate subdomains of *in-addr.arpa* delegated to you. Each ISP uses a different process for setting up *in-addr.arpa* delegation. Your ISP's web page is a good place to research that process. If you can't find the information there, try looking up the SOA record for the *in-addr.arpa* domain that corresponds to your ISP's network. For example, if your network is part of UUnet's 153.35/16 network, you could look up the SOA record of *35.153.in-addr.arpa* to find the email address of the technical contact for the zone.

If your network is registered directly with one of the regional registries, contact them to get your *in-addr.arpa* domain registered. Each registry makes information on their delegation process available on its web site. ARIN's template for requesting *in-addr.arpa* delegation, *inaddrtemplate.txt*, is included in this book as Appendix E, *in-addr.arpa Registration Form*, and available online at *http://rs.arin.net/templates/inaddrtemplate.txt*.

Now that you've sent your prospective parent word that you'd like to be adopted, you'd better take some time to get your things in order. You've got a domain to set up, and in the next chapter, we'll show you how.

4

Setting Up BIND

"It seems very pretty," she said when she had finished it, "but it's rather hard to understand!" (You see she didn't like to confess, even to herself, that she couldn't make it out at all.) "Somehow it seems to fill my head with ideas—only I don't exactly know what they are!"

If you have been diligently reading each chapter of this book, you're probably anxious to get a name server running. This chapter is for you. Let's set up a couple of name servers. Others of you may have read the table of contents and skipped directly to this chapter. (Shame on you!) If you are one of those people who cut corners, be aware that we may use concepts from earlier chapters and expect you to understand them already.

There are several factors that influence how you should set up your name servers. The biggest factor is what sort of access you have to the Internet: complete access (e.g., you can *ftp* to *ftp.uu.net*), limited access (limited by a security firewall), or no access at all. This chapter assumes you have complete access. We'll discuss the other cases in Chapter 15, *Miscellaneous.*

In this chapter, we'll set up two name servers for a fictitious domain, as an example for you to follow in setting up your own domain. We'll cover the topics in this chapter in enough detail to get your first two name servers running. Subsequent chapters will fill in the holes and go into greater depth. If you already have your name servers running, skim through this chapter to familiarize yourself with the terms we use or just to verify that you didn't miss something when you set up your servers.

Our Domain

Our fictitious domain is for a college. Movie University studies all aspects of the film industry and researches novel ways to distribute films. One of the most promising projects is research into using IP as the distribution medium. After talking with the folks at the InterNIC, we have decided on the domain name *movie.edu*. A recent grant has enabled us to connect to the Internet.

Movie U. currently has two Ethernets, and they have plans for another network or two. The Ethernets have network numbers 192.249.249 and 192.253.253. A portion of their host table shows the following entries:

```
127.0.0.1       localhost

# These are our killer machines

192.249.249.2  robocop.movie.edu robocop
192.249.249.3  terminator.movie.edu terminator bigt
192.249.249.4  diehard.movie.edu diehard dh

# These machines are in horror(ible) shape and will be replaced
# soon.

192.253.253.2  misery.movie.edu misery
192.253.253.3  shining.movie.edu shining
192.253.253.4  carrie.movie.edu carrie

# A wormhole is a fictitious phenomenon that instantly transports
# space travelers over long distances and is not known to be
# stable.  The only difference between wormholes and routers is
# that routers don't transport packets as instantly--especially
# ours.

192.249.249.1  wormhole.movie.edu wormhole wh wh249
192.253.253.1  wormhole.movie.edu wormhole wh wh253
```

And the network is pictured in Figure 4-1.

Setting Up DNS Data

Our first step in setting up the Movie U. name servers is to translate the host table into equivalent DNS data. The DNS version of the data has multiple files. One file maps all the host names to addresses. Other files map the addresses back to host names. The address-to-name lookup is sometimes called *reverse mapping*. Each network has its own file for the reverse mapping.

As a convention in this book, a file mapping host names to addresses is called *db.DOMAIN*. In *movie.edu*, this file is *db.movie*. The files mapping addresses to host names are called *db.ADDR*, where *ADDR* is the network number without the trailing

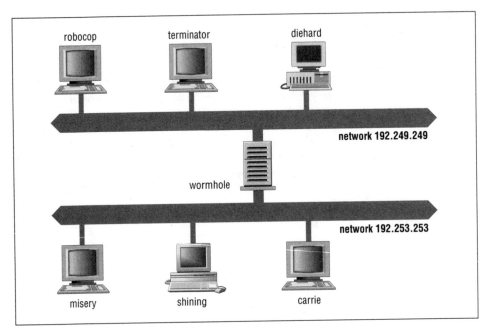

Figure 4-1. The Movie University network

zeros. In our example, the files are *db.192.249.249* and *db.192.253.253*; there's one for each network. The *db* is short for database. We'll call the collection of *db.DOMAIN* and *db.ADDR* files *db files* or *DNS database files*. There are a couple of other data files: *db.cache* and *db.127.0.0*. These files are overhead. Each name server must have them, and they are, more or less, the same for each server.

To tie all the db files together, a name server needs a startup file—for BIND version 4, this file is usually */etc/named.boot*. For BIND version 8, this file is usually */etc/named.conf*. The db files are DNS-specific. The startup file is specific to the name server implementation—in this case, BIND.

The db Files

Most entries in db files are called DNS *resource records*. DNS lookups are case-insensitive, so you can enter names in your db files in uppercase, lowercase, or mixed case. We tend to use all lowercase. Even though lookups are case-insensitive, case is preserved.

Resource records must start in column one. The resource records in the example files we present in this book do start in column one, but they may look indented because of the way this book is formatted. In the DNS RFCs, the examples present the resource records in a certain order. Most people have chosen to follow that ordering, as we have here, but this ordering is not a requirement. The ordering of resource records in the db files is as follows:

SOA record
> Indicates *authority* for this zone data

NS record
> Lists a *name server* for this zone

Other records
> Data about hosts in this zone

Of the other records, this chapter covers:

A
> Name-to-address mapping

PTR
> Address-to-name mapping

CNAME
> Canonical name (for aliases)

Those of you who have some experience with the DNS file format will look, no doubt, at our data and say to yourselves, "It would have been shorter to specify it this other way...." We are not using abbreviations or shortcuts in our data, at least not initially. Once you understand the long version, we'll go back and "tighten up" the files.

Comments

The db files are easier to read if they contain comments and blank lines. Comments start with a semicolon and finish at the end of the line. As you might guess, the name server ignores comments and blank lines.

SOA Records

The first entry in each of these files is the SOA (start of authority) resource record. The SOA record indicates that this name server is the best source of information for the data within this zone. Our name server is *authoritative* for the zone *movie.edu* because of the SOA record. An SOA record is required in each *db.DOMAIN* and *db.ADDR* file. There can be one, and only one, SOA record in a db file.

We added the following SOA record to the *db.movie* file:

```
movie.edu. IN SOA terminator.movie.edu. al.robocop.movie.edu. (
                    1          ; Serial
                    10800      ; Refresh after 3 hours
                    3600       ; Retry after 1 hour
```

```
604800    ; Expire after 1 week
86400 )   ; Minimum TTL of 1 day
```

The name *movie.edu.* must start in column one of the file. Make sure the names end with a trailing dot, as we have done here, or you will be surprised at the result! (We'll explain later in this chapter.)

The IN stands for Internet. This is one *class* of data. Other classes exist, but none of them are currently in widespread use. Our examples use only the IN class. The class field is optional. If the class is omitted, the class IN is assumed.

The first name after SOA (*terminator.movie.edu.*) is the name of the primary master name server for this data. The second name (*al.robocop.movie.edu.*) is the mail address of the person in charge of the data (if you replace the first "." with an "@"). Often you'll see *root, postmaster,* or *hostmaster* as the email address. Name servers won't use these names—they are meant for human consumption. If you have a problem with someone's domain, you can send an email message to the listed email address. BIND 4.9 and later versions provide another resource record type, RP (responsible person), for this purpose also. The RP record is discussed in Chapter 7, *Maintaining BIND*.

The parentheses allow the SOA record to span more than one line. Most of the fields within the parentheses of the SOA record are for use by slave name servers and are discussed when we introduce slave name servers later in this chapter. For now, assume these are reasonable values.

We added similar SOA records to the beginning of the *db.192.249.249* and *db.192.253.253* files. In these files, we changed the first name in the SOA record from *movie.edu.* to the name of the appropriate *in-addr.arpa* domain: *249.249.192.in-addr.arpa.* and *253.253.192.in-addr.arpa.*, respectively.

NS Records

The next entries we added to each file are NS (name server) resource records. We added one NS record for each name server for our zone. Here are the NS records from the *db.movie* file:

```
movie.edu.    IN NS  terminator.movie.edu.
movie.edu.    IN NS  wormhole.movie.edu.
```

These records indicate that there are two name servers for the zone *movie.edu.* The name servers are on the hosts *terminator* and *wormhole.* Multihomed hosts, like *wormhole,* are excellent choices for name servers since they are "well-connected." They are directly accessible by hosts on more than one network and, if they also serve as routers, they are not often down because they are closely monitored. We'll cover more on where to place your name servers in Chapter 8, *Growing Your Domain.*

As with the SOA record, we added NS records to the *db.192.249.249* and *db.192.253.253* files.

Address and Alias Records

Next, we created the name-to-address mappings. We added the following resource records to the *db.movie* file:

```
;
; Host addresses
;
localhost.movie.edu.    IN A    127.0.0.1
robocop.movie.edu.      IN A    192.249.249.2
terminator.movie.edu.   IN A    192.249.249.3
diehard.movie.edu.      IN A    192.249.249.4
misery.movie.edu.       IN A    192.253.253.2
shining.movie.edu.      IN A    192.253.253.3
carrie.movie.edu.       IN A    192.253.253.4
;
; Multi-homed hosts
;
wormhole.movie.edu.     IN A    192.249.249.1
wormhole.movie.edu.     IN A    192.253.253.1
;
; Aliases
;
bigt.movie.edu.         IN CNAME terminator.movie.edu.
dh.movie.edu.           IN CNAME diehard.movie.edu.
wh.movie.edu.           IN CNAME wormhole.movie.edu.
wh249.movie.edu.        IN A    192.249.249.1
wh253.movie.edu.        IN A    192.253.253.1
```

The first two blocks are probably not a surprise. The A stands for address, and each resource record maps a name to an address. *wormhole* acts as a router. It has two addresses associated with its name and therefore two address records. Unlike host table lookups, a DNS lookup can return more than one address for a name. A lookup of *wormhole* will return two. If the requestor and name server are on the same network, some name servers will place the "closest" address first in the response for better performance. This feature is called *address sorting* and is covered in Chapter 10, *Advanced Features and Security*. If address sorting does not apply, the addresses are *rotated* between queries so subsequent responses list them in a different order. This "round robin" feature shows up first in BIND 4.9.

The third block has the host table aliases. For the first three aliases, we created CNAME (canonical name) resource records. However, we created address records for the other two aliases—more on this in a moment. A CNAME record maps an alias to its canonical name. The name server handles CNAME records in a different manner than aliases are handled in the host table. When a name server looks up a name and finds a CNAME record, it replaces the name with the canonical name and looks up the new name. For example, when the name server looks up *wh*, it finds a CNAME record pointing to *wormhole*. *wormhole* is then looked up, and both addresses are returned.

There is one thing you need to remember about aliases like *bigt*—they should never appear on the right-hand side of a resource record. Stated differently: always use the canonical name (*terminator*) in the data portion of the resource record. Notice that the NS records we just created use the canonical name.

The final two entries solve a special problem. Suppose you have a router, like *wormhole*, and you want to check one of the interfaces. One common troubleshooting technique is to *ping* the interface to verify that it is responding. If you *ping* the name *wormhole*, the name server returns both addresses when the name is looked up. *ping* uses the first address in the list. But which address is first?

With the host table, we chose the address we wanted by using either *wh249* or *wh253*—each name referred to *one* of the host's addresses. To provide equivalent capability with DNS, we didn't make *wh249* and *wh253* into aliases (CNAME records). That would result in both addresses for *wormhole* being returned when the alias was looked up. Instead, we used address records. Now, to check the operation of the 192.253.253.1 interface on *wormhole*, we *ping wh253* since it refers to only one address. The same applies to *wh249*.

To state this as a general rule: if a host is multihomed (has more than one network interface), create an address (A) record for each alias unique to one address. Create a CNAME record for each alias common to all the addresses.

Now, don't tell your users about names like *wh249* and *wh253*. Those names are meant for system-administration purposes only. If users learn to use names like *wh249*, they will be confused when the name doesn't work for them in some places, like *.rhosts* files. That's because these places want the name that results from looking up the address, and that name is going to be the canonical name, *wormhole*.

Since we used A (address) records for the *wh249* and *wh253* aliases, you might ask: "Is it okay to use address records instead of CNAME records in *all* cases?" Well, using address records instead of CNAME records doesn't cause problems with most applications, since the application only cares that it finds the IP address. There is one application—*sendmail*—whose behavior changes, though. *sendmail* usually replaces aliases in mail headers with their canonical name; this *canonicalization* only happens if the name in the mail header has CNAME data associated with it. Without CNAME records for aliases, your *sendmail* will have to understand all of the possible aliases your host might be known by, which will require extra *sendmail* configuration work on your part.

In addition to the problem with *sendmail*, users might be confused when they try to figure out the canonical name to enter in their *.rhosts* file. Looking up a name that has CNAME data leads them to the canonical name, whereas address data won't. In this case, users *should* instead be looking up the IP *address* to get the canonical name, as *rlogind* does, but users like these never seem to be on systems we administer.

PTR Records

Next we created the address-to-name mappings. The file *db.192.249.249* maps addresses to host names for the 192.249.249 network. The DNS resource records used for this mapping are PTR (pointer) records. There is one record for each host interface on this network. (Recall that addresses are looked up as names in DNS. The address is reversed and *in-addr.arpa* is appended.)

Here are the PTR records we added for network 192.249.249:

```
1.249.249.192.in-addr.arpa.   IN PTR wormhole.movie.edu.
2.249.249.192.in-addr.arpa.   IN PTR robocop.movie.edu.
3.249.249.192.in-addr.arpa.   IN PTR terminator.movie.edu.
4.249.249.192.in-addr.arpa.   IN PTR diehard.movie.edu.
```

There are a couple of things to notice about this data. First, addresses should only point to a single name: the canonical name. Thus, 192.249.249.1 maps to *wormhole* and not to *wh249*. You *can* create two PTR records, one for *wormhole* and one for *wh249*, but most systems are not prepared to see more than one name for an address. Second, even though *wormhole* has two addresses, you only see one of them here. That's because this file shows only the direct connections to network 192.249.249, and *wormhole* has only one connection there.

We created similar data for the 192.253.253 network.

The Completed Data Files

Now that the various resource records of the db files have been explained, we'll show you what they look like when all the data are in one place. Again, the actual order of these resource records does not matter.

Here are the contents of the file *db.movie*:

```
movie.edu. IN SOA terminator.movie.edu. al.robocop.movie.edu. (
                    1         ; Serial
                    10800     ; Refresh after 3 hours
                    3600      ; Retry after 1 hour
                    604800    ; Expire after 1 week
                    86400 )   ; Minimum TTL of 1 day
```

```
;
; Name servers
;
movie.edu.  IN NS  terminator.movie.edu.
movie.edu.  IN NS  wormhole.movie.edu.


;
; Addresses for the canonical names
;
localhost.movie.edu.   IN A    127.0.0.1
robocop.movie.edu.     IN A    192.249.249.2
terminator.movie.edu.  IN A    192.249.249.3
diehard.movie.edu.     IN A    192.249.249.4
misery.movie.edu.      IN A    192.253.253.2
shining.movie.edu.     IN A    192.253.253.3
carrie.movie.edu.      IN A    192.253.253.4
wormhole.movie.edu.    IN A    192.249.249.1
wormhole.movie.edu.    IN A    192.253.253.1


;
; Aliases
;
bigt.movie.edu.        IN CNAME terminator.movie.edu.
dh.movie.edu.          IN CNAME diehard.movie.edu.
wh.movie.edu.          IN CNAME wormhole.movie.edu.


;
; Interface specific names
;
wh249.movie.edu.       IN A    192.249.249.1
wh253.movie.edu.       IN A    192.253.253.1
```

Here are the contents of the file *db.192.249.249*:

```
249.249.192.in-addr.arpa. IN SOA terminator.movie.edu. al.robocop.movie.edu.(
                          1         ; Serial
                          10800     ; Refresh after 3 hours
                          3600      ; Retry after 1 hour
                          604800    ; Expire after 1 week
                          86400 )   ; Minimum TTL of 1 day


;
; Name servers
;
249.249.192.in-addr.arpa.  IN NS  terminator.movie.edu.
249.249.192.in-addr.arpa.  IN NS  wormhole.movie.edu.


;
; Addresses point to canonical name
;
1.249.249.192.in-addr.arpa.  IN PTR wormhole.movie.edu.
2.249.249.192.in-addr.arpa.  IN PTR robocop.movie.edu.
3.249.249.192.in-addr.arpa.  IN PTR terminator.movie.edu.
4.249.249.192.in-addr.arpa.  IN PTR diehard.movie.edu.
```

Here are the contents of the file *db.192.253.253*:

```
253.253.192.in-addr.arpa. IN SOA terminator.movie.edu. al.robocop.movie.edu.(
                          1        ; Serial
                          10800    ; Refresh after 3 hours
                          3600     ; Retry after 1 hour
                          604800   ; Expire after 1 week
                          86400 )  ; Minimum TTL of 1 day


;
; Name servers
;
253.253.192.in-addr.arpa.    IN NS   terminator.movie.edu.
253.253.192.in-addr.arpa.    IN NS   wormhole.movie.edu.


;
; Addresses point to canonical name
;
1.253.253.192.in-addr.arpa.   IN PTR wormhole.movie.edu.
2.253.253.192.in-addr.arpa.   IN PTR misery.movie.edu.
3.253.253.192.in-addr.arpa.   IN PTR shining.movie.edu.
4.253.253.192.in-addr.arpa.   IN PTR carrie.movie.edu.
```

The Loopback Address

A name server needs one additional *db.ADDR* file to cover the *loopback* network: the special address that hosts use to direct traffic to themselves. This network is (almost) always 127.0.0, and the host number is (almost) always 127.0.0.1. Therefore, the name of this file is *db.127.0.0*. No surprise here; it looks like the other *db.ADDR* files.

Here are the contents of the file *db.127.0.0*:

```
0.0.127.in-addr.arpa. IN SOA terminator.movie.edu. al.robocop.movie.edu. (
                      1        ; Serial
                      10800    ; Refresh after 3 hours
                      3600     ; Retry after 1 hour
                      604800   ; Expire after 1 week
                      86400 )  ; Minimum TTL of 1 day

0.0.127.in-addr.arpa.   IN NS   terminator.movie.edu.
0.0.127.in-addr.arpa.   IN NS   wormhole.movie.edu.

1.0.0.127.in-addr.arpa.  IN PTR localhost.
```

Why do name servers need this silly little file? Think about it for a second. No one was given responsibility for network 127, yet systems use it for a loopback address. Since no one has direct responsibility, everyone who uses it is responsible for it individually. You could omit this file and your name server would operate. However, a lookup of 127.0.0.1 might fail because the root name server contacted wasn't configured itself to map 127.0.0.1 to a name. You ought to provide the mapping yourself so there are no surprises.

The Root Cache Data

Besides your local information, the name server also needs to know where the name servers are for the root domain. This information must be retrieved from the Internet host *ftp.rs.internic.net* (198.41.0.7). Use anonymous *ftp* to retrieve the file *named.root* from the *domain* subdirectory. (*named.root* is the same file we've been calling *db.cache*. Just rename *named.root* to *db.cache* after you've retrieved it.)

```
;       This file holds the information on root name servers needed to
;       initialize cache of Internet domain name servers
;       (e.g. reference this file in the "cache  . <file>"
;       configuration file of BIND domain name servers).
;
;       This file is made available by InterNIC registration services
;       under anonymous FTP as
;           file                /domain/named.root
;           on server           FTP.RS.INTERNIC.NET
;       -OR- under Gopher at    RS.INTERNIC.NET
;           under menu          InterNIC Registration Services (NSI)
;             submenu           InterNIC Registration Archives
;           file                named.root
;
;       last update:    Aug 22, 1997
;       related version of root zone:   1997082200
;
;
; formerly NS.INTERNIC.NET
;
.                           3600000   IN   NS   A.ROOT-SERVERS.NET.
A.ROOT-SERVERS.NET.         3600000        A    198.41.0.4
;
; formerly NS1.ISI.EDU
;
.                           3600000        NS   B.ROOT-SERVERS.NET.
B.ROOT-SERVERS.NET.         3600000        A    128.9.0.107
;
; formerly C.PSI.NET
;
.                           3600000        NS   C.ROOT-SERVERS.NET.
C.ROOT-SERVERS.NET.         3600000        A    192.33.4.12
;
; formerly TERP.UMD.EDU
;
.                           3600000        NS   D.ROOT-SERVERS.NET.
D.ROOT-SERVERS.NET.         3600000        A    128.8.10.90
;
; formerly NS.NASA.GOV
;
.                           3600000        NS   E.ROOT-SERVERS.NET.
E.ROOT-SERVERS.NET.         3600000        A    192.203.230.10
;
; formerly NS.ISC.ORG
;
```

```
.                              3600000    NS    F.ROOT-SERVERS.NET.
F.ROOT-SERVERS.NET.            3600000    A     192.5.5.241
;
; formerly NS.NIC.DDN.MIL
;
.                              3600000    NS    G.ROOT-SERVERS.NET.
G.ROOT-SERVERS.NET.            3600000    A     192.112.36.4
;
; formerly AOS.ARL.ARMY.MIL
;
.                              3600000    NS    H.ROOT-SERVERS.NET.
H.ROOT-SERVERS.NET.            3600000    A     128.63.2.53
;
; formerly NIC.NORDU.NET
;
.                              3600000    NS    I.ROOT-SERVERS.NET.
I.ROOT-SERVERS.NET.            3600000    A     192.36.148.17
;
; temporarily housed at NSI (InterNIC)
;
.                              3600000    NS    J.ROOT-SERVERS.NET.
J.ROOT-SERVERS.NET.            3600000    A     198.41.0.10
;
; housed in LINX, operated by RIPE NCC
;
.                              3600000    NS    K.ROOT-SERVERS.NET.
K.ROOT-SERVERS.NET.            3600000    A     193.0.14.129
;
; temporarily housed at ISI (IANA)
;
.                              3600000    NS    L.ROOT-SERVERS.NET.
L.ROOT-SERVERS.NET.            3600000    A     198.32.64.12
;
; housed in Japan, operated by WIDE
;
.                              3600000    NS    M.ROOT-SERVERS.NET.
M.ROOT-SERVERS.NET.            3600000    A     202.12.27.33
; End of File
```

The domain name "." refers to the root domain. Since the root domain's name servers change over time, don't assume *this* list is current. Pull a new version of *named.root*.

How is this file kept up to date? As the network administrator, you must keep it up to date. Some versions of BIND did update this file periodically. That feature was disabled: apparently, it didn't work as well as the authors had hoped. Sometimes the changed *db.cache* file is mailed to the *bind-users* or *namedroppers* mailing list. If you are on one of these lists, you are likely to hear about changes.

Can you put data other than root name server data in this file? You can, but it won't be used. Originally, the name server installed this data in its cache. However, the cache file has changed (subtly) to be the root name server *hints* (but the name "cache file" stuck). The name server stores the hints data in a special place and does not discard the hints if their TTLs drop to zero, as it would with cache data. The name server uses the hint data to query the root name servers for the current list of root name servers, which it caches. When the cached list of root name servers times out, the name server again uses the hints to get a new list.

What are the 3600000s for? In older versions of this file, this number used to be 99999999. Since this file was originally cache data, the name server needed to know how long to keep these records active. The 99999999s meant a very long time. The root name server data was to be kept active for as long as the server ran. Since the name server now stores this data in a special place and doesn't discard it if it times out, the TTL is unnecessary. But it's not harmful to have the 3600000s, and it makes for interesting BIND folklore when you pass responsibility to the next name server administrator.

Setting Up a BIND Configuration File

Now that the db files have been created, a name server must be instructed to read each of the files. For BIND, the mechanism for pointing the server to its db files is the configuration file. Up to this point, we've been discussing files whose data and format are described in the DNS specification. The configuration file, though, is specific to BIND and is not defined in the DNS RFCs.

The BIND configuration file syntax changed significantly between version 4 and version 8. We'll first show you the BIND 4 syntax and then we'll show you the equivalent BIND 8 syntax. You'll have to check the *named** manual page to find out which you need to use. If you already have a version 4 configuration file, you can convert it to a version 8 configuration file by running the Perl script *src/bin/named/ named-bootconf.pl* that is distributed with the BIND source.

In BIND 4, comments in the configuration file are the same as in the db files—they start with a semicolon and finish at the end of the line:

```
; This is a comment
```

In BIND 8, you can use any of 3 styles of comments: C-style, C++-style, or shell-style:

```
/* This is a C-style comment */
// This is a C++-style comment
# This is a shell-style comment
```

Don't use a version 4 style comment in a version 8 configuration file because it won't work—the semicolon ends a configuration statement instead of starting a comment statement.

---

* *named* is pronounced "name-dee" and stands for "name server daemon." BIND is pronounced to rhyme with "kind." Some creative people have noticed the similarities in the names and choose to mispronounce them "bin-dee" and "named" (like "tamed").

Usually, configuration files contain a line indicating the directory where the files are located. The name server changes its directory to this location before reading the files. This allows the filenames to be relative to the current directory instead of being complete path names. Here is how a version 4 directory line looks:

```
directory /usr/local/named
```

Here is how a version 8 directory line looks:

```
options {
        directory "/usr/local/named";
        // Place additional options here.
};
```

NOTE   Only one *options* statement is allowed in the configuration file, so any
              additional options mentioned later in this book must be added along
              with the *directory* option.

On a primary master server, the configuration file contains one line for each file to be read. For version 4, this line comprises three fields: the word *primary*, starting in the first column, the domain name of the zone, and the filename:

```
primary movie.edu              db.movie
primary 249.249.192.in-addr.arpa db.192.249.249
primary 253.253.192.in-addr.arpa db.192.253.253
primary 0.0.127.in-addr.arpa    db.127.0.0
```

For version 8, the line starts with the keyword *zone* followed by the domain name and the class (*in* stands for Internet). The *type master* is the same as the version 4 *primary*. The last field is the filename:

```
zone "movie.edu" in {
        type master;
        file "db.movie";
};
```

Here is the version 4 configuration file line to read the cache file:

```
cache   .   db.cache
```

and the equivalent version 8 configuration file line:

```
zone "." in {
        type hint;
        file "db.cache";
};
```

As mentioned earlier, this file is not for general cache data. It only contains the root name server *hints*.

By default, BIND 4 expects the configuration file to be named */etc/named.boot*, but it can be changed with a command-line option. BIND 8 expects the configuration file to be named */etc/named.conf* instead of */etc/named.boot*. The db files for our example are in the directory */usr/local/named*. Which directory you use does not matter. Avoid putting the directory in the root filesystem if the root filesystem is short on space. Here is the complete version 4 */etc/named.boot* file:

```
; BIND configuration file

directory /usr/local/named

primary  movie.edu                  db.movie
primary  249.249.192.in-addr.arpa db.192.249.249
primary  253.253.192.in-addr.arpa db.192.253.253
primary  0.0.127.in-addr.arpa       db.127.0.0
cache    .                          db.cache
```

Here is the complete version 8 */etc/named.conf* file:

```
// BIND configuration file

options {
        directory "/usr/local/named";
        // Place additional options here.
};

zone "movie.edu" in {
        type master;
        file "db.movie";
};

zone "249.249.192.in-addr.arpa" in {
        type master;
        file "db.192.249.249";
};

zone "253.253.192.in-addr.arpa" in {
        type master;
        file "db.192.253.253";
};

zone "0.0.127.in-addr.arpa" in {
        type master;
        file "db.127.0.0";
};

zone "." in {
        type hint;
        file "db.cache";
};
```

Abbreviations

At this point, we have created all the files necessary for a primary master name server. Let's go back and revisit the DNS database files; there are shortcuts we didn't use. Unless you see and understand the long form first, though, the short form can look very cryptic. Now that you know the long form and have seen the BIND configuration file, we'll show you the shortcuts.

Appending Domains

The second field of a *primary* (version 4) or *zone* (version 8) configuration file line specifies a domain name. This domain is the key to the most useful shortcut. This domain is the *origin* of all the data in the db file. The origin is appended to all names in the db file not ending in a dot. The origin will be different for each db file.

Since the origin is appended to names, instead of entering *robocop*'s address in *db.movie* as this:

```
    robocop.movie.edu.    IN A    192.249.249.2
```

we could have entered it like this:

```
    robocop    IN A    192.249.249.2
```

In the *db.192.24.249* file we entered this:

```
    2.249.249.192.in-addr.arpa.   IN PTR robocop.movie.edu.
```

Since *249.249.192.in-addr.arpa* is the origin, we could have entered:

```
    2   IN PTR robocop.movie.edu.
```

Remember we warned you earlier not to omit the trailing dot when using the long names? Suppose you forgot the trailing dot. An entry like:

```
    robocop.movie.edu    IN A    192.249.249.2
```

turns into an entry for *robocop.movie.edu.movie.edu*, and you didn't intend that at all.

@ Notation

If the domain name is the *same* as the origin, the name can be specified as "@". This is most often seen in the SOA record of the db files. The SOA records could have been entered this way:

```
@ IN SOA terminator.movie.edu. al.robocop.movie.edu. (
                    1        ; Serial
                    10800    ; Refresh after 3 hours
                    3600     ; Retry after 1 hour
                    604800   ; Expire after 1 week
                    86400 )  ; Minimum TTL of 1 day
```

Repeat Last Name

If a resource record name (that starts in column one) is a space or tab, then the name from the last resource record is used. You would use this if there were multiple resource records for a name. Here is an example where there are two address records for one name:

```
wormhole    IN A     192.249.249.1
            IN A     192.253.253.1
```

In the second address record, the name *wormhole* is implied. You can use this shortcut even if the resource records are of different types.

The Shortened db Files

Now that we have shown you the abbreviations, we'll repeat the db files, making use of these shortcuts.

Here are the contents of the file *db.movie*:

```
;
; Origin added to names not ending
; in a dot: movie.edu
;

@ IN SOA terminator.movie.edu. al.robocop.movie.edu. (
                        1          ; Serial
                        10800      ; Refresh after 3 hours
                        3600       ; Retry after 1 hour
                        604800     ; Expire after 1 week
                        86400 )    ; Minimum TTL of 1 day


;
; Name servers (The name '@' is implied)
;
            IN NS   terminator.movie.edu.
            IN NS   wormhole.movie.edu.


;
; Addresses for the canonical names
;
localhost   IN A     127.0.0.1
robocop     IN A     192.249.249.2
terminator  IN A     192.249.249.3
diehard     IN A     192.249.249.4
misery      IN A     192.253.253.2
shining     IN A     192.253.253.3
carrie      IN A     192.253.253.4

wormhole    IN A     192.249.249.1
            IN A     192.253.253.1
```

```
;
; Aliases
;
bigt          IN CNAME terminator
dh            IN CNAME diehard
wh            IN CNAME wormhole


;
; Interface specific names
;
wh249         IN A     192.249.249.1
wh253         IN A     192.253.253.1
```

Here are the contents of the file *db.192.249.249*:

```
;
; Origin added to names not ending
; in a dot: 249.249.192.in-addr.arpa
;

@ IN SOA terminator.movie.edu. al.robocop.movie.edu. (
                        1        ; Serial
                        10800    ; Refresh after 3 hours
                        3600     ; Retry after 1 hour
                        604800   ; Expire after 1 week
                        86400 )  ; Minimum TTL of 1 day


;
; Name servers (The name '@' is implied)
;
    IN NS  terminator.movie.edu.
    IN NS  wormhole.movie.edu.


;
; Addresses point to canonical name
;
1  IN PTR wormhole.movie.edu.
2  IN PTR robocop.movie.edu.
3  IN PTR terminator.movie.edu.
4  IN PTR diehard.movie.edu.
```

Here are the contents of the file *db.192.253.253*:

```
;
; Origin added to names not ending
; in a dot: 253.253.192.in-addr.arpa
;

@ IN SOA terminator.movie.edu. al.robocop.movie.edu. (
                        1        ; Serial
                        10800    ; Refresh after 3 hours
                        3600     ; Retry after 1 hour
                        604800   ; Expire after 1 week
                        86400 )  ; Minimum TTL of 1 day
```

```
;
; Name servers (The name '@' is implied)
;
    IN NS  terminator.movie.edu.
    IN NS  wormhole.movie.edu.


;
; Addresses point to canonical name
;
1  IN PTR wormhole.movie.edu.
2  IN PTR misery.movie.edu.
3  IN PTR shining.movie.edu.
4  IN PTR carrie.movie.edu.
```

Here are the contents of the file *db.127.0.0*:

```
@ IN SOA terminator.movie.edu. al.robocop.movie.edu. (
                        1          ; Serial
                        10800      ; Refresh after 3 hours
                        3600       ; Retry after 1 hour
                        604800     ; Expire after 1 week
                        86400 )    ; Minimum TTL of 1 day

    IN NS  terminator.movie.edu.
    IN NS  wormhole.movie.edu.

1  IN PTR localhost.
```

While looking at the new *db.movie* file, you may notice that we could have removed *movie.edu* from the host names of the SOA and NS records like this:

```
@ IN SOA terminator al.robocop (
                        1          ; Serial
                        10800      ; Refresh after 3 hours
                        3600       ; Retry after 1 hour
                        604800     ; Expire after 1 week
                        86400 )    ; Minimum TTL of 1 day

    IN NS  terminator
    IN NS  wormhole
```

You *can't* do this in the other db files because their origins are different. In *db.movie*, we left these names as fully qualified domain names so that the NS and SOA records are exactly the same for *all* the db files.

Host Name Checking (BIND 4.9.4 and Later Versions)

If your name server is older than BIND 4.9.4, skip to the next section.

If your name server is BIND 4.9.4 or newer, you have to pay extra attention to how your hosts are named. Starting with version 4.9.4, BIND checks host names for conformance to RFC 952. If a host name does not conform, BIND considers the zone to have a syntax error.

Before you panic, you need to know that this checking only applies to names that are considered host names. Remember, resource records have a *name* field and a *data* field, for example:

```
<name>      <class>  <type>  <data>
terminator  IN       A       192.249.249.3
```

Host names are in the *name* field of A (address) and MX (covered in Chapter 5, *DNS and Electronic Mail*) records. Host names are in the *data* fields of SOA and NS records. At least in version 4.9.4, CNAMEs do not have to conform to the *host* naming rules because they can point to names that are not host names.

Here are the host naming rules: host names are allowed to have alphabetic characters and numeric characters in each label. The following are valid host names:

```
ID4           IN A 192.249.249.10
postmanring2x IN A 192.249.249.11
```

A hyphen is allowed if it is in the middle of a label:

```
fx-gateway    IN A 192.249.249.12
```

NOTE   Underscores are not allowed in host names.

Names that are not host names can consist of any printable ASCII character.

If the resource record *data* field calls for a *mail address* (SOA records), the first label can contain any printable character, since it is not a host name, but the rest of the labels must follow the host name syntax described above. For example, a mail address has the following syntax:

```
<ASCII-characters>.<hostname-characters>
```

For example, if your mail address is *key_grip@movie.edu*, you can still use it in an SOA record, even with the underscore. Remember, in a mail address you replace the "@" with a ".":

```
movie.edu. IN SOA terminator.movie.edu. key_grip.movie.edu. (
                    1        ; Serial
                    10800    ; Refresh after 3 hours
                    3600     ; Retry after 1 hour
                    604800   ; Expire after 1 week
                    86400 )  ; Minimum TTL of 1 day
```

This extra level of checking might cause dramatic problems to sites that upgrade from a liberal version of BIND to a conservative one, especially sites that standardized on names containing an underscore. If you need to postpone changing names until later (you will still change them, right?), this feature can be toned down to warning messages or simply ignored altogether. The following version 4 configuration file statement turns the errors into warning messages:

```
check-names primary warn
```

Here is the equivalent version 8 line:

```
options {
        check-names master warn;
};
```

The warning messages are logged with *syslog*, which we will explain shortly. The following version 4 configuration file statement ignores the errors:

```
check-names primary ignore
```

Here is the equivalent version 8 line:

```
options {
        check-names master ignore;
};
```

If the nonconforming names came from a zone that you back up (and have no control over), then add a similar statement that specifies *secondary* instead of *primary*:

```
check-names secondary ignore
```

For version 8, use *slave* instead of *secondary*:

```
options {
        check-names slave ignore;
};
```

And if the names came in responses to queries, and not in zone transfers, specify *response* instead:

```
check-names response ignore
```

For version 8:

```
options {
        check-names response ignore;
};
```

Here are the 4.9.4 defaults:

```
check-names primary fail
check-names secondary warn
check-names response ignore
```

Here are the version 8 defaults:

```
options {
        check-names master fail;
```

```
            check-names slave warn;
            check-names response ignore;
    };
```

For version 8, the name checking can be specified on a per-zone basis, in which case it overrides the options statement:

```
    zone "movie.edu" in {
            type master;
            file "db.movie";
            check-names fail;
    };
```

NOTE   The options line contains 3 fields (check-names master fail), whereas the zone line check contains only 2 fields (check-names fail). This is because the zone line already specifies the type (type master).

Tools

Wouldn't it be handy to have a tool to translate your host table into name server file format? There is such a beast, written in Perl: *h2n*—a host table to name server file converter. You can use *h2n* to create your data the first time and then maintain your DNS data manually. Or, you can use *h2n* over and over again. As you have seen, the format of the host table is much simpler to understand and to modify correctly. So, you could maintain */etc/hosts* and rerun *h2n* to update your DNS data after each modification.

If you plan to use *h2n*, you might as well start with it, since it uses */etc/hosts*—not your hand-crafted DNS data—to generate the new DNS files. We could have saved ourselves lots of work by generating the sample data in this chapter with the following:

```
    % h2n -d movie.edu -s terminator -s robocop \
      -n 192.249.249 -n 192.253.253 \
      -u al.robocop.movie.edu
```

(To generate a version 8 configuration file, add -v 8 to the option list.)

The -d and -n options specify the domain name and network numbers. You'll notice that the db filenames are derived from these options. The -s options list the name servers for the NS records. The -u (user) is the email address in the SOA record. We'll cover *h2n* in more detail in Chapter 7, after we've covered how DNS affects email.

Running a Primary Master Name Server

Now that you've created your DNS database files, you are ready to start a couple of name servers. You'll need to set up two name servers: a primary master name server and a slave name server. Before you start a name server, though, make sure the syslog daemon is running. If the name server sees an error, it logs a message to the syslog daemon. If the error is bad enough, the name server will exit.

Starting Up the Name Server

At this point, we assume the machine you are running on has the BIND name server and the support tool *nslookup*. Check the *named* manual page to find the directory the server is in and verify that the executable is on your system. On BSD systems, the name server started its life in */etc*, but may have migrated elsewhere. Other places to look for *named* are */usr/etc/in.named* and */usr/sbin/in.named*. The descriptions below assume that the name server is still in */etc*.

To start up the name server, you must become root. The name server operates on a reserved port requiring root privileges. The name server doesn't require root access for anything else. Start the name server from the command line the first time you run it, to test that it is operating correctly. Later, we'll show you how to start up the name server automatically when your system boots.

The following command starts the name server. In the *movie.edu* domain, we ran this command on the host *terminator*.

```
# /etc/named
```

This command assumes that your configuration file is */etc/named.boot* (version 4) or */etc/named.conf* (version 8). You can have your configuration file elsewhere, but you have to tell the name server where it is using the *-b* command-line option:

```
# /etc/named -b conf-file
```

Check for Syslog Errors

The first thing to do after starting your name server is to check the *syslog* file for error messages. If you are not familiar with syslog, look at the *syslog.conf* manual page for a description of the syslog configuration file, or the *syslogd* manual page for a description of the syslog daemon. The name server logs messages as *daemon* under the name *named*. You might be able to find out where syslog messages are logged by looking for *daemon* in */etc/syslog.conf*:

```
% grep daemon /etc/syslog.conf
*.err;kern.debug;daemon,auth.notice /var/adm/messages
```

On this host, the name server syslog messages are logged to */var/adm/messages*, and *syslog* only saves the ones that are LOG_NOTICE or higher. Some useful messages are sent at LOG_INFO—you might like to see some of these. You can decide if you want to change the log level after reading Chapter 7, where we cover *syslog* messages in more detail.

When the name server starts, it logs a *starting* message:

```
% grep named /var/adm/messages
Jan 10 20:48:32 terminator named[3221]: starting.
```

The starting message is not an error message, but there might be other messages with it that are error messages. (If your server used *restarted* instead of *starting*, that's okay too. The message changed at BIND 4.9.3.) The most common errors are syntax errors in the db files or configuration file. For example, if you forgot the resource record type in an address record:

```
robocop  IN  192.249.249.2
```

you'll see the following syslog error messages:

```
Jan 10 20:48:32 terminator named[3221]: Line 13: Unknown type:
                192.249.249.2
Jan 10 20:48:32 terminator named[3221]: db.movie Line 13:
                database format error (192.249.249.2)
```

Or, if you misspelled the word "zone" in */etc/named.conf*:

```
zne "movie.edu" in {
```

you'll see the following syslog error message:

```
Mar 22 20:14:21 terminator named[1477]: named.conf:10:
                syntax error near `zne'
```

If BIND version 4.9.4 or later finds a name that doesn't conform to RFC 952, you'll see the following syslog error message:

```
Jul 24 20:56:26 terminator named[1496]: owner name "ID_4.movie.edu IN"
                              (primary) is invalid - rejecting
```

If you have a syntax error, check the line mentioned in the syslog error message to see if you can figure out the problem. You've seen what the db files are supposed to look like; that should be enough to figure out most simple syntax errors. Otherwise, you'll have to go through Appendix A, *DNS Message Format and Resource Records*, to see the gory syntax details of all the resource records. If you can fix the syntax error, do so and then send the name server a HUP signal:

```
# kill -HUP <pid>
```

so that it rereads the data files. You'll see more information in Chapter 7 on sending signals to the name server.

Testing Your Setup with nslookup

If you have correctly set up your local domain, and your connection to the Internet is up, you should be able to look up a local and a remote name. We'll step you through the lookups below with *nslookup*. There is a whole chapter in this book on *nslookup* (Chapter 11, *nslookup*), but we will cover *nslookup* in enough detail here to do basic name server testing.

Initialize the default domain name

Before running *nslookup*, you need to initialize the default domain name. With this in place, you can look up a name like *carrie* instead of spelling out *carrie.movie.edu*—the system adds the domain for you.

There are two ways to initialize the default domain: *hostname*(1) or */etc/resolv.conf*. Some people say that, in practice, more sites initialize the default domain in */etc/ resolv.conf*. You can use either. Throughout the book, we assume the default domain comes from *hostname*(1).

Create a file called */etc/resolv.conf* with the following line starting in column one (substitute your domain name for *movie.edu*):

```
domain movie.edu
```

Or, set *hostname*(1) to be a domain name. On the host *terminator*, we set *hostname*(1) to *terminator.movie.edu*. Don't add a trailing dot to the name.

Look up a local name

nslookup can be used to look up any type of resource record, and it can be directed to query any name server. By default, it looks up A (address) records using the name server on the local system. To look up a host's address with *nslookup*, run *nslookup* with the host's name as the only argument. A lookup of a local name should return almost instantly.

We ran *nslookup* to look up *carrie*:

```
% nslookup carrie
Server: terminator.movie.edu
Address: 192.249.249.3

Name:    carrie.movie.edu
Address: 192.253.253.4
```

If looking up a local name works, your local name server has been configured properly for your domain. If the lookup fails, you'll see something like this:

```
*** terminator.movie.edu can't find carrie: Non-existent domain
```

This means that either *carrie* is not in your data—check your db file—or you didn't set your default domain in *hostname*(1), or some name server error occurred (but you should have caught the error when you checked the syslog messages).

Look up a local address

When *nslookup* is given an address to look up, it knows to make a PTR query instead of an address query. We ran *nslookup* to look up *carrie*'s address:

```
% nslookup 192.253.253.4
Server: terminator.movie.edu
Address: 192.249.249.3

Name:    carrie.movie.edu
Address: 192.253.253.4
```

If looking up an address works, your local name server has been configured properly for your *in-addr.arpa* domain. If the lookup fails, you'll see the same error messages as when you looked up a name.

Look up a remote name

The next step is to try using the local name server to look up a remote name, like *ftp.uu.net*, or another system you know on the Internet. This command may not return as quickly as the last one. If *nslookup* fails to get a response from your name server, it will wait a little longer than a minute before giving up:

```
% nslookup ftp.uu.net.
Server: terminator.movie.edu
Address: 192.249.249.3

Name:      ftp.uu.net
Addresses: 192.48.96.9
```

If this works, your name server knows where the root name servers are and knows how to contact them to find information about domains other than your own. If it fails, either you forgot to initialize the cache file (and a syslog message will show up) or the network is broken somewhere and you can't reach the name servers for the remote domain. Try a different remote domain name.

If these first lookups succeeded, congratulations! You have a primary master name server up and running. At this point, you are ready to start configuring your slave name server.

One more test

While you are testing, though, run one more test. Try having a remote name server look up a name in your domain. This is only going to work if your parent name servers have already delegated your domain to the name server you just set up. If your parent required you to have your two name servers running before delegating your domain, skip ahead to the next section, "Editing the Startup Files."

To make *nslookup* use a remote name server to look up a local name, give the local host's name as the first argument, and the remote server's name as the second argument. Again, if this doesn't work, it may take a little longer than a minute before *nslookup* gives you an error message. For instance, to have *gatekeeper.dec.com* look up *carrie*:

```
% nslookup carrie gatekeeper.dec.com.
Server: gatekeeper.dec.com.
Address: 204.123.2.2

Name:    carrie.movie.edu
Address: 192.253.253.4
```

If the first two lookups worked, but using a remote name server to look up a local name failed, your domain may not be registered with your parent name server. That is not a problem, at first, because systems within your domain can look up the names of other systems within your domain and outside of your domain. You'll be able to send email and to *ftp* to local and remote systems. Some systems won't allow *ftp* connections if they can't map your address back to a name. But not being registered will shortly become a problem. Hosts outside of your domain cannot look up names within your domain. You will be able to send email to friends in remote domains, but you won't get their responses. To fix this problem, contact someone responsible for your parent domain and have them check the delegation of your domain.

Editing the Startup Files

Once you have confirmed that your name server is running properly and can be used from here on, you'll need to start it automatically and set *hostname*(1) to a domain name in your system's startup files. Check to see if your vendor has already set up the name server to start on bootup. You may have to remove comment characters from the startup lines, or the startup file may test to see if */etc/named.conf* exists. To look for automatic startup lines, use:

```
% grep named /etc/*rc*
```

or, if you have System V style *rc* files, use:

```
% grep named /etc/rc*/S*
```

If you don't find anything, add lines like the following to the appropriate startup file somewhere after your interfaces are initialized by *ifconfig*:

```
if test -x /etc/named -a -f /etc/named.conf
then
        echo "Starting named"
        /etc/named
fi
```

You may want to wait to start the name server until after the default route is installed or your routing daemon (*routed* or *gated*) is started, depending upon whether these services need the name server or can get by with */etc/hosts.*

Find out which startup file initializes the host name. Change *hostname*(1) to a domain name. For example, we changed:

```
hostname terminator
```

to:

```
hostname terminator.movie.edu
```

Running a Slave Name Server

You need to set up another name server for robustness. You can (and probably will) set up more than two name servers. Two servers are the minimum. If you have only one name server and it goes down, no one can look up names. A second name server splits the load with the first server or handles the whole load if the first server is down. You *could* set up another primary master name server, but we don't recommend it. Set up a slave name server. You can always change a slave name server into a primary master name server later if you decide that you want to expend the extra work it takes to run multiple primary master name servers.

How does a server know if it is a primary master or a slave for a zone? The *named.conf* file tells the server it is a primary master or a slave on a per-zone basis. The NS records don't tell us which servers are the primary master for a zone and which servers are slave for a zone—they only say who the servers are. (Globally, DNS doesn't care; as far as the actual name resolution goes, slave servers are as good as primary master servers.)

What is different between a primary master name server and a slave name server? The crucial difference is where the server gets its data. A primary master name server reads its data from files. A slave name server loads its data over the network from another name server. This process is called a *zone transfer.*

A slave name server is not limited to loading zones from a *primary master* name server; a slave server can load from another *slave* server.

The big advantage of slave name servers is that you only maintain one set of the DNS database files, the ones on the primary master name server. You don't have to worry about synchronizing the files among name servers; the slaves do that for you. The caveat is that a slave does not resynchronize instantly. It polls to see if it is current. The polling interval is one of those numbers in the SOA record that we haven't explained yet. (BIND version 8 speeds up the distribution of zone data, which we will describe later.)

A slave name server doesn't need to retrieve *all* of its db files over the network; the overhead files, *db.cache* and *db.127.0.0*, are the same as on a primary master, so keep a local copy on the slave. That means that a slave name server is a *primary master* for *0.0.127.in-addr.arpa*. Well, you *could* make it a slave for *0.0.127.in-addr.arpa*, but that data never changes—it might as well be a primary master.

Setup

To set up your slave name server, create a directory for the db files on the slave name server host (e.g., */usr/local/named*) and copy over the files */etc/named.conf*, *db.cache*, and *db.127.0.0*:

```
# rcp /etc/named.conf host:/etc
# rcp db.cache db.127.0.0 host:db-file-directory
```

You must modify */etc/named.conf* on the slave name server host. For version 4, change every occurrence of primary to secondary except for *0.0.127.in-addr.arpa*. Before the filename on each of these lines, add the IP address of the primary master server you just set up. For example, if the original version 4 configuration file line was this:

```
primary  movie.edu     db.movie
```

then the modified line looks like:

```
secondary  movie.edu     192.249.249.3 db.movie
```

If the original version 8 configuration file line was:

```
zone "movie.edu" in {
     type master;
     file "db.movie";
};
```

change master to slave and add a masters line with the IP address of the master server:

```
zone "movie.edu" in {
     type slave;
     file "db.movie";
     masters { 192.249.249.3; };
};
```

This tells the name server that it is a slave for the zone *movie.edu* and that it should track the version of this zone that is being kept on the host 192.249.249.3. The slave name server will keep a backup copy of this zone in the local file *db.movie*.

For Movie U., we set up our slave name server on *wormhole*. Recall that the configuration file on *terminator* (the primary master) looked like this:

```
directory /usr/local/named

primary  movie.edu              db.movie
```

```
primary   249.249.192.in-addr.arpa  db.192.249.249
primary   253.253.192.in-addr.arpa  db.192.253.253
primary   0.0.127.in-addr.arpa      db.127.0.0
cache     .                         db.cache
```

We copied */etc/named.conf, db.cache,* and *db.127.0.0* to *wormhole* and edited the configuration file as described above. The version 4 configuration file on *wormhole* now looks like this:

```
directory /usr/local/named

secondary  movie.edu                192.249.249.3 db.movie
secondary  249.249.192.in-addr.arpa 192.249.249.3 db.192.249.249
secondary  253.253.192.in-addr.arpa 192.249.249.3 db.192.253.253
primary    0.0.127.in-addr.arpa     db.127.0.0
cache      .                        db.cache
```

The equivalent version 8 configuration file looks like this:

```
options {
        directory "/usr/local/named";
};

zone "movie.edu" in {
        type slave;
        file "db.movie";
        masters { 192.249.249.3; };
};

zone "249.249.192.in-addr.arpa" in {
        type slave;
        file "db.192.249.249";
        masters { 192.249.249.3; };
};

zone "253.253.192.in-addr.arpa" in {
        type slave;
        file "db.192.253.253";
        masters { 192.249.249.3; };
};

zone "0.0.127.in-addr.arpa" in {
        type master;
        file "db.127.0.0";
};

zone "." in {
        type hint;
        file "db.cache";
};
```

This causes the name server on *wormhole* to load *movie.edu, 249.249.192.in-addr.arpa,* and *253.253.192.in-addr.arpa* over the network from 192.249.249.3

(*terminator*). It also saves a backup copy of these files in */usr/local/named*. You may find it handy to isolate the backup files in a subdirectory or to name them with a unique suffix like *.bak*; on rare occasions, you may have to delete all of the backup files manually. We'll cover more on backup files later.

Start up the slave name server. Check for error messages in the *syslog* file as you did for the primary master server. As on the primary master, the command to start up a name server is:

```
# /etc/named
```

One extra check to make on the slave that you didn't have to make on the primary master is to see that the name server created the backup files. Shortly after we started our slave name server on *wormhole*, we saw *db.movie, db.192.249.249*, and *db.192.253.253* show up in the */usr/local/named* directory. This means the slave has successfully loaded these zones from the primary master and has saved a backup copy.

To complete setting up your slave name server, try looking up the same names you looked up when the primary master server was started. This time *nslookup* must be run on the slave name server host so that the slave server is queried. If your slave is working fine, add the proper lines to your system startup files so that the slave name server is started when your system boots up and *hostname*(1) is set to a domain name.

Backup Files

Slave servers are not *required* to save a backup copy of the zone data. If there is a backup copy, the slave server reads it on startup and later checks with the master server to see if the master server has a newer copy, instead of loading a new copy of the zone immediately. If the master server has a newer copy, the slave pulls it over and saves it in the backup file.

Why save a backup copy? Suppose the master server is down when the slave starts up. The slave will be unable to transfer the zone and therefore won't function as a server for that zone until the master server is up. With a backup copy, the slave has some data, although it might be slightly out of date. Since the slave does not rely on the master server always being up, it is a more robust system.

To run without a backup copy, omit the filename at the end of the *secondary* lines in the version 4 configuration file. In version 8, remove the *file* line. We recommend having all your slave servers save backup copies, though. There is very little extra cost to having a backup file, but there is a very high cost if you get caught without a backup file when you need it most.

Multiple Master Servers

Are there other ways to make your slave server configuration more robust? Yes, you can specify up to ten IP addresses of master servers. In a version 4 configuration file, just add them after the first IP address, before the backup filename. In a version 8 configuration file, add them after the first IP address and terminate them with semicolons:

```
masters { 192.249.249.3; 192.249.249.4; };
```

The slave will try the master server at each IP address, in the order listed, until it successfully transfers the zone. The intent of this feature is to allow you to list all the IP addresses of the host running the primary master for the zone if that host is multihomed. But, since there is no check made that the contacted server is a primary master or slave, you can list the IP addresses of hosts running slave servers for the zone, if that makes sense for your setup.

SOA Values

Remember this SOA record?

```
movie.edu. IN SOA terminator.movie.edu. al.robocop.movie.edu. (
                    1        ; Serial
                    10800    ; Refresh after 3 hours
                    3600     ; Retry after 1 hour
                    604800   ; Expire after 1 week
                    86400 )  ; Minimum TTL of 1 day
```

We never explained what the values in between the parentheses were for.

The serial number applies to all the data within the zone. We chose to start our serial number at 1, a logical place to start. But, many people find it more useful to use the date in the serial number instead, like 1997102301. This format is YYYYMMDDNN, where Y is the year, M is the month, D is the day, and NN is a count of how many times the zone data were modified that day. Whatever you choose, it's important that this number always increase when you update your zone data.

When a slave name server contacts a master server for zone data, it first asks for the serial number on the data. If the slave's serial number is lower than the master server's, the slave's zone data are out of date. In this case, the slave pulls a new copy of the zone. When a slave starts up and there is no backup file to read, it always loads the zone. As you might guess, when you modify the db files on the primary master, you must increment the serial number. Updating your db files is covered in Chapter 7.

The next four fields specify various time intervals in seconds:

refresh

> The refresh interval tells the slave how often to check that its data are up to date. To give you an idea of the system load this feature causes, a slave will make one SOA query per zone per refresh interval. The value we choose, three hours, is reasonably aggressive. Most users will tolerate a delay of half of a working day for things like name server data to propagate when they are waiting for their new workstation to be operational. If you provide one-day service for your site, consider raising this value to eight hours. If your data don't change very often, or if all of your slaves are spread over long distances (as the root name servers are), consider a value that is even longer: 24 hours.

retry

> If the slave fails to reach the master name server(s) after the refresh period (the host(s) could be down), then it starts trying to connect every *retry* seconds. Normally, the retry interval is shorter than the refresh interval, but it doesn't have to be.

expire

> If the slave fails to contact the master server(s) for *expire* seconds, the slave expires its data. Expiring the data means the slave stops giving out answers about the data because the data are too old to be useful. Essentially, this field says: at some point, the data are so old that having *no* data is better than having stale data. Expire times on the order of a week are common—longer (up to a month) if you frequently have problems reaching your updating source. The expiration time should always be much larger than the retry and refresh intervals; if the expire time is smaller than the refresh interval, your slaves will expire their data before trying to load new data.

TTL

> TTL stands for *time to live*. This value applies to all the resource records in the db file. The name server supplies this TTL in query responses, allowing other servers to cache the data for the TTL interval. If your data don't change much, you might consider using a minimum TTL of several days. One week is about the longest value that makes sense. A value as short as one hour can be used, but it is not recommended because of the amount of DNS traffic it causes.

What values you choose for your SOA record will depend upon the needs of your site. In general, longer times cause less load on your systems and lengthen the propagation of changes; shorter times increase the load on your systems and speed up the propagation of changes. The values we use in this book should work well for most sites. RFC 1537 recommends the following values for top-level domain servers:

```
86400 ;  Refresh        24 hours
 7200 ;  Retry           2 hours
```

```
2592000 ;  Expire        30 days
 345600 ;  Minimum TTL    4 days
```

There is one implementation feature you need to be aware of. Older versions (pre-4.8.3) of BIND slaves stopped answering queries during a zone load. As a result, BIND was modified to spread out the zone loads, reducing the periods of unavailability. So, even if you set a low refresh interval, your slaves may not check as often as you request. BIND attempts a certain number of zone loads and then waits 15 minutes before trying another batch.

Now that we've told you all about how slave servers poll to keep their data up-to-date, BIND version 8 changed how zone data propagates! The polling feature is still there, but version 8 adds a notification when zone data changes. If both your primary master server and your slaves are version 8, the primary master will notify the slave that a zone has changed within 15 minutes of loading a new copy of that zone. The notification causes the slave server to shorten the refresh interval and attempt to load the zone immediately. We'll discuss this more in Chapter 10.

Adding More Domains

Now that you have your name servers running, you might want to support more domains. What needs to be done? Nothing special, really. All you need to do is add more primary or secondary statements (version 4) or zone statements (version 8) to your configuration file. You can even add secondary lines to your primary master server, and primary lines to your slave server. (You may have already noticed that your slave server was primary master for *0.0.127.in-addr.arpa.*)

At this point, it's useful to repeat something we said in an earlier chapter. Calling a *given* name server a primary master name server or a slave name server is a little silly. Name servers can be authoritative for more than one zone. A name server can be a primary master for one zone, and a slave for another. Most name servers, however, are either primary master for most of the zones they load or slave for most of the zones they load. So if we call a particular name server a primary master or a slave, we mean that it's the primary master or a slave for *most* of the zones it loads.

What Next?

In this chapter, we showed you how to create name server data files by translating */etc/hosts* to equivalent name server data, and how to set up a primary master and a slave name server. There is more work to do to complete setting up your local domain: you need to modify your DNS data for email, configure the other hosts in your domain to use name servers, and you may need to start up more name servers. These topics are covered in the next few chapters.

5

DNS and Electronic Mail

And here Alice began to get rather sleepy, and went on saying to herself, in a dreamy sort of way, "Do cats eat bats? Do cats eat bats?" and sometimes "Do bats eat cats?" for, you see, as she couldn't answer either question, it didn't much matter which way she put it.

I'll bet you're drowsy too, after that looong chapter. Thankfully, this next chapter discusses a topic that will probably be very interesting to you system administrators and postmasters: how DNS impacts electronic mail. And even if it isn't interesting to you, at least it's shorter than the last chapter.

One of the advantages of the Domain Name System over host tables is its support of advanced mail routing. When mailers only had the *HOSTS.TXT* file (and its derivative, */etc/hosts*) to work with, the best they could do was to attempt delivery to a host's IP address. If that failed, they could either defer delivery of the message and try again later, or bounce the message back to the sender.

DNS offers a mechanism for specifying backup hosts for mail delivery. The mechanism also allows hosts to assume mail handling responsibilities for other hosts. This lets diskless hosts that don't run mailers, for example, have mail addressed to them processed by their server. Together, these features give administrators much more flexibility in configuring electronic mail on their network.

MX Records

DNS uses a single type of resource record to implement enhanced mail routing, the MX record. Originally, this functionality was split between two records, the MD (mail destination) and MF (mail forwarder) records. MD specified the final destination to which a message addressed to a given domain name should be delivered. MF specified a host that would forward mail on to the eventual destination, should that destination be unreachable.

Early experience with DNS on the Internet showed that separating the functionality didn't work very well. A mailer needed both the MD and MF records attached to a domain name (if both existed) to decide where to send the mail—one or the other alone wouldn't do. But an explicit lookup of one type or another (either MD or MF) would cause a name server to cache just that record type. So mailers either had to do two queries, one for MD and one for MF data, or they could no longer accept cached answers. This meant that the overhead of running mail was higher than that of running other services, and was eventually deemed unacceptable.

The two records were integrated into a single record type, MX, to solve this problem. Now a mailer just needed all the MX records for a particular domain name destination to make a mail routing decision. Using cached MX records was fine, as long as the TTLs matched.

MX records specify a *mail exchanger* for a domain name: a host that will *either* process *or* forward mail for the domain name (through a firewall, for example). "Processing" the mail means either delivering it to the individual it's addressed to, or gatewaying it to another mail transport, like UUCP. "Forwarding" means sending it to its final destination or to another mail exchanger "closer" to the destination via SMTP, the Internet's Simple Mail Transfer Protocol. Sometimes forwarding the mail involves queuing it for some amount of time, too.

In order to prevent mail routing loops, the MX record has an extra parameter, besides the domain name of the mail exchanger: a preference value. The preference value is an unsigned 16-bit number (between 0 and 65535) that indicates the mail exchanger's priority. For example, the MX record:

```
peets.mpk.ca.us.    IN    MX    10 relay.hp.com.
```

specifies that *relay.hp.com* is a mail exchanger for *peets.mpk.ca.us* at preference value 10.

Taken together, the preference values of a host's mail exchangers determine the order in which a mailer should use them. The preference value itself isn't important, only its relationship to the values of other mail exchangers: is it higher or lower than the values of this host's other mail exchangers? Unless there are other records involved:

```
plange.puntacana.dr.    IN    MX    1 listo.puntacana.dr.
plange.puntacana.dr.    IN    MX    2 hep.puntacana.dr.
```

does exactly the same thing as:

```
plange.puntacana.dr.    IN    MX    50   listo.puntacana.dr.
plange.puntacana.dr.    IN    MX    100 hep.puntacana.dr.
```

Mailers should attempt delivery to the mail exchangers with the *lowest* preference values first. This seems a little counterintuitive at first—the *most* preferred mail exchanger has the *lowest* preference value. But since the preference value is an unsigned quantity, this lets you specify a "best" mail exchanger at preference value 0.

If delivery to the most preferred mail exchanger(s) fails, mailers should attempt delivery to less preferred mail exchangers (those with *higher* preference values), in order of increasing preference value. That is, mailers should try more preferred mail exchangers before they try less preferred mail exchangers. More than one mail exchanger may share the same preference value, too. This gives the mailer its choice of which to send to first.* The mailer should try all the mail exchangers at a given preference value before proceeding to the next higher value, though.

For example, the MX records for *ora.com* might be:

```
ora.com.    IN    MX    0 ora.ora.com.
ora.com.    IN    MX    10 ruby.ora.com.
ora.com.    IN    MX    10 opal.ora.com.
```

Interpreted together, these MX records instruct mailers to attempt delivery to *ora.com* by sending to:

1. *ora.ora.com* first

2. Either *ruby.ora.com* or *opal.ora.com* next, and finally

3. The remaining preference 10 mail exchanger (the one not used in 2)

Of course, once the mailer successfully delivers the mail to one of *ora.com*'s mail exchangers, it can stop. A mailer successfully delivering *ora.com* mail to *ora.ora.com* doesn't need to try *ruby* or *opal.*

What if a host doesn't have any MX records? Will a mailer simply not deliver mail to that host? Actually, you can compile recent versions of *sendmail* to do just that. Most vendors, however, have compiled their *sendmail*s to be more forgiving: if no MX records exist, they'll at least attempt delivery to the host's address. *sendmail* version 8, compiled "out of the box," will try the address of a mail destination without MX records. Check your vendor's documentation if you're not sure which variety your *sendmail* is.

Even though nearly all mailers will deliver mail to a host with just an address, and no MX records, it's still a good idea to have at least one MX record for each host. *sendmail* will request MX records for a host each time it needs to deliver mail. If the host doesn't have any MX records, a name server—usually one of your authoritative name servers—still ends up answering that query. If you simply add an MX record

---

* The newest version of *sendmail*, version 8, will actually choose randomly among mail exchangers at the same preference.

for the host pointing to itself, *sendmail* will have its first query answered, and the mailer's local name server will cache the MX record for future use.

What's a Mail Exchanger, Again?

The idea of a mail exchanger is probably new to many of you, so let's go over it in a little more detail. A simple analogy should help here: imagine that a mail exchanger is an airport, and instead of setting up MX records to instruct mailers where to send messages, you're advising your in-laws on which airport to fly into when they come visit you.

Say you live in Los Gatos, California. The closest airport for your in-laws to fly into is San Jose, the second closest is San Francisco, and the third Oakland. (We'll ignore other factors like price of the ticket, Bay Area traffic, etc.) Don't see the parallel? Then picture it like this:

```
los-gatos.ca.us.    IN    MX    1 san-jose.ca.us.
los-gatos.ca.us.    IN    MX    2 san-francisco.ca.us.
los-gatos.ca.us.    IN    MX    3 oakland.ca.us.
```

The MX list is just an ordered list of destinations that tells mailers (your in-laws) where to send messages (fly) if they want to reach a given domain (your house). The preference value tells them how desirable it is to use that destination—you can think of it as a logical "distance" from the eventual destination (in any units you choose), or simply as a "top-ten"-style ranking of the proximity of those mail exchangers to the final destination.

With this list, you're saying, "Try to fly into San Jose, and if you can't get there, try San Francisco and Oakland, in that order." It *also* says that if you reach San Francisco, you should take a commuter flight to San Jose. If you wind up in Oakland, you should try to get a commuter to San Jose, or at least to San Francisco.

What makes a good mail exchanger, then? The same qualities that make a good airport:

Size

> You wouldn't want to fly into tiny Reid-Hillview Airport to get to Los Gatos, because the airport's not equipped to handle large planes or many people. (You'd probably be better off landing a big jet on Highway 280 than at Reid-Hillview.) Likewise, you don't want to use an emaciated, underpowered host as a mail exchanger; it won't be able to handle the load.

Uptime

> You know better than to fly through Denver International Airport in the winter, right? Then you should know better than to use a host that's rarely up or available as a mail exchanger.

Connectivity

If your relatives are flying in from far away, you've got to make sure they can get a direct flight to at least one of the airports in the list you give them. You can't tell them their only choices are San Jose and Oakland if they're flying in from Helsinki. Similarly, you've got to make sure that at least one of your hosts' mail exchangers is reachable to anyone who might conceivably send you mail.

Management and administration

How well an airport is managed has a bearing on your safety while flying into or just through the airport, and on how easy it is to use. Think of these factors when choosing a mail exchanger. The privacy of your mail, the speed of its delivery during normal operations, and how well your mail is treated when your hosts go down all hinge upon the quality of the administrators who manage your mail exchangers.

Keep this example in mind, because we'll use it again later.

The MX Algorithm

That's the basic idea behind MX records and mail exchangers, but there are a few more wrinkles you should know about. To avoid routing loops, mailers need to use a slightly more complicated algorithm than what we've described when they determine where to send mail.*

Imagine what would happen if mailers didn't check for routing loops. Let's say you send mail from your workstation to *nuts@ora.com*, raving (or raging) about the quality of this book. Unfortunately, *ora.ora.com* is down at the moment. No problem! Recall *ora.com*'s MX records:

```
ora.com.    IN    MX    0  ora.ora.com.
ora.com.    IN    MX    10 ruby.ora.com.
ora.com.    IN    MX    10 opal.ora.com.
```

Your mailer falls back and sends your message to *ruby.ora.com*, which is up. *ruby*'s mailer then tries to forward the mail on to *ora.ora.com*, but can't, because *ora.ora.com* is down. Now what? Unless *ruby* checks the sanity of what she is doing, she'll try to forward the message to *opal.ora.com*, or maybe even to herself. That's certainly not going to help get the mail delivered. If *ruby* sends the message to herself, we have a mail routing loop. If *ruby* sends the message to *opal*, *opal* will either send it back to *ruby* or send it to herself, and we again have a mail routing loop.

---

* This algorithm is based on RFC 974, which describes how Internet mail routing works.

To prevent this from happening, mailers discard certain MX records before they decide where to send a message. A mailer sorts the list of MX records by preference value and looks in the list for the canonical domain name of the host it's running on. If the local host appears as a mail exchanger, the mailer discards that MX record and all MX records in which the preference value is higher (that is, less preferred mail exchangers). That prevents the mailer from sending messages to itself or to mailers "farther" from the eventual destination.

Let's think about this in the context of our airport analogy. This time, imagine you're an airline passenger (a message), and you're trying to get to Greeley, Colorado. You can't get a direct flight to Greeley, but you can fly to either Fort Collins or Denver (the two next highest mail exchangers). Since Fort Collins is closer to Greeley, you opt to fly to Fort Collins.

Now, once you've arrived in Fort Collins, there's no sense in flying to Denver, away from your destination (a lower preference mail exchanger). (And flying from Fort Collins to Fort Collins would be silly, too.) So the only acceptable flight to get you to your destination is now a Fort Collins-Greeley flight. You eliminate flights to less preferred destinations to prevent frequent flyer looping and wasteful travel time.

One caveat: most mailers will *only* look for their local host's *canonical* domain name in the list of MX records. They don't check for aliases (domain names on the left side of CNAME records). Unless you always use canonical names in your MX records, there's no guarantee a mailer will be able to find itself in the MX list, and you'll run the risk of having your mail loop. If you send mail addressed to a particular domain name to a mailer that isn't configured to accept mail for that domain name, and it finds itself as the most preferred mail exchanger, it may bounce the mail with the error:

```
554 MX list for movie.edu points back to relay.isp.com
554 <root@movie.edu>... Local configuration error
```

This replaces the quainter "I refuse to talk to myself" error in newer versions of *sendmail*. The moral: in an MX record, always use the mail exchanger's canonical name.

One more caveat: the hosts you list as mail exchangers *must* have address records. A mailer needs to find an address for each mail exchanger you name, or else it can't attempt delivery there.

To go back to our *ora.com* example, when *ruby* received the message from your workstation, her mailer would have checked the list of MX records:

```
ora.com.    IN    MX    0  ora.ora.com.
ora.com.    IN    MX    10 ruby.ora.com.
ora.com.    IN    MX    10 opal.ora.com.
```

Finding the local host's domain name in the list at preference value 10, *ruby*'s mailer would discard all the records at preference value 10 or higher (the records in bold):

```
ora.com.    IN    MX    0 ora.ora.com.
ora.com. IN MX 10 ruby.ora.com.
ora.com. IN MX 10 opal.ora.com.
```

leaving only:

```
ora.com.    IN    MX    0 ora.ora.com.
```

Since *ora.ora.com* is down, *ruby* would defer delivery until later, and queue the message.

What happens if a mailer finds *itself* at the highest preference (lowest preference value), and has to discard the whole MX list? Some mailers attempt delivery directly to the destination host's IP address, as a last-ditch effort. In most mailers, however, it's an error. It may indicate that DNS thinks the mailer should be processing (not just forwarding) mail for the destination, but the mailer hasn't been configured to know that. Or it may indicate that the administrator has ordered the MX records incorrectly by using the wrong preference values.

Say, for example, the folks who run *acme.com* add a mail exchanger record to direct mail addressed to *acme.com* to a mailer at their Internet Service Provider:

```
acme.com.    IN    MX    10 mail.isp.net.
```

Many mailers need to be configured to identify their aliases and the names of other hosts they process mail for. Unless the mailer on *mail.isp.net* is configured to recognize email addressed to *acme.com* as local mail, it will assume it's being asked to relay the mail and attempt to forward the mail to a mail exchanger closer to the final destination.* When it looks up the MX records for *acme.com*, it'll find itself as the most preferred mail exchanger, and return the mail to the sender. Then it will bounce the mail with the familiar error:

```
554 MX list for acme.com points back to mail.isp.com
554 <root@acme.com>... Local configuration error
```

Many versions of *sendmail* use class *w* or fileclass *w* as the list of "local" destinations. Depending on your *sendmail.cf* file, adding an alias can be as easy as adding the line

```
Cw acme.com
```

to *sendmail.cf*. If your mailer uses another mail transport, such as UUCP, to deliver mail to the hosts it acts as a mail exchanger for, this will probably require more involved configuration.[†]

---

* Unless, of course, *mail.isp.net*'s mailer is configured not to relay mail for unknown domains.

† Configuring UUCP, while beyond the scope of this book, is covered in *Using & Managing uucp*, by Ed Ravin, published by O'Reilly & Associates (1996).

You may have noticed that we tend to use multiples of ten for our preference values. Ten is convenient because it allows you to insert other MX records temporarily at intermediate values without changing the other weights, but otherwise there's nothing magical about it.

6

Configuring Hosts

In this chapter:
- *The Resolver*
- *Sample Resolver Configurations*
- *Minimizing Pain and Suffering*
- *Vendor-Specific Options*

*They were indeed a queer-looking party that
assembled on the bank—the birds with draggled
feathers, the animals with their fur clinging close to
them, and all dripping wet, cross, and
uncomfortable.*

Now that you or someone else in your organization has set up name servers for your zones, you'll want to configure the hosts on your network to use them. That involves configuring those hosts' resolvers. You should also check files like *hosts.equiv* and *.rhosts* and make any changes dictated by using DNS; you may need to convert some of the host names in these files to domain names. And you may also want to add aliases, both for your users' convenience and to minimize the shock of the conversion to DNS.

This chapter covers these topics, and also describes configuring the resolver in many common versions of UNIX and in Microsoft's Windows 95 and Windows NT.

The Resolver

We introduced resolvers way back in Chapter 2, *How Does DNS Work?*, but we didn't say much more about them. The resolver, you'll remember, is the client half of the Domain Name System. It's responsible for translating a program's request for host information into a query to a name server and for translating the response into an answer for the program.

We haven't done any resolver configuration yet, because the occasion for it hasn't arisen. When we set up our name servers in Chapter 4, *Setting Up BIND*, the resolver's default behavior worked just fine for our purposes. But if we'd needed the resolver to do more than what it does by default, or to behave differently from the default, we would have had to configure the resolver.

There's one thing we should mention up front: what we'll describe in the next few sections is the behavior of the vanilla BIND 8.1.2 resolver in the absence of other naming services. Not all resolvers behave quite this way; some vendors still ship resolvers based on earlier versions of the DNS code, and some have implemented special resolver functionality that lets you modify the resolver algorithm. Whenever we think it's important, we'll point out differences between the behavior of the 8.1.2 BIND resolver and that of earlier resolvers, particularly the 4.8.3 resolver, which is what many vendors were shipping when we last updated this book. We'll cover various vendors' extensions later in this chapter.

So what exactly does the resolver allow you to configure? Most resolvers let you configure at least three aspects of the resolver's behavior: the default domain, the search list, and the name server(s) that the resolver queries. Many UNIX vendors allow you to configure other resolver behavior, too, through nonstandard extensions to DNS. Sometimes these extensions are necessary to cope with other software, like Sun's Network Information Service (NIS); sometimes they're simply value added by the vendor.[*]

Almost all resolver configuration is done in the file */etc/resolv.conf* (this may be */usr/etc/resolv.conf* or something similar on your host—check the *resolver* manual page, usually in section 4 or 5, to make sure). There are five main *directives* you can use in *resolv.conf*: the *domain* directive, the *search* directive, the *nameserver* directive, the *sortlist* directive, and the *options* directive. These directives control the behavior of the resolver. There are other, vendor-specific directives available on some versions of UNIX—we'll discuss them at the end of this chapter.

The Default Domain

The default domain is the domain considered "local" to the host. For example, when you add an entry like:

```
relay mark
```

to your *.rhosts* file, the name *relay* is assumed to be in your default domain. This makes a lot more sense than allowing access to every host on the Internet whose domain name starts with *relay*. Other authorization files like *hosts.equiv* and *hosts.lpd* work the same way.

Normally, the default domain is determined from the host's *hostname*; the default domain is everything after the first "." in the name. If the name doesn't contain a ".", the default domain is assumed to be the root domain. So the *hostname asylum.sf.ca.us* implies a default domain of *sf.ca.us*, while the *hostname dogbert*

---

[*] NIS used to be called "Yellow Pages," or "YP," but was changed to NIS because the British phone company had a copyright on the name Yellow Pages.

implies a root default domain—which probably isn't correct, given that there are no hosts immediately under the root domain.

You can also set the default domain with the *domain* directive in *resolv.conf.* If the *domain* directive is specified, it overrides the domain in the *hostname.*

The domain directive has a very simple syntax, but you've got to get it right, since the resolver doesn't report errors. The keyword *domain* starts the line in column one, followed by whitespace (one or more blanks or tabs), then the name of the default domain. The default domain should be written without a trailing dot, like this:

```
domain colospgs.co.us
```

In older versions of the BIND resolver (those before BIND 4.9.3), trailing spaces *are not allowed* on the line, and will cause your default domain to be set to a name ending with one or more spaces, which is almost certainly not what you want. And there's yet another way to set the default domain—via the *LOCALDOMAIN* environment variable. *LOCALDOMAIN* is handy because you can set it on a per-user basis. For example, you might have a big, massively parallel box in your corporate computing center to which employees from all over the world log in. Each may do most of his work in a different company subdomain. With *LOCALDOMAIN*, each employee can set his default domain to the appropriate domain in his shell startup file.

Which method should you use—*hostname*, the *domain* directive, or *LOCALDOMAIN?* We prefer using *hostname*, but primarily because that's the way Berkeley does it, and it seems "cleaner" in that it requires less explicit configuration. Also, some Berkeley software, particularly software that uses the *ruserok()* library call to authenticate users, allows short host names in files like *hosts.equiv* only if *hostname* is set to the full domain name.

If you run software that can't tolerate long *hostnames*, though, you can use the *domain* directive. The *hostname* command will continue to return a short name, and the resolver will fill in the domain from *resolv.conf.* You may even find occasion to use *LOCALDOMAIN* on a host with lots of users.

The Search List

The default domain, whether derived from *hostname* or *resolv.conf*, also determines the default *search list.* The search list was designed to make users' lives a little easier by saving them some typing. The idea is to search one or more domains for names typed at the command line that might be incomplete—that is, that might not be fully qualified domain names.

Most UNIX networking commands that take a domain name as an argument, like *telnet, ftp, rlogin,* and *rsh,* apply the search list to those arguments.

Both the way the default search list is derived and the way the search list is applied changed from BIND 4.8.3 to BIND 4.9. If your resolver is an older make, you'll still see the 4.8.3 behavior, but if you've got a newer model, including BIND 8.1.2,[*] you'll see the improvements in the 4.9 resolver.

With any BIND resolver, a user can indicate that a domain name is fully qualified by adding a trailing dot to it.[†] For example, the trailing dot in the command:

```
% telnet ftp.ora.com.
```

means "don't bother searching any other domains; this domain name is fully qualified." This is analogous to the leading slash in full pathnames in the UNIX and MS-DOS filesystems. Pathnames without a leading slash are interpreted as relative to the current working directory, while pathnames with a leading slash are absolute, anchored at the root.

The BIND 4.8.3 search list

With BIND 4.8.3 resolvers, the default search list includes the default domain and each of its parent domains with two or more labels. Therefore, on a host running a 4.8.3 resolver and configured with:

```
domain cv.hp.com
```

the default search list would contain first *cv.hp.com,* the default domain, then *hp.com,* the default domain's parent, but not *com,* as it only has one label.[‡] The name is looked up as is, after the resolver appends each element of the search list, and only if the name typed contains at least one dot. Thus, a user typing:

```
% telnet pronto.cv.hp.com
```

will cause lookups of *pronto.cv.hp.com.cv.hp.com* and *pronto.cv.hp.com.hp.com* before the resolver looks up *pronto.cv.hp.com* by itself. A user typing:

```
% telnet asap
```

---

[*] Though the ISC added lots of new server functionality in BIND 8, the resolver is nearly identical to the BIND 4.9 resolver.

[†] Note that we said that the resolver can handle a trailing dot. Some programs, particularly UNIX mail user agents, don't deal correctly with a trailing dot in email addresses. They cough even before they hand the domain name in the address to the resolver.

[‡] One reason older BIND resolvers didn't append just the top-level domain is that there were—and still are—very few hosts at the second level of the Internet's name space, so tacking on just *com* or *edu* to *foo* is unlikely to result in the domain name of a real host. Also, looking up the address of a *foo.com* or *foo.edu* might well require sending a query to a root name server, which taxes the roots and can be time-consuming.

on the same host would cause the resolver to look up *asap.cv.hp.com* and *asap.hp.com*, but not just *asap*, since the name typed ("*asap*") contains no dots.

Note that application of the search list stops as soon as a prospective domain name turns up the data being looked up. In the *asap* example, the search list would never get around to appending *hp.com* if *asap.cv.hp.com* resolved to an address.

The BIND 4.9 and later search list

With BIND 4.9, the default search list includes just the default domain. So, if you configure a host with:

```
domain cv.hp.com
```

the default search list would contain just *cv.hp.com*. Also, in a change from earlier resolvers, the search list is usually applied *after* the name is tried as is. As long as the argument you type has at least one dot in it, it's looked up exactly as you typed it *before* any element of the search list is appended. If that lookup fails, the search list is applied. Even if the argument has no dots in it (that is, it's a single label name), it's tried as-is, after the resolver appends the elements of the search list.

Why is it better to try the argument *literatim* first? From experience, the designers of DNS found that, more often than not, if a user bothered to type in a name with even a single dot in it, he was probably typing in a fully qualified domain name without the trailing dot. With older search list behavior, the resolver would send several fruit-less queries before ever trying the name as typed.

Therefore, with a 4.9 resolver, a user typing:

```
% telnet pronto.cv.hp.com
```

would have *pronto.cv.hp.com* looked up first (there are three dots in the argument). If that query failed, the resolver would try *pronto.cv.hp.com.cv.hp.com*. A user typing:

```
% telnet asap
```

on the same host would cause the resolver to look up *asap.cv.hp.com* first, since the name doesn't contain a dot, and then just *asap*.

The search Directive

What if you don't like the default search list you get when you set your default domain? In BIND 4.8.3 and all newer resolvers, you can set the search list explicitly, domain by domain, in the order you want the domains searched. You do this with the *search* directive.

The syntax of the *search* directive is very similar to that of the *domain* directive, except that it can take multiple domain names as arguments. The keyword *search* starts the line in column one, followed by from one to six domain names, in the order you want them searched. The first domain in the list is interpreted as the default domain, so the *search* and *domain* directives are mutually exclusive. If you use both in *resolv.conf*, the one that appears last will override the other.

The directive:

```
search corp.hp.com paloalto.hp.com hp.com
```

for example, would instruct the resolver to search the *corp.hp.com* domain first, then *paloalto.hp.com*, and then both domains' parent, *hp.com*.

This directive might be useful on a host whose users access hosts in both *corp.hp.com* and *paloalto.hp.com* frequently. On the other hand, on a BIND 4.8.3 resolver, the directive:

```
search corp.hp.com
```

would have the resolver skip searching the default domain's parent domain when the search list is applied. (On a 4.9 resolver, the parent domain isn't in the search list, so this is no different from the default behavior.) This might be useful if the host's users only access hosts in the local domain, or if connectivity to the parent name servers isn't good (because it minimizes unnecessary queries to the parent name servers).

NOTE   If you use the *domain* directive and update your resolver to BIND version 4.9 or later, users who relied on your default domain's parent being in the search list may believe the resolver has suddenly broken. You can restore the old behavior by using the *search* directive to configure your resolver to use the same search list that it would have built before. For example, under BIND 4.9 or BIND 8, you can replace *domain nsr.hp.com* with *search nsr.hp.com hp.com* and get the same functionality.

The nameserver Directive

Back in Chapter 4, we talked about two types of name servers: primary master name servers and slave name servers. But what if you don't want to run a name server on a host, yet still want to use DNS? Or, for that matter, what if you *can't* run a name server on a host (because the operating system doesn't support it, for example)? Surely you don't have to run a name server on *every* host, right?

No, of course you don't. By default, the resolver looks for a name server running on the local host—which is why we could use *nslookup* on *terminator* and *wormhole* right after we configured their name servers. You can, however, instruct the resolver to look to another host for name service. This configuration is called a *DNS client* in the *BIND Operations Guide*.

The *nameserver* directive (yep, all one word) tells the resolver the IP address of a name server to query. For example, the line:

```
nameserver 15.32.17.2
```

instructs the resolver to send queries to the name server running at IP address 15.32.17.2, instead of to the local host. This means that on hosts that don't run name servers, you can use the *nameserver* directive to point them at a remote name server. Typically, you would configure the resolvers on your hosts to query your own name servers.

However, since name servers before BIND 4.9 don't have any notion of access control, you can configure your resolver to query almost anyone's name server. Of course, configuring your host to use someone else's name server without first asking permission is presumptuous, if not downright rude, and using one of your own will usually give you better performance, so we'll consider this only an emergency option.

You can also configure the resolver to query the host's local name server, by using either the local host's IP address or the zero address. The zero address, 0.0.0.0, is interpreted by most TCP/IP implementations to mean "this host." The host's real IP address, of course, also means "this host." On hosts that don't understand the zero address, you can use the loopback address, 127.0.0.1.

Now what if the name server your resolver queries is down? Isn't there any way to specify a backup? Do you just fall back to using the host table?

The resolver will also allow you to specify up to three (count 'em, three) name servers using multiple *nameserver* directives. The resolver will query those name servers, in the order listed, until it receives an answer or times out. The number of name servers you configure dictates other aspects of the resolver's behavior, too.

NOTE   If you use multiple *nameserver* directives, *don't* use the loopback address! There's a bug in some Berkeley-derived TCP/IP implementations that can cause problems with BIND if the local name server is down. The resolver's connected datagram socket won't rebind to a new local address if the local name server isn't running, and consequently the resolver will send query packets to the fallback remote name servers with a source address of 127.0.0.1. When the remote name servers try to reply, they'll end up sending the reply packets to themselves.

One name server configured

If there's only one name server configured, the resolver queries that name server with a timeout of five seconds. The timeout is the length of time the resolver will wait for a response from the name server before sending another query. If the resolver encounters an error that indicates the name server is really down or unreachable, or if it times out, it will double the timeout and query the name server again. The errors that would cause this include:[*]

- Receipt of an ICMP `port unreachable` message, which means that no name server is listening on the name server port

- Receipt of an ICMP `host unreachable` or `network unreachable` message, which means that queries can't be sent to the destination IP address

If the domain name or data don't exist, the resolver doesn't retry the query. Theoretically, at least, each name server should have an equivalent "view" of the name space; there's no reason to believe one and not another. So if one name server tells you that a given domain name doesn't exist, or that the type of data you're looking for doesn't exist for the domain name you specified, any other name server should give you the same answer.[†] If the resolver receives a network error *each* time it sends a query (for a total of four errors), it falls back to using the host table. Note that these are *errors*, not timeouts. If it times out on even one query, the resolver returns a null answer and does not fall back to */etc/hosts*.

More than one name server configured

With more than one name server configured, the behavior is a little different. Here's what happens: the resolver starts by querying the first name server in the list, with a timeout of five seconds, just as in the single name server case. If the resolver times out or receives a network error, it will fall back to the next name server, waiting the same five seconds for that name server. Unfortunately, the resolver won't receive many of the possible errors; the socket the resolver uses is "unconnected," since it must be able to receive responses from any of the name servers it queries, and unconnected sockets don't receive ICMP error messages. If the resolver queries all the configured name servers, to no avail, it updates the timeouts and cycles through them again.

---

[*] When we say "one name server configured," that means either one *nameserver* directive in *resolv.conf* or no *nameserver* directive with a name server running locally.

[†] The built-in latency of DNS makes this a small fib—a primary can have authority for a zone and have different data from a slave that also has authority for the zone. The primary may have just loaded new zone data from disk, while the slave may not have had time to transfer the new zone data from the primary. Both name servers return authoritative answers for the zone, but the primary may know about a brand-new host that the slave doesn't yet know about.

The resolver timeout for the next round of queries is based on the number of name servers configured in *resolv.conf.* The timeout for the second round of queries is ten seconds divided by the number of name servers configured, rounded down. Each successive round's timeout is double the previous timeout. After three sets of retransmissions (a total of four timeouts for every name server configured), the resolver gives up trying to query name servers.

For you mathophobes, Table 6-1 shows what the timeouts look like when you have one, two, or three name servers configured.

Table 6-1. Resolver Timeouts

Retry	Name Servers Configured		
	1	2	3
0	5s	(2x) 5s	(3x) 5s
1	10s	(2x) 5s	(3x) 3s
2	20s	(2x) 10s	(3x) 6s
3	40s	(2x) 20s	(3x) 13s
Total	75s	80s	81s

(Note that this is how BIND versions 4.9 and later behave. The behavior of older versions of BIND is similar, but not necessarily identical.)

So if you configure three servers, the resolver queries the first server, with a timeout period of five seconds. If that query times out, the resolver queries the second server with the same timeout, and similarly for the third. If the resolver cycles through all three servers, it doubles the timeout period and divides by three (to three seconds, 10/3 rounded down) and queries the first server again.

Do these times seem awfully long? Remember, this describes a worst-case scenario. With properly-functioning name servers running on tolerably fast hosts, your resolvers should get their answers back in well under a second. Only if all the configured servers are really busy or they or your network is down will the resolver ever make it all the way through the retransmission cycle and give up.

What does the resolver do after it gives up? It times out and returns an error. Typically this results in an error like:

```
% telnet tootsie
tootsie: Host name lookup failure
```

Of course, it'll take at least 75 seconds of waiting to see this message, so be patient.

The sortlist Directive

The *sortlist* directive is a mechanism in BIND 4.9 and later resolvers that lets you specify subnets and networks for the resolver to prefer if it receives multiple addresses as the result of a query. In some cases, you'll have reason to want your host to use a particular network to get to certain destinations. For example, say your workstation and your NFS server have two network interfaces each: one on an Ethernet, subnet 128.32.1; and one on an FDDI ring, subnet 128.32.42. If you leave your workstation's resolver to its own devices, it's anybody's guess which of the NFS server's IP addresses you'll use for a mount—presumably, the first one in a reply packet from the name server. To make sure you try the interface on the FDDI ring first, you can add a *sortlist* directive to *resolv.conf* that sorts the address on 128.32.42 to the preferred position in the structure passed back to programs:

```
sortlist 128.32.42.0/255.255.255.0
```

The argument after the slash is the subnet mask for the subnet in question. To prefer an entire network, you can omit the slash and the subnet mask:

```
sortlist 128.32.0.0
```

The resolver will assume you mean the entire class B network 128.32. (The resolver derives the default unsubnetted net mask for the network from the first few bits of the IP address.)

And, of course, you can specify several subnets and networks to prefer over others:

```
sortlist 128.32.42.0/255.255.255.0 15.0.0.0
```

The resolver sorts any addresses in a reply that match these arguments into the order in which they appear in the directive, and appends addresses that don't match to the end.

The options Directive

The *options* directive was introduced with BIND 4.9. *options* will let you tweak two internal resolver settings. The first is the debug flag, *RES_DEBUG*. The directive:

```
options debug
```

sets *RES_DEBUG*, producing lots of exciting debugging information on standard output, assuming your resolver was configured with *DEBUG* defined. (Actually, that may not be a good assumption, since most vendors compile their stock resolvers without *DEBUG* defined.) This is very useful if you're attempting to diagnose a problem with your resolver or with name service in general, but very annoying otherwise.

The second setting you can modify is *ndots*, which sets the minimum number of dots a domain name argument must have so that the resolver will look it up *before* applying the search list. By default, one or more dots will do; this is equivalent to *ndots:1*. The resolver will try the domain name as typed first as long as the name has any dots in it. You can raise the threshold if you believe your users are more likely to type partial domain names that will need the search list applied. For example, if your default domain is *mit.edu* and your users are accustomed to typing:

```
% ftp prep.ai
```

and having *mit.edu* automatically appended to produce *prep.ai.mit.edu*, then you may want to raise *ndots* to two so that your users won't unwittingly cause lookups to the root name servers for names in the top-level *ai* domain. You could do this with:

```
options ndots:2
```

You can combine both option settings on the same line in *resolv.conf*, like so:

```
options debug ndots:2
```

Comments

Also introduced with BIND 4.9 resolvers, and about time, if you ask us, is the ability to put comments in the *resolv.conf* file. Lines that begin with a pound sign or semicolon in the first column are interpreted as comments and ignored by the resolver.

A Note on the 4.9 Resolver Directives

If you're just moving to a BIND 4.9.3 or 4.9.4 resolver, be careful when using the new directives. You may still have older resolver code statically linked into programs on your host. Often, this isn't a problem because UNIX resolvers ignore directives they don't understand. But don't count on all programs on your host obeying the new directive.

If you're running on a host with programs that include really old resolver code, before 4.8.3, and you'd still like to use the *search* directive with programs that can take advantage of it, here's a trick: use both a *domain* directive and a *search* directive in *resolv.conf*, with the *domain* directive first. Old resolvers will read the *domain* directive and ignore the *search* directive, because they won't recognize it. New resolvers will read the *domain* directive, but the following *search* directive will override its behavior.

Sample Resolver Configurations

So much for the theory—let's go over what *resolv.conf* files look like on real hosts. Resolver configuration needs vary depending on whether or not a host runs a local name server, so we'll cover both cases: hosts with local name servers, and hosts with remote name servers.

Resolver Only

We, as the administrators of *movie.edu*, have just been asked to configure a professor's new standalone workstation, which doesn't run a name server. Deciding which domain the workstation belongs in is easy—there's only *movie.edu* to choose from. However, she *is* working with researchers at Pixar on new shading algorithms, so perhaps it'd be wise to put *pixar.com* in her workstation's search list. The *search* directive:

```
search movie.edu pixar.com
```

will put her workstation in the *movie.edu* domain, and will search *pixar.com* for names not found in *movie.edu.*

The new workstation is on the 192.249.249.0 network, so the closest name servers are *wormhole.movie.edu* (192.249.249.1) and *terminator.movie.edu* (192.249.249.3). As a rule, you should configure hosts to use the closest name server available first. (The closest possible name server is a name server on the local host; the next closest is a name server on the same network or subnet.) In this case, both name servers are equally close, but we know that *wormhole* is bigger (it's a faster host, with more capacity). So the first *nameserver* directive in *resolv.conf* should be:

```
nameserver 192.249.249.1
```

Since this particular professor is known to get awfully vocal when she has problems with her computer, we'll also add *terminator.movie.edu* (192.249.249.3) as a backup name server. That way, if *wormhole* is down for any reason, the professor's workstation can still get name service (assuming *terminator* and the rest of the network are up).

The *resolv.conf* file ends up looking like this:

```
search movie.edu pixar.com
nameserver 192.249.249.1
nameserver 192.249.249.3
```

Local Name Server

Next, we have to configure the university mail hub, *postmanrings2x*, to use domain name service. *postmanrings2x* is shared by all groups in the *movie.edu* domain. We've recently configured a name server on the host to help cut down the load on the other name servers, so we should make sure the resolver queries the name server on the local host first.

The simplest resolver configuration for this case is no configuration at all: don't create a *resolv.conf* file, and let the resolver default to using the local name server. The *hostname* should be set to the full domain name of the host, so the resolver can determine the local domain.

If we decide we need a backup name server—a prudent decision—we can use *resolv.conf*. Whether or not we configure a backup name server depends largely on the reliability of the local name server. A good implementation of the BIND *named* will keep running for longer than some operating systems, so there may be no need for a backup. If the local name server has a history of problems, though—say it hangs occasionally and stops responding to queries—it's prudent to add a backup name server.

To add a backup name server, just list the local name server first in *resolv.conf* (at the host's IP address or the zero address, 0.0.0.0—either will do), then one or two backup name servers. Remember not to use the loopback address unless you know your system's TCP/IP stack doesn't have the problem we mentioned earlier.

Since we'd rather be safe than sorry, we're going to add two backup name servers. *postmanrings2x* is on the 192.249.249.0 network, too, so *terminator* and *wormhole* are the closest name servers to it (besides its own). We'll reverse the order in which they're tried from the previous resolver-only example, to help balance the load between the two. The *resolv.conf* file ends up looking like this:

```
domain movie.edu
nameserver 0.0.0.0
nameserver 192.249.249.3
nameserver 192.249.249.1
```

Minimizing Pain and Suffering

Now that you've configured your host to use DNS, what's going to change? Will your users be forced to type long domain names? Will they have to change their mail addresses and mailing lists?

Thanks to the search list, much of this will continue working as before. There are some exceptions, though, and there are notable differences in the way that some programs behave when they use DNS. We'll try to cover all of the common ones.

Differences in Service Behavior

As you've seen earlier in this chapter, programs like *telnet, ftp, rlogin,* and *rsh* apply the search list to domain name arguments that aren't dot-terminated. That means that if you're in *movie.edu* (i.e., your default domain is *movie.edu* and your search list includes *movie.edu*), you can type either:

```
% telnet misery
```

or:

```
% telnet misery.movie.edu
```

or even:

```
% telnet misery.movie.edu.
```

and get to the same place. The same holds true for the other services, too. There's one other behavioral difference you may benefit from: because a name server may return more than one IP address when you look up an address, modern versions of *telnet* and *ftp* will try to connect to the first address returned, and if the connection is refused or times out, for example, it will try the next, and so on:

```
% ftp tootsie
ftp: connect to address 192.249.249.244: Connection timed out
Trying 192.253.253.244...
Connected to tootsie.movie.edu.
220 tootsie.movie.edu FTP server (Version 16.2 Fri Apr 26
    18:20:43 GMT 1991) ready.
Name (tootsie: guest):
```

And remember that with the *resolv.conf sortlist* directive, you can even control the order in which your applications try those IP addresses.

One oddball service is NFS. The *mount* command can handle domain names just fine, and you can put domain names into */etc/fstab* (your vendor may call it */etc/checklist*), too. But watch out for */etc/exports* and */etc/netgroup*. */etc/exports* controls which filesystems you allow various clients to NFS-mount. You can also assign a name to a group of hosts in *netgroup* and then allow them access via *exports* by using the name of the group.

Unfortunately, older versions of NFS don't *really* use DNS to check *exports* or *netgroup*—the client tells the NFS server its identity in an RPC (Remote Procedure Call) packet. Consequently, the client's identity is whatever the client claims it is. And the identity a host uses in Sun RPC is the local host's *hostname*. So the name you use in either file needs to match the client's *hostname*, which isn't necessarily its domain name.

Electronic Mail

Some electronic mail programs, including *sendmail*, also don't work as expected; *sendmail* doesn't use the search list quite the same way other programs do. Instead, when configured to use a name server, it uses a process called *canonicalization* to convert names in electronic mail addresses to full, canonical domain names.

In canonicalization, *sendmail* applies the search list to a name and looks up data of type ANY, which matches any type of record. If the name server queried finds a

CNAME record (an alias), it replaces the name looked up with the canonical name the alias points to. If the name server queried finds an A record (an address), *sendmail* uses the domain name that resolved to the address as the canonical name. If the name server doesn't find an address, but finds one or more MX records:

- If the search list has not yet been appended, *sendmail* uses the domain name that resolved to the MX record(s) as the canonical name.

- If one or more elements of the search list have been appended, *sendmail* notes that the domain name is a potential canonical name, and continues appending elements of the search list. If a subsequent element of the search list turns up an address, the domain name that turned up the address is the canonical name. Otherwise, the domain name that found the first MX record is used as the canonical name.[*]

sendmail uses canonicalization several times when processing an SMTP message; it canonicalizes the destination address and several fields in the SMTP headers.[†]

sendmail also sets macro *w* (not to be confused with class *w*) to the canonicalized *hostname* when you freeze the *sendmail.cf* file, or, if you don't freeze your configuration file, when the *sendmail* daemon starts up. So even if you set your *hostname* to a short, single-part name, *sendmail* will canonicalize the *hostname* using the search list defined in *resolv.conf.*

This is important because the local host's canonical name is the only name *sendmail* recognizes, by default, as the local host's name. *sendmail* will attempt to forward mail that's addressed to a domain name it thinks isn't local. So, for example, unless you configure *sendmail* to recognize the host's aliases (using class *w* or fileclass *w*, as we showed in Chapter 5, *DNS and Electronic Mail*), the host will try to forward messages that arrive addressed for anything other than the canonical domain name.

There's another important implication of the way *sendmail* canonicalizes the local *hostname*—*sendmail* recognizes only the local host's canonical name in MX lists. Consequently, if you use anything other than a host's canonical name in an MX record, you run the risk that the host will not recognize it. This can cause mail to loop and then be returned to the sender.

One last note on *sendmail*: when you start running a name server, if you're running an older version of *sendmail* (before version 8), you should also set the *I* option in your *sendmail.cf* file. Option *I* determines what *sendmail* does if a lookup for a

---

[*] All this complexity is necessary to deal with wildcard MX records, which we'll discuss in Chapter 15, *Miscellaneous.*

[†] Some older versions of *sendmail* use a different technique for doing canonicalization: they apply the search list and query the name server for type CNAME records for the name in question. CNAME matches only CNAME records. If a record is found, the name is replaced with the domain name on the right-hand side of the CNAME record.

destination host fails. When using */etc/hosts*, a failed lookup is fatal. If you search the host table once for a name and don't find it, it's doubtful it'll miraculously appear later, so the mailer may as well return the message. When using DNS, however, a lookup failure may be temporary, because of intermittent networking problems, for example. Setting option *I* instructs *sendmail* to queue mail if a lookup fails, instead of returning it to the sender. Just add OI to your *sendmail.cf* file and refreeze it, if you use a frozen configuration file.

Updating .rhosts, hosts.equiv, etc.

Once you start using DNS, you may also need to disambiguate host names in your host's authorization files. Entries that use simple, one-part host names will now be assumed to be in the local domain. For example, the *lpd.allow* file on *wormhole* might include:

```
wormhole
terminator
diehard
robocop
mash
twins
```

If we move *mash* and *twins* into the *comedy.movie.edu* domain, though, they won't be allowed to access *lpd*; the entries in *lpd.allow* only allow *mash.movie.edu* and *twins.movie.edu*. So we'd have to add the proper domains to host names outside of the local host's default domain:

```
wormhole
terminator
diehard
robocop
mash.comedy.movie.edu
twins.comedy.movie.edu
```

Some other files you should check for host names in need of domain-ification are:

```
hosts.equiv
.rhosts
X0.hosts
sendmail.cf
```

Sometimes, simply running these files through a canonicalization filter—a program that translates host names to domain names using the search list—is enough to disambiguate them. Here's a short canonicalization filter in Perl to help you out:

```
#!/usr/bin/perl

# Perl canonicalization filter
#
# Expects one hostname per line, in the first field (a la .rhosts,
# X0.hosts)
```

```
use Socket;

while( < >)
    if(($hostname, $null) = split){
      ($domainname, $aliases, $addrtype, $length, @addrs) =
           gethostbyname($hostname);
      if($domainname) {s/$hostname/$domainname/;}
    }
    print;
}
```

Providing Aliases

Even if you cover all your bases and convert all your *.rhosts*, *hosts.equiv*, and *send-mail.cf* files after you configure your host to use DNS, your users will still have to adjust to using domain names. Hopefully, the confusion they feel will be minimal, and will be more than offset by the benefits of DNS.

One way to make your users' lives less confusing after configuring DNS is to provide aliases for well-known hosts that are no longer reachable using their familiar names. For example, our users are accustomed to typing *telnet doofy* or *rlogin doofy* to get to the bulletin board system run by the movie studio on the other side of town. Now they'll have to start using *doofy*'s full domain name, *doofy.maroon.com*. But most of our users don't know the full domain name, and it'll be some time before we can tell all of them and they get used to it.

Luckily, BIND will let you define aliases for your users. All we need to do is set the environment variable *HOSTALIASES* to the pathname of a file that contains mappings between aliases and domain names. For example, to set up a system-wide alias for *doofy*, we could set *HOSTALIASES* to */etc/host.aliases* in the system's shell startup files, and add:

```
doofy    doofy.maroon.com
```

to */etc/host.aliases*. The alias file format is simple: the alias starts the line in column one, followed by whitespace, and then the domain name that corresponds to the alias. The domain name is written without a trailing dot. The alias can't contain dots.

Now, when our users type *telnet doofy* or *rlogin doofy*, the resolver will transparently substitute *doofy.maroon.com* for *doofy* in the name server query. The message the users see will look something like:

```
Trying...
Connected to doofy.maroon.com.
Escape character is '^]'.
IRIX System V.3 (sgi)
login:
```

If the resolver falls back to using */etc/hosts*, though, our *HOSTALIASES* won't have any effect. So we should also keep a similar alias in */etc/hosts*.

With time, and perhaps a little instruction, the users will start to associate the full domain name they see in the *telnet* banner with the bulletin board they use.

With *HOSTALIASES*, if you know the domain names your users are likely to have trouble with, you can save them a little frustration. If you don't know which hosts they're trying to get to, you can let your users create their own alias files, and have each point the *HOSTALIASES* variable in his shell startup file to his personal alias file.

Vendor-Specific Options

UNIX is ostensibly a standard operating system, but there are almost as many UNIX standards as flavors of UNIX. Likewise, there are almost as many different styles of resolver configuration as there are UNIXes. Almost all support the original Berkeley syntax, but most add nonstandard enhancements or variations, too. We'll cover as many of the major styles of resolver configuration as we can.

Sun's SunOS 4.x

Configuring a host running SunOS can be a challenge. The behavior of the SunOS resolver is arguably as different from that of standard BIND as major vendors get—primarily because SunOS's resolver is integrated with Sun's Network Information Service, or NIS (née Yellow Pages).

NIS, briefly, provides a mechanism for keeping important files synchronized between hosts on a network. This includes not just */etc/hosts*, but also */etc/services*, */etc/passwd*, and others. Sun positions DNS as a backup option to NIS; if the NIS resolver can't find a host name (or IP address) in the NIS hosts map, you can configure it to query a name server.

Note that the resolver functionality is implemented as part of the *ypserv* program, which also handles other types of NIS queries. So if *ypserv* isn't running, neither is your resolver! (Mercifully, the resolver in Solaris 2 doesn't require that you run *ypserv*.) One benefit of using *ypserv* to resolve all queries is that you don't need to configure the resolvers on NIS clients, only on NIS servers.[*] The NIS clients will query an NIS server for host data, and the NIS server will query DNS, if necessary.

If you run SunOS 4.X (Solaris 1), you can (1) follow the party line and configure your resolver to use DNS as a backup to NIS, (2) choose to run NIS without host maps, or (3) buck convention and recompile your resolver to use DNS exclusively—or you

---

[*] Actually, you also need to configure the resolver on hosts on which you use *sendmail.mx*, Sun's MX-smart version of *sendmail*.

can pick up free copies of modified resolvers on the Internet. However, we must warn you that, according to our sources, Sun *will not support* the modified resolver option.

If you run Solaris 2, you can simply configure the resolver like a normal human being. You also have control over the order in which the resolver consults various naming services via the *nsswitch.conf* file.

Modified resolvers

We won't go into much detail about this option here, primarily because this process is now well-documented and nearly automated in the newest BIND distribution. The process itself usually involves creating a new *libc.so*—the standard, shared C library—by pulling out routines that call NIS and replacing them with pure DNS versions. Although Sun generously provides the necessary replacement routines, they don't support them. Worse, the routines supplied with SunOS 4.1 were based on BIND 4.8.1.

If you have the latest DNS source distribution, look for instructions on installing the BIND 8.1.2 resolver routines under SunOS in the package's *src/port/sunos/shres* subdirectory, currently in a file called *INSTALL*.

If you'd rather skip the potentially edifying experience of creating your own shared C library and leverage someone else's efforts, you can check out *resolv+*, based on the BIND 4.8.3 resolver.

resolv+ is an enhanced version of the 4.8.3 resolver routines for SunOS, written by Bill Wisner, which allows administrators to choose the order in which NIS and DNS are queried (much like the extensions other vendors have added to UNIX, which we'll discuss later). The new routines are available, with instructions on how to build them into *libc.so*, from *ftp.uu.net* as the file */networking/ip/dns/resolv+2.1.1.tar.Z*. For more information on the functionality *resolv+* provides, see the Linux section later in this chapter.

Using DNS with NIS

If you go the socially acceptable route, though, you'll need to make NIS and DNS coexist peacefully. That's a little tricky, so we'll go over it in some detail. We won't cover how to set up NIS—that's already been covered in gory detail in Hal Stern's *Managing NFS and NIS* (O'Reilly & Associates, 1991). Note that these instructions only apply to versions of SunOS after 4.1. If you run an older version of SunOS, consider the replacement libraries on *ftp.uu.net*.

First, you'll need to modify the *Makefile* NIS uses to build its maps—the files that it distributes to other hosts on the network. You should make this modification on the master NIS server, not on the slaves.

The NIS *Makefile* lives in */var/yp/Makefile* on a SunOS host. The change you need to make is simple: you need to uncomment one line and comment another. Find the lines that read:

```
#B=-b
B=
```

and change them to read:

```
B=-b
#B=
```

Then rebuild your NIS hosts map:

```
# cd /var/yp
# rm hosts.time
# make hosts.time
updated hosts
pushed hosts
```

This will insert a "magic cookie" into the hosts map that instructs NIS to query DNS if it can't find a host name in the hosts map. Now, when the *ypserv* program looks up a name, it will check the appropriate hosts map for the local NIS *domainname*, and if it can't find the name there, it will query a name server. The search list *ypserv* uses when it queries the name server is derived from either the local NIS *domainname* or from the *domain* directive in *resolv.conf.*

Next, you should create a *resolv.conf* file, if you need one. The rules for configuring the resolver change slightly with SunOS:

- You *can't* set the *hostname* to a domain name and have the resolver infer the local domain.

- You also can't use the *search* directive in *resolv.conf,* since the SunOS 4.1.1 resolver is based on BIND 4.8.1. The resolver will silently ignore it.

- You *can* set the NIS *domainname* to a domain name (you have to set it to the name of your NIS domain if you're using NIS), and the resolver will derive the name of the local DNS domain from it. However, this doesn't work quite the same way it does with BIND; if you set *domainname* to *fx.movie.edu*, for example, the search list will only include *movie.edu.* Why doesn't the search list include *fx.movie.edu?* Because NIS assumes it's already checked an authoritative source of *fx.movie.edu* host data—the *fx.movie.edu* hosts map.

- If you want to set the default domain to the same name as your NIS *domainname,* you can prepend a dot or a plus ("+") to the *domainname.* To set your default domain to *fx.movie.edu*, you could set *domainname* to either *+fx.movie.edu* or *.fx.movie.edu.*

- You can also override NIS's normal behavior by setting the local domain with the *domain* directive in *resolv.conf.* So if you wanted to force the resolver to include *fx.movie.edu* in the search list, you could add domain *fx.movie.edu* to *resolv.conf.*

- You can even set the *domain* directive in *resolv.conf* to a DNS domain name totally unrelated to your NIS *domainname*. In some unfortunate situations, the local NIS *domainname* isn't the same as, or even similar to, the DNS domain name. Say the Information Technology Department at Movie U. originally set up the NIS domain *it.dept.movieu*, and still uses it. To prevent spurious DNS queries in the nonexistent *dept.movieu* domain, hosts in this NIS domain should be configured with domain *movie.edu* (or something similar) in *resolv.conf.*

Finally, Sun's *resolv.conf* treats the *nameserver* directive just as vanilla BIND does. So once you're done inserting magic cookies and configuring your NIS *domainname* and possibly your DNS domain, you can add any name servers to *resolv.conf* and be done.

Ignoring NIS

If you want to retain Sun's support but would rather not use icky NIS, you still have an option: you can run NIS with an empty hosts map. First, set up your *resolv.conf* file, then insert the magic cookie into the NIS *Makefile* as we described in the preceding section, "Using DNS with NIS," and create an empty hosts map. Creating an empty hosts map just requires moving the NIS master server's */etc/hosts* file aside temporarily, generating your hosts NIS map, then replacing the */etc/hosts* file:

```
% mv /etc/hosts /etc/hosts.tmp
% touch /etc/hosts # to keep make from complaining
% cd /var/yp
% make hosts.time
updated hosts
pushed hosts
% mv /etc/hosts.tmp /etc/hosts
```

Now, when the resolver checks NIS, it won't find anything, and will go directly to querying a domain name server.

If you periodically rebuild your NIS maps, you should make sure the hosts map doesn't accidentally get rebuilt from */etc/hosts*. The best way to do this is to remove the hosts target from the NIS *Makefile.* You can just comment out everything in the *Makefile* from the line that begins with:

```
hosts.time: $(DIR)/hosts
```

to the next blank line.

Sun's Solaris 2.x

The resolver in Solaris 2 through 2.5.1 is based on the BIND 4.8.3 resolver, with extensions to give you the ability to determine the order in which the resolver consults the "sources:" DNS, NIS, and */etc/hosts*. The resolver in Solaris 2.6 is based on the BIND 4.9.3 resolver, with the same extensions.[*] This service order is configured in a file called *nsswitch.conf*, which lives in the */etc* directory.

Actually, *nsswitch.conf* is used to configure the order in which a number of different services are resolved. Individual services, called *databases* in Sun's parlance, are selected by a keyword. For naming services, the database name is *hosts*. The possible sources are *dns*, *nis*, *nisplus*, and *files* (which refers to */etc/hosts*, in this case). Configuring the order in which the sources are consulted is a simple matter of listing them after the database name in that order. For example:

```
hosts:  dns files
```

has the resolver try DNS (i.e., query a name server) first, then check */etc/hosts*. By default, resolution moves from one source to the next (e.g., falls back to */etc/hosts* from DNS) only if the first source isn't available. You can modify this behavior by using several other criteria to determine when to move on to the next source. The possible criteria are:

UNAVAIL
The service hasn't been configured (in DNS's case, there is no *resolv.conf* file, and there is no name server running on the local host).

NOTFOUND
The service can't find the name or address in question.

TRYAGAIN
The service isn't currently available (for example, because the resolver has timed out while trying to look up a name).

SUCCESS

For each of these criteria, you can specify that the resolver should either *continue* or *return*. For example, if you want the resolver to check */etc/hosts* if DNS isn't configured or if DNS can't find the name, you can use:

```
hosts:  dns [NOTFOUND=continue UNAVAIL=continue] files
```

If you want a DNS NXDOMAIN (no such domain name) answer to halt the search for the name, you'd use:

```
hosts:  dns [NOTFOUND=return]
```

The default Solaris resolver behavior, by the way, is determined by the answers you give SunInstall.

---

[*] You can get patches to update Solaris 2.5 and 2.5.1 to BIND 4.9.3 via anonymous *ftp* from *sunsolve1.sun.com* in */pub/patches*. Check *http://sunsolve.sun.com/sunsolve/pubpatches/patches.html* for the current patch numbers.

nscd

In recent versions of Solaris 2.X, including 2.5 and later, Sun introduced a name service cache daemon, called *nscd*. *nscd* caches the results of lookups in the *passwd*, *group*, and *hosts* databases. You can think of *nscd* as very similar to a caching-only name server, except that it also works for information in *passwd* and *group* databases. Sun's intent with *nscd* was to speed up performance by caching frequently-looked-up names. Unfortunately, word on the street is that *nscd* sometimes slows DNS lookups, and many people disable it. Moreover, *nscd* interferes with round robin (*nscd* caches records in one order and doesn't rotate them).

nscd is started by default during a multiuser bootup, and reads the configuration file */etc/nscd.conf*. Administrators can tune a number of parameters in *nscd.conf*. The most important of these are:

enable-cache hosts (yes | no)
> Determines whether or not *nscd* caches the results of host lookups

positive-time-to-live hosts value
> Determines how long *nscd* caches positive results (e.g., addresses), in seconds

negative-time-to-live hosts value
> Determines how long *nscd* caches negative results (e.g., NXDOMAIN), in seconds

If you're not convinced of *nscd*'s usefulness, at least with DNS lookups, you can use:

```
enable-cache hosts no
```

to turn caching off for the hosts database.

HP's HP-UX

HP's resolver implementation is basically straight BIND; the HP-UX 8.0 and 9.0 resolvers are based on BIND 4.8.3, and support the standard *domain, nameserver,* and *search* directives. The order in which a host consults DNS, NIS, and the host table is hard-wired. The host will use DNS if DNS is configured. If DNS isn't configured, and NIS is running, the host will use NIS. If neither DNS nor NIS is running, the host will use the host table. The host only falls back to using the other services under the circumstances described earlier in the chapter (i.e., the resolver only uses one name server—either listed in *resolv.conf* or on the local host by default—and four errors are received while contacting that name server).

The hard-wired algorithm is less flexible than what other vendors provide, but it's easy to troubleshoot. When you can consult DNS, NIS, and the host table in any order, diagnosing user problems can be awfully difficult.

The HP-UX 10.30 resolver is based on BIND 4.9.3, and patches are available for all versions of 10.X to upgrade the server and ancillary programs to BIND 4.9.6. To gain access to the patches, visit the HP-UX patch archive at *http://us-support.external.hp.com/* and register. You can then search the patch database for the latest patches.

HP-UX 10.0 introduced Solaris's *nsswitch.conf* functionality; that is, you can use *nsswitch.conf* to control the order in which the resolver consults the various naming services.* The syntax is exactly the same as that used in Solaris's *nsswitch.conf.* The default settings for the *hosts* database under HP-UX are:

```
hosts: dns nis files
```

This functionality is also available in patches for HP-UX 9.0. Check the web-based HP-UX patch archive for these. You may need quite a few patches:

- One for the standard, shared C library, *libc.so*, which contains the resolver routines in HP-UX
- One for the *mount* command, which is statically linked
- One for *nslookup*
- One for the *ifconfig* and *route* commands
- One for HP's Visual User Environment (VUE), which is shipped statically linked

The HP-UX 10.30 resolver also supports the BIND 4.9.3 search list behavior and the *options ndots* directive.

IBM's AIX

The resolver shipped with the current version of AIX, 4.2.1, is also relatively standard. The code is based on BIND 4.9.3, so it understands the *domain, search, nameserver, options,* and *sortlist* directives; AIX supports up to three *nameserver* directives. AIX versions 4 and 4.1 were based on BIND 4.8.3, so they handle all the directives AIX 4.2.1's resolver does except *options* and *sortlist.*

One difference between AIX's behavior and the stock BSD behavior is that AIX uses the existence of the *resolv.conf* file to determine whether to query a name server. If *resolv.conf* doesn't exist on the local host, the resolver reads */etc/hosts.* This means that on a host running a name server, you should create a zero-length */etc/resolv.conf* file, even if you don't intend to put any directives in it.

---

* Before HP-UX 10.10, you could only use *nsswitch.conf* to configure order of resolution for the *hosts* database. From 10.10 on, you can also use *nsswitch.conf* to configure resolution order for the *services, networks, protocols, rpc,* and *netgroup* databases.

IBM has also modified the resolver so that it checks NIS and then */etc/hosts*, even if DNS claims there's no such domain name or no such data. This gives you the ability to add hosts to */etc/hosts* temporarily, before they make it into the name server, and will let you maintain your own host-specific name-to-address mappings.

AIX 4.2.1 also includes a mechanism to control resolution order similar to Solaris's *nsswitch.conf*. AIX uses a file called */etc/netsvc.conf*. Like *nsswitch.conf*, *netsvc.conf* calls the database *hosts*, but uses an equals sign between the database name and the sources instead of a colon, uses commas between sources, uses *bind* for DNS, and uses *local* for */etc/hosts*. So:

```
hosts = local,nis,bind
```

has the AIX resolver check the local */etc/hosts* first, then check the NIS *hosts* map, and finally try DNS. Individual users or processes can override the system-wide resolution order configured with *netsvc.conf* by setting an environment variable, *NSORDER*. NSORDER uses the same syntax *netsvc.conf* does, minus the database name and equal sign. So to change the resolution order for your user to check DNS first and then */etc/hosts*, ignoring NIS, you could run:

```
% NSORDER=bind,local; export NSORDER
```

AIX 3.2's resolver was based on the BIND 4.8.1 resolver, so it doesn't understand the *search* directive. It exhibits the same peculiarities with respect to the existence of *resolv.conf* that the 4.1 resolver does. For those of you with older AIX 3.2 installations, there is a patch, PTF U412845, that will let you shorten the resolver timeout so that AIX will fall back to */etc/hosts* more quickly than normal. There are also instructions on using Bill Wisner's *resolv+* package with AIX in the AIX FAQ, posted periodically to *comp.unix.aix* and archived on *rtfm.mit.edu* in */pub/usenet/news.answers/aix-faq/*. Use at your own risk. For more information on *resolv+*'s functionality, see the Linux section later in this chapter.

We should also note that you can configure the resolver using AIX's System Management Interface Tool (SMIT).

Digital's Digital UNIX

The resolver shipped with the most recent version of Digital UNIX, 4.0D, is based on the BIND 4.9.3 resolver. As such, it understands all five resolver directives covered in this chapter.

Digital UNIX allows you to configure the order in which the resolver checks NIS, DNS, and the host table via a file called *svc.conf* (see the *svc.conf*(5) manpage).[*] *svc.conf* also allows you to configure which services are consulted for other

---

[*] Digital's "other" UNIX operating system, Ultrix, also supports *svc.conf*.

"databases," including mail aliases, authentication checks (mapping from IP address to host or domain names), password and group information, and a slew of other things.

To configure the resolver with *svc.conf,* use the database name *hosts,* followed by an equals sign and the keywords for the services you want checked, separated by commas, in the order you want them checked. The legal keywords for *hosts* are *local* (the local host table), *yp* (for "Yellow Pages," the old name for NIS), and *bind* (for DNS). *local* must be the first service listed for *hosts.* Don't use any whitespace on the line, except (optionally) after commas and at the end of the line.

The line:

```
hosts=local,bind
```

instructs the resolver to check */etc/hosts* for host names first, and if no match is found, to use domain name service. This is very useful when the host has a small local host table that includes the local host's domain name and IP address, the host's default router, and any other hosts referenced during startup. Checking the local host table first avoids any problems using domain name service during startup, when networking and *named* may not have started.

Digital UNIX also includes a utility called *svcsetup* (see the *svcsetup*(8) manpage), which allows you to set up the *svc.conf* file interactively, without the aid of an editor. Typing *svcsetup* will throw you into a mode where you can choose the database you'd like to configure, and will prompt you for the order of the services you want checked.

Silicon Graphics' IRIX

As of IRIX 6.2, IRIX has a BIND 4.9.3 name server, but the resolver is still essentially 4.8.3. There are also patches available to bring the server up to BIND 4.9.4. For the current patch numbers, see *http://support.sgi.com/surfzone/patches/browse/index.html* (you'll need to register if you aren't already a SurfZone member).

The IRIX *resolv.conf* file, which lives in */usr/etc/resolv.conf,* adds a *hostresorder* directive. The *hostresorder* directive allows the administrator to determine the order in which NIS, DNS, and the local host table are searched. Individual users can set the environment variable *HOSTRESORDER* to determine the order in which the services are used for their commands.

hostresorder takes one or more of the keywords *nis, bind,* and *local* as arguments. (The keywords correspond to the obvious services.) The keywords may be separated by either whitespace or a slash. Whitespace indicates that the next service should be tried if the previous service doesn't return an answer (e.g., the name isn't found in the host table, or the name server returns "no such domain") or isn't available (e.g., the name server isn't running). A slash indicates that the preceding service is authoritative, and if no answer is returned, resolution should stop. The next service is tried only if the previous isn't available.

SCO's Open Server 5.0

The newest release of SCO's UNIX operating system, Open Server 5.0.X, has a resolver based on the BIND 4.9.2 resolver. As a 4.9.2-derived resolver, it understands all of the normal directives (including *sortlist* and *options!*) in *resolv.conf* plus *hostresorder. hostresorder* works exactly the same way it does in IRIX (see the section on IRIX immediately preceding this section); the keywords are the same (*bind, nis,* and *local*), and a slash, instead of a space, indicates that the preceding service is authoritative and the search should return if that service doesn't find the name. The default setting (without *hostresorder* configured) is equivalent to:

```
hostresorder bind nis local
```

Also, even if resolution order isn't explicitly configured, if DNS and NIS aren't available, the resolver will use */etc/hosts*.

You can override anything configured with *domain, options,* or *hostresorder* in *resolv.conf* with the environment variables *LOCALDOMAIN, RES_OPTIONS,* and *HOSTRESORDER*, respectively. For example, to change resolution order to DNS-only and the options to set *ndots* to 1 before starting sendmail, you could run:

```
% HOSTRESORDER="dns"; RES_OPTIONS="ndots:1"
% export HOSTRESORDER RES_OPTIONS
% /usr/lib/sendmail -bd -q1h
```

Linux

Since we first published this book, Linux has taken the computing world by storm. A couple of the reasons are that Linux is freeware, and that it does a better job of keeping up with developments in the UNIX and Internet communities than any vendor's version of UNIX. Attesting to that is the fact that RedHat Linux 5.1, the latest version of one of the predominant strains of Linux, ships with a BIND 4.9.6 resolver and server. The resolver also supports Sun's *nsswitch.conf* file.

However, some older Linux resolvers are based on Bill Wisner's *resolv+* library, which is in turn based on BIND 4.8.3. Consequently, the *resolv.conf* file can include any legit 4.8.3 resolver directives (*domain, search,* and *nameserver,* but not *options*) and has the older default search list described in this chapter.

resolv+, as the name suggests, also provides several enhancements over the standard 4.8.3 resolver. They include the ability to determine the order in which DNS, NIS, and */etc/hosts* are consulted (replaced by the more standard *nsswitch.conf* in newer versions), the ability to detect certain types of DNS spoofing, and the ability to reorder address records in replies to favor local subnets.

All of these enhancements are controlled by the */etc/hosts.conf* file. The most interesting keywords that *hosts.conf* accepts are:

order

> Controls the order in which the various name services are consulted; the valid arguments are *bind*, *hosts*, and *nis*, at least one of which must follow the keyword. Multiple arguments must be separated by commas.

nospoof

> Takes the single argument *on* or *off. nospoof* instructs the resolver to check any reverse mapping (PTR) information it gets from remote name servers by issuing a forward (address) query for the domain name in the reply. If the address returned by the address query isn't the same as the address the resolver originally tried to reverse map, the PTR record is ignored.

reorder

> Takes the single argument *on* or *off.* With *reorder* on, the resolver sorts the addresses of multiply-homed hosts so that any address on a local subnet appears first.

Windows 95

Windows 95, the successor to the popular Windows operating system, includes its own TCP/IP stack with a DNS resolver. In fact, Windows 95 actually includes two TCP/IP stacks: one for TCP/IP over LANs, and another for TCP/IP over dialup connections. Configuration of the resolver in Windows 95 is, naturally enough, graphical. To get to the main DNS configuration panel, start the Control Panel, then select *Network*, then choose the TCP/IP protocol. This brings up a new dialog, which looks similar to the one in Figure 6-1. Choose the tab labeled DNS *Configuration.*

Configuration using this panel is fairly self-explanatory: you check *Enable* DNS to turn on DNS resolution, then fill in the PC's hostname (in this case, the first label of its domain name) in the *Host* field, and the local domain (everything after the first dot) in the *Domain* field. You add the IP addresses of the name servers you want to query, in the order in which you want to query them, under DNS *Server Search Order.* Finally, you fill in the domains in the search list under *Domain Suffix Search Order* in the order in which you want them applied.

One interesting note about the current version of Windows 95: you can configure a different set of name servers for each dial-up connection you might have to an Internet service provider (ISP) in the Dial-Up Networking (DUN) configuration. To configure DUN-specific resolver settings, double-click on the *My Computer* icon on

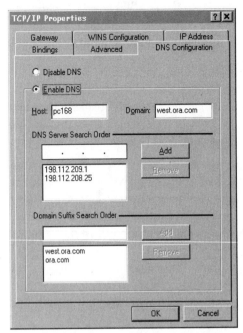

Figure 6-1. Resolver configuration under Windows 95

your desktop, then double-click on *Dial-Up Networking*, right-click on the name of the connection whose resolver settings you'd like to configure, then select *Properties*. Select the *Server Types* tab and click on TCP/IP *Settings*. You'll see the window shown in Figure 6-2.

If you leave the *Server assigned name server addresses* radio button checked, the resolver will retrieve the name servers it should query from the DHCP server you dial into. If you check *Specify name server addresses* and specify the addresses of one or two name servers, Windows 95 will try to use those name servers when the DUN connection is active.

This is really useful if you use multiple ISPs and each has its own name servers. However, configuring name servers in the TCP/IP Properties panel *overrides* the DUN-specific name servers. To use the DUN-specific name server feature, you must leave the TCP/IP Properties panel blank except for enabling DNS and specifying the local hostname. This limitation is probably just an oversight due to a lack of integration between the dial-up and LAN TCP/IP stacks, and should be corrected in a future release of Windows 95.

Lest you think this is the only idiosyncrasy in the way that DNS resolution works on Windows 95, we'll point you to the Windows 95 Networking FAQ, maintained by Rich Graves, at *http://www-leland.stanford.edu/~llurch/win95netbugs/faq.html*. This

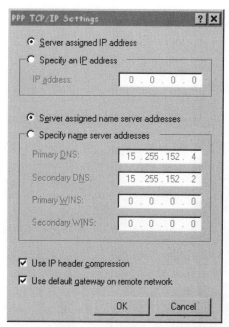

Figure 6-2. DUN resolver configuration under Windows 95

FAQ contains lots of valuable DNS information, including how to change the order in which the Win95 resolver uses the LMHOSTS file, WINS, and DNS.

Windows NT

In Windows NT, LAN resolver configuration is done from a single panel that looks remarkably similar to Windows 95's now that NT 4.0—which includes the Windows 95 "shell"—has been released. In fact, other than the presence of handy little arrows that allow you to reorder name servers and elements of the search list, there's really no semantic difference between them, as shown in Figure 6-3.

To get to the DNS configuration panel, start the Control Panel, click on *Network*, and select the *Protocols* tab. Double-click on *TCP/IP Protocol*, then select the *DNS* tab.

Windows NT also allows the user to configure resolver settings specific to particular dialup networking connections. To configure these, click on the *My Computer* icon, start *Dial Up Networking*, pull down the top selection box and choose the name of the DUN connection whose resolver you'd like to configure. Then click on the *More* pull-down and select *Edit Entry and Modem Properties*. Select the *Server* tab on the resulting window, and click on the *TCP/IP Settings* button. You'll see the very same window you'd see in Windows 95 (shown earlier). If you leave the *Server assigned name server addresses* radio button checked, the resolver will retrieve the name

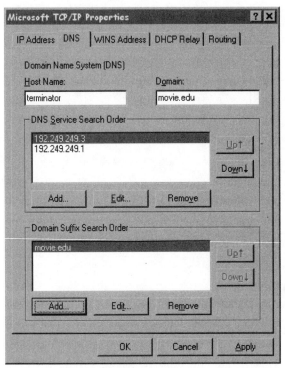

Figure 6-3. Resolver configuration under Windows NT

servers it should query from the DHCP server you dial into. If you check *Specify name server addresses* and specify the addresses of one or two name servers, Windows NT will use those name servers when the DUN connection is active. When you drop the DUN connection, NT will revert to using the LAN resolver's settings.

7

Maintaining BIND

"Well, in our country," said Alice, still panting a little, "you'd generally get to somewhere else—if you ran very fast for a long time as we've been doing."

"A slow sort of country!" said the Queen. "Now, here, you see, it takes all the running you can do, to keep in the same place. If you want to get somewhere else, you must run at least twice as fast as that!"

This chapter discusses a number of related topics pertaining to name server maintenance. We'll talk about sending signals to name servers, modifying the db files, and keeping *db.cache* up to date. We'll list common syslog error messages and explain the statistics BIND keeps.

This chapter doesn't cover troubleshooting problems. Maintenance involves keeping your data current and watching over your name servers as they operate. Troubleshooting involves putting out fires—those little DNS emergencies that flare up periodically. Firefighting is covered in Chapter 13, *Troubleshooting DNS and BIND*.

BIND Name Server Signals

In day-to-day operation, the BIND name server, *named*, is manipulated with signals. We'll use them in this chapter and in other chapters. Here's a list of the signals you can send to a name server and a short description of the action each signal causes. Each of these signals will be discussed in more detail elsewhere in this book. (On some systems, the files listed below will be found in */var/tmp* instead of */usr/tmp*.)

HUP

Reload the name server. Send this signal to a primary master name server after modifying its configuration file or one of its database files. Send this signal to a

4.9 or later slave name server to cause it to update its slave zones if they are not current.

INT

Dump a copy of the name server's internal database to *named_dump.db* in */usr/tmp* (version 4) or in the name server's current directory (version 8).

ABRT (version 4)

Append the name server's statistics to */usr/tmp/named.stats*. This signal may be called IOT on your system.

ILL (version 8)

Append the name server's statistics to *named.stats* in the name server's current directory.

USR1

Append debugging information to *named.run* in */usr/tmp* (version 4) or in the name server's current directory (version 8). Each subsequent USR1 signal increases the amount of detail in the debugging information. For information on what is logged at each level, see Chapter 12, *Reading BIND Debugging Output.*

USR2

Turn off debugging.

WINCH

Toggle logging all queries with syslog. Logging takes place at priority LOG_INFO. *named* must be compiled with QRYLOG defined (it is defined by default). This feature did not exist in version 4.8.3.

TERM (version 8)

Exit and save dynamic zones to files.

The 4.9 and later distributions provide a handy shell script for sending these signals, called *ndc*. Check out the manpage for the command syntax or just run *ndc* without any options and it will display a usage message. Be careful not to use a BIND 4 version of *ndc* with a BIND 8 name server since the signal to send for statistics has changed. If you don't have *ndc*, you'll have to send the signals manually. Read on.

To send a name server a signal, you must first find the name server's process ID. The BIND name server leaves its process ID in a disk file, making it easier to chase the critter down—you don't have to use *ps*. The most common place for the process ID to be left is */etc/named.pid*. On some systems, the process ID is in */var/run/named.pid*. Check the *named* manual page to see which directory *named.pid* is in on your system. Since the name server process ID is in a file, sending a HUP signal can be as simple as:

```
# kill -HUP `cat /etc/named.pid`
```

If you can't find the process ID in a file, you can always find the process ID with *ps*. On a BSD-based system use:

```
% ps -ax | grep named
```

On a SYS V-based system use:

```
% ps -ef | grep named
```

However, you may find more than one name server running if you use *ps*, since name servers spawn children to perform zone transfers. During a zone transfer, the name server pulling the zone data starts a child process, and the name server providing the zone data may start a child process. We'll digress a little here and explain why child processes are used.

A slave name server starts a child process to perform a zone transfer. This allows the slave name server to keep answering queries while the zone data is being transferred from the master server to the local disk by the child process. Once the zone is on the local disk, the slave name server reads in the new data. Using a child process to do the zone transfer fixed a problem with pre-4.8.3 versions of BIND, in which slave name servers wouldn't answer queries during a zone transfer. This could be a real nuisance on name servers that loaded lots of zones or large zones: they'd go silent for long periods of time.

A version 8 primary master name server does *not* spawn a child process to provide a zone to a slave name server. Instead, the primary master server transfers the zone at the same time it is answering queries. If the primary master server loads a new copy of the zone from a disk file while a zone transfer is in progress, it will abort the zone transfer in progress and load the new zone from the disk file. The slave server will have to attempt the zone transfer again after the primary master has completed loading the new zone.

A version 4 primary master name server starts a child process to provide a zone to a slave name server. This creates extra load on the host running the primary master server, especially if the zones are very large or many zone transfers are active at one time.

If the *ps* output shows multiple name servers, you should be able to tell easily which name server process is the parent and which processes are children. A child name server started by a slave server to pull a copy of a zone is called *named-xfer* instead of *named*:

```
root  548 547  0 22:03:17 ?    0:00 named-xfer -z movie.edu
       -f /usr/tmp/NsTmp0 -s 0 -P 53 192.249.249.3
```

A child name server started by a master name server changes its command-line options to indicate which slave server it is providing the zone to:

```
root 1137 1122 6 22:03:18 ?    0:00 /etc/named -zone XFR
       to [192.249.249.1]
```

You may encounter a version of *named* that doesn't change its command line, but you can still figure out the relationship between multiple *named* processes by examining their process IDs and parent process IDs. All the child processes will have the parent name server's process ID as their parent process ID. This may seem like stating the obvious, but only send signals to the *parent* name server process. The child processes will go away after the zone transfers complete.

Updating db Files

Something is always changing on your network—the new workstations arrive, you finally retire or sell the relic, or you move a host to a different network. Each change means the db files must be modified. Should you make the changes manually? Should you wimp out and use a tool to help you?

First, we'll discuss how to make the changes manually. Then we'll talk about a tool to help out: *h2n*. Actually, we recommend that you use a tool to create the db files— we were kidding about that wimp stuff, okay? Or, at least use a tool to increment the serial number for you. The syntax of the DNS files lends itself to making mistakes. It doesn't help that the address and pointer records are in different files, which must agree with each other. However, even when you use a tool, it is critical to know what goes on when the files are updated, so we'll start with the manual method.

Adding and Deleting Hosts

After creating your db files initially, it should be fairly apparent what needs to be changed when you add a new host. We'll go through the steps here in case you weren't the one to set up those files, or if you'd just like a checklist to follow. Make these changes to your *primary* master name server's DNS database files. If you make the change to your *slave* name server's backup files, the slave's data will change, but the next zone transfer will overwrite it.

1. Update the serial number in *db.DOMAIN*. The serial number is likely to be at the top of the file, so it's easy to do first and reduces the chance that you'll forget.

2. Add any A (address), CNAME (alias), and MX (mail exchanger) records for the host to the *db.DOMAIN* file. We added the following resource records to the *db.movie* file when a new host (*cujo*) was added to our network:

```
cujo  IN  A   192.253.253.5  ; cujo's internet address
      IN MX  10 cujo          ; if possible, mail directly to cujo
      IN MX  20 terminator     ; otherwise, deliver to our mail hub
```

3. Update the serial number and add PTR records to *each db.ADDR* file for which the host has an address. *cujo* only has one address, on network *192.253.253*; therefore, we added the following PTR record to the *db.192.253.253* file:

```
5  IN PTR cujo.movie.edu.
```

4. Restart the primary master name server by sending it a HUP signal; this forces it to load the new information:

```
# kill -HUP `cat /etc/named.pid`
```

After it has been restarted, the primary master name server will load the new data. Slave name servers will load this new data sometime within the time interval defined in the SOA record for refreshing their data.

Sometimes your users won't want to wait for the slaves to pick up the new data—they'll want it available right away. (Are you wincing or nodding knowingly as you read this?) Can you force a slave to load the new information right away? With version 8 masters and slaves, the slaves will pick up the new data quickly because the primary master notifies the slave of changes within 15 minutes of the change. If your name server is 4.9 or later, you can send it a HUP signal just as you did for your primary master name server. If your name server is 4.8.3 or earlier, remove all of the slave's backup files (or just the ones you want to force), kill the slave server, and start up a new one. Since the backup files are gone, the slave must immediately pull new copies of the zones.

To delete a host, remove the resource records from the *db.DOMAIN* and from each *db.ADDR* file pertaining to that host. Increment the serial number in each file you changed and restart your primary master name server.

SOA Serial Numbers

Each of the DNS database files has a serial number. Every time the data in the db file is changed, the serial number must be incremented. If the serial number is not incremented, slave name servers for the zone will not pick up the updated data. The change is simple. If the original db file had the following SOA record:

```
movie.edu. IN SOA terminator.movie.edu. al.robocop.movie.edu. (
                        100      ; Serial
                        10800    ; Refresh
                        3600     ; Retry
                        604800   ; Expire
                        86400 )  ; Minimum TTL
```

the updated db file would have the following SOA record:

```
movie.edu. IN SOA terminator.movie.edu. al.robocop.movie.edu. (
                        101      ; Serial
                        10800    ; Refresh
                        3600     ; Retry
```

```
604800  ; Expire
86400 ) ; Minimum TTL
```

This simple change is the key to distributing the data to all of your secondaries. Failing to increment the serial number is the most common mistake made when updating a name server. The first few times you make a change to a DNS database file, you'll remember to update the serial number because this process is new and you are paying close attention. After the db file modifications become second nature, you'll make some "quickie" little change, forget to update the serial number...and none of the slaves will pick up the new data. That's why you should use a tool that updates the serial number for you! Your tool could be *h2n* or something written locally, but use a tool.

BIND does allow you to use a decimal serial number, like 1.1, but we recommend that you stay with integer values. Here's how BIND version 4 handles decimal serial numbers: if there is a decimal point in the serial number, BIND multiplies the digits to the left of the decimal by 1000. The digits to the right of the decimal point are then concatenated to the digits on the left. Therefore, a number like 1.1 is converted to 10001 internally. 1.10 is converted to 100010. This creates certain anomalies; for example, 1.1 is "greater" than 2, and 1.10 is "greater" than 2.1. Because this is so counterintuitive, it's best to stick with integer serial numbers.

There are several good ways to manage integer serial numbers. The obvious way is just to use a counter: increment the serial number by one each time the file is modified. Another method is to derive the serial number from the date. For example, you could use the eight-digit number formed by *YYYYMMDD*. Suppose today is January 15, 1997. In this form, your serial number would be 19970115. This scheme only allows one update per day, though, and that may not be enough. Add another two digits to this number to indicate how many times the file has been updated that day. The first number for January 15, 1997, would then be 1997011500. The next modification that day would change the serial number to 1997011501. This scheme allows 100 updates per day. *h2n* will generate the serial number from the date if you use the *-y* option. Whatever scheme you choose, the serial number must fit in a 32-bit integer.

Starting Over with a New Serial Number

What do you do if the serial number on one of your zones accidentally becomes very large and you want to change it back to a more reasonable value? There is a way that works with all versions of BIND, and a couple of ways that work with version 4.9 and later.

The way that always works with all versions is to purge your slaves of any knowledge of the old serial number. Then you can start numbering from one (or any convenient point). Here's how. First, change the serial number on your primary master server and restart it; now the primary master server has the new integer serial number. Log onto one of your slave name server hosts and kill the server process with the command *kill `cat /etc/named.pid`*. Remove its backup copies of the db files (e.g., *rm db.movie db.192.249.249 db.192.253.253*). Start up your slave name server. Since the backup copies were removed, the slave must load a new version of the DNS database files—picking up the new serial numbers. This process must be repeated for each slave server. If there are any servers not under your control backing up your zones, you'll have to contact their administrators to get them to do the same.

If all of your secondaries are version 4.9 and later, you have two choices, and both involve two steps. One method involves synchronizing the serial number at zero, and the other involves incrementing the serial number by the largest amount possible.

If you set the zone serial number to zero, each 4.9 slave will transfer the zone the next time it checks. Serial number zero is special in that way. In fact, the zone will be transferred *every* time the slave checks, so don't forget to increment the serial number once all the slaves have synchronized on serial number zero. But there is a limit to how far you can increment the serial number. Read on.

The other method of fixing the serial number (with 4.9 and later slaves) will be easier to understand if we first cover some background material. The DNS serial number is a 32-bit unsigned integer. Its value ranges from 0 to 4,294,967,295. The DNS serial number uses *sequence space arithmetic*, which means that for any serial number, half of the numbers in the number space (2,147,483,647 numbers) are less than the serial number, and half of the numbers are larger.

Let's go over an example of sequence space numbers. Suppose the serial number is 5. Serial numbers 6 through (5 + 2,147,483,647) are larger than serial number 5. Serial numbers (5 + 2,147,483,649) through 4 are smaller serial numbers. Notice that the serial number wrapped around to 4 after reaching 4,294,967,295. Notice also that we didn't include the number (5 + 2,147,483,648) because this is exactly halfway around the number space, and it could be larger or smaller than 5, depending on the implementation. To be safe, don't use it.

Now back to the original problem. If your zone serial number is 25,000 and you want to start numbering at 1 again, you can speed through the serial number space in two steps. First, add the largest increment possible to your serial number (25,000 + 2,147,483,647 = 2,147,508,647). If the number you come up with is larger than 4,294,967,295 (the largest 32-bit value), you'll have wrap around to the beginning of the number space by subtracting 4,294,967,296 from it. After changing the serial number, you must wait for all of your secondaries to pick up a new copy of the zone. Second, change the zone serial number to its target value (1), which is now *larger* than the current serial number (2,147,508,647). After the secondaries pick up a new copy of the zone, you're done!

Additional db File Entries

After you've been running a name server for a while, you may want to add data to your name server to help you manage your zone. Have you ever been stumped when someone asked you *where* one of your hosts is? Maybe you don't even remember what kind of host it is. Administrators have to manage larger and larger populations of hosts these days, making it easy to lose track of this information. The name server can help you out. And if one of your hosts is acting up and someone notices remotely, the name server can help them get in touch with you.

So far in the book, we've covered SOA, NS, A, CNAME, PTR, and MX records. These records are critical to everyday operation—name servers need them to operate, and applications look up data of these types. DNS defines more data types. The next most useful resource record types are TXT and RP; these can be used to tell you the machine's location and responsible person. For a complete list of the resource records, see Appendix A, *DNS Message Format and Resource Records.*

General text information

TXT stands for TeXT. These records are simply a list of strings, each less than 256 characters in length. Versions of BIND prior to 4.8.3 do not support TXT records. In version 4, BIND limits the db file TXT record to a single string of almost 2K of data.

TXT records can be used for anything you want; one use is to list a host's location:

```
cujo  IN  TXT  "Location: machine room dog house"
```

BIND version 8 has the same 2K limit, but you can specify the TXT record as multiple strings:

```
cujo  IN  TXT  "Location:" "machine room dog house"
```

Responsible Person

Domain administrators will undoubtedly develop a love/hate relationship with the Responsible Person, or RP, record. The RP record can be attached to any domain name, internal or leaf, and indicates who is responsible for that host or zone. This will enable you to locate the miscreant responsible for the host peppering you with DNS queries, for example. But it will also lead people to you when one of your hosts acts up.

The record takes two arguments as its record-specific data: an electronic mail address, in domain name format, and a domain name, which points to additional data about the contact. The electronic mail address is in the same format the SOA record uses: it substitutes a "." for the "@". The next argument is a domain name, which must have a TXT record associated with it. The TXT record then contains free-format information about the contact, like full name and phone number. If you omit either field, you must specify the root domain (".") as a placeholder instead.

Here are some example RP (and associated) records:

```
robocop      IN  RP   root.movie.edu.  hotline.movie.edu.
             IN  RP   richard.movie.edu.  rb.movie.edu.
hotline      IN  TXT  "Movie U. Network Hotline, (415) 555-4111"
rb           IN  TXT  "Richard Boisclair, (415) 555-9612"
```

Note that TXT records for *root.movie.edu* and *richard.movie.edu* aren't necessary, since they're only the domain-name encoding of electronic mail addresses, not real domain names.

This resource record didn't exist when BIND 4.8.3 was implemented, but BIND 4.9 supports it. Check the documentation for your version of the name server to see if it supports RP before trying to use it.

Generating the BIND Database from the Host Tables

As you saw in Chapter 4, *Setting Up BIND*, we defined a well-structured process for converting host table information to name server information. We've written a tool in Perl to automate this process, called *h2n*. Using a tool to generate your data has one big advantage: there will be no syntax errors or inconsistencies in your database files—assuming we wrote *h2n* correctly! One common inconsistency is having an A (address) record for a host, but no corresponding PTR (pointer) record, or the other way around. Because these data are in separate files, it is easy to err.

What does *h2n* do? Given the */etc/hosts* file and some command-line options, *h2n* creates the db files for your domain. As a system administrator, you keep the host table current. Each time you modify the host table, you run *h2n* again. *h2n* rebuilds each db file from scratch, assigning each new file the next higher serial number. It can be run manually, or from a *cron* script each night. If you use *h2n*, you'll never need to worry about forgetting to update the serial number.

First, *h2n* needs to know the name of your domain and your network numbers. These map conveniently into the db filenames: *movie.edu* data goes in *db.movie*, and network 192.249.249 data goes into *db.192.249.249*. The domain name and network number are specified with the *-d* and *-n* flags, as follows:

-d domain

    The domain name of your zone.

-n network

> The network number of your network. If you are generating files for several networks, use several *-n* options on the command line. Omit trailing zeros from the network numbers.

The *h2n* command requires the *-d* flag and at least one *-n* flag; they have no default values. For example, to create the BIND database for the zone *movie.edu*, which consists of two networks, give the command:

```
% h2n -d movie.edu -n 192.249.249 -n 192.253.253
```

For greater control over the data, you can use other options:

-s server

> The servers for the NS records. As with *-n*, use several *-s* options if you have multiple primary master or slave servers. A version 8 server will NOTIFY this list of servers when a zone changes. The default is the host on which you run *h2n*.

-h host

> The host for the SOA record. *host* must be the primary master server to ensure proper operation of the version 8 NOTIFY feature. The default is the host on which you run *h2n*.

-u user

> The mail address of the person in charge of the domain's data. This defaults to *root* on the host on which you run *h2n*.

-o other

> Other SOA values, not including the serial number, as a colon-separated list. These default to 10800:3600:604800:86400.

-f file

> Read the *h2n* options from the named `file`, rather than from the command line. If you have lots of options, keep them in a file.

-v 4|8

> Generate configuration files for version 4 or version 8. Version 4 is the default.

-y

> Generate the serial number from the date.

Here is an example that uses all the options mentioned so far:

```
% h2n -f opts
```

Contents of file *opts*:

```
-d movie.edu
-n 192.249.249
-n 192.253.253
-s terminator.movie.edu
-s wormhole
```

```
-u al
-h terminator
-o 10800:3600:604800:86400
-v 8
-y
```

If an option requires a host name, you can provide either a full domain name (e.g., *terminator.movie.edu*), or just the host's name (e.g., *terminator*). If you give the host name only, *h2n* will form a complete domain name by adding the domain name given with the *-d* option. (If a trailing dot is necessary on the name, *h2n* will add it also.)

There are more options to *h2n* than we've shown here. For the complete list of options, you'll have to look at the manpage.

Of course, a few kinds of resource records aren't easy to generate from */etc/hosts*—the necessary data simply aren't there. You may need to add these records manually. But since *h2n* always rewrites db files, won't your changes be overwritten?

h2n provides a "back door" for inserting this kind of data. Put these special records in a file named *spcl.DOMAIN*, where *DOMAIN* is the domain name of your zone. When *h2n* finds this file, it will "include" it within the database files by adding the line:

```
$INCLUDE spcl.DOMAIN
```

to the end of the *db.DOMAIN* file. (The *$INCLUDE* directive is described later in this chapter.) For example, the administrator of *movie.edu* may add extra MX records into the file *spcl.movie* so that users can mail to *movie.edu* directly instead of sending mail to hosts within *movie.edu*. Upon finding this file, *h2n* would put the line:

```
$INCLUDE spcl.movie
```

at the end of the database file *db.movie*.

Keeping db.cache Current

As explained in Chapter 4, the *db.cache* file tells your server where the servers for the "root" zone are. It must be updated periodically. The root name servers do not change very often, but they do change. A good practice is to check your *db.cache* file every month or two. In Chapter 4, we told you to get the servers by *ftp*ing to *ftp.rs.internic.net*. And that's probably your best method to keep current.

If you have on your system a copy of *dig*, a utility that works a lot like *nslookup* and is included in the BIND distribution, you can retrieve the current list of roots just by running:

```
% dig @a.root-servers.net  .  ns > db.cache
```

Organizing Your Files

When you first set up your domain, organizing your files was simple—you put them all in a single directory. There was one configuration file and a handful of *db* files. Over time, your responsibilities grew. More networks were added. Maybe a few subdomains were started. You started backing up zones for other sites. After a while, an *ls* of your name server directory no longer fits on a single screen. It's time to reorganize. BIND has a few features that will help with your organization.

The configuration file for a 4.9 or later server can have a *control* entry, called *include*, which allows you to insert a new configuration file into the current configuration file. This allows you to take a very large configuration file and break it into smaller pieces. The database files (for all BIND versions) allow two control entries: *$ORIGIN* and *$INCLUDE*. $ORIGIN changes the origin, and $INCLUDE inserts a new file into the current file. The database control entries are not resource records; they facilitate the maintenance of DNS data. In particular, these statements make it easier for you to divide your domain into subdomains: they allow you to store the data for each subdomain in a separate database file.

Using Several Directories

One way to organize your db files is to store them in separate directories. If your server is a primary master for several sites (both forward and reverse maps), you could store each site's db files in its own directory. Another division might be to store all the primary master files in one directory and all the slave backup files in a different directory. Let's look at what the version 4 configuration file might look like if you chose the primary/slave division:

```
directory /usr/local/named
;
; These files are not specific to any zone
;
cache     .                        db.cache
primary   0.0.127.in-addr.arpa     db.127.0.0
;
; These are our primary zone files
;
primary   movie.edu                primary/db.movie
primary   249.249.192.in-addr.arpa primary/db.192.249.249
primary   253.253.192.in-addr.arpa primary/db.192.253.253
;
; These are our slave zone files
;
secondary ora.com                  198.112.208.25 slave/bak.ora
secondary 208.112.198.in-addr.arpa 198.112.208.25 slave/bak.198.112.208
```

Here's the same configuration file in version 8 format:

```
options { directory "/usr/local/named"; };
//
// These files are not specific to any zone
//
zone "." {
        type hint;
        file "db.cache";
};
zone "0.0.127.in-addr.arpa" {
        type master;
        file "db.127.0.0";
};
//
// These are our primary zone files
//
zone "movie.edu" {
        type master;
        file "primary/db.movie";
};
zone "249.249.192.in-addr.arpa" {
        type master;
        file "primary/db.192.249.249";
};
zone "253.253.192.in-addr.arpa" {
        type master;
        file "primary/db.192.253.253";
};
//
// These are our slave zone files
//
zone "ora.com" {
        type slave;
        file "slave/bak.ora";
        masters { 198.112.208.25; };
};
zone "208.112.192.in-addr.arpa" {
        type slave;
        file "slave/bak.198.112.208";
        masters { 198.112.208.25; };
};
```

Another variation on this division is to break the configuration file into three files:
the main file, a file that contains all the primary entries, and a file that contains all
the *secondary* entries. Here's what the version 4 main configuration file might look
like:

```
directory /usr/local/named
;
; These files are not specific to any zone
;
cache    .                         db.cache
primary  0.0.127.in-addr.arpa      db.127.0.0
;
include  conffile.primary
```

```
            include  conffile.slave
```

Here is *conffile.primary* (version 4):

```
            ;
            ; These are our primary zone files
            ;
            primary  movie.edu                     primary/db.movie
            primary  249.249.192.in-addr.arpa      primary/db.192.249.249
            primary  253.253.192.in-addr.arpa      primary/db.192.253.253
```

Here is *conffile.slave* (version 4):

```
            ;
            ; These are our slave zone files
            ;
            secondary ora.com                      198.112.208.25 slave/bak.ora
            secondary 208.112.198.in-addr.arpa 198.112.208.25 slave/bak.198.112.208
```

Here are the same files in version 8 format:

```
            options { directory "/usr/local/named"; };
            //
            // These files are not specific to any zone
            //
            zone "." {
                    type hint;
                    file "db.cache";
            };
            zone "0.0.127.in-addr.arpa" {
                    type master;
                    file "db.127.0.0";
            };
            //
            include "conffile.primary";
            include "conffile.slave";
```

Here is *conffile.primary* (version 8):

```
            //
            // These are our primary zone files
            //
            zone "movie.edu" {
                    type master;
                    file "primary/db.movie";
            };
            zone "249.249.192.in-addr.arpa" {
                    type master;
                    file "primary/db.192.249.249";
            };
            zone "253.253.192.in-addr.arpa" {
                    type master;
                    file "primary/db.192.253.253";
            };
```

Here is *conffile.slave* (version 8):

```
//
// These are our slave zone files
//
zone "ora.com" {
        type slave;
        file "slave/bak.ora";
        masters { 198.112.208.25; };
};
zone "208.112.192.in-addr.arpa" {
        type slave;
        file "slave/bak.198.112.208";
        masters { 198.112.208.25; };
};
```

You might think the organization would be better if you put the configuration file with the *primary* entries into the *primary* subdirectory, add a new *directory* line to change to this directory, and remove the *primary/* from each of the file names, since the server is now in that directory. Then make comparable changes in the configuration file with the *secondary* lines. But things get rather confused when the name server keeps switching around to different directories—the slave backup files end up in the last directory the name server changed to, and when the name server is sent a HUP signal, it may not be able to find the main configuration file if it is not left in the directory where it started (if the configuration file is specified with a relative path name).

Changing the Origin in a Database File

With BIND, the default origin for the DNS database files is the second field of the primary or secondary statement in the version 4 *named.boot* file or the second field of the zone statement in the version 8 *named.conf* file. The origin is a domain name that is appended automatically to all names not ending in a dot. This origin can be changed in the db file with *$ORIGIN*. In the db file, *$ORIGIN* is followed by a domain name. (Don't forget the trailing dot if you give the full domain name!) From this point on, all names not ending in a dot have the new origin appended. If your name server (e.g., *movie.edu*) is responsible for a number of subdomains, you can use the *$ORIGIN* entry to reset the origin and simplify the files. For example:

```
$ORIGIN classics.movie.edu.
maltese      IN  A  192.253.253.100
casablanca   IN  A  192.253.253.101

$ORIGIN comedy.movie.edu.
mash         IN  A  192.253.253.200
twins        IN  A  192.253.253.201
```

We'll cover more on creating subdomains in Chapter 9, *Parenting*.

Including Other Database Files

Once you've subdivided your domain like this, you might find it more convenient to keep the subdomain records in separate files. The $INCLUDE statement lets you do this:

```
$ORIGIN classics.movie.edu.
$INCLUDE db.classics

$ORIGIN comedy.movie.edu.
$INCLUDE db.comedy
```

To simplify the file even further, the new origin can be specified on the $INCLUDE line:

```
$INCLUDE db.classics classics.movie.edu.
$INCLUDE db.comedy   comedy.movie.edu.
```

When you specify the origin on the $INCLUDE line, it only applies to the particular file that you're including. For example, the *comedy.movie.edu* origin only applies to the names in *db.comedy*. After *db.comedy* has been included, the origin returns to what it was before $INCLUDE, even if there was an $ORIGIN entry within *db.comedy*.

Changing BIND 8 System File Locations

Version 8 allows you to change the name and location of the following system files: *named.pid*, *named-xfer*, *named_dump.db*, and *named.stats*. Most of you will not need to use this feature. Don't feel obligated to change the names or locations of these files just because you can change them.

If you do change the default location of the files written by the name server (*named.pid*, *named_dump.db*, or *named.stats*), for security reasons, you should choose a directory that is not world-writable. While we don't know of any break-ins caused by these files, you should follow this guideline just to be safe.

named.pid is usually */etc/named.pid* or */var/run/named.pid*. One reason you might change the default location of this file is if you find yourself running more than one name server on a single host. (Yikes! Why would someone do that?) Chapter 10, *Advanced Features and Security*, gives an example of running two name servers on one host. You can specify a different *named.pid* file in the configuration file for each server:

```
options { pid-file "server1.pid"; };
```

named-xfer is usually */etc/named-xfer* or */usr/sbin/named-xfer*. It's used by a slave server for inbound zone transfers. One reason you might change the default location is to build and test a new version of BIND 8 in a local directory—your local version of *named* can be configured to use the local version of *named-xfer.*

```
options { named-xfer "/home/rudy/named/named-xfer"; };
```

named_dump.db is left in the name server's current directory (version 8) when the name server dumps its database. Here is an example of to change its location:

```
options { dump-file "/home/rudy/named/named_dump.db"; };
```

named.stats is left in the name server's current directory (version 8) when the name server writes its statistics to a file. Here is an example how to change its location:

```
options { statistics-file "/home/rudy/named/named.stats"; };
```

BIND 8 Logging

BIND 4 had an extensive logging system, writing information to a debug file and sending information to syslog. But, BIND 4 gave you limited control over this logging process—you could turn debugging on to a certain level. That's it. BIND 8 has the same logging system as BIND 4, but BIND 8 gives you control you didn't get with BIND 4.

This control has its cost though—there's a lot to learn before you can be effective configuring this subsystem. If you don't have some time you can spend to experiment with logging, use the defaults and come back to this topic later. Most of you do not need to change the default logging behavior.

Logging has two major topics you need to understand: channels and categories. A channel specifies where the logging data goes: to syslog, to a file, to stderr, or to the bit bucket. A category specifies what data is logged.

Each category of data can be sent to a single channel or to multiple channels. In Figure 7-1, queries are logged to a file, statistics data is logged to a file and logged to syslog.

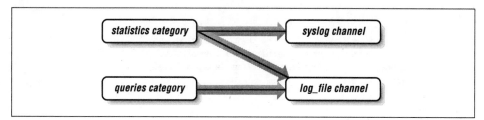

Figure 7-1. Logging categories to channels

Channels allow you to filter by message severity. Here is the list of severities:

```
critical
error
```

```
warning
notice
info
debug [level]
dynamic
```

The top five severities (critical, error, warning, notice, and info) are the familiar severity levels used by syslog. The other two (debug and dynamic) are unique to BIND 8.

`debug` is name server debugging for which you can specify a debug level. If you omit the debug level, then the level is assumed to be one. If you specify a debug level, you will see messages of that level when name server debugging is turned on (i.e., if you specify "debug 3", then you will see level three debugging messages even when you only send one USR1 signal to the name server). If you specify `dynamic` severity, then the name server will log messages that match its debug level (i.e., if you send one USR1 signal to the name server, it will log messages from level one. If you send three USR1 signals to the name server, it will log messages from levels one through three.) The default severity is `info`, which means you won't see debug messages unless you specify the severity.

NOTE   You can configure a channel to log both debug messages and syslog
              messages to a file. However the converse is not true—you cannot
              configure a channel to log both debug messages and syslog messages
              with syslog—only syslog messages can be sent to syslog.

Let's configure a couple of channels to show you how this works. The first channel will go to syslog and will log with facility `daemon`, sending those messages of severity `info` and above. The second channel will go to a file, logging debug messages at any level as well as syslog messages. Here is the `logging` statement for the BIND 8 configuration file:

```
logging {
  channel my_syslog {
     syslog daemon;
     // Debug messages will not be sent to syslog, so
     // there is no point to setting the severity to
     // debug or dynamic; use the lowest syslog level: info.
     severity info;
  };
  channel my_file {
     file "log.msgs";
     // Set the severity to dynamic to see all the debug messages.
     severity dynamic;
  };
};
```

Now that we've configured a couple of channels, we have to tell the name server exactly what to send to those channels. Let's implement what was pictured in Figure 7-1 with statistics going to syslog and to the file, and queries going to the file. The category specification is part of the **logging** statement, so we'll build on the previous **logging** statement:

```
logging {
   channel my_syslog {
      syslog daemon;
      severity info;
   };
   channel my_file {
      file "log.msgs";
      severity dynamic;
   };

   category statistics { my_syslog; my_file; };
   category queries { my_file; };
};
```

With this **logging** statement in your configuration file, start your name server and send it a few queries. But nothing is written to *log.msgs*! (Well, if you wait long enough, the name server's statistics will show up in *log.msgs*.) You had expected those queries to be logged. Alas, you have to turn on name server debugging to get queries logged:

```
# kill -USR1 `cat /etc/named.pid`
```

Now send your name server some queries and they are logged in *log.msgs*. But look around: there's a new file called *named.run*. It has all the other debugging information written to it. You didn't want all this other debugging, though; you just wanted the statistics and queries. How do you get rid of *named.run*?

There's a special category we haven't told you about: **default**. If you don't specify any channels for a category, the **default** category is used. Let's change the **default** category to discard all logging messages (there's a channel called **null** for this purpose):

```
logging {
   channel my_syslog {
      syslog daemon;
      severity info;
   };
   channel my_file {
      file "log.msgs";
      severity dynamic;
   };

   category default { null; };
   category statistics { my_syslog; my_file; };
```

```
    category queries { my_file; };
};
```

Now, start your server, turn on debugging to level one, and send some queries. The queries end up in *log.msgs* and *named.run* was created but the file is empty. Great! We're getting the hang of this after all.

A few days pass. One of your co-workers notices that the name server is sending many fewer messages to syslog than it used to. In fact, the only syslog messages are statistics messages. The ones your co-worker watched, the zone transfer messages, are gone. What happened?

Well, the **default** category is set up, by default, to send messages to both syslog and to the debug file (*named.run*). When the **default** category was configured to the **null** channel, the other syslog messages were turned off. Here's what we should have used:

```
    category default { my_syslog; };
```

This sends the syslog messages to syslog, but does not write debug or syslog messages to a file.

Remember, we said you'd have to experiment for a while with logging to get exactly what you want. We hope this example gives you a clue what you might run into. Now, let's go over the details of logging.

The Logging Statement

Here's the syntax of the **logging** statement. It's rather intimidating. We'll go over some more examples as we explain what each clause means:

```
logging {
  [ channel channel_name {
    ( file path_name
       [ versions ( number | unlimited ) ]
       [ size size_spec ]
     | syslog ( kern | user | mail | daemon | auth | syslog | lpr |
                news | uucp | cron | authpriv | ftp |
                local0 | local1 | local2 | local3 |
                local4 | local5 | local6 | local7 )
     | null );

    [ severity ( critical | error | warning | notice |
                 info | debug [ level ] | dynamic ); ]
    [ print-category yes_or_no; ]
    [ print-severity yes_or_no; ]
    [ print-time yes_or_no; ]
  }; ]

  [ category category_name {
```

```
        channel_name; [ channel_name; ... ]
    }; ]
    ...
};
```

Here are the default channels. The name server will make these channels even if you do not want them. You cannot redefine these channels. You can only add more channels:

```
channel default_syslog {
    syslog daemon;          // send to syslog's daemon facility
    severity info;          // only send priority info and higher
};

channel default_debug {
    file "named.run";       // write to named.run in the
                            // working directory
    severity dynamic;       // log at the server's current debug level
};

channel default_stderr {    // writes to stderr
    file "<stderr>";        // this is illustrative only;
                            // there's currently no way of
                            // specifying an internal file
                            // descriptor in the configuration language.
    severity info;          // only send priority info and higher
};

channel null {
    null;                   // toss anything sent to this channel
};
```

If you do not assign channels to the categories **default**, **panic**, **packet**, and **eventlib**, the name server will assign these channels by default:

```
logging {
    category default { default_syslog; default_debug; };
    category panic { default_syslog; default_stderr; };
    category packet { default_debug; };
    category eventlib { default_debug; };
};
```

As we mentioned earlier, the **default** category logs to both syslog and to the debug file (which by default is *named.run*). This means that all syslog messages of severity **info** and above are sent to syslog, and when debugging is turned on, the syslog messages and debug messages are written to *named.run*. This more or less matches the BIND 4 behavior.

Channel Details

A channel may be defined to go to a file, to syslog, or to null.

File channels

If a channel goes to a file, you must specify the file's path name. Optionally, you can specify how many versions of the file can exist at one time and how big the file may grow.

If you specify that there can be three versions, BIND 8 will keep around *file, file.0, file.1,* and *file.2.* After the name server starts or after it is restarted by a HUP signal, it will move *file.1* to *file.2, file.0* to *file.1, file* to *file.0,* and start a new copy of *file.* If you specify unlimited versions, BIND 8.1.2 will keep 99 versions.

If you specify a maximum file size, BIND 8 will stop writing to the file after it reaches the specified size. Unlike the versions clause (mentioned in the last paragraph), the file will not be rolled over and a new file opened when the specified size is reached. The name server just stops writing to the file. If you do not specify a file size, the file will grow indefinitely.

Here is an example file channel using the **versions** and **size** clauses:

```
logging{
  channel my_file {
     file "log.msgs" versions 3 size 10k;
     severity dynamic;
  };
};
```

The size can include a scaling factor as in the example. K or k is kilobytes. M or m is megabytes. G or g is gigabytes.

It's important to specify the severity as either **debug** or **dynamic** if you want to see debug messages. The default severity is **info**, which will only show you syslog messages.

Syslog channels

If a channel goes to syslog, you can specify the facility to be any of the following: **kern, user, mail, daemon, auth, syslog, lpr, news, uucp, cron, authpriv, ftp, local0, local1, local2, local3, local4, local5, local6, local7.** The default is **daemon.** We recommend that you use the default.

Here's an example syslog channel using the facility **local0** instead of **daemon:**

```
logging {
    channel my_syslog {
        syslog local0;          // send to syslog's local0 facility
        severity info;          // only send priority info and higher
    };
};
```

Null channel

There is a predefined channel called `null` for those messages you want to throw away.

Stderr channel

There is a predefined channel called `default_stderr` for any messages you'd like written to the *stderr* file descriptor of the name server. You cannot configure any other file descriptors.

Data formatting for all channels

The BIND 8 logging facility also allows you some control over the formatting of messages. You can add to the messages: a time stamp, the category, or the severity.

Here's an example debug message that has all the extra goodies:

```
01-Feb-1998 13:19:18.889 config: debug 1: source = db.127.0.0
```

The category for this message is `config` and the severity is `debug` level one.

Here's an example channel configuration that includes all three additions:

```
logging {
  channel my_file {
    file "log.msgs";
    severity debug;
    print-category yes;
    print-severity yes;
    print-time yes;
  };
};
```

There is not much point in adding the time stamp for messages to a syslog channel since syslog adds the time and date itself.

Category Details

There are lots of categories—lots! We'll list them here so you can see them all. Rather than trying to figure out which you want to see, we recommend that you configure your name server to print out all of its log messages, with their category and severity, and then pick out the ones you want to see. We'll show you how to do this after telling you about the categories:

default

> If you don't specify any channels for a category, the `default` category is used instead. In that sense, `default` is synonymous with all categories. However, there are some messages that didn't end up in a category. So, even if you specify

channels for each category individually, you'll still want to specify a channel for the `default` category for all the uncategorized messages.

If you do not specify a channel for the `default` category, one will be specified for you:

```
category default { default_syslog; default_debug; };
```

cname
> CNAME errors (e.g., "... has CNAME and other data")

config
> Configuration file processing

db
> Database operations

eventlib
> System events; must point to a file channel

insist
> Internal consistency check failures

lame-servers
> Detection of bad delegation

load
> Zone loading messages

maintenance
> Maintenance events (e.g., system queries)

ncache
> Negative caching events

notify
> Asynchronous change notifications

os
> Problems with the operating system

packet
> Decodes of packets received and sent; must point to a file channel

panic
> Problems that cause the shutdown of the server

parser
> Parsing of the configuration file

queries
> Analogous to BIND 4's query logging

response-checks
> Malformed responses, unrelated additional information, etc.

security

> Approved/unapproved requests

statistics

> Periodic reports of activities

update

> Dynamic update events

xfer-in

> Zone transfers from remote name servers to the local name server

xfer-out

> Zone transfers from the local name server to remote name servers

Viewing all category messages

A good activity to start your foray into logging is to configure your name server to log all of its messages to a file, with the category and severity, and then pick out which messages you are interested in.

Earlier we listed the categories that are configured by default:

```
logging {
    category default { default_syslog; default_debug; };
    category panic { default_syslog; default_stderr; };
    category packet { default_debug; };
    category eventlib { default_debug; };
};
```

By default, the category and severity are not included with messages written to the `default_debug` channel. In order for you to see all the log messages, with their category and severity, you'll have to configure each of these categories yourself.

Here is a logging statement that does just that:

```
logging {
  channel my_file {
      file "log.msgs";
      severity dynamic;
      print-category yes;
      print-severity yes;
  };

  category default  { default_syslog; my_file; };
  category panic    { default_syslog; my_file; };
  category packet   { my_file; };
  category eventlib { my_file; };
  category queries  { my_file; };
};
```

Notice that we've defined each category to include the channel `my_file`. We also added one category that wasn't in the default logging statement above—`queries`. Queries aren't printed unless you configure the `queries` category.

Start your server and turn on debugging to level one. You'll see messages in *log.msgs* that look like the following:

```
queries: info: XX /192.253.253.4/foo.movie.edu/A
default: debug 1: req: nlookup(foo.movie.edu) id 4 type=1 class=1
default: debug 1: req: found 'foo.movie.edu' as 'foo.movie.edu' (cname=0)
default: debug 1: ns_req: answer -> [192.253.253.4].2338 fd=20 id=4 size=87
```

Once you see the messages that interest you, configure your server to log only those messages.

Keeping Everything Running Smoothly

A significant part of maintenance is being aware when something has gone wrong, before it becomes a real problem. If you catch a problem early, chances are it'll be that much easier to fix. As the old adage says, an ounce of prevention is worth a pound of cure.

This isn't quite troubleshooting—we'll devote an entire chapter to troubleshooting later—think of it as "pre-troubleshooting." Troubleshooting (the pound of cure) is what you have to do if you ignore maintenance, after your problem has developed complications, and you need to identify the problem by its symptoms.

The next two sections deal with preventative maintenance: looking periodically at the *syslog* file and at the BIND name server statistics to see whether any problems are developing. Consider this a name server's medical checkup.

Common Syslog Messages

There are a large number of syslog messages *named* can emit. In practice, you'll only see a few of them. We'll cover the most common syslog messages here, excluding reports of syntax errors in DNS database files.

Every time you start *named*, it sends out this message at priority LOG_NOTICE:

```
Jan 10 20:48:32 terminator named[3221]: starting.  named 8.1.2
```

This message logs the fact that *named* started at this time, and tells you the version of BIND you're running. This is, of course, nothing to be concerned about. It *is* a good place to look if you're not sure what version of BIND your operating system supports. (Older versions of BIND used "restarted" instead of "starting.")

Every time you send the name server a HUP signal, it sends out this message at priority LOG_NOTICE:

```
Jan 10 20:50:16 terminator named[3221]: reloading nameserver
```

The "reloading" message just tells you that *named* reloaded its database (as a result of a HUP signal) at this time. Again, this is nothing to be concerned about. This message will most likely be of interest when you are tracking down how long a bad resource record has been in your name server data or how long a whole zone has been missing because of a mistake during an update.

Another message you may see shortly after your name server starts is:

```
Jan 10 20:50:20 terminator named[3221]: cannot set resource limits on
                this system
```

This means that your name server thinks your operating system does not support the *getrlimit()* and *setrlimit()* system calls, which are used when you try to define *coresize, datasize, stacksize* or *files* on a BIND 8 name server. It doesn't matter whether you're actually using any of these substatements in your configuration file; BIND will print the message anyway. If you're not *using* these substatements, ignore the message. If you are, and you think your operating system does support *getrlimit()* and *setrlimit()*, you'll have to recompile BIND with *HAVE_GETRUSAGE* defined. This message in logged at priority LOG_INFO.

If you run your name server on a host with many network interfaces, especially virtual network interfaces, you may see this message soon after startup, or even after your name server has run well for a while:

```
Jan 10 20:50:31 terminator named[3221]: fcntl(dfd, F_DUPFD, 20): Too
                many open files
Jan 10 20:50:31 terminator named[3221]: fcntl(sfd, F_DUPFD, 20): Too
                many open files
```

This means that BIND has run out of file descriptors. BIND uses a fair number of file descriptors: two for each network interface it's listening on (one for UDP and one for TCP), and one for opening zone data files. If that's more than the limit your operating system places on processes, BIND won't be able to get any more file descriptors and you'll see this message. The priority will depend on which part of BIND fails to get the file descriptor: the more critical the subsystem, the higher the priority.

The next step is to either get BIND to use fewer file descriptors, or to raise the limit the operating system places on the number of file descriptors BIND can use:

• If you don't need BIND listening on all of your network interfaces (particularly the virtual ones), use the *listen-on* substatement to configure BIND to listen only on those interfaces it needs to. See Chapter 10 for details on the syntax of *listen-on*.

- If your operating system supports *getrlimit()* and *setrlimit()* (see above), configure your name server to use a larger number of files with the *files* substatement. See Chapter 10 for details on using the *files* substatement.

- If your operating system places too restrictive a limit on open files, raise that limit before you start *named* with the *ulimit* command.

Every time a BIND 8 name server loads a zone, it sends out a message at priority LOG_INFO:

```
Jan 10 21:49:50 terminator named[3221]: master zone "movie.edu" (IN)
                loaded(serial 1996011000)
```

(BIND 4.9 name servers call it a "primary zone" instead of a "master zone.") This tells you when the name server loaded the zone, the class (in this case, IN) of the zone, and the serial number in the zone's SOA record.

About every hour, a BIND 8 name server will send a message at priority LOG_INFO that snapshots the current statistics:

```
Feb 18 14:09:02 terminator named[3565]: USAGE 824681342 824600158
                CPU=13.01u/3.26s CHILDCPU=9.99u/12.71s
Feb 18 14:09:02 terminator named[3565]: NSTATS 824681342 824600158
                A=4 PTR=2
Feb 18 14:09:02 terminator named[3565]: XSTATS 824681342 824600158
                RQ=6 RR=2 RIQ=0 RNXD=0 RFwdQ=0 RFwdR=0 RDupQ=0 RDupR=0
                RFail=0 RFErr=0 RErr=0 RTCP=0 RAXFR=0 RLame=0 Ropts=0
                SSysQ=2 SAns=6 SFwdQ=0 SFwdR=0 SDupQ=5 SFail=0 SFErr=0
                SErr=0 RNotNsQ=6 SNaAns=2 SNXD=1
```

(This feature was also present in BIND 4.9 through 4.9.3, then turned off in the 4.9.4 server.) The first two numbers for each message are time. If you subtract the second number from the first number, you'll find out how many seconds your server has been running. (You'd think the name server could do that for you.) The CPU entry tells you how much time your server has spent in user mode (13.01 seconds) and system mode (3.26 seconds). Then it tells you the same statistic for child processes. The NSTATS message lists the query types your server has received and the counts for each. The XSTATS message lists additional statistics. The statistics under NSTATS and XSTATS are explained in more detail later in this chapter.

If BIND version 4.9.4 or later finds a name that doesn't conform to RFC 952, it logs a syslog error:

```
Jul 24 20:56:26 terminator named[1496]: owner name "ID_4.movie.edu IN"
                                        (primary) is invalid - rejecting
```

This message is logged at level LOG_NOTICE. See Chapter 4 for the host naming rules.

Another syslog message, sent at priority LOG_INFO, is a warning message about the zone data:

```
Jan 10 20:48:38 terminator named[3221]: terminator2 has CNAME
                and other data (invalid)
```

This message means that there's a problem with your zone data. For example, you may have entries like these:

```
terminator2   IN   CNAME t2
terminator2   IN   MX    10 t2
t2            IN   A     192.249.249.10
t2            IN   MX    10 t2
```

The MX record for *terminator2* is incorrect, and would cause the message given above. *terminator2* is an alias for *t2*, which is the canonical name. As described earlier, when DNS looks up a name and finds a CNAME, it replaces the original name with the canonical name, and then tries looking up the canonical name. Thus, when the server looks up the MX data for *terminator2*, it finds a CNAME record and then looks up the MX record for *t2*. Since the server follows the CNAME record for *terminator2*, it will never use the MX record for *terminator2*; in fact, this record is illegal. In other words, all resource records for a host have to use the *canonical name*; it's an error to use an alias in place of the canonical name.

The following message indicates that a slave was unable to reach any master server when it tried to do a zone transfer:

```
Jan 10 20:52:42 wormhole named[2813]: zoneref: Masters for
                secondary zone "movie.edu" unreachable
```

This message is sent at priority LOG_NOTICE, and is only sent the first time the zone transfer fails. When the zone transfer finally succeeds, a 4.9 or later server will tell you that the zone transferred by issuing another syslog message. Older servers don't tell you when the zone transferred. When this message first appears, you don't need to take any immediate action. The name server will continue to attempt to transfer the zone, according to the retry period in the SOA record. After a few days (or half the expire time), you might check that the server was able to transfer the zone. On servers that don't issue the syslog message when the zone transfers, you can verify that the zone transferred by checking the timestamp on the backup file. When a zone transfer succeeds, a new backup file is created. When a zone is found to be up to date, the backup file is *touched* (à la the UNIX *touch* command). In both cases, the timestamp on the backup file is updated, so go to the slave and give the command *ls -l /usr/local/named/db.**. This will tell you when the slave last synchronized each zone with the master server. We'll cover how to troubleshoot slaves failing to transfer zones in Chapter 13.

If you are watching the syslog messages on your 4.9 or later master server, you'll see a LOG_INFO syslog message when the slave does pick up the new zone data or when a tool, like *nslookup*, transfers a zone:

```
Mar  7 07:30:04 terminator named[3977]: approved AXFR from
                [192.249.249.1].2253 for "movie.edu"
```

If you are using the version 4 *xfrnets* configuration file statement or version 8 *allow-transfer* option statement (explained in Chapter 10) to limit which servers can load zones, you may see this message saying *unapproved* instead of *approved*.

This syslog message is seen only if you capture LOG_INFO syslog messages:

```
Jan 10 20:52:42 wormhole named[2813]: Malformed response
                  from 192.1.1.1
```

Most often, this message means that some bug in a name server caused it to send an erroneous response packet. The error probably occurred on the remote name server (192.1.1.1) rather than the local server (*wormhole*). Diagnosing this kind of error involves capturing the response packet in a network trace and decoding it. Decoding DNS packets manually is beyond the scope of this book, so we won't go into much detail. You see this type of error when the response packet says it has several answers in the answer section (like four address resource records), and yet the answer section only contains a single answer. The only course of action is to notify the hostmaster (or root) of the offending host via email (assuming you can get the name of the host by looking up the address). You would also see this message if the underlying network altered (damaged) the UDP response packets in some way. Checksumming of UDP packets is optional, so this error might not be caught at a lower level.

named logs this message when you try to sneak into your zone file data that belongs in another zone:

```
Jun 13 08:02:03 terminator named[2657]: db.movie:28: data "foo.bar.edu"
                  outside zone "movie.edu" (ignored)
```

For instance, if we tried to use this zone data:

```
robocop        IN A   192.249.249.2
terminator     IN A   192.249.249.3

; Add this entry to the name server's cache
foo.bar.edu.   IN A   10.0.7.13
```

we'd be adding data for the *bar.edu* zone into our *movie.edu* zone file. A 4.8.3 vintage name server would blindly add *foo.bar.edu* to its cache. It wouldn't check that all the data in the *db.movie* file was in the *movie.edu* zone. You can't fool a name server newer than 4.9, though. This *syslog* message is logged at priority LOG_INFO.

Earlier in the book we said that you can't use a CNAME in the data portion of a resource record. BIND versions 4.9 and later will catch this misuse:

```
Jun 13 08:21:04 terminator named[2699]: "movie.edu IN NS" points to a
                  CNAME (dh.movie.edu)
```

Here is an example of the guilty resource records:

```
@                               NS        terminator.movie.edu.
                                NS        dh.movie.edu.
terminator.movie.edu.   IN A        192.249.249.3
diehard.movie.edu.      IN A        192.249.249.4
dh                              IN CNAME diehard
```

The second NS record should have listed *diehard.movie.edu* instead of *dh.movie.edu*. This syslog message won't show up immediately when you start your name server.

NOTE   You'll only see the syslog message when the offending data is looked up. This syslog message is logged by a 4.9.3 or BIND 8 server at priority LOG_INFO, and by a 4.9.4 to 4.9.7 server at priority LOG_DEBUG.

This message indicates that your name server may be guarding itself against one type of network attack:

```
Jun 11 11:40:54 terminator named[131]: Response from unexpected source
                                ([204.138.114.3].53)
```

Your name server sent a query to a remote name server, and a response came, but it wasn't from any of the addresses your name server had listed for the remote name server. The potential security breach is this: an intruder causes your name server to query a remote name server, and at the same time the intruder sends responses (pretending the responses are from the remote name server) that the intruder hopes your name server will add to its cache. Perhaps he sends along a false PTR record, pointing the IP address of one of his hosts to the domain name of a host you trust. Once the false PTR record is in your cache, the intruder uses one of the BSD "r" commands (e.g., *rlogin*) to gain access to your system.

Less paranoid admins will realize that this situation can also happen if the parent name server only knows about one of the IP addresses of a multihomed name server host. The parent tells your name server the one IP address it knows about, and when your server queries the remote name server, the remote name server responds from the other IP address. This shouldn't happen if BIND is running on the remote name server host, because BIND makes every attempt to use the same IP address in the response as the query was sent to. This syslog message is logged at priority LOG_INFO.

Here's an interesting syslog message:

```
Jun 10 07:57:28 terminator named[131]: No root nameservers for
                class 226
```

The only classes defined to date are: class 1, Internet (IN); class 3, Chaos (CH); and class 4, Hesiod (HS). Where does class 226 come from? That's exactly the point your name server is making with this syslog message. Something is wrong in the world because there is no class 226. What can you do about it? Nothing, really. This message doesn't give you enough information—you don't know who the query is from or what the query was for. Then again, if the class field is corrupted, the query name may be garbage too. The actual cause of the problem could be a broken remote name server or resolver, or it could be a corrupted UDP datagram. This syslog message is logged at priority LOG_INFO.

This message might happen if you are backing up some other zone:

```
Jun  7 20:14:26 wormhole named[29618]: Zone "253.253.192.in-addr.arpa"
                (class 1) SOA serial# (3345) rcvd from [192.249.249.10]
                is < ours (563319491)
```

Ah, the pesky admin for *253.253.192.in-addr.arpa* changed the serial number format and neglected to tell you about it. Some thanks you get for running a slave for this zone, huh? Drop the admin a note to see if this change was intentional or just a typo. If the change was intentional, or you don't want to contact the admin, then you have to deal with it locally—kill your slave, remove the backup copy of this zone, and restart your server. This procedure removes all knowledge your slave had of the old SOA serial number, at which point it is quite happy with the new serial number. This syslog message is logged at priority LOG_NOTICE.

By the way, if that pesky admin was running a BIND 8 name server, then he must have missed (or ignored) a message his server logged, telling him that he'd rolled the zone's serial number back:

```
Jun 7 19:35:14 terminator named[3221]: WARNING: new serial number < old
               (zp->z_serial < serial)
```

This message is logged at LOG_NOTICE.

You might want to remind him of the wisdom of checking syslog after making any changes to the name server.

This message will undoubtedly become familiar to you:

```
Aug 21 00:59:06 jade named[12620]: Lame server on 'foo.movie.edu'
                (in 'MOVIE.EDU'?): [10.0.7.125].53 'NS.HOLLYWOOD.LA.CA.US':
                learnt (A=10.47.3.62,NS=10.47.3.62)
```

"Aye, Captain, she's sucking mud!" There's some mud out there in the Internet waters in the form of bad delegations. A parent name server is delegating a subdomain to a child name server, and the child name server is not authoritative for the subdomain. In this case, the *edu* name server is delegating *movie.edu* to 10.0.7.125, and the name server on this host is not authoritative for *movie.edu*. Unless you know the admin for *movie.edu*, there's probably nothing for you to do about this. The syslog message is logged by a 4.9.3 server at priority

LOG_WARNING, by a 4.9.4 to 4.9.7 server at priority LOG_DEBUG, and by a BIND 8 server at LOG_INFO.

If your version 4.9 or later name server's configuration file has:

```
options query-log
```

or your version 8 configuration file has:

```
logging { category queries { default_syslog; }; };
```

you will get a LOG_INFO syslog message for every query your name server receives:

```
Feb 20 21:43:25 terminator named[3830]:
            XX /192.253.253.2/carrie.movie.edu/A
Feb 20 21:43:32 terminator named[3830]:
            XX /192.253.253.2/4.253.253.192.in-addr.arpa/PTR
```

These messages include the IP address of the host that made the query and the query. Make sure you have lots of disk space if you log all the queries to a busy name server. (On a running server, you can toggle query logging on and off with the WINCH signal.)

Starting with version 8.1.2, you might see this set of syslog messages:

```
May 19 11:06:08 named[21160]: bind(dfd=20, [10.0.0.1].53):
            Address already in use
May 19 11:06:08 named[21160]: deleting interface [10.0.0.1].53
May 19 11:06:08 named[21160]: bind(dfd=20, [127.0.0.1].53):
            Address already in use
May 19 11:06:08 named[21160]: deleting interface [127.0.0.1].53
May 19 11:06:08 named[21160]: not listening on any interfaces
May 19 11:06:08 named[21160]: Forwarding source address
            is [0.0.0.0].1835
May 19 11:06:08 named[21161]: Ready to answer queries.
```

What has happened is that you had a name server running and you started up a second name server without killing the first one. Unlike what you might expect, the second name server continues to run; it just isn't listening on any interfaces.

Understanding the BIND Statistics

Periodically, you should look over the statistics on some of your name servers, if only to see how busy they are. We will show you an example of the name server statistics and discuss what each line means. Name servers handle many queries and responses during normal operation, so first, we need to show you what a typical exchange might look like.

Reading the explanations for the statistics is hard without a mental picture of what goes on during a lookup. To help you understand the name server's statistics, Figure 7-2 shows what might go on when an application tries to look up a name. The application, *ftp*, queries a local name server. The local name server had previously looked up data from this domain and knows where the remote name servers are. It queries each of the remote name servers—one of them twice—trying to find the answer. In the meantime, the application times out and sends yet another query, asking for the same information.

Keep in mind that even though a name server has sent a query to a remote name server, the remote name server may not receive the query right away. The query might be delayed or lost by the underlying network, or perhaps the remote name server host might be busy with another application.

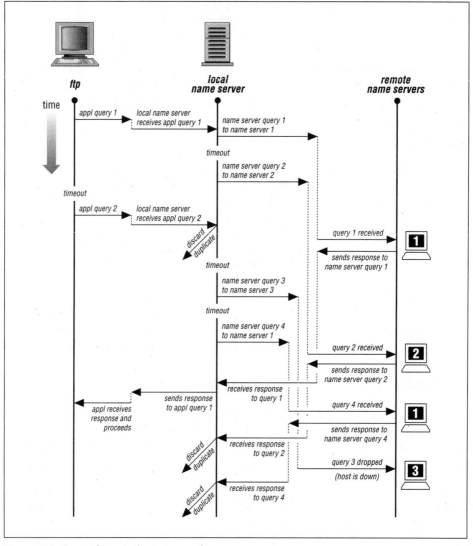

Figure 7-2. Example query/response exchange

Notice that a BIND name server is able to detect duplicate queries only while it is still trying to answer the original query. The local name server detects the duplicate query from the application because the local name server is still working on it. But, remote name server 1 does not detect the duplicate query from the local name server because it answered the previous query. After the local name server receives the first response from remote name server 1, all other responses are discarded as duplicates. This dialog required the following exchanges:

Exchange	Number
Application to local name server	2 queries
Local name server to application	1 response
Local name server to remote name server 1	2 queries
Remote name server 1 to local name server	2 responses
Local name server to remote name server 2	1 query
Remote name server 2 to local name server	1 response
Local name server to remote name server 3	1 query
Remote name server 3 to local name server	0 responses

These exchanges would make the following contributions to the local name server's statistics:

Statistic	Cause
2 queries received	From the application on the local host
1 duplicate query	From the application on the local host
1 answer sent	To the application on the local host
3 responses received	From remote name servers
2 duplicate responses	From remote name servers
2 A queries	Queries for address information

In our example, the local name server received queries only from an application, yet it sent queries to remote name servers. Normally, the local name server would also receive queries from remote name servers (that is, in addition to asking remote servers for information it needs to know, the local server would also be asked by remote servers for information they need to know), but we didn't show any remote queries, for the sake of simplicity.

Now that you've seen a typical exchange between applications and name servers, and the statistics it generated, let's go over a more extensive example of the statistics. To get the statistics from your name server, send the version 4 name server an ABRT signal (on many systems, called IOT):

```
% kill -ABRT `cat /etc/named.pid`
```

Or send a version 8 name server an ILL signal instead of ABRT:

```
% kill -ILL `cat /etc/named.pid`
```

(The process ID is stored in */var/run/named.pid* on an SVR4 filesystem.) Wait a few seconds and look at the file */usr/tmp/named.stats* (or */var/tmp/named.stats*). A version 8 name server leaves the file *named.stats* in its current directory (*/usr/local/ named* in most of our examples). If the statistics are not dumped to this file, your server may not have been compiled with STATS defined and, thus, may not be collecting statistics. Following are the statistics from one of Paul Vixie's name servers. These statistics came from a 4.9.3 name server. An 8.1.2 name server has all of the same items as below except RNotNsQ and the items are arranged in a different order. If your name server is newer than 8.1.2, the statistics may not look at all like those shown here—the BIND statistics may be replaced with the DNS server and resolver MIB extensions defined in RFC 1611 and RFC 1612.

```
+++ Statistics Dump +++ (800708260) Wed May 17 03:57:40 1995
746683    time since boot (secs)
392768    time since reset (secs)
14        Unknown query types
268459    A queries
3044      NS queries
5680      CNAME queries
11364     SOA queries
1008934   PTR queries
44        HINFO queries
680367    MX queries
2369      TXT queries
40        NSAP queries
27        AXFR queries
8336      ANY queries
++ Name Server Statistics ++
(Legend)
        RQ      RR      RIQ     RNXD     RFwdQ
        RFwdR  RDupQ  RDupR  RFail     RFErr
        RErr    RTCP   RAXFR  RLame    ROpts
        SSysQ  SAns   SFwdQ  SFwdR    SDupQ
        SFail   SFErr  SErr   RNotNsQ  SNaAns
        SNXD
(Global)
    1992938 112600 0 19144 63462 60527 194 347 3420 0  5 2235 27 35289 0
    14886 1927930 63462 60527 107169  10025 119 0 1785426 805592  35863
[15.255.72.20]
    485 0 0 0 0  0 0 0 0  0 0 0 0  0 485 0 0 0  0 0 0 0 485  0
[15.255.152.2]
    441 137 0 1 2 108 0 0 0 0  0 0 0 0 0  13 439 85 7 84  0 0 0 0 431  0
[15.255.152.4]
    770 89 0 1 4  69 0 0 0 0  0 0 0 0 0  14 766 68 5 7  0 0 0 0 755  0
...  <lots of entries deleted>
```

Let's look at these statistics one line at a time:

```
746683     time since boot (secs)
```

This is how long the local name server has been running. To convert to days, divide by 86400 (60x60x24, the number of seconds in a day). This server has been running for about 8.5 days.

```
392768     time since reset (secs)
```

This is how long the local name server has run since the last HUP signal—i.e., the last time it loaded its database. You'll probably see this number differ from the time since boot only if the server is a primary master name server for some zone. Name servers that are slaves for a zone automatically pick up new data with zone transfers and are not usually sent HUP signals. Since *this* server has been reset, it is probably a primary master name server for some zone.

```
14         Unknown query types
```

This name server received 14 queries for data of a type the name server didn't recognize. Either someone is experimenting with new types, or there is a defective implementation somewhere.

```
268459     A queries
```

There have been 268459 address lookups. Address queries are normally the most common type of query.

```
3044       NS queries
```

There have been 3044 name server queries. Internally, name servers generate NS queries when they are trying to look up servers for the root domain. Externally, applications like *dig* or *nslookup* can also be used to look up NS records.

```
5680       CNAME queries
```

Some versions of *sendmail* make CNAME queries in order to canonicalize a mail address (replace an alias with the canonical name). Other versions of *sendmail* use ANY queries instead (we'll get to those shortly). Otherwise, the CNAME lookups are most likely from *dig* or *nslookup*.

```
11364      SOA queries
```

SOA queries are made by slave name servers to check if their zone data are current. If the data are not current, an AXFR query follows to cause the zone transfer. Since this set of statistics does show AXFR queries, we can conclude that slave name servers load zone data from this server.

```
1008934    PTR queries
```

The pointer queries map addresses to names. Many kinds of software look up IP addresses: *inetd, rlogind, rshd,* network management software, and network tracing software.

```
  44      HINFO queries
```

The host-information queries are most likely from someone interactively looking up HINFO records.

```
680367   MX queries
```

Mail exchanger queries are made by mailers like *sendmail* as part of the normal electronic mail delivery process.

```
  2369  .  TXT queries
```

Some application must be making text queries for this number to be this large. It might be a tool like *Harvest*, which is an information search and retrieval technology developed at the University of Colorado.

```
  40      NSAP queries
```

This is a relatively new data type used to map domain names to OSI Network Service Access Point addresses.

```
  27      AXFR queries
```

An AXFR query is made by a slave name server to cause a zone transfer.

```
  8336    ANY queries
```

ANY queries request data of any type for a name. This query type is used most often by *sendmail*. Since *sendmail* looks up CNAME, MX, and address records for a mail destination, it will make a query for ANY data type so that all the resource records are cached right away at the local name server.

The rest of the statistics are kept on a per-host basis. If you look over the list of hosts your name server has exchanged packets with, you'll find out just how garrulous your name server is—you'll see hundreds or even thousands of hosts in the list. While the size of the list is impressive, the statistics themselves are only somewhat interesting. We will explain *all* of the statistics, even the ones with zero counts, although you'll probably only find a handful of the statistics useful. To make the statistics easier to read, you'll need a tool to expand the statistics because the output format is rather compact. We wrote a tool, called *bstat*, to do just this. Here's what its output looks like:

```
hpcvsop.cv.hp.com
        485 queries received
        485 responses sent to this name server
        485 queries answered from our cache
relay.hp.com
        441 queries received
        137 responses received
          1 negative response received
          2 queries for data not in our cache or authoritative data
        108 responses from this name server passed to the querier
```

```
 13 system queries sent to this name server
439 responses sent to this name server
 85 queries sent to this name server
  7 responses from other name servers sent to this name server
 84 duplicate queries sent to this name server
431 queries answered from our cache
```
hp.com
```
770 queries received
 89 responses received
  1 negative response received
  4 queries for data not in our cache or authoritative data
 69 responses from this name server passed to the querier
 14 system queries sent to this name server
766 responses sent to this name server
 68 queries sent to this name server
  5 responses from other name servers sent to this name server
  7 duplicate queries sent to this name server
755 queries answered from our cache
```

In the raw statistics (not the *bstat* output), each host IP address is followed by a table of counts. The column heading for this table is the cryptic legend at the beginning. The legend is broken into several lines, but the host statistics are all on a single line. In the following section, we'll explain briefly what each column means as we look at the statistics for one of the hosts this server conversed with—15.255.152.2 (*relay.hp.com*). For the sake of our explanation, we'll first show you the column heading from the legend (e.g., RQ) followed by the count for this column for *relay*.

```
RQ 441
```

RQ is the count of queries received from *relay*. These queries were made because *relay* needed information about a domain served by this name server.

```
RR 137
```

RR is the count of responses received from *relay*. These are responses to queries made from this name server. Don't try to correlate this number to RQ, because they are not related. RQ counts questions *asked* by *relay*; RR counts *answers relay* gave to this name server (because this name server *asked relay* for information).

```
RIQ 0
```

RIQ is the count of inverse queries received from *relay*. Inverse queries were originally intended to map addresses to names, but that function is now handled by PTR records. Older versions of *nslookup* use an inverse query on startup, so you may see a nonzero RIQ count.

```
RNXD 1
```

RNXD is the count of "no such domain" answers received from *relay*.

```
RFwdQ 2
```

RFwdQ is the count of queries received (RQ) from *relay* that needed further processing before they could be answered. This count is much higher for hosts that configure their resolver (with *resolv.conf*) to send all queries to your name server.

```
RFwdR 108
```

RFwdR is the count of responses received (RR) from *relay* that answered the original query and were passed back to the application that made the query.

```
RDupQ 0
```

RDupQ is the count of duplicate queries from *relay*. You'll only see duplicates when the resolver is configured (with *resolv.conf*) to query this name server.

```
RDupR 0
```

RDupR is the count of duplicate responses from *relay*. A response is a duplicate when the name server can no longer find the original query in its list of pending queries that caused the response.

```
RFail 0
```

RFail is the count of SERVFAIL responses from *relay*. A SERVFAIL response indicates some sort of server failure. Server failure responses often occur because the remote server read a db file and found a syntax error. Any queries for data in that zone (the one from the erroneous db file) will result in a server failure answer from the remote name server. This is probably the most common bad response. Server failure responses also occur when the remote name server tries to allocate more memory and can't, or when the remote name server's zone data expire.

```
RFErr 0
```

RFErr is the count of FORMERR responses from *relay*. FORMERR means that the remote name server said the local name server's query had a format error.

```
RErr  0
```

RErr is the count of errors that weren't either SERVFAIL or FORMERR.

```
RTCP  0
```

RTCP is the count of queries received on TCP connections from *relay*. (Most queries use UDP.)

```
RAXFR 0
```

RAXFR is the count of zone transfers initiated. The 0 count indicates that *relay* is not a slave for any zones served by this name server.

```
RLame 0
```

RLame is the count of lame delegations received. If this count is not 0, it means that some zone is delegated to the name server at this IP address, and the name server is not authoritative for the zone.

```
ROpts 0
```

ROpts is the count of packets received with IP options.

```
SSysQ 13
```

SSysQ is the count of system queries sent to *relay*. System queries are queries *initiated* by the local name server. Most system queries will go to root name servers, because system queries are used to keep up-to-date on who the root name servers are. But system queries are also used to find out the address of a name server if the address record timed out before the name server record did. Since *relay* is not a root name server, these queries must have been sent for the latter reason.

```
SAns  439
```

SAns is the count of answers sent to *relay*. This name server answered 439 out of the 441 (RQ) queries *relay* sent to it. I wonder what happened to the 2 queries it didn't answer...

```
SFwdQ 85
```

SFwdQ is the count of queries that were sent (forwarded) to *relay* when the answer was not in this name server's zone data or cache.

```
SFwdR 7
```

SFwdR is the count of responses from some name server that were sent (forwarded) to *relay*.

```
SDupQ 84
```

SDupQ is the count of the duplicate queries sent to *relay*. It's not as bad as it looks, though. The duplicate count is incremented if the query was sent to any other name server first. So, *relay* might have answered all the queries it received the first time it received them, and the query still counted as a duplicate because it was sent to some other name server before *relay*.

```
SFail 0
```

SFail is the count of SERVFAIL responses sent to *relay*.

```
SFErr 0
```

SFErr is the count of FORMERR responses sent to *relay*.

```
SErr  0
```

SErr is the count of *sendto()* system calls that failed when the destination was *relay*.

```
RNotNsQ 0
```

RNotNsQ is the count of queries received that were not from port 53, the name server port. Prior to version 8, all name server queries would come from port 53. Any queries from ports other than 53 came from a resolver. Now, name servers will query from ports other than 53, which makes this statistic useless since you can no longer distinguish resolver queries from name server queries. Hence, version 8 dropped RNotNsQ from its statistics.

```
SNaAns 431
```

SNaAns is the count of nonauthoritative answers sent to *relay*. Out of the 439 answers (SAns) sent to *relay*, 431 were from cached data.

```
SNXD  0
```

SNXD is the count of "no such domain" answers sent to *relay*.

Is this name server "healthy"? How do you know what "healthy" operation is? From this one snapshot, we really couldn't say if the name server is healthy. You have to watch the statistics generated by your server over a period of time to get a feel for what sorts of numbers are normal for your configuration. These numbers will vary markedly among servers, depending on the mix of applications generating lookups, the type of server (primary, slave, caching-only), and the level in the domain tree it is serving.

One thing to watch for in the statistics is how many queries per second your server receives. Take the number of queries received (from the "Global" statistics) and divide by the number of seconds the name server has been running. This server received 1992938 queries in 746683 seconds, or approximately 2.7 queries per second—a pretty busy server. If the number you come up with for your server seems out of line, look at which hosts are making all the queries and decide if it makes sense for them to be making all those queries. At some point you may decide that you need more servers to handle the load; we cover that situation in the next chapter.

8

Growing Your Domain

"What size do you want to be?" it asked.

"Oh, I'm not particular as to size," Alice hastily replied; "only one doesn't like changing so often, you know..."

"Are you content now?" said the Caterpillar.

"Well, I should like to be a little larger, sir, if you wouldn't mind...."

How Many Name Servers?

We set up two name servers in Chapter 4, *Setting Up BIND*. Two servers are as few as you'll ever want to run. Depending on the size of your network, you may need to run many more than just two servers. It is not uncommon to run from five to seven servers, with one of them off-site. How many name servers are enough? You'll have to decide that based on your network. Here are some guidelines to help out:

- Have at least one name server available directly on each network or subnet you have. This removes routers as a point of failure. Make the most of any multihomed hosts you may have, since they're (by definition) attached to more than one network.

- If you have a file server and some diskless nodes, run a name server on the file server to serve this group of machines.

- Run name servers near, but not necessarily on, large time-sharing machines. The users and their processes probably generate a lot of queries, and, as administrators, you will work harder to keep a multiuser host up. But balance their needs against the risk of running a name server—a security-critical server—on a system that lots of people have access to.

- Run one name server off-site. This makes your data available when your network isn't. You might argue that it's useless to look up an address when you can't reach the host. Then again, the off-site name server may be available if your network is reachable, but your other name servers are down. If you have a close relationship with an organization on the Internet—say another university or a business partner—they may consent to run a slave for you.

Figure 8-1 shows a sample topology and a brief analysis to show you how this might work.

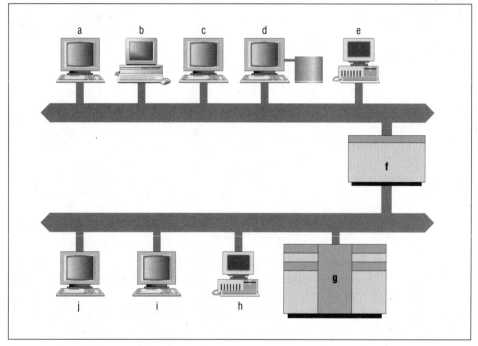

Figure 8-1. Sample network topology

Notice that if you follow our guidelines, there are still a number of places you could choose to run a name server. Host *d*, the file server for hosts *a*, *b*, *c*, and *e*, could run a name server. Host *g*, a big, multiuser host, is another good candidate. But probably the best choice is host *f*, the smaller host with interfaces on both networks. You'll only need to run one name server, instead of two, and it'll run on a closely-watched host. If you want more than one name server on either network, you can also run one on *d* or *g*.

Where Do I Put My Name Servers?

In addition to giving you a rough idea of how many name servers you'll need, these criteria should also help you decide *where* to run name servers (e.g., on file servers, multihomed hosts). But there are other important considerations when choosing the right host.

Other factors to keep in mind are the host's connectivity, the software it runs (BIND and otherwise), and maintaining the homogeneity of your name servers:

Connectivity

It's important that name servers be well connected. Having a name server running on the fastest, most reliable host on your network won't do you any good if the host is mired in some backwater subnet of your network behind a slow, flaky serial line. Try to find a host close to your link to the Internet (if you have one), or find a well-connected Internet host to act as a slave for your zone. And on your own network, try to run name servers near the hubs of your network.

It's doubly important that your primary master name server be well connected. The primary needs good connectivity to all the slaves that update from it, for reliable zone transfers. And, like any name server, it'll benefit from fast, reliable networking.

Software

Another factor to consider in choosing a host for a name server is the software the host runs. Software-wise, the best candidate for a name server is a host running a vendor-supported version of BIND 8.1.2 or 4.9.7 and a robust implementation of TCP/IP (preferably based on 4.3 or 4.4 BSD UNIX's networking—we're Berkeley snobs). You can compile your own 8.1.2 BIND from the sources—it's not hard, and the latest versions are very reliable—but you'll probably have a tough time getting your vendor to support it. If you don't absolutely need a feature of BIND 8.1.2, you may be able to get away with running your vendor's port of older BIND code, like 4.9.4, which will give you the benefit of your vendor's support, for what that's worth.

Homogeneity

One last thing to take into account is the homogeneity of your name servers. As much as you might believe in "open systems," hopping between different versions of UNIX can be frustrating and confusing. Avoid running name servers on lots of different platforms, if you can. You can waste a lot of time porting your scripts (or ours!) from one operating system to another, or looking for the location of *nslookup* or *named.conf* on three different UNIXes. Moreover, different vendors' versions of UNIX tend to support different versions of BIND, which can cause all sorts of frustration. If you need BIND 8.1.2's security features on all your name servers, for example, choose a platform that supports 8.1.2 for all your name servers.

Security

Since you would undoubtedly prefer that hackers not commandeer your name server to assist them in attacking your own hosts or other networks across the Internet, it's important to run your name server on a secure host. Don't run a name server on a big, multiuser system whose users you can't trust. If you have certain computers that are dedicated to hosting network services, but don't permit general logins, those are good candidates for running name servers. If you only have one or a few really secure hosts, consider running the primary master name server on one of those, since its compromise would be more significant than the compromise of the slaves.

Though these are really secondary considerations—it's more important to have a name server on a given subnet than to have it running on the perfect host—do keep these criteria in mind when making a choice.

Capacity Planning

If you have heavily populated networks, or users who do a lot of name-server-intensive work, you may find you need more name servers than we've recommended to handle the load. Or our recommendations may be fine for a little while, but as people add hosts to your nets or install new name-server-intensive programs, you may find your name servers bogged down by queries.

Just which tasks are "name-server-intensive"? Surfing the web can be name-server-intensive. Sending electronic mail, especially to large mailing lists, can be name-server-intensive. Programs that make lots of remote procedure calls to different hosts can be name-server-intensive. Even running certain graphical user environments can tax your name server. X Window-based user environments query the name server to check access lists (among other things).

The astute (and precocious) among you may be asking, "But how do I know when my name servers are overloaded? What do I look for?" An excellent question!

Memory utilization is probably the most important aspect of a name server's operation to monitor. *named* can get very large on a name server that is authoritative for many zones. If *named*'s size, plus the size of the other processes you run, exceeds your real memory, your host may swap furiously ("thrash") and not get anything done. Even if your host has more than enough memory to run all its processes, large name servers are slow to start and slow to spawn new *named* processes (e.g., to handle zone transfers). Another problem: since *named* creates new *named* processes to handle zone transfers, it's quite possible to have more than one *named* process running at one time—one answering queries, and one or more servicing zone transfers. If your master name server already consumes five or ten megabytes of memory, count on two or three times that amount being used occasionally.

Another criterion you can use to measure the load on your name server is the load the name server process places on the host's CPU. Correctly configured name servers don't use much CPU time, so high CPU usage is often symptomatic of a configuration error. Programs like *top* can help you characterize your name server's average CPU utilization. Unfortunately, there are no absolute rules when it comes to acceptable CPU utilization. We offer a rough rule of thumb, though: 5% average CPU utilization is probably acceptable; 10% is a bit high, unless the host is dedicated to providing name service.[*]

To get an idea of what normal figures are, here's what *top* might show for a relatively quiet name server:

```
last pid: 14299; load averages: 0.11, 0.12, 0.12        18:19:08
68 processes: 64 sleeping, 3 running, 1 stopped
Cpu states: 11.3% usr, 0.0% nice, 15.3% sys, 73.4% idle, 0.0% intr, 0.0% ker
Memory: Real: 8208K/13168K act/tot Virtual: 16432K/30736K act/tot Free: 4224K


  PID USERNAME PRI NICE   SIZE  RES STATE  TIME  WCPU    CPU COMMAND
   89 root       1    0  2968K 2652K sleep  5:01  0.00%  0.00% named
```

Okay, that's *really* quiet. Here's what *top* shows on a busy (though not overloaded) name server:

```
load averages: 0.30, 0.46, 0.44                 system: relay 16:12:20
39 processes: 38 sleeping, 1 waiting
Cpu states: 4.4% user, 0.0% nice, 5.4% system, 90.2% idle, 0.0% unk5, 0.0% unk6,
0.0% unk7, 0.0% unk8
Memory: 31126K (28606K) real, 33090K (28812K) virtual, 54344K free Screen #1/3


   PID USERNAME PRI NICE  SIZE  RES  STATE   TIME  WCPU   CPU  COMMAND
 21910 root       1    0 2624K 2616K sleep 146:21  0.00% 1.42% /etc/named
```

Another statistic to look at is the number of queries the name server receives per minute (or second, if you have a busy name server). Again, there are no absolutes here: an HP9000 K460 can handle hundreds of queries per second without breaking into a sweat, while a 386 PC might have problems with more than a few queries a second.

To check the volume of queries your name server is receiving, it's easiest to look at the name server's internal statistics, which you can configure the server to write to

---

[*] *top* is a very handy program, written by Bill LeFebvre, that gives you a continuous report of which processes are sucking up the most CPU time on your host. The most recent version of *top* is available via anonymous *ftp* from *eecs.nwu.edu* as */pub/top/top-3.4.tar.Z.*

syslog at regular intervals.* For example, you could configure your name server to dump statistics every hour (actually, that's the default for BIND 8 servers), and compare the number of queries received between hours:

```
options {
        statistics-interval 60;
};
```

You should pay special attention to peak periods. Monday morning is often busy, because many people like to respond to mail they've received over the weekend first thing on Mondays.

You might also want to take a sample starting just after lunch, when people are returning to their desks and getting back to work—all at about the same time. Of course, if your organization is spread across several time zones, you'll have to use your own good judgment to determine a busy time.

Here's a snippet from the *syslog* file on a BIND 8.1.2 name server:[†]

```
    Apr 22 07:40:37 denver named[150]: NSTATS 830180437 829791665 A=131686
    PTR=8554 MX=187 ANY=339
Apr 22 07:40:37 denver named[150]: XSTATS 830180437 829791665 RQ=140766
RR=4111 RIQ=0 RNXD=2045 RFwdQ=3671 RFwdR=3839 RDupQ=0 RDupR=7 RFail=0
RFErr=0 RErr=0 RTCP=0 RAXFR=0 RLame=0 ROpts=0 SSysQ=285 SAns=137097
SFwdQ=3671 SFwdR=3839 SDupQ=92 SFail=4 SFErr=0 SErr=0 RNotNsQ=140721
SNaAns=7728 SNXD=55787
    Apr 22 08:40:37 denver named[150]: NSTATS 830184037 829791665 A=132968
    PTR=8633 MX=187 ANY=342
Apr 22 08:40:37 denver named[150]: XSTATS 830184037 829791665 RQ=142130
RR=4144 RIQ=0 RNXD=2062 RFwdQ=3698 RFwdR=3870 RDupQ=0 RDupR=7 RFail=0
RFErr=0 RErr=0 RTCP=0 RAXFR=0 RLame=0 ROpts=0 SSysQ=287 SAns=138434
SFwdQ=3698 SFwdR=3870 SDupQ=92 SFail=4 SFErr=0 SErr=0 RNotNsQ=142085
SNaAns=7778 SNXD=56284
```

The number of queries received is dumped in the *RQ* field (in bold). To calculate the number of queries received in the hour, just subtract the first *RQ* value from the second one: 142130 − 140766 = 1364.

Even if your host is fast enough to handle the number of queries it receives, you should make sure the DNS traffic isn't placing undue load on your network. On most LANs, DNS traffic will be too small a proportion of the network's bandwidth to worry about. Over slow leased lines or dial-up connections, though, DNS traffic could consume enough bandwidth to merit concern.

---

* Some older BIND name servers needed coercion to dump their statistics: the ABRT signal (IOT on older systems). BIND 4.9 name servers automatically dumped stats every hour, but 4.9.4 and later name servers, once again, need to be coerced with ABRT.

† On a 4.9.4 through 4.9.7 server, you could dump stats like these to the *named.stats* file by sending *named* a SIGABRT, then move *named.stats* to another filename, wait an hour (with *sleep 3600*, for example), then send SIGABRT again.

To get a rough estimate of the volume of DNS traffic on your LAN, multiply the number of queries received (RQ) plus the number of answers sent (SAns) in an hour by 800 bits (100 bytes, a rough average size for a DNS packet), and divide by 3600 (seconds per hour) to find the bandwidth utilized. This should give you a feeling for how much of your network's bandwidth is being consumed by DNS traffic.[*]

To give you an idea of what's normal, the last NSFNET traffic report (in April, 1995) showed that DNS traffic constituted just over 5% of the total traffic volume (in bytes) on their backbone. The NSFNET's figures are based upon actual traffic sampling, not calculations like ours using the name server's statistics.[†] If you want to get a more accurate idea of the traffic your name server is receiving, you can always do your own traffic sampling with a LAN protocol analyzer.

Once you've found that your name servers are overworked, what then? First, it's a good idea to make sure that your name servers aren't being bombarded with queries by a misbehaving program. To do that, you'll need to find out where all the queries are coming from.

If you're running a BIND 4.9 or 8.1.2 name server, you can find out which resolvers and name servers are querying your name server just by dumping the statistics. A modern server keeps statistics on a host-by-host basis, which is really useful in tracking down heavy users of your name server. For example, take these statistics:

```
+++ Statistics Dump +++ (829373099) Fri Apr 12 23:24:59 1996
970779    time since boot (secs)
471621    time since reset (secs)
0     Unknown query types
185108    A queries
6     NS queries
69213    PTR queries
669     MX queries
2361     ANY queries
++ Name Server Statistics ++
(Legend)
    RQ       RR      RIQ     RNXD      RFwdQ
    RFwdR    RDupQ   RDupR   RFail     RFErr
    RErr     RTCP    RAXFR   RLame     ROpts
    SSysQ    SAns    SFwdQ   SFwdR     SDupQ
    SFail    SFErr   SErr    RNotNsQ   SNaAns
    SNXD
(Global)
    257357 20718 0 8509 19677  19939 1494 21 0 0  0 7 0 1 0
    824 236196 19677 19939 7643  33 0 0 256064 49269  155030
```

---

[*] For a nice package that automates the analysis of BIND's statistics, look for Nigel Campbell's *bindgraph* in the DNS Resources Directory's tools page, URL *http://www.dns.net/dnsrd/tools.html.*

[†] We're not sure how representative of the current state of the Internet these numbers are, but it's extremely difficult to wheedle equivalent numbers out of the commercial backbone providers that succeeded the NSFNET.

```
      [15.17.232.4]
        8736 0 0 0 717  24 0 0 0 0  0 0 0 0 0  0 8019 0 717 0
        0 0 0 8736 2141  5722
      [15.17.232.5]
        115 0 0 0 8  0 21 0 0 0  0 0 0 0 0  0 86 0 1 0  0 0 0 115 0  7
      [15.17.232.8]
        66215 0 0 0 6910  148 633 0 0 0  0 5 0 0 0  0 58671 0 6695 0
        15 0 0 66215 33697  6541
      [15.17.232.16]
        31848 0 0 0 3593  209 74 0 0 0  0 0 0 0 0  0 28185 0 3563 0
        0 0 0 31848 8695  15359
      [15.17.232.20]
        272 0 0 0 0  0 0 0 0 0  0 0 0 0 0  0 272 0 0 0  0 0 0 272 7  0
      [15.17.232.21]
        316 0 0 0 52  14 3 0 0 0  0 0 0 0 0  0 261 0 51 0  0 0 0 316 30  30
      [15.17.232.24]
        853 0 0 0 65  1 3 0 0 0  0 2 0 0 0  0 783 0 64 0  0 0 0 853 125  337
      [15.17.232.33]
        624 0 0 0 47  1 0 0 0 0  0 0 0 0 0  0 577 0 47 0  0 0 0 624 2  217
      [15.17.232.94]
        127640 0 0 0 1751  14 449 0 0 0  0 0 0 0 0  0 125440 0 1602 0
        0 0 0 127640 106  124661
      [15.17.232.95]
        846 0 0 0 38  1 0 0 0 0  0 0 0 0 0  0 809 0 37 0  0 0 0 846 79  81
      -- Name Server Statistics --
      --- Statistics Dump --- (829373099) Fri Apr 12 23:24:59 1996
```

Each host is broken out, after the *Global* entry, by IP address, in brackets. Looking at the legend, you can see that the first field in each record is RQ, or queries received. That gives us a very good reason to go look at the hosts 15.17.232.8, 15.17.232.16, and 15.17.232.94, which appear to be responsible for about 88% of our queries.

If you're running an older name server, the only way to find out which resolvers and name servers are sending all those darned queries is to turn on name server debugging. (We'll cover this in depth in Chapter 12, *Reading BIND Debugging Output.*) All you're really interested in is the source IP addresses of the queries your name server is receiving. When poring over the debugging output, look for hosts sending repeated queries, especially for the same or similar information. That may indicate a misconfigured or buggy program running on the host, or a foreign name server pelting your name server with queries.

If all the queries appear to be legitimate, add a new name server. Don't put the name server just anywhere, though; use the information from the debugging output to help you decide where best to run one. In cases where DNS traffic is gobbling up your Ethernet, it won't help to choose a host at random and create a name server there. You need to consider which hosts are sending all the queries, then figure out how to best provide them name service. Here are some hints to help you decide:

- Look for queries from resolvers on hosts that share the same file server. You could run a name server on the file server.

- Look for queries from resolvers on large, multiuser hosts. You could run a name server there.

- Look for queries from resolvers on another subnet. Those resolvers should be configured to query a name server on their local subnet. If there isn't one on that subnet, create one.

- Look for queries from resolvers on the same bridged segment (assuming you use bridging). If you run a name server on the bridged segment, the traffic won't need to be bridged to the rest of the network.

- Look for queries from hosts connected to each other via another, lightly loaded network. You could run a name server on the other network.

Adding More Name Servers

When you need to create new name servers for your domain, the simplest recourse is to add slaves. You already know how—we went over it in Chapter 4—and once you've set one slave up, cloning it is a piece of cake. But you can run into trouble indiscriminately adding slaves.

If you run a large number of slave servers for a zone, the primary master name server can take quite a beating just keeping up with the slaves' polling to check that their data are current. There are a number of courses of action to take for this problem:

- Make more primary master name servers.

- Increase the refresh interval so that the slaves don't check so often.

- Direct some of the slave name servers to load from other slave name servers.

- Create caching-only name servers (described later).

- Create "partial-slave" name servers (also described later).

Primary Master and Slave Servers

Creating more primaries will mean extra work for you, since you have to keep the db files synchronized manually. Whether or not this is preferable to your other alternatives is your call. You can use tools like *rdist* to simplify the process of distributing the files. A *distfile* to synchronize files between primaries might be as simple as the following[*]

---

[*] The file *rdist* reads to find out which files to update.

```
dup-primary:

# copy named.boot file to dup'd primary

/etc/named.conf  -> wormhole
    install ;

# copy contents of /usr/local/named (db files, etc.) to dup'd primary

/usr/local/named -> wormhole
    install ;
```

or for multiple primaries:

```
dup-primary:

primaries =  ( wormhole carrie )
/etc/named.conf  -> {$primaries}
    install ;

/usr/local/named -> {$primaries}
    install ;
```

You can even have *rdist* trigger your name server's reload using the *special* option by adding lines like:

```
special /usr/local/named/* "kill -HUP `cat /etc/named.pid`" ;
special /etc/named.conf "kill -HUP `cat /etc/named.pid`" ;
```

These tell *rdist* to execute the quoted command if any of the files change.

Increasing your name servers' refresh interval is another option. This slows down the propagation of new information, however. In some cases, this is not a problem. If you rebuild your DNS data with *h2n* only once each day at 1 a.m. (run from *cron*) and then allow six hours for the data to distribute, all the slaves will be current by 7 a.m.[*] That may be acceptable to your user population. See the section called "Changing Other SOA Values" later in this chapter for more detail.

You can even have some of your slaves load from other slaves. Slave name servers *can* load zone data from other slave name servers instead of loading from a primary name server. The slave name server can't tell if it is loading from a primary or another slave. It's only important that the name server serving the zone transfer is authoritative for the zone. There's no trick to configuring this. Instead of specifying the IP address of the primary in the slave's conf file, you simply specify the IP address of another slave.

Here are the contents of the file *named.conf*:

---

[*] And, of course, if you're using BIND 8's NOTIFY, they'll catch up much sooner than that.

```
// this slave updates from wormhole, another
// slave
zone "movie.edu" {
            type slave;
            file "db.movie";
            masters { 192.249.249.1; };
};
```

For a BIND 4 server, this would look slightly different.

Here are the contents of the file *named.boot*:

```
; this slave updates from wormhole, another slave
secondary   movie.edu   192.249.249.1   db.movie
```

When you go to this second level of distribution, though, it can take up to twice as long for the data to percolate from the primary name server to all the slaves. Remember that the *refresh interval* is the period after which the slave servers will check to make sure that their zone data are still current. Therefore, it can take the first-level slave servers the entire refresh interval before they get their copy of the zone files from the primary master server. Similarly, it can take the second-level slave servers the entire refresh interval to get their copy of the files from the first-level slave servers. The propagation time from the primary master server to all of the slave servers can therefore be twice the refresh interval.

One way to avoid this to use BIND 8's NOTIFY feature. This is on by default, and will trigger zone transfers soon after the zone is updated on the primary master. Unfortunately, it only works on version 8 BIND slaves.[*]

If you decide to configure your network with two (or more) tiers of slave servers, be careful to avoid updating loops. If we were to configure *wormhole* to update from *diehard*, and then we accidentally configured *diehard* to update from *wormhole*, neither would ever get data from the primary. They would merely check their out-of-date serial numbers against each other, and perpetually decide that they were both up-to-date.

Caching-Only Servers

Creating *caching-only name servers* is another alternative when you need more servers. Caching-only name servers are name servers not authoritative for any domains (except *0.0.127.in-addr.arpa*). The name doesn't imply that primary and slave name servers don't cache—they do. The name means that the *only* function this server performs is looking up data and caching them. As with primary and slave name servers, a caching-only name server needs a *db.cache* file and a *db.127.0.0* file. The *named.conf* file for a caching-only server contains these lines:

---

[*] And, incidentally, on the Microsoft DNS Server.

```
options {
          directory "/usr/local/named";
// or your data directory
};

zone "0.0.127.in-addr.arpa" {
          type master;
          file "db.127.0.0";
};

zone "." {
          type hint;
          file "db.cache";
};
```

On a BIND 4 server, the *named.boot* file looks like this:

```
directory /usr/local/named   ; or your data directory

primary 0.0.127.in-addr.arpa  db.127.0.0  ; for loopback address
cache   .                     db.cache
```

A caching-only name server can look up names inside and outside your zone, as can primary and slave name servers. The difference is that when a caching-only name server initially looks up a name within your zone, it ends up asking one of the primary or slave name servers for your zone for the answer. A primary or slave would answer the same question out of its authoritative data. Which primary or slave does the caching-only server ask? As with name servers outside of your domain, it finds out which name servers serve your zone from the name server for your parent zone. Is there any way to prime a caching-only name server's cache so it knows which hosts run primary and slave name servers for your zone? No, there isn't. You can't use *db.cache*—the *db.cache* file is only for *root* name server hints.

A caching-only name server's real value comes after it builds up its cache. Each time it queries an authoritative name server and receives an answer, it caches the records in the answer. Over time, the cache will grow to include the information most often requested by the resolvers querying the caching-only name server. And you avoid the overhead of zone transfers—a caching-only name server doesn't need to do them.

Partial-Slave Servers

In between a caching-only name server and a slave name server is another variation: a name server that is a slave for only a few of the local zones. We call this a *partial-slave name server* (and probably nobody else does). Suppose *movie.edu* had twenty class C networks (and a corresponding twenty *in-addr.arpa* zones). Instead of creating a slave server for all 21 zones (all the *in-addr.arpa* subdomains plus *movie.edu*), we could create a partial-slave server for *movie.edu* and only those *in-*

addr.arpa zones the host itself is in. If the host had two network interfaces, then its name server would be a slave for three zones: *movie.edu* and the two *in-addr.arpa* zones.

Let's say we scare up the hardware for another name server. We'll call the new host *zardoz.movie.edu*, with IP addresses 192.249.249.9 and 192.253.253.9. We'll create a partial-slave name server on *zardoz*, with this *named.conf* file:

```
options {
                directory "/usr/local/named";
};

zone "movie.edu" {
                type slave;
                file "db.movie";
                masters { 192.249.249.3; };
};

zone "249.249.192.in-addr.arpa" {
                type slave;
                file "db.192.249.249";
                masters { 192.249.249.3; };
};

zone "253.253.192.in-addr.arpa" {
                type slave;
                file "db.192.253.253";
                masters { 192.249.249.3; };
};

zone "0.0.127.in-addr.arpa";
                type master;
                file "db.127.0.0";
};

zone "." {
                type hint;
                file "db.cache";
};
```

For a BIND 4 server, the *named.boot* file would look like this:

```
directory    /usr/local/named
secondary    movie.edu                      192.249.249.3 db.movie
secondary    249.249.192.in-addr.arpa 192.249.249.3 db.192.249.249
secondary    253.253.192.in-addr.arpa 192.249.249.3 db.192.253.253
primary      0.0.127.in-addr.arpa         db.127.0.0
cache        .                              db.cache
```

This server is a slave for *movie.edu* and only two of the 20 *in-addr.arpa* zones. A "full" slave would have 21 different *zone* statements in *named.conf.*

What's so useful about a partial-slave name server? They're not much work to administer, because their *named.conf* files don't change much. On a server authoritative for all the *in-addr.arpa* zones, we'd need to add and delete *in-addr.arpa* zones (and their corresponding entries in *named.conf*) as our network changed. That can be a surprising amount of work on a large network.

A partial slave can still answer most of the queries it receives, though. Most of these queries will be for data in the *movie.edu* and two *in-addr.arpa* zones. Why? Because most of the hosts querying the name server are on the two networks it's connected to, 192.249.249 and 192.253.253. And those hosts probably communicate primarily with other hosts on their own network. This generates queries for data within the *in-addr.arpa* zone that corresponds to the local network.

Registering Name Servers

When you get around to setting up more and more name servers, a question may strike you—must I register *all* of my primary and slave name servers with my parent zone? No, only those servers you want to make available to servers outside of your zone need to be registered with the parent. For instance, if you run nine name servers for your zone, you may choose to tell the parent zone about only four of them. Within your zone, all nine servers are used. Five of those nine servers, however, are only queried by resolvers on hosts that are configured to query them (in *resolv.conf,* for example). Their parent name servers will never delegate to them, since they're not registered in the domain name space. Only the four servers registered with your parent zone are queried by other name servers, including caching-only and partial-slave name servers within your domain. This setup is shown in Figure 8-2.

Besides being able to pick and choose which of your name servers are hammered by outside queries, there's a technical motivation for registering only some of your zone's name servers: there is a limit to how many servers will fit in a UDP response packet. In practice, around ten name server records should fit. Depending on the data (how many servers are in the same domain), you could get more or fewer.[*] There's not much point in registering more than ten servers, anyway—if none of the ten servers can be reached, it's unlikely the destination host can be reached.

If you've set up a new authoritative name server, and you decide it should be registered, make a list of the parents of the zones it's authoritative for. You'll need to contact the administrators for each of these parent zones. For example, let's say we want to register the name server we set up on *zardoz* above. In order to get this slave registered in all the right zones, we'll need to contact the administrators of *edu*

---

[*] The domain names of the Internet's root name servers were changed because of this. All of the roots were moved into the same domain, *root-servers.net,* to take the most advantage of domain name compression and store as many roots as possible in a single UDP packet.

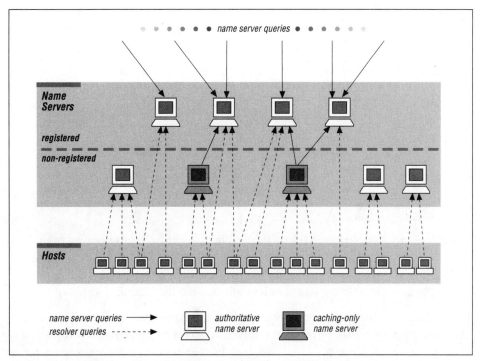

Figure 8-2. Registering only some of your name servers

and *in-addr.arpa*. (For help determining who runs your parent zones, turn back to Chapter 3, *Where Do I Start?*)

When you contact the administrators of a parent zone, be sure to fill out the form they specify (if any) on their web site. If there's no standard form, give them the domain name of the zone the new name server is authoritative for. If the new name server is in the new zone, you'll also need to give them the IP address(es) of the new name server. In fact, if there's no official format for submitting the information, it's often best just to send your parent the complete list of registered name servers for the zone, plus any addresses necessary, in data file format. That avoids any potential confusion.

Since our networks were originally assigned by the InterNIC, we submitted the form at *http://www.arin.net/templates/inaddrtemplate.txt* to *hostmaster@arin.net*, per their web site, to change our registration. If they hadn't had a template for us to use, our message to the administrator of *in-addr.arpa* might have read something like this:

```
Howdy!

I've just set up a new slave name server on
zardoz.movie.edu for the 249.249.192.in-addr.arpa
```

```
and 253.253.192.in-addr.arpa zones.  Would you
please add NS records for this name server to the
in-addr.arpa zone?  That would make our delegation
information look like:

253.253.192.in-addr.arpa. 86400 IN NS terminator.movie.edu.
253.253.192.in-addr.arpa. 86400 IN NS wormhole.movie.edu.
253.253.192.in-addr.arpa. 86400 IN NS zardoz.movie.edu.

249.249.192.in-addr.arpa. 86400 IN NS terminator.movie.edu.
249.249.192.in-addr.arpa. 86400 IN NS wormhole.movie.edu.
249.249.192.in-addr.arpa. 86400 IN NS zardoz.movie.edu.

Thanks!

Albert LeDomaine
al@robocop.movie.edu
```

Notice we specified explicit TTLs on the NS and A records? That's because our parent name servers aren't authoritative for those records; *our* name servers are. By including them, we're indicating our choice of a TTL for our zone's delegation. Of course, our parent may have other ideas about what the TTL should be.

In this case, glue data—A records for each of the name servers—aren't necessary, since the domain names of the name servers aren't within the *in-addr.arpa* zones. They're within *movie.edu*, so a name server that was referred to *terminator* or *wormhole* could still find their addresses by following delegation to the *movie.edu* name servers.

Is a partial-slave name server a good name server to register with your parent zone? Actually, it's not *ideal*, because it's only authoritative for *some* of your *in-addr.arpa* zones. Administratively, it may be easier to register only servers backing up *all* the local zones; that way, you don't need to keep track of which name servers are authoritative for which zones. All of your parent zones can delegate to the same set of name servers: your primary and your "full" slaves.

If you don't have many name servers, though, or if you're good at remembering which name servers are authoritative for what, go ahead and register a partial-slave.

Caching-only name servers, on the other hand, must *never* be registered. A caching-only name server rarely has complete information for any given zone, just the bits and pieces of it that it has looked up recently. If a parent name server were mistakenly to refer a foreign name server to a caching-only name server, the foreign name server would send the caching-only name server a nonrecursive query. The caching-only name server might have the data cached, but then again, it might not. If it didn't have the data, it would refer the querier to the best name servers it knew (those closest to the domain in the query)—which might include the caching-only name server itself! The poor foreign name server might never get an answer. This kind of misconfiguration—actually, delegating a zone to any name server not authoritative for that zone—is known as *lame delegation.*

Changing TTLs

An experienced domain administrator needs to know how to set the time to live on his zone's data to his best advantage. The TTL on a resource record, remember, is the time in seconds any server can cache that record. So if the TTL for a particular resource record is 3600 (seconds), and a server outside your domain caches that record, it will have to remove the entry from its cache after an hour. If it needs the same data after the hour is up, it'll have to query your name servers again.

When we introduced TTLs, we emphasized that your choice of a TTL would dictate how current you'd keep copies of your data, at the cost of increased load on your name servers. A low TTL would mean that name servers outside your domain would have to get data from your name servers often, and would therefore keep current. On the other hand, your name servers would be peppered by their queries.

You don't *have* to choose a TTL once and for all, though. You can—and experienced administrators do—change TTLs periodically to suit your needs.

Suppose we know that one of our hosts is about to be moved to another network. This host is the *movie.edu* film library. It houses a large collection of files our site makes available to hosts on the Internet. During normal operation, outside name servers cache the address of our host according to the minimum TTL in the SOA record. (We set the *movie.edu* TTL to be one day in our sample files.) A name server caching the old address record just before the change could have the wrong address for as long as a day. A loss of connectivity for a day is unacceptable, though. What can we do to minimize the loss of connectivity? We can lower the TTL, so that outside servers cache the address record for a shorter period. By reducing the TTL, we force the outside servers to update their data more frequently, which means that any changes we make when we actually move the system will be propagated to the outside world quickly. How long can we make the TTL? Unfortunately, we can't use a TTL of zero, which should mean "don't cache this record at all." Some older BIND 4 name servers can't return records with a TTL of zero, instead returning null answers or SERVFAIL errors. Small TTLs, like 30 seconds, are okay, though. The easiest change is to lower the TTL in the SOA record in the *db.movie* file. If you don't place an explicit TTL on resource records in the db files, the name server applies this *minimum* TTL from the SOA record to each resource record. If you lower the minimum TTL field, though, the new, lower TTL applies to all addresses, not just the address of the host being moved. The drawback to this approach is that your name server will be answering a lot more queries, since the querying servers will cache *all* the data in your zone for a shorter period. A better alternative is to put a different TTL only on the affected address record.

To add an explicit TTL on an individual resource record, place it before the IN in the class field. The TTL value is in seconds. Here's an example of an explicit TTL from *db.movie*:

```
cujo  3600 IN  A   192.253.253.5  ; explicit TTL of 1 hour
```

If you're observant, you may have noticed a potential problem: the explicit TTL on *cujo*'s address is 3600 seconds, but the TTL field in the SOA record—ostensibly the *minimum* TTL for the zone—is *higher*. Which takes precedence?

If BIND followed the DNS RFCs, the TTL field in the SOA record would really define the minimum TTL value for all resource records in the zone. Thus, you could only specify explicit TTLs larger than this minimum. BIND name servers don't work this way, though. In other words, in BIND, "minimum" is not really minimum. Instead, BIND implements the minimum TTL field in the SOA record as a "default" TTL. If there is no TTL on a record, the minimum applies. If there is a TTL on the resource record, BIND allows it even if it is smaller than the minimum. That one record is sent out in responses with the smaller TTL, while all other records are sent out with the "minimum" TTL from the SOA record.

You should also know that when giving out answers, a slave supplies the same TTL a primary does—that is, if a primary gives out a TTL of 86400 for a particular record, a slave will, too. The slave doesn't decrement the TTL according to how long it has been since it loaded the zone. So, if the TTL of a single resource record is set smaller than the SOA minimum, both the primary and slave name servers give out the resource record with the same, smaller TTL. If the slave name server has reached the expiration time for the zone, it expires the whole zone. It will never expire an individual resource record within a zone.

So BIND does allow you to put a small TTL on an individual resource record if you know that the data is going to change shortly. Thus, any server caching that data only caches it for a brief time. Unfortunately, while BIND makes tagging records with a small TTL possible, most domain administrators don't spend the time to do it. When a host changes address, you often lose connectivity to it for a while.

More often than not, the host having its address changed is not one of the main hubs on the site, so the outage impacts few people. If one of the mail hubs or a major *ftp* repository—like the film library—is moving, though, a day's loss of connectivity may be unacceptable. In cases like this, the domain administrator should plan ahead and reduce the TTL on the data to be changed.

Remember that the TTL on the affected data will need to be lowered *before* the change takes place. Reducing the TTL on a workstation's address record and changing the workstation's address simultaneously may do you little or no good; the address record may have been cached minutes before you made the change, and may linger until the old TTL times out. *And* be sure to factor in the time it'll take your slaves to load from your primary. For example, if your minimum TTL is 12 hours, and your refresh interval is 3 hours, be sure to lower the TTLs at least 15 hours ahead of time, so that by the time you move the host, all the long TTL records will have timed out. Of course, if all of your slaves are BIND 8 servers that use NOTIFY, the slaves shouldn't take the full refresh interval to synch up.

Changing Other SOA Values

We briefly mentioned increasing the refresh interval as a way of offloading your primary name server. Let's discuss refresh in a little more detail and go over the remaining SOA values, too.

The *refresh* value, you'll remember, controls how often a slave checks whether its data is up-to-date. The *retry* value then becomes the refresh time after the first failure to reach a master name server. The *expire* value determines how long data can be held before it's discarded, when a master is unreachable. Finally, the *minimum* TTL sets how long domain information may be cached.

Suppose we've decided we want the slaves to pick up new information every hour instead of every three hours. We change the refresh value to 3600 in each of the db files (or with the *-o* option to *h2n*). Since the retry is related to refresh, we should probably reduce retry, too—to every 15 minutes or so. Typically, the retry is less than the refresh, but that's not required.[*] Although lowering the refresh value will speed up the distribution of data, it will also increase the load on the server being loaded from since the slaves will check more often. The added load isn't much, though; each slave makes a single SOA query during each zone's refresh interval to check its master's copy of the zone. So with two slave name servers, changing the refresh time from three hours to one hour will only generate four more queries (per zone) to the primary in any three-hour span.

If all of your slaves run BIND 8 and you use NOTIFY, of course, refresh doesn't mean as much. But if you have even one BIND 4 slave, your zone data will take up to the refresh interval to reach it.

Some older versions of BIND slaves stopped answering queries during a zone load. As a result, BIND was modified to spread out the zone loads, reducing the periods of unavailability. So, even if you set a low refresh interval, your slaves may not check exactly as often as you request. BIND name servers attempt a certain number of zone loads and then wait 15 minutes before trying another batch. On the other hand,

---

[*] Actually, BIND 8 servers will warn you if refresh is set to less than ten times the retry interval.

BIND 4.9 and later may also refresh *more often* than the refresh interval. These newer BINDs will wait a random number of seconds between one-half the refresh interval and the full refresh interval to check serial numbers.

Expiration times on the order of a week are common—longer if you frequently have problems reaching your updating source. The expiration time should always be much larger than the retry and refresh interval; if the expire time is smaller than the refresh interval, your slaves will expire their data before trying to load new data. BIND 8 will complain if you set an expire time less than refresh plus retry, less than twice retry, less than seven days or greater than six months. Choosing an expire time that meets all BIND 8's criteria is a good idea in most situations.

If your data don't change much, you might consider raising the minimum TTL. The SOA's minimum TTL value is typically one day (86400 seconds), but you can make it longer. One week is about the longest value that makes sense for a TTL. Longer than that and you may find yourself unable to change bad, cached data in a reasonable amount of time.

Planning for Disasters

It's a fact of life on a network that things go wrong. Hardware fails, software has bugs, and people very occasionally make mistakes. Sometimes this results in minor inconvenience, like having a few users lose connections. Sometimes the results are catastrophic and involve the loss of important data and valuable jobs.

Because the Domain Name System relies so heavily on the network, it is vulnerable to network outages. Thankfully, the design of DNS takes into account the imperfection of networks: it allows for multiple, redundant name servers, retransmission of queries, retrying zone transfers, and so on.

The Domain Name System doesn't protect itself from every conceivable calamity, though. There are types of network failure—some of them quite common—that DNS doesn't or can't protect against. But with a small investment of time and money, you can minimize the threat of these outages.

Outages

Power outages, for example, are relatively common in many parts of the world. In some parts of the U.S., thunderstorms or tornadoes may cause a site to lose power, or to have only intermittent power, for an extended period. Elsewhere, typhoons, volcanoes, or construction work may interrupt your electrical service.

If all your hosts are down, of course, you don't need name service. Quite often, however, sites have problems when power is *restored*. Following our recommendations, they run their name servers on file servers and big multiuser machines. And when the power comes up, those machines are naturally the last to boot—because all those disks need to be *fsck*ed first! Which means that all the hosts on-site that are quick to boot do so without the benefit of name service.

This can cause all sorts of wonderful problems, depending on how your hosts' startup files are written. UNIX hosts often execute some variant of:

```
/etc/ifconfig lan0 inet `hostname` netmask 255.255.128.0 up
/etc/route add default site-router 1
```

to bring up their network interface. Using host names in the commands (`` `hostname` `` expands to the local host name and **site-router** is the name of the local router) is admirable for two reasons:

- It lets the administrators change the router's IP address without changing all the startup files on-site.
- It lets the administrators change the host's IP address by changing the IP address in only one file.

Unfortunately, the *route* command will fail without name service. The *ifconfig* command will fail only if the localhost's name and IP address don't appear in the host's */etc/hosts* file, so it's a good idea to leave at least that data in each host's */etc/hosts*.

By the time the startup sequence reaches the *route* command, the network interface will be up, and the host will use name service to map the name of the router to an IP address. And since the host has no default route until the *route* command is executed, the only name servers it can reach are those on the local subnet.

If the booting host can reach a working name server on its local subnet, it can execute the *route* command successfully. Quite often, however, one or more of the name servers it can reach aren't yet running. What happens then depends on the contents of *resolv.conf*.

In BIND 4.9 and BIND 8, the resolver will only fall back to the host table if there is only one name server listed in *resolv.conf* (or if no name server is listed, and the resolver defaults to using a name server on the local host). If only one name server is configured, the resolver will query it, and if the network returns an error each time the resolver sends a query, the resolver will fall back to searching the host table. The errors that cause the resolver to fall back include:

- Receipt of an ICMP **port unreachable** message
- Receipt of an ICMP **network unreachable** message

- Inability to send the UDP packet (e.g., because networking is not yet running on the local host)[*]

If the host running the one configured name server isn't running at all, though, the resolver won't receive any errors. The name server is effectively a black hole. After about 75 seconds of trying, the resolver will just time out and return a null answer to the application that called it. Only if the name server host has actually started networking—but not yet started the name server—will the resolver get an error: an ICMP port unreachable message.

Overall, the single name server configuration does work if you have name servers available on each net, but perhaps not as elegantly as we might like. If the local name server hasn't come up when a host on its network reboots, the *route* command will fail.

This may seem awkward, but it's not nearly as bad as what happens with multiple servers. With multiple servers listed in *resolv.conf,* BIND *never* falls back to the host table after the primary network interface has been *ifconfig*ed. The resolver simply loops through the name servers, querying them until one answers or the 75-plus second timeout is reached.

This is especially problematic during bootup. If none of the configured name servers are available, the resolver will time out without returning an IP address, and adding the default route will fail.

Recommendations

Our recommendation, as primitive as it sounds, is to hardcode the IP address of the default router into the startup file, or to use an external file (many systems use */etc/defaultrouter*). This will ensure that your host's networking will start correctly.

An alternative is to list just a single, reliable name server on your host's local net in *resolv.conf.* This will allow you to use the name of the default router in the startup file, as long as you make sure that the router's name appears in */etc/hosts* (in case your reliable name server isn't running when the host reboots). Of course, if the host running the reliable name server isn't running when your host reboots, all bets are off. You won't fall back to */etc/hosts,* because there won't be any networking running to return an error to your host.

If your vendor's version of BIND allows configuration of the order in which services are queried, or will fall back from DNS to */etc/hosts* if DNS doesn't find an answer, take advantage of it! In the former case, you can configure the resolver to check */etc/*

---

[*] Check Chapter 6, *Configuring Hosts,* for vendor-specific enhancements to and variants on this resolver algorithm.

hosts first, and then keep a "stub" */etc/hosts* file on each host, including the default router and the local host's name. In the latter situation, just make sure such a "stub" */etc/hosts* exists; no other configuration should be necessary.

A last, promising prospect is to do away with setting the default route manually by using ICMP *Router Discovery Messages.* This extension to the ICMP protocol, described in RFC 1256, uses broadcast or multicast messages to dynamically discover and advertise routers on a network. Sun includes an implementation of this protocol in recent versions of Solaris as */usr/sbin/in.rdisc*, and newer versions of Cisco's Internetwork Operating System (IOS) support it too.

And what if your default route is added correctly, but the name servers still haven't come up? This can affect *sendmail*, NFS, and a slew of other services. *sendmail* won't canonicalize host names correctly without DNS, and your NFS mounts may fail.

The best solution to this problem is to run a name server on a host with uninterruptible power. If you rarely experience extended power loss, battery backup might be enough. If your outages are longer, and name service is critical to you, you should consider an uninterruptible power system (UPS) with a generator of some kind.

If you can't afford luxuries like these, you might just try to track down the fastest booting host around and run a name server on it. Hosts with filesystem journaling should boot especially quickly, since they don't need to *fsck.* Hosts with small filesystems should boot quickly, too, since they don't have as much filesystem to check.

Once you've located the right host, you'll need to make sure the host's IP address appears in the *resolv.conf* files of all the hosts that need full-time name service. You'll probably want to list the backed-up host last, since during normal operation, hosts should use the name server closest to them. Then, after a power failure, your critical applications will still have name service, albeit at a small sacrifice in performance.

Coping with Disaster

When disaster strikes, it really helps to know what to do. Knowing to duck under a sturdy table or desk during an earthquake can save you from being pinned under a toppling monitor. Knowing how to turn off your gas can save your house from conflagration.

Likewise, knowing what to do in a network disaster (or even just a minor mishap) can help you keep your network running. Living out in California, as we do, we have some experience and some suggestions.

Short Outages (Hours)

If your network is cut off from the outside world (whether "the outside world" is the rest of the Internet or the rest of your company), your name servers may start to have trouble resolving names. For example, if your domain, *corp.acme.com*, is cut off from the rest of the Acme Internet, you may not have access to your parent (*acme.com*) name servers, or to the root name servers.

You'd think this wouldn't impact communication between hosts in your local domain, but it can. For example, if you type:

```
% telnet selma.corp.acme.com
```

on a host running an older version of the resolver, the first domain name the resolver looks up will be *selma.corp.acme.com.corp.acme.com* (assuming your host is using the default search list—remember this from Chapter 6). The local domain name server, if it's authoritative for *corp.acme.com*, can tell that's not a kosher domain name. The following lookup, however, is for *selma.corp.acme.com.acme.com*. This prospective domain name is no longer in the *corp.acme.com* domain, so the query is sent to the *acme.com* name servers. Or rather your local name server *tries* to send the query there, and keeps retransmitting until it times out.

You can avoid this problem by making sure the first domain name the resolver looks up is the right one. Instead of typing:

```
% telnet selma.corp.acme.com
```

typing:

```
% telnet selma
```

or:

```
% telnet selma.corp.acme.com.
```

(note the trailing dot) will result in a lookup of *selma.corp.acme.com* first.

Note that BIND 4.9 and later resolvers don't have this problem, at least not by default. 4.9 and newer resolvers check the domain name as is first, as long as the name has more than one dot in it. So, if you tried:

```
% telnet selma.corp.acme.com
```

even without the trailing dot, the first name looked up would be *selma.corp.acme.com*.

If you are stuck running a 4.8.3 BIND or older resolver, you can avoid querying off-site name servers by taking advantage of the definable search list. You can use the *search* directive to define a search list that doesn't include your parent zone's domain name. For example, to work around the problem *corp.acme.com* is having, you could temporarily set your hosts' search lists to just:

```
search corp.acme.com
```

Now, when a user types:

```
% telnet selma.corp.acme.com
```

the resolver looks up *selma.corp.acme.com.corp.acme.com* first (which the local name server can answer), then *selma.corp.acme.com*, the correct domain name. And this works fine, too:

```
% telnet selma
```

works fine, too.

Longer Outages (Days)

If you lose network connectivity for a long time, your name servers may have other problems. If they lose connectivity to the root name servers for an extended period, they'll stop resolving queries outside their authoritative data. If the slaves can't reach their master, sooner or later they'll expire the zone.

In case your name service really goes haywire because of the connectivity loss, it's a good idea to keep a site-wide or workgroup */etc/hosts* around. In times of dire need, you can move *resolv.conf* to *resolv.bak*, kill the local name server (if there is one), and just use */etc/hosts*. It's not flashy, but it'll get you by.

As for slaves, you can reconfigure a slave that can't reach its master to run as a primary master. Just edit *named.conf* and change the type substatement in the *zone* statement from *slave* to *master*, then delete the *master* substatement. If more than one slave for the same zone is cut off, you can configure one as a primary master temporarily and reconfigure the other to load from the temporary primary.

Alternatively, you can just increase the expire time in all of your slaves' backup files and then signal the slaves to reload the files.

Really Long Outages (Weeks)

If an extended outage cuts you off from the Internet—say for a week or more—you may need to restore connectivity to root name servers artificially to get things working again. Every name server needs to talk to a root name server occasionally. It's a bit like therapy: the name server needs to contact the root to regain its perspective on the world.

To provide root name service during a long outage, you can set up your own root name servers, *but only temporarily*. Once you're reconnected to the Internet, you *must* shut off your temporary root servers. The most obnoxious vermin on the Internet are name servers that believe they're root name servers but don't know anything about most top-level domains. A close second is the Internet name server configured to query—and report—a false set of root name servers.

That said, and our alibis in place, here's what you have to do to configure your own
root name server. First, you need to create a *db.root* file. The *db.root* file will
delegate to the highest-level domain in your isolated network. For example, if
movie.edu were to be isolated from the Internet, we might create a *db.root* file for
terminator that looked like this:

```
. IN SOA terminator.movie.edu. al.robocop.movie.edu. (
                1         ; Serial
                10800     ; Refresh after 3 hours
                3600      ; Retry after 1 hour
                604800    ; Expire after 1 week
                86400 )   ; Minimum TTL of 1 day

; Refresh, retry and expire really don't matter, since all
; roots are primaries.  Minimum TTL could be longer, since
; the data are likely to be stable.

    IN NS terminator.movie.edu. ; terminator is the temp. root

; Our root only knows about movie.edu and our two
; in-addr.arpa domains

movie.edu. 86400 IN NS terminator.movie.edu.
           86400 IN NS wormhole.movie.edu.

249.249.192.in-addr.arpa. 86400 IN NS terminator.movie.edu.
                          86400 IN NS wormhole.movie.edu.

253.253.192.in-addr.arpa. 86400 IN NS terminator.movie.edu.
                          86400 IN NS wormhole.movie.edu.

terminator.movie.edu. 86400 IN A 192.249.249.3
wormhole.movie.edu.   86400 IN A 192.249.249.1
                      86400 IN A 192.253.253.1
```

Then we need to add the appropriate line to *terminator*'s *named.conf* file:

```
// Comment out hints zone
// zone . {
//              type hint;
//                      file "db.cache";
//              };

zone                 "."      {
                type master;
                file "db.root";
};
```

Or, for BIND 4's *named.boot* file:

```
; cache    .  db.cache  (comment out the cache directive)
primary  .  db.root
```

We then update all of our name servers (except the new, temporary root) with a *db.cache* file that includes just the temporary root (best to move the old cache file aside—we'll need it later, once connectivity is restored).

Here are the contents of the file *db.cache*:

```
.  99999999  IN  NS  terminator.movie.edu.

terminator.movie.edu.  IN  A  192.249.249.3
```

That will keep *movie.edu* name resolution going during the outage. Then, once Internet connectivity is restored, we can delete the *zone* statement from *named.conf* on *terminator*, and restore the original cache files on all our other name servers.

9

Parenting

The way Dinah washed her children's faces was this: first she held the poor thing down by its ear with one paw, and then with the other paw she rubbed its face all over, the wrong way, beginning at the nose: and just now, as I said, she was hard at work on the white kitten, which was lying quite still and trying to purr—no doubt feeling that it was all meant for its good.

Once your domain reaches a certain size, or you decide you need to distribute the management of parts of your domain to various entities within your organization, you'll want to divide the domain into subdomains. These subdomains will be the children of your current domain on the domain tree; your domain will be the parent. If you delegate responsibility for your subdomains to another organization, each becomes its own zone, separate from its parent zone. We like to call the management of your subdomains—your children—*parenting*.

Good parenting starts with carving up your domain sensibly, choosing appropriate names for your child domains, and then delegating the subdomains to create new zones. Responsible parents also work hard at maintaining the relationship between the name servers authoritative for their zone and its children; they ensure that delegation from parent to child is current and correct.

Good parenting is vital to the success of your network, especially as name service becomes critical to navigating between sites. Incorrect delegation to a child zone's name servers can render a site effectively unreachable, while the loss of connectivity to the parent zone's name servers can leave a site unable to reach any hosts outside the local zone.

In this chapter we present our views on when to create subdomains, and we go over how to create and delegate them in some detail. We also discuss management of the parent-child relationship and, finally, how to manage the process of carving up a large domain into smaller subdomains with a minimum of disruption and inconvenience.

When to Become a Parent

Far be it from us to *tell* you when you should become a parent, but we *will* be so bold as to offer you some guidelines. You may find some compelling reason to implement subdomains that isn't on our list, but here are some of the most common reasons:

- A need to delegate or distribute management of the domain to a number of organizations

- The large size of your domain—dividing it would make it easier to manage and offload the name servers for the domain

- A need to distinguish hosts' organizational affiliation by including them in particular domains

Once you've decided to have children, the next question to ask yourself is, naturally, how many children to have.

How Many Children?

Of course, you won't simply say, "I want to create four subdomains." Deciding how many child domains to implement is really choosing the organizational affiliation of your subdomains. For example, if your company has four branch offices, you might decide to create four subdomains, each of which corresponds to a branch office.

Should you create subdomains for each site, for each division, or even for each department? You have a lot of latitude in your choice because of DNS's scalability. You can create a few large subdomains or many small subdomains. There are trade-offs whichever you choose, though.

Delegating to a few large subdomains isn't much work for the parent domain, because there's not much delegation to keep track of. However, you wind up with larger subdomains, which require more memory and faster name servers, and administration isn't as distributed. If you implement site-level subdomains, for example, you may force autonomous or unrelated groups at a site to share a single name space and a single point of administration.

Delegating to many smaller subdomains can be a headache for the administrator of the parent. Keeping delegation data current involves keeping track of which hosts run name servers and which zones they're authoritative for. The data change each time a subdomain adds a new name server, or when the address of a name server for the subdomain changes. If the subdomains are all administered by different people, that means more administrators to train, more relationships for the parent administrator to maintain, and more overhead for the organization overall. On the other hand, the subdomains are smaller and easier to manage, and the administration is more widely distributed, allowing closer management of subdomain data.

Given the advantages and disadvantages of either alternative, it may seem difficult to make a choice. Actually, though, there's probably a natural division in your organization. Some companies manage computers and networks at the site level; others have decentralized, relatively autonomous workgroups that manage everything themselves. Here are a few basic rules to help you find the right way to carve up your name space:

- Don't shoehorn your organization into a weird or uncomfortable domain structure. Trying to fit 50 independent, unrelated U.S. divisions into 4 regional subdomains may save you work (as the administrator of the parent zone), but it won't help your reputation. Decentralized, autonomous operations demand different domains—that's the *raison d'être* of the Domain Name System.

- The structure of your domain should mirror the structure of your organization, especially your organization's *support* structure. If departments run networks, assign IP addresses, and manage hosts, then departments should manage the subdomains.

- If you're not sure or can't agree about how the namespace should be organized, try to come up with guidelines for when a group within your organization can carve off their own subdomain (e.g., how many hosts do you need to create a new subdomain, what level of support must the group provide) and grow the namespace organically, only as needed.

What to Name Your Children

Once you've decided how many subdomains you'd like to create and what they correspond to, you should choose good names for them. Rather than unilaterally deciding on your subdomains' names, it's considered polite to involve your future subdomain administrators and their constituencies in the decision. In fact, you can leave the decision entirely to them, if you like.

This can lead to problems, though. It's nice to use a relatively consistent naming scheme across your subdomains. It makes it easier for users in one subdomain, or outside your domain entirely, to guess or remember your subdomain names, and to figure out in which domain a particular host or user lives.

Leaving the decision to the locals can result in naming chaos. Some will want to use geographical names, others will insist on organizational names. Some will want to abbreviate, others will want to use full names.

Therefore, it's often best to establish a naming convention before choosing subdomain names. Here are some suggestions from our experience:

- In a dynamic company, the names of organizations can change frequently. Naming subdomains organizationally in a climate like this can be disastrous. One month the Relatively Advanced Technology (RAT) group seems stable enough, the next month they've been merged into the Questionable Computer Systems organization, and the following quarter they're all sold to a German conglomerate. Meanwhile, you're stuck with well-known hosts in a subdomain whose name no longer has any meaning.

- Geographical names are more stable than organizational names, but sometimes not as well known. You may know that your famous Software Evangelism Business Unit is in Poughkeepsie or Waukegan, but people outside your company may have no idea where it is (and might have trouble spelling either name).

- Don't sacrifice readability for convenience. Two-letter subdomain names may be easy to type, but impossible to recognize. Why abbreviate "Italy" to "it" and have it confused with your Information Technology organization, when for a paltry three more letters you can use the full name and eliminate any ambiguity?

- Too many companies use cryptic, inconvenient domain names. The general rule seems to be: the larger the company, the more indecipherable the domain names. Buck the trend: make the names of your subdomains obvious!

- Don't use existing or reserved top-level domain names as subdomain names. It might seem sensible to use two-letter country abbreviations for your international subdomains, or to use organizational top-level domain names like *net* for your networking organization, but it can cause nasty problems. For example, naming your Communications department's subdomain *com* might impede your ability to communicate with hosts under the top-level *com* domain. Imagine the administrators of your *com* subdomain naming their new Sun workstation *sun* and their new HP 9000 *hp* (they aren't the most imaginative folks): users anywhere within your domain sending mail to friends at *sun.com* or *hp.com* could have their letters end up in your *com* subdomain,[*] since the name of your parent zone may be in some of your hosts' search lists.

---

[*] Actually, not all mailers have this problem, but some popular versions of *sendmail* do. It all depends on which form of canonicalization it does, as we discussed in the section entitled "Electronic Mail" in Chapter 6, *Configuring Hosts*.

How to Become a Parent: Creating Subdomains

Once you've decided on names, creating child domains is easy. But first, you've got to decide how much autonomy you're going to give your subdomains. Odd that you have to decide that before you actually create them....

Thus far, we've assumed that if you create a subdomain, you'll want to delegate it to another organization, thereby making it a separate zone from the parent. Is this always true, though? Not necessarily.

Think carefully about how the computers and networks within a subdomain are managed when choosing whether or not to delegate it. It doesn't make sense to delegate a subdomain to an entity that doesn't manage its own hosts or nets. For example, in a large corporation, the personnel department probably doesn't run its own computers: the MIS (Management Information Systems) or IT (Information Technology—same animal as MIS) department manages them. So while you may want to create a subdomain for personnel, delegating management for that subdomain to them is probably wasted effort.

Creating a Subdomain in the Parent's Zone

You can *create* a subdomain without delegating it, however. How? By creating resource records that refer to the subdomain within the parent's zone. For example, *movie.edu* has a host that stores its complete database of employee and student records, *brazil*. To put *brazil* in the *personnel.movie.edu* domain, we could add records to *db.movie*.

Partial contents of file *db.movie*:

```
brazil.personnel      IN  A      192.253.253.10
                      IN  MX     10 brazil.personnel.movie.edu.
                      IN  MX     100 postmanrings2x.movie.edu.
employeedb.personnel  IN  CNAME  brazil.personnel.movie.edu.
db.personnel          IN  CNAME  brazil.personnel.movie.edu.
```

Now users can log into *db.personnel.movie.edu* to get to the employee database. We could make this setup especially convenient for personnel department employees by adding *personnel.movie.edu* to their PCs' or workstations' search lists; they'd only need to type *telnet db* to get to the right host.

We can make this more convenient for ourselves by using the *$ORIGIN* directive to change the origin to *personnel.movie.edu* so that we can use shorter names.

Partial contents of file *db.movie*:

```
$ORIGIN personnel.movie.edu.
brazil     IN A    192.253.253.10
           IN MX   10 brazil.personnel.movie.edu.
           IN MX   100 postmanrings2x.movie.edu.
employeedb IN CNAME brazil.personnel.movie.edu.
db         IN CNAME brazil.personnel.movie.edu.
```

If we had a few more records, we could create a separate file for them and use *$INCLUDE* to include it into *db.movie* and change the origin at the same time.

Notice there's no SOA record for *personnel.movie.edu*? There's no need for one, since the *movie.edu* SOA record indicates the start of authority for the entire *movie.edu* zone. Since there's no delegation to *personnel.movie.edu*, it's part of the *movie.edu* zone.

Creating and Delegating a Subdomain

If you decide to delegate your subdomains, to send your children out into the world, as it were, you'll need to do things a little differently. We're in the process of doing it now, so you can follow along with us.

We need to create a new subdomain of *movie.edu* for our special effects lab. We've chosen the name *fx.movie.edu*—short, recognizable, unambiguous. Because we're delegating *fx.movie.edu* to administrators in the lab, it'll be a separate zone. The hosts *bladerunner* and *outland*, both within the special effects lab, will serve as the zone's name servers (*bladerunner* will serve as the primary master). We've chosen to run two name servers for the domain for redundancy—a single *fx.movie.edu* name server would be a single point of failure that could effectively isolate the entire special effects lab. Since there aren't many hosts in the lab, though, we feel two name servers should be enough.

The special effects lab is on *movie.edu*'s new 192.253.254 subnet.

Partial contents of */etc/hosts*:

```
192.253.254.1 movie-gw.movie.edu movie-gw
# fx primary
192.253.254.2 bladerunner.fx.movie.edu bladerunner br
# fx secondary
192.253.254.3 outland.fx.movie.edu outland
192.253.254.4 starwars.fx.movie.edu starwars
192.253.254.5 empire.fx.movie.edu empire
192.253.254.6 jedi.fx.movie.edu jedi
```

First, we create a data file that includes records for all the hosts that will live in *fx.movie.edu*.

Contents of file *db.fx*:

```
@  IN  SOA  bladerunner.fx.movie.edu. hostmaster.fx.movie.edu. (
                1       ; serial
```

```
              10800   ; refresh every 3 hours
              3600    ; retry every hour
              604800  ; expire after a week
              86400 ) ; minimum TTL of 1 day


      IN  NS  bladerunner
      IN  NS  outland

; MX records for fx.movie.edu
      IN  MX  10 starwars
      IN  MX  100 wormhole.movie.edu.


; starwars handles bladerunner's mail
; wormhole is the movie.edu mail hub

bladerunner  IN  A    192.253.254.2
             IN  MX   10 starwars
             IN  MX   100 wormhole.movie.edu.

br           IN   CNAME    bladerunner

outland      IN  A    192.253.254.3
             IN  MX   10 starwars
             IN  MX   100 wormhole.movie.edu.

starwars     IN  A    192.253.254.4
             IN  MX   10 starwars
             IN  MX   100 wormhole.movie.edu.

empire       IN  A    192.253.254.5
             IN  MX   10 starwars
             IN  MX   100 wormhole.movie.edu.

jedi         IN  A    192.253.254.6
             IN  MX   10 starwars
             IN  MX   100 wormhole.movie.edu.
```

Then we create the *db.192.253.254* file:

```
@  IN  SOA  bladerunner.fx.movie.edu. hostmaster.fx.movie.edu. (
            1        ; serial
            10800    ; refresh every 3 hours
            3600     ; retry every hour
            604800   ; expire after a week
            86400 )  ; minimum TTL of 1 day

      IN    NS    bladerunner.fx.movie.edu.
      IN    NS    outland.fx.movie.edu.

1     IN    PTR   movie-gw.movie.edu.
2     IN    PTR   bladerunner.fx.movie.edu.
3     IN    PTR   outland.fx.movie.edu.
4     IN    PTR   starwars.fx.movie.edu.
5     IN    PTR   empire.fx.movie.edu.
6     IN    PTR   jedi.fx.movie.edu.
```

Notice that the PTR record for *1.254.253.192.in-addr.arpa* points to *movie-gw.movie.edu*. That's intentional. The router connects to the other *movie.edu* networks, so it really doesn't belong in the *fx.movie.edu* domain, and there's no requirement that all the PTR records in *254.253.192.in-addr.arpa* map into a single domain—though they should correspond to the canonical names for those hosts.

Next, we create an appropriate *named.conf* file for the primary master:

```
options {
                directory "/usr/local/named";
};

zone "0.0.127.in-addr.arpa" {
                type master;
                file "db.127.0.0";
};

zone "fx.movie.edu" {
                type master;
                file "db.fx";
};

zone "254.253.192.in-addr.arpa" {
                type master;
                file "db.192.253.254";
};

zone "." {
                type hint;
                file "db.cache";
};
```

Here are the contents of the corresponding *named.boot* file for BIND 4:

```
directory       /usr/local/named

primary         0.0.127.in-addr.arpa      db.127.0.0  ; loopback
primary         fx.movie.edu              db.fx
primary         254.253.192.in-addr.arpa  db.192.253.254

cache           .                         db.cache
```

Of course, if we'd used *h2n*, we could have just run:

```
% h2n -d fx.movie.edu -n 192.253.254 -s bladerunner -s outland \
-u hostmaster.fx.movie.edu -m 10:starwars -m 100:wormhole.movie.edu
```

and saved ourselves some typing. *h2n* would have created essentially the same *db.fx*, *db.192.253.254*, and *named.boot* files.

Now we need to configure *bladerunner*'s resolver. Actually, this may not require creating *resolv.conf*. If we set *bladerunner*'s *hostname* to its new domain name, *bladerunner.fx.movie.edu*, the resolver can derive the local domain from the fully qualified domain name.

Next we start up the *named* process on *bladerunner* and check for *syslog* errors. If *named* starts okay, and there are no *syslog* errors that need tending to, we'll use *nslookup* to look up a few hosts in *fx.movie.edu* and in *254.253.192.in-addr.arpa*:

```
Default Server: bladerunner.fx.movie.edu
Address:  192.253.254.2

> jedi
Server:  bladerunner.fx.movie.edu
Address:  192.253.254.2
Name:    jedi.fx.movie.edu
Address:  192.253.253.6

> set type=mx
> empire
Server:  bladerunner.fx.movie.edu
Address:  192.253.254.2

empire.fx.movie.edu       preference = 10,
                          mail exchanger = starwars.fx.movie.edu
empire.fx.movie.edu       preference = 100,
                          mail exchanger = wormhole.movie.edu
starwars.fx.movie.edu     internet address = 192.253.254.4
 > ls fx.movie.edu
[bladerunner.fx.movie.edu]
             1D IN SOA    bladerunner.fx.movie.edu.
hostmaster.fx.movie.edu.  (
                  1              ; serial
                  3H             ; refresh
                  1H             ; retry
                  1w1h           ; expire
                  1D )           ; minimum

             1D IN NS     bladerunner.fx.movie.edu.
             1D IN NS     outland.fx.movie.edu.
             1D IN MX     10 starwars.fx.movie.edu.
             1D IN MX     100 wormhole.movie.edu.
br.fx.movie.edu.        1D IN CNAME bladerunner.fx.movie.edu.
jedi.fx.movie.edu.      1D IN A     192.253.254.6
             1D IN MX     10 starwars.fx.movie.edu.
             1D IN MX     100 wormhole.movie.edu.
outland.fx.movie.edu.   1D IN A     192.253.254.3
             1D IN MX     10 starwars.fx.movie.edu.
             1D IN MX     100 wormhole.movie.edu.
starwars.fx.movie.edu.  1D IN A     192.253.254.4
             1D IN MX     10 starwars.fx.movie.edu.
             1D IN MX     100 wormhole.movie.edu.
bladerunner.fx.movie.edu.  1D IN A 192.253.254.2
             1D IN MX     10 starwars.fx.movie.edu.
             1D IN MX     100 wormhole.movie.edu.
```

```
empire.fx.movie.edu.    1D IN A    192.253.254.5
                1D IN MX    10 starwars.fx.movie.edu.
                1D IN MX    100 wormhole.movie.edu.
fx.movie.edu.       1D IN SOA    bladerunner.fx.movie.edu.
hostmaster.fx.movie.edu. (
                        1                   ; serial
                        3H                  ; refresh
                        1H                  ; retry
                        1w1h                ; expire
                        1D )                ; minimum


  > set type=ptr
  > 192.253.254.3
Server:   bladerunner.fx.movie.edu
Address:  192.253.254.2


3.254.253.192.in-addr.arpa      name = outland.fx.movie.edu


  > ls 254.253.192.in-addr.arpa.
[bladerunner.fx.movie.edu]
            1D IN SOA    bladerunner.fx.movie.edu.
hostmaster.fx.movie.edu. (
                        1                   ; serial
                        3H                  ; refresh
                        1H                  ; retry
                        1w1h                ; expire
                        1D )                ; minimum


            1D IN NS     bladerunner.fx.movie.edu.
            1D IN NS     outland.fx.movie.edu.
6.254.253.192.in-addr.arpa.  1D IN PTR  jedi.fx.movie.edu.
1.254.253.192.in-addr.arpa.  1D IN PTR  movie-gw.movie.edu.
2.254.253.192.in-addr.arpa.  1D IN PTR  bladerunner.fx.movie.edu.
3.254.253.192.in-addr.arpa.  1D IN PTR  outland.fx.movie.edu.
4.254.253.192.in-addr.arpa.  1D IN PTR  starwars.fx.movie.edu.
5.254.253.192.in-addr.arpa.  1D IN PTR  empire.fx.movie.edu.
254.253.192.in-addr.arpa.  1D IN SOA  bladerunner.fx.movie.edu.
hostmaster.fx.movie.edu. (
                        1                   ; serial
                        3H                  ; refresh
                        1H                  ; retry
                        1w1h                ; expire
                        1D )                ; minimum


  > ^D
```

The output looks reasonable, so it's safe to set up a slave name server for *fx.movie.edu* and to delegate *fx.movie.edu* from *movie.edu*.

An fx.movie.edu Slave

Setting up the slave name server for *fx.movie.edu* is simple: copy *named.conf*, *db.127.0.0*, and *db.cache* over from *bladerunner*, and edit *named.conf* and *db.127.0.0* according to the instructions in Chapter 4, *Setting Up BIND*.

Contents of file *named.conf:*

```
options {
                directory "/usr/local/named";
};

zone "0.0.127.in-addr.arpa" {
                type master;
                file "db.127.0.0";
};

zone "fx.movie.edu" {
                type slave;
                file "db.fx";
                masters { 192.253.254.2; };
};

zone "254.253.192.in-addr.arpa" {
                type slave;
                file "db.192.253.254";
                masters { 192.253.254.2; };
};

zone "." {
                type hint;
                file "db.cache";
};
```

Or, the equivalent *named.boot* file:

```
directory   /usr/local/named

primary     0.0.127.in-addr.arpa         db.127.0.0
secondary   fx.movie.edu                 192.253.254.2   db.fx
secondary   254.253.192.in-addr.arpa     192.253.254.2   db.192.253.254

cache       .                            db.cache
```

Like *bladerunner, outland* really doesn't need a *resolv.conf* file, as long as its *host-name* is set to *outland.fx.movie.edu.*

Again, we start *named* and check for errors in the *syslog* output. If the *syslog* output is clean, we'll look up a few records in *fx.movie.edu.*

On the movie.edu Primary Master

All that's left now is to delegate the *fx.movie.edu* domain to the new *fx.movie.edu* name servers on *bladerunner* and *outland.* We add the appropriate NS records to *db.movie.*

Partial contents of file *db.movie*:

```
fx    86400    IN    NS    bladerunner.fx.movie.edu.
      86400    IN    NS    outland.fx.movie.edu.
```

According to RFC 1034, the domain names in the resource record-specific portion of these two lines (*bladerunner.fx.movie.edu* and *outland.fx.movie.edu*) must be the canonical domain names for the name servers. A remote name server following delegation expects to find one or more address records attached to that domain name, not an alias (CNAME) record. Actually, the RFC extends this restriction to any type of resource record that includes a domain name as its value—all must specify the canonical domain name.

These two records alone aren't enough, though. Do you see the problem? How can a name server outside of *fx.movie.edu* look up information within *fx.movie.edu*? Well, a *movie.edu* name server would refer it to the name servers authoritative for *fx.movie.edu*, right? That's true, but the NS records in *db.movie* only give the *names* of the *fx.movie.edu* name servers. The foreign name server needs the IP addresses of the *fx.movie.edu* name servers in order to send queries to them. Who can give it those addresses? Only the *fx.movie.edu* name servers. A real chicken-and-egg problem!

The solution is to include the addresses of the *fx.movie.edu* name servers in the *db.movie* file. While these aren't strictly part of the *movie.edu* zone, they're necessary for delegation to *fx.movie.edu* to work. Of course, if the name servers for *fx.movie.edu* weren't within *fx.movie.edu*, these addresses—called *glue records*—wouldn't be necessary. A foreign name server would be able to find the address it needed by querying other name servers.

So, with the glue records, the records added look like the following partial contents of file *db.movie*:

```
fx    86400    IN    NS    bladerunner.fx.movie.edu.
      86400    IN    NS    outland.fx.movie.edu.
bladerunner.fx.movie.edu.    86400    IN    A    192.253.254.2
outland.fx.movie.edu.        86400    IN    A    192.253.254.3
```

Be sure you don't include unnecessary glue records in the file. Older BIND name servers (pre-4.9) load these records into their cache and give them out in referrals to other name servers. If the name server listed in the address record changes IP addresses and you forget to update the glue, your name server will continue giving out the outdated address information, resulting in poor resolution performance for name servers looking for data in the delegated zone, or even rendering them unable to resolve names in the delegated zone.

BIND 4.9 and BIND 8 will automatically ignore any glue you include that isn't strictly necessary, and will log the fact that it's ignored the record(s) to the slave's backup copy of the zone data. For example, if we had an NS record for *movie.edu* pointing to an off-site name server, *ns-1.isp.net*, and we made the mistake of including its address in *db.movie* on the *movie.edu* primary, we'd see:

```
; Ignoring info about ns-1.isp.net, not in zone movie.edu
; ns-1.isp.net 258983 IN     A      10.1.2.3
```

in *db.movie* on a *movie.edu* slave. Note that the extraneous A record has been commented out.

Also, remember to keep the glue up to date. If *bladerunner* gets a new network interface, and hence another IP address, then you should add another A record to the glue data.

We might also want to include aliases for any hosts moving into *fx.movie.edu* from *movie.edu*. For example, if we were to move *plan9.movie.edu*, a server with an important library of public domain special effects algorithms, into *fx.movie.edu*, we should create an alias under *movie.edu* pointing the old name to the new one:

```
plan9        IN     CNAME    plan9.fx.movie.edu.
```

This will allow people outside of *movie.edu* to reach *plan9* even though they're using its old domain name, *plan9.movie.edu*.

You shouldn't put any information about domain names in *fx.movie.edu* into the *db.movie* file. The *plan9* alias is actually in the *movie.edu* zone, so it belongs in *db.movie*. An alias pointing *p9.fx.movie.edu* to *plan9.fx.movie.edu*, on the other hand, is in the *fx.movie.edu* zone, and belongs in *db.fx*. If you were to put a record in the db file that was outside of the zone the file described, a BIND 4.9 name server would ignore it. Older name servers might load it into the cache or even into authoritative data, but since the behavior is unpredictable and is eliminated in newer versions of BIND, it's best to do it the right way even if the software doesn't force you to.

Delegating an in-addr.arpa Zone

We almost forgot to delegate the *254.253.192.in-addr.arpa* zone! This is a little trickier than delegating *fx.movie.edu*, because we don't manage the parent zone.

First, we need to figure out what *254.253.192.in-addr.arpa*'s parent zone is, and who runs it. To figure this out may take some sleuthing; we covered how to do this in Chapter 3, *Where Do I Start?*.

As it turns out, the *in-addr.arpa* zone is *254.253.192.in-addr.arpa*'s parent. And, if you think about it, that makes some sense. There's no reason for the administrators of *in-addr.arpa* to delegate *253.192.in-addr.arpa* or *192.in-addr.arpa* to a separate authority, because unless 192.0.0.0 or 192.253.0.0 is all one big CIDR block, networks like 192.253.253 and 192.253.254 don't have anything in common with each other. They may be managed by totally unrelated organizations.

You might have remembered (from Chapter 3) that the *in-addr.arpa* zone is managed by ARIN, the American Registry of Internet Numbers. (Of course, if you didn't remember, you could always use *nslookup* to find the contact address in *in-addr.arpa*'s SOA record, like we showed you in Chapter 3.) All that's left is for us to fill out *inaddrtemplate.txt* (there's a copy in Appendix E, *in-addr.arpa Registration Form*, or you can find it online at *http://www.arin.net/templates/ inaddrtemplate.txt*), and send it to the email address *hostmaster@arin.net*.

Adding a movie.edu Slave

If the special effects lab gets big enough, it may make sense to put a *movie.edu* slave somewhere on the 192.253.254 network. That way, a larger proportion of DNS queries from *fx.movie.edu* hosts can be answered locally. It seems logical to make one of the existing *fx.movie.edu* name servers into a *movie.edu* slave, too—that way, we can make better use of an existing name server, instead of setting up a brand-new name server.

We've decided to make *bladerunner* a slave for *movie.edu*. This won't interfere with *bladerunner*'s primary mission: the primary master for *fx.movie.edu*, that is. A single name server, given enough memory, can be authoritative for literally thousands of zones. One name server can load some zones as a primary master and others as a slave.[*]

The configuration change is simple: we add one line to *bladerunner*'s *named.conf* file to tell *named* to load the *movie.edu* zone from the IP address of the *movie.edu* primary master name server, *terminator.movie.edu*.

Contents of file *named.conf*:

```
options {
        directory "/usr/local/named";
};

zone "0.0.127.in-addr.arpa" {
        type master;
        file "db.127.0.0";
};

zone "fx.movie.edu" {
        type master;
        file "db.fx";
```

---

[*] Clearly, though, a name server can't be both the primary master and a slave for a single zone. Either the name server gets the data for a given zone from a local file (and is a primary master for the zone) or from another name server (and is a slave for the zone).

```
        };

        zone "254.253.192.in-addr.arpa" {
                      type master;
                      file "db.192.253.254";
        };

        zone "movie.edu" {
                      type slave;
                      file "db.movie";
                      masters { 192.249.249.3;}
        };

        zone "." {
                      type hint;
                      file "db.cache";
        };
```

Or, if you're using a BIND 4 name server, here are the contents of the *named.boot* file:

```
        directory    /usr/local/named

        primary      0.0.127.in-addr.arpa      db.127.0.0  ; loopback
        primary      fx.movie.edu              db.fx
        primary      254.253.192.in-addr.arpa  db.192.253.254
        secondary    movie.edu                 192.249.249.3     db.movie

        cache        .                          db.cache
```

Subdomains of in-addr.arpa Domains

Forward mapping domains aren't the only domains you can divide into subdomains and delegate. If your *in-addr.arpa* name space is large enough, you may need to divide it, too. Typically, you divide the domain that corresponds to your network number into subdomains to correspond to your subnets. How that works depends on the type of network you have and on your network's subnet mask.

Subnetting on an Octet Boundary

Since Movie U. just has three /24 (class C-sized) network numbers, one per segment, there's no particular need to subnet those networks. However, our sister university, Altered State, has a class B-sized network, 172.20/16. Their network is subnetted between the third and fourth octet of the IP address; that is, their subnet mask is 255.255.255.0. They've already created a number of subdomains of their domain, *altered.edu*, including *fx.altered.edu* (okay, we copied them), *makeup.altered.edu*, and *foley.altered.edu*. Since each of these departments also runs its own subnet (their special effects department runs subnet 172.20.2.0, makeup runs 172.20.15.0, and foley runs 172.20.25.0), they'd like to divvy up their *in-addr.arpa* namespace appropriately, too.

Delegating *in-addr.arpa* subdomains is no different from delegating subdomains of forward-mapping domains. Within their *db.172.20* file, they need to add NS records like these:

```
2    86400   IN   NS   gump.fx.altered.edu.
2    86400   IN   NS   toystory.fx.altered.edu.
15   86400   IN   NS   prettywoman.makeup.altered.edu.
15   86400   IN   NS   priscilla.makeup.altered.edu.
25   86400   IN   NS   blowup.foley.altered.edu.
25   86400   IN   NS   muppetshow.foley.altered.edu.
```

delegating the subdomain that corresponds to each subnet to the correct name server in each subdomain.

Two important reminders: the Altered States administrators needed to use the fully qualified domain names of the name servers in the NS records, because the default origin in this file is *20.172.in-addr.arpa*, and they *didn't* need glue address records, since the names of the name servers they delegated the zone to weren't in the zone.

Subnetting on a Non-Octet Boundary

What do you do about networks that aren't subnetted neatly on octet boundaries, like subnetted /24 (class C-sized) networks? In these cases, you can't delegate along lines that match the subnets. This forces you into one of two situations: you have multiple subnets per *in-addr.arpa* subdomain, or you have multiple *in-addr.arpa* subdomains per subnet. Neither is particularly pleasing.

Class A and B networks

Let's take the case of the /8 (class A-sized) network 15.0.0.0, subnetted with the subnet mask 255.255.248.0 (a thirteen-bit subnet field and an eleven-bit host field, or 8192 subnets of 2048 hosts). In this case, the subnet 15.1.200.0, for example, extends from 15.1.200.0 to 15.1.207.255. Therefore, the delegation for that single subdomain in *db.15*, the zone database file for *15.in-addr.arpa*, looks like this:

```
200.1.15.in-addr.arpa.    86400   IN   NS   ns-1.cns.hp.com.
200.1.15.in-addr.arpa.    86400   IN   NS   ns-2.cns.hp.com.
201.1.15.in-addr.arpa.    86400   IN   NS   ns-1.cns.hp.com.
201.1.15.in-addr.arpa.    86400   IN   NS   ns-2.cns.hp.com.
202.1.15.in-addr.arpa.    86400   IN   NS   ns-1.cns.hp.com.
202.1.15.in-addr.arpa.    86400   IN   NS   ns-2.cns.hp.com.
203.1.15.in-addr.arpa.    86400   IN   NS   ns-1.cns.hp.com.
203.1.15.in-addr.arpa.    86400   IN   NS   ns-2.cns.hp.com.
204.1.15.in-addr.arpa.    86400   IN   NS   ns-1.cns.hp.com.
204.1.15.in-addr.arpa.    86400   IN   NS   ns-2.cns.hp.com.
205.1.15.in-addr.arpa.    86400   IN   NS   ns-1.cns.hp.com.
```

```
205.1.15.in-addr.arpa.        86400    IN    NS    ns-2.cns.hp.com.
206.1.15.in-addr.arpa.        86400    IN    NS    ns-1.cns.hp.com.
206.1.15.in-addr.arpa.        86400    IN    NS    ns-2.cns.hp.com.
207.1.15.in-addr.arpa.        86400    IN    NS    ns-1.cns.hp.com.
207.1.15.in-addr.arpa.        86400    IN    NS    ns-2.cns.hp.com.
```

That's a lot of delegation for one subnet!

/24 (class C-sized) networks

In the case of a subnetted /24 (class C-sized) network, say 192.253.254.0, subnetted with the mask 255.255.255.192, you have a single *in-addr.arpa* zone, *254.253.192.in-addr.arpa*, that corresponds to subnets 192.253.254.0/26, 192.253.254.64/26, 192.253.254.128/26, and 192.253.254.192/26. You can solve this one of three ways, none of them pretty.

Solution 1. The first is to administer the *254.253.192.in-addr.arpa* zone as a single entity and not even try to delegate. This requires either cooperation between the administrators of the four subnets involved or the use of a tool like MIT's WebDNS (*http://hem.passagen.se/hno/webdns/*) to allow each of the four administrators to take care of their own data.

Solution 2. The second is to delegate at the *fourth* octet. That's even nastier than the /8 delegation we just showed. You'll need at least a couple of NS records per IP *address* in the file *db.192.253.254*, like this:

```
1.254.253.192.in-addr.arpa.       86400    IN    NS    ns1.foo.com.
1.254.253.192.in-addr.arpa.       86400    IN    NS    ns2.foo.com.

2.254.253.192.in-addr.arpa.       86400    IN    NS    ns1.foo.com.
2.254.253.192.in-addr.arpa.       86400    IN    NS    ns2.foo.com.

. . .

65.254.253.192.in-addr.arpa.      86400    IN    NS    relay.bar.com.
65.254.253.192.in-addr.arpa.      86400    IN    NS    gw.bar.com.

66.254.253.192.in-addr.arpa.      86400    IN    NS    relay.bar.com.
66.254.253.192.in-addr.arpa.      86400    IN    NS    gw.bar.com.

. . .

129.254.253.192.in-addr.arpa.     86400    IN    NS    mail.baz.com.
130.254.253.192.in-addr.arpa.     86400    IN    NS    www.baz.com.

194.254.253.192.in-addr.arpa.     86400    IN    NS    mail.baz.com.
194.254.253.192.in-addr.arpa.     86400    IN    NS    www.baz.com.
```

and so on, all the way down to *254.254.253.192.in-addr.arpa*. Of course, in *ns1.foo.com*'s *named.conf*, you'd also expect to see:

```
zone "1.254.253.192.in-addr.arpa" {
                type master;
                file "db.192.253.254.1";
};

zone "2.254.253.192.in-addr.arpa" {
                type master;
                file "db.192.253.254.2";
};
```

Or, if *ns1.foo.com* were running BIND 4, you'd expect to see these directives in *named.boot*:

```
primary     1.254.253.192.in-addr.arpa     db.192.253.254.1
primary     2.254.253.192.in-addr.arpa     db.192.253.254.2
```

and in *db.192.253.254.1*, just the one PTR record:

```
@      IN      SOA     ns1.foo.com.     root.ns1.foo.com.     (
                                1        ; Serial
                                10800    ; Refresh
                                3600     ; Retry
                                608400   ; Expire
                                86400    ; Default TTL

       IN      NS      ns1.foo.com.
       IN      NS      ns2.foo.com.

       IN      PTR     thereitis.foo.com.
```

Note that the PTR record is attached to the zone's domain name, since the zone's domain name corresponds to just one IP address. Now, when a *254.253.192.in-addr.arpa* name server receives a query for the PTR record for *1.254.253.192.in-addr.arpa*, it will refer the querier to *ns1.foo.com* and *ns2.foo.com*, which will respond with the one PTR record in the zone.

Solution 3. Finally, there's a clever technique that obviates the need to maintain a separate zone data file for each IP address.[*] The organization responsible for the overall /24 network creates CNAME records for each of the domain names in the zone, pointing to domain names in new subdomains, called *0-63, 64-127, 128-191,* and *192-255,* which are then delegated to the proper servers. Each subdomain will contain only the PTR records in the range the subdomain is named for.

Partial contents of file *db.192.253.254*:

```
1.254.253.192.in-addr.arpa.    IN   CNAME   1.0-63.254.253.192.in-addr.arpa.
2.254.253.192.in-addr.arpa.    IN   CNAME   2.0-63.254.253.192.in-addr.arpa.
```

---

[*] We first saw this explained by Glen Herrmansfeldt at CalTech in the newsgroup *comp.protocols.tcp-ip.domains*. It's now codified as RFC 2317.

```
...

0-63.254.253.192.in-addr.arpa.      86400    IN    NS    ns1.foo.com.
0-63.254.253.192.in-addr.arpa.      86400    IN    NS    ns2.foo.com.

65.254.253.192.in-addr.arpa. IN  CNAME 65.64-127.254.253.192.in-addr.arpa.
66.254.253.192.in-addr.arpa. IN  CNAME 66.64-127.254.253.192.in-addr.arpa.

...

64-127.254.253.192.in-addr.arpa.    86400    IN    NS    relay.bar.com.
64-127.254.253.192.in-addr.arpa.    86400    IN    NS    gw.bar.com.

129.254.253.192.in-addr.arpa. IN  CNAME 129.128-191.254.253.192.in-addr.arpa.
130.254.253.192.in-addr.arpa. IN  CNAME 130.128-191.254.253.192.in-addr.arpa.

...

128-191.254.253.192.in-addr.arpa.   86400    IN    NS    mail.baz.com.
128-191.254.253.192.in-addr.arpa.   86400    IN    NS    www.baz.com.
```

The zone data file for *0-63.254.253.192.in-addr.arpa*, *0-63.254.253.192.in-addr.arpa.dns*, can contain just PTR records for IP addresses 192.253.254.1 through 192.253.254.63.

Partial contents of file *0-63.254.253.192.in-addr.arpa*:

```
@    IN    soa   ns1.foo.com.    root.ns1.foo.com.    (
                           1        ; Serial
                           10800    ; Refresh
                           3600     ; Retry
                           608400   ; Expire
                           86400 )  ; Default TTL

     in   NS    ns1.foo.com.
     in   NS    ns2.foo.com.

1    IN   PTR   thereitis.foo.com.
2    IN   PTR   setter.foo.com.
3    IN   PTR   mouse.foo.com.
...
```

When a resolver requests the PTR record for *1.254.253.192.in-addr.arpa*, a *254.253.192.in-addr.arpa* name server will transparently (to the resolver) map this to a request for the PTR record for *1.0-63.254.253.192.in-addr.arpa*. This request will wind up at one of the *0-63.254.253.192.in-addr.arpa* name servers, run by the organization that runs the low (addresses 0-63) subnet.

Good Parenting

Now that the delegation to the *fx.movie.edu* name servers is in place, we—responsible parents that we are—should check that delegation using *check_del*.

What? We haven't given you *check_del* yet? Unfortunately, *check_del* is too long to include in this book, but we've made it available via anonymous *ftp*. See the preface for details. Feel free to snatch the code there and compile it if you want to follow along.

check_del "knows" delegation. *check_del* reads NS records. For each NS record, *check_del* issues a query to the name server listed for the zone's SOA record. The query is nonrecursive, so the name server queried doesn't query other name servers to find the SOA record. If the name server replies, *check_del* checks the reply to see whether the *aa*—authoritative answer—bit in the reply packet is set. If it is, the name server checks to make sure that the packet contains an answer. If both these criteria are met, the name server is flagged as authoritative for the zone. Otherwise, the name server is not authoritative, and *check_del* reports an error.

Why all the fuss over bad delegation? Incorrect delegation can cause the propagation of old and erroneous root name server information. When a name server is queried for data in a zone it isn't authoritative for, it does its best to provide useful information to the querier. This "useful information" comes in the form of NS records for the closest ancestor domain the name server knows. (We mentioned this briefly in Chapter 8, *Growing Your Domain*, when we discussed why you shouldn't register a caching-only name server.)

For example, say one of the *fx.movie.edu* name servers mistakenly receives an iterative query for the address of *carrie.horror.movie.edu*. It knows nothing about the *horror.movie.edu* domain (except for what it might have cached), but it likely has NS records for *movie.edu* cached, since those are its parent name servers. So it would return those records to the querier.

In that scenario, the NS records may help the querying name server get an answer. However, it's a fact of life on the Internet that not all administrators keep their cache files up to date. If one of your name servers follows a bad delegation and queries a remote name server for records it doesn't have, look what can happen:

```
% nslookup
Default Server:  terminator.movie.edu
Address:  192.249.249.3

> set type=ns
> .
Server:  terminator.movie.edu
Address:  192.249.249.3

Non-authoritative answer:
(root)    nameserver = D.ROOT-SERVERS.NET
(root)    nameserver = E.ROOT-SERVERS.NET
(root)    nameserver = I.ROOT-SERVERS.NET
(root)    nameserver = F.ROOT-SERVERS.NET
(root)    nameserver = G.ROOT-SERVERS.NET
```

```
(root)   nameserver = A.ROOT-SERVERS.NET
(root)   nameserver = H.ROOT-SERVERS.NETNIC.NORDU.NET
(root)   nameserver = B.ROOT-SERVERS.NET
(root)   nameserver = C.ROOT-SERVERS.NET
(root)   nameserver = A.ISI.EDU              —These three name
(root)   nameserver = SRI-NIC.ARPA           —servers are no longer
(root)   nameserver = GUNTER-ADAM.ARPA       —roots
```

A remote name server tried to "help out" our local name server by sending it the current list of roots. Unfortunately, the remote name server was corrupt, and returned NS records that were incorrect. And our local name server, not knowing any better, cached that data.

Queries to misconfigured *in-addr.arpa* name servers often result in bad root NS records, because the *in-addr.arpa* and *arpa* domains are the closest ancestors of most *in-addr.arpa* subdomains, and name servers very seldom cache either *in-addr.arpa* or *arpa*'s NS records. (The roots seldom give them out, since they delegate directly to lower-level subdomains.) Once your name server has cached bad root NS records, your name resolution may suffer.

Those root NS records may have your name server querying a root name server that is no longer at that IP address, or a root name server that no longer exists at all. If you're having an especially bad day, the bad root NS records may point to a real, non-root name server that is close to your network. Even though it won't return authoritative root data, your name server will favor it because it will have a low RTT due to its proximity to your network.

Using check_del

If our little lecture has convinced you of the importance of maintaining correct delegation, you'll be eager to learn how to use *check_del* to ensure that you don't join the ranks of the miscreants.

check_del usually takes two arguments: the name of a data file to check, and the default origin in the data file. The default origin tells *check_del* the domain name to append to relative names in the file. (When *named* reads the db file, it learns the default origin in the *named.conf* or *named.boot* file; it's at the beginning of the *zone* statement, and always the second field in a *primary* or *secondary* directive. *check_del* doesn't read the conf or boot file, though, so you need to specify the domain name on the command line. If it read the conf or boot file, it'd be limited to checking only db files listed in it.)

To check whether the *db.movie* file contains proper delegation to *fx.movie.edu* (and any other subdomains), we'd run:

```
% check_del -o movie.edu -f db.movie
```

If the delegation is correct, we'd see this:

```
5 domains properly delegated
```

Actually, it's one domain delegated to three authoritative servers (*movie.edu* delegated to *terminator, wormhole,* and *zardoz*), and one subdomain delegated to two authoritative servers (*fx.movie.edu* delegated to *bladerunner* and *outland*), but *check_del* doesn't know that. The point is that all the NS records in *db.movie* are correct.

If one of the *fx.movie.edu* name servers—say *outland*—were misconfigured, we'd see this:

```
Server outland.fx.movie.edu is not authoritative for fx.movie.edu

4 domains properly delegated
1 domains improperly delegated
```

Okay, *check_del* doesn't really understand plurals, either.

If one of the *fx.movie.edu* name servers weren't running at all, we'd see:

```
4 domains properly delegated
1 servers not running

Servers not running:
        outland.fx.movie.edu
```

In this case, not running really means that *check_del* tried to send the name server a query and got an ICMP port unreachable error back, which indicated that nothing was listening on the name server port.

And if the name server didn't answer in an acceptable amount of time, you'd see:

```
4 domains properly delegated
1 servers not responding

Servers not responding:
        outland.fx.movie.edu
```

Managing Delegation

If the special effects lab gets bigger, we may find that we need additional name servers. We dealt with setting up new name servers in Chapter 8, and even went over what information to send to the parent zone's administrator. But we never explained what the parent needed to do.

It turns out that the parent's job is relatively easy, especially if the administrators of the subdomain send complete information. Imagine that the special effects lab expands to a new network, 192.254.20. They have a passel of new, high-powered graphics workstations. One of them, *alien.fx.movie.edu,* will act as the network's name server.

The administrators of *fx.movie.edu* (we delegated it to the folks in the lab) send their parent zones' administrators (that's us) a short note:

```
Hi!

We've just set up alien.fx.movie.edu (192.254.20.3) as a name
server for fx.movie.edu.  Would you please update your
delegation information?  I've attached the NS records you'll
need to add.

Thanks,

Arty Segue
ajs@fx.movie.edu

----- cut here -----

fx.movie.edu.  86400  IN  NS  bladerunner.fx.movie.edu.
fx.movie.edu.  86400  IN  NS  outland.fx.movie.edu.
fx.movie.edu.  86400  IN  NS  alien.fx.movie.edu.

bladerunner.fx.movie.edu.  86400  IN  A  192.253.254.2
outland.fx.movie.edu.      86400  IN  A  192.253.254.3
alien.fx.movie.edu.        86400  IN  A  192.254.20.3
```

Our job as the *movie.edu* administrator is straightforward: add the NS and A records to *db.movie*.

What if we're using *h2n* to create our name server data? We can stick the delegation information into the *spcl.movie* file, which *h2n* $INCLUDEs at the end of the *db.movie* file it creates.

The final step for the *fx.movie.edu* administrator is to send a similar message to *hostmaster@internic.net* (administrator for the *in-addr.arpa* domain), requesting that the *20.254.192.in-addr.arpa* domain be delegated to *alien.fx.movie.edu*, *bladerunner.fx.movie.edu*, and *outland.fx.movie.edu*.

Another way to manage delegation: stubs

If you're running BIND 4.9 or BIND 8 name servers, you don't have to manage delegation information manually. BIND 4.9 and BIND 8 name servers support an experimental feature, called *stub*, which enables a name server to pick up changes to delegation information automatically.

Name servers that act as stubs for a subdomain do periodic zone transfers of the subdomain's data, but they ignore everything in it except for the NS records and the SOA record. The NS records are "promoted" into the parent zone, and the SOA record governs how often the stub does zone transfers. Now, when the administrators of a subdomain make changes to the subdomain's name servers, they simply update their NS records. The parent zone's authoritative name servers will pick up the updated records within the refresh interval.

On the *movie.edu* name servers running BIND 8, here's what we'd add to *named.conf*:

```
zone "fx.movie.edu" {
                type stub;
                file "db.fx";
                masters { 192.253.254.2; };
};
```

On a BIND 4.9 name server, we'd use this directive:

```
stub    fx.movie.edu    192.253.254.2    db.fx
```

Note that we should configure all of the *movie.edu* name servers as stubs for *fx.movie.edu*, because if the *fx.movie.edu* delegation information changes, that won't change the *movie.edu* zone's serial number.

Managing the Transition to Subdomains

We won't lie to you—the *fx.movie.edu* example we showed you was unrealistic for several reasons. The main one is the magical appearance of the special effects lab's hosts. In the real world, the lab would have started out with a few hosts, probably in the *movie.edu* zone. After a generous endowment, an NSF grant, or a corporate gift, they might expand the lab a little and buy a few more computers. Sooner or later, the lab would have enough hosts to warrant the creation of a new subdomain. By that point, however, many of the original hosts would be well known by their names under *movie.edu*.

We briefly touched on using CNAME records under the parent domain (in our *plan9.movie.edu* example) to help people adjust to a host's change of domain. But what happens when you move a whole network or subnet into a new subdomain?

The strategy we recommend uses CNAME records in much the same way, but on a larger scale. Using a tool like *h2n*, you can create CNAMEs for hosts *en masse*. This allows users to continue using the old domain names for any of the hosts that have moved. When they *telnet* or *ftp* (or whatever) to those hosts, however, the command will report that they're connected to a host in *fx.movie.edu*:

```
% telnet plan9
Trying...
Connected to plan9.fx.movie.edu.
Escape character is '^]'.

HP-UX plan9.fx.movie.edu A.09.05 C 9000/735 (ttyu1)

login:
```

Some users, of course, don't notice subtle changes like this, so you should also do some public relations work and notify folks of the change.

On *fx.movie.edu* hosts running old versions of *sendmail*, we may also need to configure mail to accept mail addressed to the new domain names. Modern versions of *sendmail* canonicalize the host names in addresses in message headers using a name server before sending the messages. This will turn a *movie.edu* alias into a canonical name in *fx.movie.edu*. If, however, the *sendmail* on the receiving end is older and hardcodes the local host's domain name, we'd have to change the name to the new domain name by hand. This usually requires a simple change to class *w* or fileclass *w* in *sendmail.cf*; see the section "The MX Algorithm" in Chapter 5, *DNS and Electronic Mail*.

How do you create all these aliases? You simply need to tell *h2n* to create the aliases for hosts on the *fx.movie.edu* networks (192.253.254 and 192.254.20), and indicate (in the */etc/hosts* file) what the new domain names for the hosts are. For example, using the *fx.movie.edu* host table, we could easily generate the aliases under *movie.edu* for all the hosts in *fx.movie.edu*.

Partial contents of file */etc/hosts*:

```
192.253.254.1 movie-gw.movie.edu movie-gw
# fx primary
192.253.254.2 bladerunner.fx.movie.edu bladerunner br
# fx secondary
192.253.254.3 outland.fx.movie.edu outland
192.253.254.4 starwars.fx.movie.edu starwars
192.253.254.5 empire.fx.movie.edu empire
192.253.254.6 jedi.fx.movie.edu jedi
192.254.20.3  alien.fx.movie.edu alien
```

h2n's *-c* option takes a zone's domain name as an argument. When *h2n* finds any hosts in that zone on networks it's building data for, it'll create aliases for them in the current zone (specified with *-d*). So by running:

```
% h2n -d movie.edu -n 192.253.254 -n 192.254.20 \
-c fx.movie.edu -f options
```

(where *options* contains other command-line options for building data from other *movie.edu* networks), we could create aliases under *movie.edu* for all *fx.movie.edu* hosts.

Removing Parent Aliases

Although parent-level aliases are useful for minimizing the impact of moving your hosts, they're also a crutch of sorts. Like a crutch, they'll restrict your freedom. They'll clutter up your parent name space, when one of your motivations for implementing a subdomain may have been making the parent zone smaller. And they'll prevent you from using the names of hosts in the subdomain as names for hosts in the parent zone.

After a grace period—which should be well advertised to users—you should remove all the aliases, with the possible exception of aliases for extremely well-known Internet hosts. During the grace period, users can adjust to the new domain names, and modify scripts, *.rhosts* files, and the like. But don't get suckered into leaving all those aliases in the parent zone; they defeat part of the purpose of the DNS, because they prevent you and your subdomain administrator from naming hosts autonomously.

You might want to leave CNAME records for well-known Internet hosts or central network resources intact, because of the potential impact of a loss of connectivity. On the other hand, rather than moving the well-known host or central resource into a subdomain at all, it might be better to leave it at the parent zone level.

h2n gives you an easy way to delete the aliases you created so simply with the *-c* option, even if the records for the subdomain's hosts are mixed in the host table or on the same network as hosts in other zones. The *-e* option takes a zone's domain name as an argument, and tells *h2n* to exclude (hence *-e*) all records containing that domain name on networks it would otherwise create data for. This command line, for example, would delete all the CNAME records for *fx.movie.edu* hosts created earlier, while still creating an A record for *movie-gw* (which is on the 192.253.254 network):

```
% h2n -d movie.edu -n 192.253.254 -n 192.254.20 \
-e fx.movie.edu -f options
```

The Life of a Parent

That's a lot of parental advice to digest in one sitting, so let's recap the highlights of what we've talked about. The life cycle of a typical parent goes something like this:

1. You have a single zone, with all of your hosts in that zone.

2. You break your zone into a number of subdomains, some of them in the same zone as the parent, if necessary. You provide CNAME records in the parent zone for well-known hosts that have moved into subdomains.

3. After a grace period, you delete any remaining CNAME records.

4. You handle subdomain delegation updates, either manually or by using stubs, and periodically check delegation.

Okay, now that you know all there is to parenting, let's go on to talk about more advanced name server features. You may need some of these tools to keep those kids in line.

10

Advanced Features and Security

*"What's the use of their having names," the Gnat
said, "if they won't answer to them?"*

The latest BIND name server, version 8.1.2, has *lots* of new features. Two of the most prominent introductions are support for asynchronous zone change notification (DNS NOTIFY) and DNS Dynamic Update. Of the rest, the most important are related to security: they'll let you tell your name server whom to answer queries from, whom to offer zone transfers to, and whom to permit dynamic updates from. Many of the security features aren't necessary inside a corporate network, but the other mechanisms will help out the administrators of any name servers.

In this chapter, we'll cover these features and suggest how they might come in handy in your DNS infrastructure. (We do save some of the hard-core firewall material 'til the last chapter, though.)

Address Match Lists and ACLs

Before we introduce many of the new features, however, we'd better cover address match lists. BIND 8 uses address match lists for nearly every security feature, and for some features that aren't security-related at all.

An address match list is a list (what else?) of terms that specify one or more IP addresses. The elements in the list can be individual IP addresses, IP prefixes, or a named access control list. An IP prefix has the format:

```
network in dotted-octet format/bits in netmask
```

For example, the network 15.0.0.0, with the network mask 255.0.0.0 (eight contiguous ones), would be written 15/8. Traditionally, this would have been thought of as the "class A" network 15. The network consisting of IP addresses 192.168.1.192 through 192.168.1.255, on the other hand, would be written 192.168.1.192/26 (network 192.168.1.192 with the netmask 255.255.255.192, which has 26 contiguous ones).

A named ACL must have been previously defined with an *acl* statement. The *acl* statement has a simple structure:

```
acl "name" {
                { address_match list; };
};
```

Any time you're going to use one or more terms in a few access lists, it's a good idea to use an *acl* statement to associate them with a name. You can then refer to the name in the address match list. For example, let's call 15/8 what it is: HP-NET. And we'll call 192.168.1.192/26 "internal":

```
acl "HP-NET" {
                { 15/8; };
};

acl "internal" {
                { 192.168.1.192/26; };
};
```

Now we can refer to these ACLs by name in address match lists.

There are also four predefined access lists:

None
    No IP addresses

Any
    All IP addresses

Localhost
    Any of the local host's IP addresses

Localnets

> Any of the networks the local host has a network interface on (found by using each network interface's IP address and using the netmask to mask off the host bits in the address)

DNS NOTIFY (Zone Change Notification)

Traditionally, BIND slaves have used a polling scheme to determine when they need a zone transfer. The polling interval is called the *refresh time*. Other parameters in the zone's SOA record govern other aspects of the polling mechanism.

Wouldn't it be nice if the primary master name server could *tell* its slave servers when the information in a zone changed? After all, the primary master name server *knows* the data has changed: Someone signaled it with a SIGHUP, and it checked the *mtime* (the UNIX file modification time) of all of its zone data files to determine which had been changed. The primary's notification could come soon after the actual modification, instead of waiting for the refresh interval to expire.

RFC 1996 proposed a mechanism that would allow primary master servers to notify their slaves of changes to a zone's data. BIND 8 implements this scheme, called DNS NOTIFY for short.

DNS NOTIFY works like this: when a primary master name server notices a change to data in a zone, it sends a special request to all of the slave servers for that zone. It determines which servers are the slaves for the zone by looking at the list of NS records in the zone and taking out the one that points to the name server listed in the first record-specific field in the zone's SOA record as well as the local host.

The special NOTIFY request is identified by its opcode in the query header. The opcode for most queries is QUERY. NOTIFY messages have a special opcode, NOTIFY (duh). Other than that, the request looks very much like a query for the SOA record for the zone: it specifies the zone's domain name, class, and a type of SOA. The authoritative answer bit is also set.

When a slave receives a NOTIFY request for a zone from one of its configured master name servers, it responds with a NOTIFY response. The response tells the master that the slave received the NOTIFY request, so that it can stop sending it NOTIFY messages for the zone. Then the slave proceeds just as if the refresh timer had expired: it queries the master server for the SOA record for the zone that the master claimed has changed. If the serial number is higher, the slave transfers the zone.

Why doesn't the slave simply take the master's word that the zone has changed? It's possible that a miscreant could forge NOTIFY requests to our slaves, causing lots of unnecessary zone transfers, amounting to a denial of service attack against our master server.

If the slave actually transfers the zone, RFC 1996 says that it should issue its own NOTIFY requests to the other authoritative name servers for the zone. The idea is that the primary master may not be able to notify all of the slave servers for the zone itself, since it's possible some slaves can't communicate directly with the primary master and use another slave as their master. However, BIND 8 doesn't implement this, and BIND 8 slaves don't send NOTIFY messages unless explicitly configured to.

Here's how that works in practice. On our network, *terminator.movie.edu* is the primary master for *movie.edu*, and *wormhole.movie.edu* and *zardoz.movie.edu* are slaves, as shown in Figure 10-1.

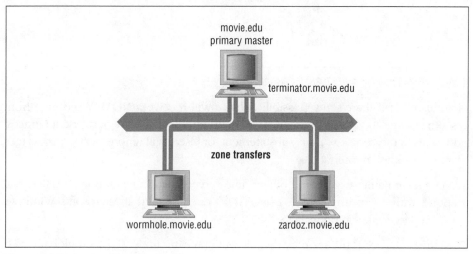

Figure 10-1. movie.edu zone transfers

When we update *movie.edu* on *terminator, terminator* sends NOTIFY messages to *wormhole* and *zardoz*. Both slaves check to see whether *movie.edu*'s serial number has incremented, and when they find it has, perform a zone transfer.

Let's also look at a more complicated zone transfer scheme. Here, *a* is the primary master name server for the zone, and *b*'s master server, but *b* is *c*'s master server. Moreover, *b* has two network interfaces, as shown in Figure 10-2.

In this scenario, *a* notifies both *b* and *c* after the zone is updated. *b* checks to see whether the zone's serial number has incremented and initiates a zone transfer. However, *c* ignores *a*'s NOTIFY message, because *a* is not *c*'s configured master name server (*b* is). If *b* is explicitly configured to notify *c*, then after *b*'s zone transfer completes, it sends *c* a NOTIFY message, which prompts *c* to check the serial number *b* holds for the zone.

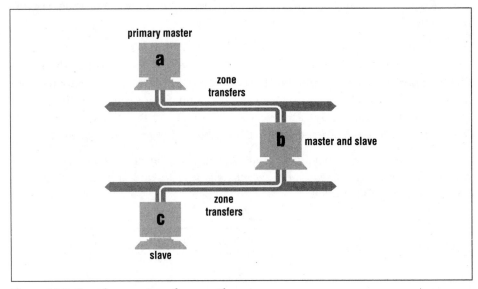

Figure 10-2. Complex zone transfer example

Note also that if there's any possibility that *c* will receive a NOTIFY message from *b*'s other network interface, *c* must be configured with both network interfaces' addresses in the zone's *masters* substatement, or else *c* will ignore NOTIFY messages from the unknown interface.

BIND 4 slave name servers, and other name servers that don't support NOTIFY, will respond with a Not Implemented (NOTIMP) error. Note that Microsoft's Windows NT DNS Server *does* support DNS NOTIFY.

In BIND 8, DNS NOTIFY is on by default, but you can turn NOTIFY off globally with the substatement:

```
options {
            notify no;
};
```

You can also turn NOTIFY on or off for a particular zone. For example, say you know that all of the slave servers for your *acmebw.com* zone are running BIND 4, and therefore don't understand NOTIFY requests. The *zone* statement:

```
zone "acmebw.com" {
            type master;
            file "db.acmebw";
            notify no;
};
```

avoids sending useless NOTIFY messages to the slaves for *acmebw.com*. A zone-specific NOTIFY setting overrides any global setting for that zone. Unfortunately, the current version of BIND doesn't allow you to turn off NOTIFY on a server-by-server basis.

BIND 8 even has a provision for adding servers to your "NOTIFY list" besides those in your zone's NS records. For example, you may have one or more unregistered slave servers (described in Chapter 8, *Growing Your Domain*) that you'd still like to pick up zone changes quickly. Or the server you're configuring may be a slave for the zone, but is the master server for another slave, and needs to send NOTIFY messages to it.

To add a server to your NOTIFY list, use the *also-notify* substatement of the *zone* statement:

```
zone "acmebw.com" {
            type master;
            file "db.acmebw.com";
            notify yes;
            also-notify { 15.255.152.4; };
};
```

DNS Dynamic Update

BIND 8 also supports the dynamic update facility described in RFC 2136. This permits authorized updaters to add and delete resource records from a zone for which the server is authoritative. An updater can find the authoritative name servers for a zone by retrieving the zone's NS records. If the server receiving an authorized update message is not the primary master for the zone, it will forward the update "upstream" to its master server(s). If they, in turn, are slaves for the zone, they will also forward the update upstream.

Dynamic update permits more than the simple addition and deletion of records. Updaters can add or delete individual resource records, delete RRsets (a set of resource records with the same domain name, class and type, such as all Internet addresses for *www.acmebw.com*), or even delete all records associated with a given name. An update can also stipulate that certain prerequisite records exist or not exist in the zone before the update takes effect. For example, an update can add the address record:

```
dakota.west.acmebw.com.        in      a      192.168.1.4
```

only if the name *dakota.west.acmebw.com* isn't currently being used, or only if *dakota.west.acmebw.com* currently has no address records.

For the most part, dynamic update functionality is used by programs like DHCP servers that assign IP addresses automatically to computers, and then need to register the resulting name-to-address and address-to-name mappings. These programs use the *ns_update()* routine to create update messages and send them to an authoritative server for the zone that contains the domain name.

However, it is possible to create updates manually with the command-line program *nsupdate*, which is part of the standard BIND distribution. *nsupdate* reads one-line commands that it then translates into an update message. Commands can be specified on standard input (the default) or in a file, whose name must be given as an argument to *nsupdate*. Commands not separated by a blank line are incorporated into the same update message.

The commands *nsupdate* understands are:

`prereq yxrrset` *domain name type* [*rdata*]
> Makes the existence of an RRset of type *type* owned by *domain name* a prerequisite to performing the update

`prereq nxrrset`
> Makes the non-existence of an RRset of type *type* owned by *domain name* a prerequisite to performing the update specified in successive *update* commands

`prereq yxdomain` *domain name*
> Makes the existence of the domain name specified a prerequisite to performing the update

`prereq nxdomain`
> Makes the non-existence of the domain name specified a prerequisite to performing the update

`update delete` *domain name* [*type*] [*rdata*]
> Deletes the domain name specified or, if *type* is also specified, deletes the RRset specified or, if *rdata* is also specified, deletes the record matching *domain name*, *type*, and *rdata*

`update add` *domain name ttl* [*class*] *type rdata*
> Adds the record specified to the zone. Note that the TTL, in addition to the type and resource-record-specific data, must be included, but the class is optional, and defaults to IN

So, for example, the command:

```
% nsupdate
> prereq nxdomain dakota.west.acmebw.com.
> update add dakota.west.acmebw.com. 333 in a 192.168.0.4
>
```

tells the server to add an address for *dakota.west.acmebw.com* only if the domain name does not already exist. Note that the last blank line is *nsupdate*'s cue to send the update.

The command:

```
% nsupdate
> prereq yxrrset dakota.west.acmebw.com. in mx
> update delete dakota.west.acmebw.com. in mx
> update add dakota.west.acmebw.com. in mx 10 dakota.west.acmebw.com.
> update add dakota.west.acmebw.com. in mx 50 store-forward.mindspring.com.
>
```

checks to see whether *dakota.west.acmebw.com* already has MX records, and if it
does, deletes them and adds two in their place.

Given the fearsome control that dynamic updates obviously give an updater over a
zone, you clearly need to restrict them, if you use them at all. By default, BIND 8
servers don't allow dynamic updates to authoritative zones. In order to use them,
you add an *allow-update* substatement to the *zone* statement for the zone that you'd
like to allow updates to.

allow-update takes an address match list as an argument. The address or addresses
matched by the list are the only addresses that are allowed to send your server
updates to that zone. It's prudent to make this access list as restrictive as possible:

```
zone "acmebw.com" {
            type master;
            file "db.acmebw";
            allow-update { 192.168.0.1; };
};
```

System Tuning

While the default configuration values will work fine for most sites, yours may be
one of the rare sites that needs some further tuning.

Zone Transfers

Zone transfers can place a heavy load on a name server. On BIND 4 name servers,
outbound zone transfers (transfers of a zone the server is master for), in particular,
require *fork()*ing the *named* process, thereby using a significant amount of extra
memory. BIND 4.9 introduced mechanisms for limiting the zone transfer load that
your name server places on its master servers. BIND 8 has these mechanisms and
more.

Limiting transfers initiated per name server

With BIND 4.9 and later, you can limit how many zones your name server requests
from a single remote name server. This will make the administrator of the remote
name server host happy because their machine won't be pounded for zone transfers
if all of the zones change—important if hundreds of zones are involved.

In BIND 8, the conf file statement is:

```
options {
            transfers-per-ns 2;
};
```

The equivalent BIND 4 boot file directive is:

```
limit transfers-per-ns 2
```

With a forthcoming version of BIND 8 (we're not sure which), you'll also be able to set the limit on a server-by-server basis, instead of globally. To do this, you'd use the *transfers* substatement inside a *server* statement, where the server is the server you'd like to specify the limit for:

```
server 192.168.1.2 {
            transfers 2;
};
```

The default limit is two active zone transfers per name server. That limit may seem small, but it works. Here is what happens. Suppose your name server needs to load four zones from a remote name server. Your name server will start transferring the first two zones and wait on the third and fourth zone. After one of the first two zone transfers completes, the third zone will be requested. After another transfer completes, the fourth zone will be started. The net result is the same as before there were limits—all the zones are transferred—but the work is spread out.

When might you want to increase this limit? You might want to increase this limit if you notice that it is taking too long to synch up with the remote name server, and you know that the reason is the serializing of transfers—not just that the network between the machines is slow. This probably only matters if you're maintaining hundreds or thousands of zones. And you need to make sure that the remote name server and the networks between can handle the additional workload of more simultaneous zone transfers.

Limiting the total number of zone transfers initiated

The last limit dealt with a single remote name server. This one deals with more than one remote name server. BIND versions 4.9 and later let you limit the total number of zones your server will request at any one time. The default limit is ten. As we explained above, your server will only pull two zones from any given remote name server by default. If your server is transferring two zones from each of five name servers, your server will have hit the limit, and it will postpone any further transfers until one of the current transfers finishes.

The BIND 8 *named.conf* file statement is:

```
options {
            transfers-in 10;
};
```

The equivalent BIND 4 boot file directive is:

```
limit transfers-in 10
```

If your host or network cannot handle ten active zone transfers, you should decrease this number. If you run a server supporting hundreds or thousands of zones, and your host and network can support the load, you might want to raise this limit. If you raise this limit, you may also need to also raise the limit for the number of transfers per name server. (For example, if your name server loads from only four remote name servers, and your name server will only start two transfers per remote name server, then your server will have at most eight active zone transfers. Increasing the limit for the total number of zone transfers will not have any effect unless the limit per server is also increased.)

Limiting the duration of a zone transfer

BIND 8 will also let you limit the duration of an inbound zone transfer. By default, zone transfers are limited to 120 minutes, or two hours. The idea is that a zone transfer that's taking longer than 120 minutes is probably hung and won't complete, and the *named-xfer* process is taking up resources unnecessarily. If you'd like a smaller or larger limit, perhaps because you know that your server is a slave for a zone that normally takes more than 120 minutes to transfer, you can use this statement:

```
options {
               max-transfer-time-in 180;
};
```

You can even place the limit on transfers of a particular zone by using the *max-transfer-time-in* substatement inside a *zone* statement. For example, if you know that the *rinkydink.com* zone always takes a long time (say three hours) to transfer, either because of its size or because the links to the master server are so slow, but you'd still like a shorter time limit (maybe an hour) on other zone transfers, you could use:

```
options {
               max-transfer-time-in 60;
};

zone "rinkydink.com" {
               type slave;
               file "db.rinkydink";
               masters { 192.168.1.2; };
               max-transfer-time-in 180;
};
```

More efficient zone transfers

A zone transfer, we said earlier, is composed of many DNS messages sent end-to-end over a TCP connection. Traditional zone transfers only put a single resource record in each DNS message. That's a waste of space: you need a full header on each

DNS message, even though you're only carrying a single record. It's like being the only person in a Chevy Suburban. A DNS message could carry many more records.

BIND 8 servers understand a new zone transfer format, called *many-answers*. The *many-answers* format puts as many records as possible into a single DNS message. The result is that a *many-answers* zone transfer takes less bandwidth, because there's less overhead, and less CPU time, because less time is spent unmarshaling DNS messages.

The BIND 8 *transfer-format* subcommand controls which zone transfer format the server uses for zones that it is a master for. That is, it determines the format of the zones that your server transfers to its slaves. *transfer-format* is both an *options* subcommand and a *server* subcommand: as an *options* subcommand, *transfer-format* controls the server's global zone transfer behavior. The default is to use the old *one-answer* zone transfer format, for interoperability with BIND 4 name servers.

```
options {
        transfer-format many-answers;
};
```

changes the server's settings to use the *many-answers* format for all servers, unless explicitly told not to in a *server* statement, like this:

```
server 192.168.1.2 {
        transfer-format one-answer;
};
```

The one downside to using the *many-answers* format is that zone transfers can actually take longer using the new format. They're more efficient from a bandwidth and CPU utilization point of view, but your zone transfers may take longer to complete.

If you'd like to take advantage of the new, more efficient zone transfers, set your server's global zone transfer format setting to *many-answers*, if most of your slaves run BIND 8 or Microsoft's DNS Server, which also understands the format, or *one-answer*, if most of your slaves run BIND 4. Then use the *transfer-format* server substatement to adjust the global setting for exceptional servers.

Resource Limits

Sometimes, you just want to tell the server to stop being so greedy: don't use more than this much memory, don't open more than this many files. BIND 4.9 introduced these limits, and as with so many features, BIND 8 gives you several variations.

Changing the data segment size limit

Some operating systems have a default limit to stop processes from using too much memory. If your OS is limiting the name server from growing to the size it wants to grow to, the name server may not operate efficiently, and it may even panic or exit. Unless your name server handles an extremely large amount of data, you won't run into this limit. But if you do, BIND 4.9 and 8 have configuration options to change the system's default limit on data segment size. You might use these options to set a higher limit than the default system limit for the *named* process.

For BIND 8, the statement is:

```
options {
                datasize size
};
```

For BIND 4, the directive is:

```
limit datasize size
```

size is an integer value in bytes. You can specify a different unit than bytes by appending a character: k (kilobyte), m (megabyte), or g (gigabyte). For example, 64m is 64 megabytes.

NOTE   Not all systems support increasing the data segment size. If your system is one that does not, the name server will issue a syslog message at level LOG_WARNING to tell you that this feature is not implemented.

Changing the stack size limit

In addition to allowing you to change the limit on the size of the server's data segment, BIND 8 will let you adjust the limit the system places on the amount of memory the *named* process' stack can use. The syntax is:

```
options {
                stacksize size;
};
```

where *size* is specified as in *datasize*. As with *datasize*, this feature only works on systems that permit modification of the stack size limit.

Changing the core size limit

If you don't appreciate *named*'s leaving huge *core* files around on your filesystem, you can at least make them smaller by using *coresize*. Conversely, if *named* hasn't been able to dump an entire core file because of a tight operating system limit, you may be able to raise that limit with *coresize*.

coresize's syntax is:

```
options {
                coresize size;
};
```

Again, as with *datasize*, this feature only works on operating systems that support modifying the limit on core file size.

Changing the open files limit

On hosts with many IP addresses, or a low limit on the maximum number If your name server is authoritative for a lot of zones, the *named* process will open lots of files when it starts up—one per authoritative zone, assuming you use backup files on the zones you're a slave for. Likewise, if the host running your name server has lots of virtual network interfaces,[*] *named* will require one file descriptor per interface. Most UNIX operating systems place a limit on the number of files any process can open simultaneously. If your name server tries to open more files than this limit permits, you'll see this message in your syslog output:

```
named[pid]: socket(SOCK_RAW): Too many open files
```

If your operating system also permits changing that limit on a per-process basis, you can increase it using BIND 8's *files* substatement:

```
options {
                files number;
};
```

The default is *unlimited* (which is also a valid value), although this just means that the server doesn't place any limit on the number of simultaneously open files; the operating system, however, may.

Maintenance Intervals

BIND name servers have always done periodic housekeeping: refreshing zones the server is a slave for, for example. With BIND 8, you can now control how often these chores happen, or whether they happen at all.

Cleaning interval

Name servers older than BIND 4.9 only passively remove stale entries from the cache. Before such a name server returns a record to a querier, it checks to see whether the TTL on that record has expired. If it has, the name server starts the resolution process to find more current data. This means that a BIND 4 server may cache a lot of records in a flurry of name resolution, and then just let those records spoil in the cache, taking up valuable memory, even though the records are stale.

BIND 8 now actively walks through the cache and removes stale records once each cleaning interval. This means that a BIND 8 name server will tend to use less memory for caching than a BIND 4 server in the same role. On the other hand, the cleaning

---

[*] Chapter 15, *Miscellaneous*, describes a better solution to the "Too many open files" problem than bumping up the limit on files.

process takes CPU time, and on very slow or very busy name servers, you may not want it running every hour.

By default, the cleaning interval is 60 minutes. You can tune the interval with the *cleaning-interval* substatement to the *options* statement. For example:

```
options {
            cleaning-interval 120;
};
```

sets the cleaning interval to 120 minutes. To turn off cache cleaning entirely, use a cleaning interval of zero.

Interface interval

We've said already that BIND, by default, listens on all of a host's network interfaces. BIND 8 is actually smart enough to notice when a network interface on the host it's running on comes up or goes down. To do this, it periodically scans the host's network interfaces. This happens once each interface interval, which is 60 minutes by default. If you know the host your name server runs on has no dynamic network interfaces, you can disable scanning for new interfaces by setting the interface interval to zero to avoid unnecessary hourly overhead:

```
options {
            interface-interval 0;
};
```

On the other hand, if your host brings up or tears down network interfaces more often than every hour, you may want to reduce the interval.

Statistics interval

Okay, adjusting the statistics interval—the frequency at which the BIND 8 server dumps statistics to the statistics file—won't have much effect on performance. But it fits better here, with the other maintenance intervals, than anywhere else in the book.

The syntax of the *statistics-interval* substatement is exactly analogous to the other maintenance intervals:

```
options {
            statistics-interval 60;
};
```

And, as with the other maintenance intervals, the default is 60 minutes, and a setting of zero disables the periodic dumping of statistics.

Name Server Address Sorting

When you are contacting a host that has multiple network interfaces, using a particular interface may give you better performance. If the multihomed host is local and shares a network with your host, one of the multihomed host's addresses is "closer." If the multihomed host is remote, you *may* see better performance by using one of the interfaces instead of another, but often it doesn't matter much which address is used. In days past, net 10 (the former ARPAnet "backbone") was always closer than any other remote address. The Internet has improved drastically since those days, so you won't often see a marked improvement by preferring one network over another for remote multihomed hosts, but we'll cover that case anyway.

Before we get into address sorting by a name server, you should first look at whether address sorting by the resolver better suits your needs. (See the section called "The sortlist Directive" in Chapter 6, *Configuring Hosts.*) Since your resolver and name server may be on different networks, it often makes more sense for the resolver to sort addresses optimally for its host. Address sorting at the name server works fairly well, but it won't be optimal for every resolver it services. Resolver address sorting was added at 4.9. If your resolver (not your name server) is older than 4.9, you are out of luck. You'll have to make do with address sorting at the name server, which was introduced in 4.8.3.

We should also mention that address sorting is not supported in BIND 8. For BIND 8, the developers removed address sorting because they believed that it had no place in the server.

Local Multihomed Hosts

Let's deal with the local multihomed host first. Suppose you have a source host (i.e., a host that keeps your master sources) on two networks, cleverly called network A and network B, and this host uses NFS to export filesystems to hosts on both networks. Hosts on network A will experience better performance if they use the source host's interface to network A. Likewise, hosts on network B would benefit from using the source host's interface to network B for the address of the NFS mount.

In Chapter 4, *Setting Up BIND*, we mentioned that BIND returns all the addresses for a multihomed host. There was no guarantee of the order in which a DNS server would return the addresses, so we assigned aliases (*wh249* and *wh253* for *wormhole*) to the individual interfaces. If one interface was preferable, you (or more realistically, a DNS client) could use an appropriate alias to get the correct address. You *can* use aliases to choose the "closer" interface (e.g., for setting up NFS mounts), but because of address sorting, they are not always necessary.

BIND 4 servers, by default, sort addresses if one condition holds: if the host that sent the query to the name server *shares* a network with the name server host (e.g., both are on network A), then BIND sorts the addresses in the response. How does BIND know when it shares a network with the querier? It knows because when BIND starts up, it finds out all the interface addresses of the host it is running on. BIND extracts the network numbers from these addresses to create the default sort list. When a query is received, BIND checks if the sender's address is on a network in the default sort list. If it is, then the query is local and BIND sorts the addresses in the response.

In Figure 10-3, assume that there is a BIND 4 name server on *notorious*. The name server's default sort list would contain network A and network B. When *spellbound* sends a query to *notorious* looking up the addresses of *notorious*, it will get an answer back with *notorious*'s network A address first. That's because *notorious* and *spellbound* share network A. When *charade* looks up the addresses of *notorious*, it will get an answer back with *notorious*'s network B address first. Both hosts are on network B. In both of these cases, the name server sorts the addresses in the response because the hosts share a network with the name server host. The sorted address list has the "closer" interface first (see Figure 10-3).

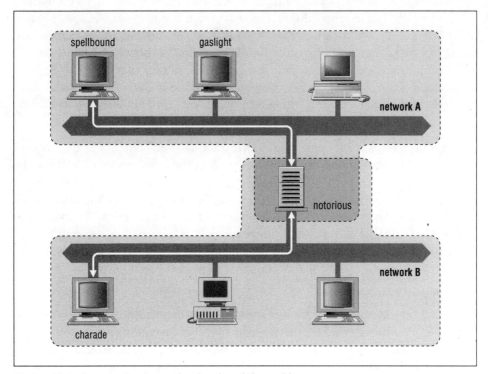

Figure 10-3. Communicating with a local multihomed host

Let's change the situation slightly. Suppose the name server is running on *gaslight*. When *spellbound* queries *gaslight* for *notorious*'s address, *spellbound* will see the same response as in the last case because *spellbound* and *gaslight* share network A, which means that the name server will sort the response. However, *charade* may see a differently-ordered response, since it does not share a network with *gaslight*. The closer address for *notorious* may still be first in the response to *charade*, but only because of luck, not name server address sorting. In this case, you'd have to run an additional name server on network B for *charade* to benefit from BIND 4's default address sorting.

As you can see, you benefit by running a name server on each network; not only is your name server available if your router goes down, it also sorts addresses of multihomed hosts. Because the name server sorts addresses, you do not need to specify aliases for NFS mounts or network logins to get the best response.

Remote Multihomed Hosts

Suppose that your site often contacts a particular remote site or a "distant" local site, and that you get better performance by favoring addresses on one of the remote site's networks. For instance, the *movie.edu* domain has networks 192.249.249 and 192.253.253. Let's add a connection to net 10 (the old ARPAnet). The remote host being contacted has two network connections, one to network 10 and one to network 26. This host does not route to network 26, but for special reasons it has a network 26 connection. Since the router to network 26 is always overloaded, you'll get better performance by using the remote host's net 10 address. Figure 10-4 shows this situation.

If a user on *terminator* is contacting *reanimator*, it's preferable to use the network 10 address, because access through *gateway B* to the network 26 address will be slower than the direct route. Unfortunately, the name server running on *terminator* will not *intentionally* place network address 10 first in the list when it looks up the addresses for *reanimator*; the only network that *terminator* is attached to is 192.249.249, and so it doesn't know that network 10 is "closer" than network 26. This is where the *sortlist* boot file entry comes into play. To indicate a preference for network 10 addresses, add the following line to *named.boot*:

```
sortlist 10.0.0.0
```

The *sortlist* entries are *appended* to the default sort list. With this *sortlist* entry, the sort list on *terminator* now contains networks 192.249.249 and 10. Now, when a user on *terminator* queries the name server on *terminator*, and the name server sorts the response because the query is local, the name server will check for addresses on the 192.249.249 network and place them first in the response. If there are no addresses on network 192.249.249, it will check for network 10 addresses and place them first

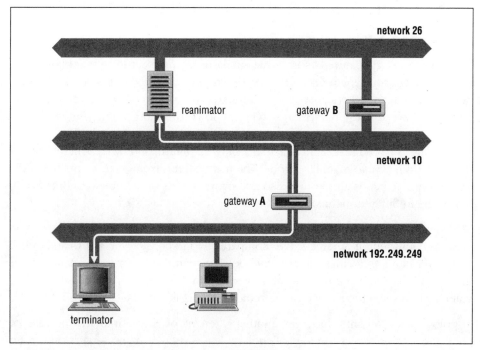

Figure 10-4. Communicating with a remote multihomed host

in the response. This solves the problem we described earlier—when *reanimator* is looked up, its network 10 address will be placed first in the response.

Address Sorting on Subnetted Networks

Subnetted networks change address sorting only slightly. When the name server creates its default sort list, it adds both the subnet number and the network number to the list. Like before, when the query is local and the name server sorts the response, the common subnet address will be placed first. Unfortunately, not everything is perfect—you can't add *sortlist* entries for other subnets of your network. Here's why: the name server assumes all the *sortlist* entries are network numbers (not subnet numbers), and your network number is already on the sort list. Since your network number is already on the list, the subnet *sortlist* entry is discarded.

Multiple Sortlist Entries

One last thing—if you want to add more than one *sortlist* entry, you must specify them all on the same line, like this:

```
sortlist 10.0.0.0 26.0.0.0
```

Preferring Name Servers on Certain Networks

BIND 8's topology feature is somewhat similar to *sortlist*, but it only applies to the process of choosing name servers. We described how BIND chooses between a number of name servers that are authoritative for the same zone earlier in the book—by selecting the name server with the lowest roundtrip time. But we lied—a little. BIND 8 actually places remote name servers in 64 millisecond bands when comparing RTT. The first band is actually only 32 milliseconds wide (there! We did it again), from zero to 32 milliseconds. The next extends from 33 to 96 milliseconds, and so on. The bands are designed so that name servers on different continents will always be in different bands.

The idea is to favor name servers in lower bands but to treat servers in the same band as equivalent. If a name server compares two remote servers' RTTs and one is in a lower band, the name server will choose to send the query to the name server in the lower band. But if the remote servers are in the same band, the name server will check to see whether one of the remote servers is topologically closer.

Topology lets you introduce yet another element of fudge into the process of choosing a name server to query. Topology lets you favor name servers on certain networks over others. Topology takes as an argument an address match list, where the entries are networks, listed in the order in which the local name server should prefer them (highest to lowest). Therefore:

```
topology {
              15/8;
              172.88/16;
    };
```

tells the local name server to prefer name servers on the network 15.0.0.0 over other name servers, and name servers on the network 172.88.0.0 over name servers on networks other than network 15.0.0.0. So if the name server has a choice between a name server on network 15.0.0.0, a name server on 172.88.0.0, and a name server on 192.168.1.0, assuming all three have RTT values in the same band, it will choose to query the name server on 15.0.0.0.

You can also negate entries in the topology address match list to penalize name servers on certain networks. The higher in the address match list the negated entry matches, the greater the penalty.

Building Up a Large Site-wide Cache with Forwarders

Certain network connections discourage sending large volumes of traffic off-site, either because the network connection is pay-per-packet or because the network connection is a slow link with a high delay, like a remote office's satellite connection to the company's network. In these situations, you'll want to limit the off-site DNS traffic to the bare minimum. BIND provides a mechanism to do this: *forwarders*.

If you designate one or more servers at your site as forwarders, all the off-site queries are sent to the forwarders first. The idea is that the forwarders handle all the off-site queries generated at the site, building up a rich cache of information. For any given query in a remote domain, there is a high probability that the forwarder can answer the query from its cache, avoiding the need for the other servers to send packets off-site. Nothing special is done to these servers to make them forwarders; you modify all the *other servers* at your site to direct their queries through the forwarders.

A primary master or slave name server's mode of operation changes slightly when it is directed to use a forwarder. If the requested information is already in its database of authoritative data and cache data, it answers with this information; this part of the operation hasn't changed. However, if the information is not in its database, the name server will send the query to a forwarder and wait a short period for an answer before resuming normal operation and contacting the remote servers itself. What the name server is doing that's different is sending a *recursive* query to the forwarder, expecting it to find the answer. At all other times, the name server sends out *nonrecursive* queries to other name servers and deals with responses that only refer to other name servers.

For example, here is the *forwarders* conf file statement—and the equivalent BIND 4 boot file directive—for name servers in the *movie.edu* domain. Both *wormhole* and *terminator* are the site forwarders. This *forwarders* statement is added to every name server conf file *except* the conf files for the forwarders, *wormhole* and *terminator.*

```
options {
        forwarders { 192.249.249.1; 192.249.249.3; };
};
```

The equivalent BIND 4 directive is:

```
forwarders 192.249.249.1 192.249.249.3
```

When you use forwarders, try to keep your site configuration simple. You *can* end up with configurations that are really twisted.

Avoid having "mid-level" servers forward packets (i.e., avoid having a *forwarders* line in your mid-level name server's conf file). Mid-level servers mostly refer name servers to subdomain name servers. If they have been configured to forward packets, do they refer to subdomain name servers or do they contact the subdomain name server to find out the answer? Whichever way it works, you're probably making your site configuration too hard for mere mortals (and subdomain administrators) to understand.

NOTE   Avoid chaining your forwarders. Don't configure server A to forward to server B, and configure server B to forward to server C (or worse yet, back to server A).

A More Restricted Name Server

You may want to restrict your name servers even further—stopping them from even *trying* to contact an off-site server if their forwarder is down or doesn't respond. You can do this by making the server a *forward-only* server. (A forward-only server is still a primary master, slave, or caching-only server; don't get confused here. We call it a forward-only server because calling it a primary master, slave, or caching-only forward-only server is just too long a name.) A *forward-only* server is a variation on a server that uses *forwarders*. It still answers queries from its authoritative data and cache data. However, it relies *completely* on its forwarders; it *doesn't* try to contact other servers to find out information if the forwarders don't give it an answer. Here is an example of what a forward-only server's conf file would contain:

```
options {
               forwarders { 192.249.249.1; 192.249.249.3; };
               forward only;
};
```

On a BIND 4 name server, that would look like:

```
forwarders 192.249.249.1 192.249.249.3
options forward-only
```

BIND name servers before 4.9 provide the same functionality, using the *slave* directive instead of the options *forward-only* directive:

```
forwarders 192.249.249.1 192.249.249.3
slave
```

Don't confuse this old use of the term "slave" with the modern use. "Slave" now means a name server that gets the data that describes a zone from a master server via a zone transfer.

You must have the *forwarders* line in the conf or boot file. It does not make sense to have only the forward-only line. If you do create a forward-only name server, you might want to consider including the forwarders' IP addresses more than once. On a BIND 8 server, that would look like:

```
options {
                forwarders { 192.249.249.1; 192.249.249.3;
                        192.249.249.1; 192.249.249.3; };
                forward only;
};
```

On a BIND 4 server, that's:

```
forwarders 192.249.249.1 192.249.249.3 192.249.249.1 192.249.249.3
options forward-only
```

The forward-only server contacts each forwarder only once, and it waits a short time for the forwarder to respond. Listing the forwarders multiple times directs the forward-only server to *retransmit* queries to the forwarders, and increases the overall length of time that the forward-only name server will wait for an answer from forwarders.

However, you must ask yourself if it *ever* makes sense to use a forward-only server. A forward-only server is completely dependent on the forwarders. You can achieve much the same configuration (and dependence) by not running a forward-only server at all; instead, create a *resolv.conf* file that contains *nameserver* directives that point to the forwarders you were using. Thus, you are still relying on the forwarders, but now your applications are querying the forwarders directly instead of having a forward-only name server query them for the applications. You lose the local caching that the forward-only server would have done, and the address sorting, but you reduce the overall complexity of your site configuration by running fewer "restricted" name servers.

A Nonrecursive Name Server

By default, BIND resolvers send recursive queries, and BIND name servers do the work required to answer recursive queries. (If you don't remember how recursion works, look in Chapter 2, *How Does DNS Work?*) In the process of finding the answer to recursive queries, the name server builds up a cache of nonauthoritative information about other domains.

In some circumstances, it is *undesirable* for name servers to do the extra work required to answer a recursive query or to build up a cache of data. The root name servers are an example of one of these circumstances. The root name servers are so busy that they should not be spending the extra effort to recursively find the answer to a request. Instead, they send a response based only on the authoritative data they have. The response may contain the answer, but it is more likely that the response contains a referral to other name servers. And since the root servers do not support recursive queries, they do not build up a cache of nonauthoritative data, which is good because their cache would be huge.*

You can induce BIND to run as a nonrecursive name server with the following conf file statement:

```
options {
              recursion no;
};
```

On a BIND 4.9 server, that's the directive:

```
options no-recursion
```

Now the server will respond to recursive queries as though they were nonrecursive.

In conjunction with *recursion no*, there is one more configuration option necessary if you want to stop your server from building a cache:

```
options {
              fetch-glue no;
};
```

Or, on BIND 4.9:

```
options no-fetch-glue
```

This stops the server from fetching missing glue when constructing the *additional data* section of a response.

If you choose to make one of your servers nonrecursive, do not list this name server in any host's *resolv.conf* file. While you can make your name server nonrecursive, there is no corresponding option to make your resolver work with a nonrecursive name server.†

You can list a nonrecursive name server as one of the servers authoritative for your zone data (i.e., you can tell a parent name server to refer queries about your zone to this server). This works because name servers send nonrecursive queries between themselves.

Do not list a nonrecursive name server as a *forwarder.* When a name server is using another server as a forwarder, it sends the query to the forwarder as a recursive query instead of a nonrecursive query.

---

* Note that a root name server wouldn't normally receive recursive queries, unless a name server's administrator configured it to use a root server as a forwarder, a host's administrator configured its resolver to use the root server as a name server, or a user pointed *nslookup* at the root server.

† In general. Clearly, programs designed to send nonrecursive queries, or that can be configured to send nonrecursive queries, like *nslookup*, would still work.

Avoiding a Bogus Name Server

In your term as name server administrator, you might find some remote name server that responds with bad information. You can attempt to find an administrator to fix the problem. Or, you can save yourself some grief and configure your name server to not ask questions of this server, which is possible with BIND 4.9 and later. Here is the conf file statement:

```
server 10.0.0.2 {
                bogus yes;
};
```

Or, on a BIND 4.9 server:

```
bogusns 10.0.0.2
```

Of course, you fill in the correct IP address.

If this is the only server for a zone, and you just told your name server to stop talking to that server, don't expect to be able to look up names in that zone. Hopefully, there are other servers for that zone that can provide good information.

Securing Your Name Server

BIND 4.9 introduced several important security features that help you protect your name server. BIND 8 continued the tradition by introducing several more. These features are particularly important if your name server is running on the Internet, but they may also be useful on purely internal name servers.

We'll start by discussing measures you should take on all name servers for which security is important. Then we'll describe a model in which your name servers are split into two communities, one for serving only resolvers and one for answering other name servers' queries.

BIND Version

One of the most important ways you can enhance the security of your name server is to run the latest version of BIND. All versions of BIND before 4.9.7 are susceptible to at least a few known attacks.[*] BIND 8.1.2 is an even better bet, because of the many new security mechanisms it introduced.

But don't stop there: New attacks are being thought up all the time, so you'll have to do your best to keep abreast of BIND's vulnerabilities and the latest "safe" version

---

[*] In fact, part of the reason there *is* a BIND 4.9.7, and the BIND 4 release stream didn't stop with 4.9.6, was 4.9.6's vulnerability to a particular attack.

of BIND. One good way to do that is to read the newsgroup *comp.protocols.dns.bind* regularly.

Restricting Queries

Up until BIND 4.9, domain administrators had no way to control who could look up data on their name servers. That makes a certain amount of sense; the original idea behind DNS was to make information easily available all over the Internet.

The neighborhood is not such a friendly place anymore, though. In particular, people who run Internet firewalls may have a legitimate need to hide certain parts of their name space from most of the world but to make it available to a limited audience.

The BIND 8 *allow-query* substatement allows you to place an IP address-based access list on queries. The access list can apply to a particular zone, or to any queries received by the server. In particular, the access list specifies which IP addresses are allowed to send queries to the server.

Restricting all queries

The global form of the *allow-query* substatement looks like this:

```
options {
                allow-query { address_match_list; };
};
```

So to restrict our name server to answering queries from the two main Movie U. networks, we'd use:

```
options {
                allow-query { 192.249.249/24; 192.253.253/24; };
};
```

Restricting queries in a particular zone

BIND 8 also allows you to apply an access list to a particular zone. In this case, just use *allow-query* as a substatement of the *zone* statement for the zone you want to protect:

```
zone "hp.com" {
                type slave;
                file "db.hp";
                masters { 15.255.152.2; };
                allow-query { "HP-NET"; };
};
```

Any kind of authoritative name server, master or slave, can apply an access list to the zone. Zone-specific access lists take precedence over global access lists for that zone. The zone-specific access list may even be more permissive than the global access list. If there's no zone-specific access list defined, any global access list will apply.

In BIND 4.9, this functionality is provided by the *secure_zone* record. Not only does it limit queries for individual resource records, it limits zone transfers, too. (In BIND 8, restricting zone transfers is done separately.) However, 4.9 servers have no mechanism for restricting who can send your server queries for data in zones your server *isn't* authoritative for; the secure zones mechanism only works with authoritative zones.

To use secure zones, you include one or more special TXT (text) records in your zone data on the primary master name server. The records are conveniently transferred to the zone's slave servers automatically. Of course, only BIND 4.9 slaves will understand them.

The TXT records are special because they're attached to the pseudo-domain name *secure_zone*, and the resource record-specific data has a special format, either:

    address:mask

or:

    address:H

In the first form, **address** is the dotted-octet form of the IP network to which you want to *allow* access to the data in this zone. The mask is the netmask for that address. If you want to allow all of net 15 access to your zone data, use 15.0.0.0:255.0.0.0. If you only want to allow the range of IP addresses from 15.254.0.0 to 15.255.255.255 access to your zone data, use 15.254.0.0:255.254.0.0.

The second form specifies the address of a particular host you'd like to allow access to your zone data. The H is equivalent to the mask 255.255.255.255; in other words, each bit in the 32-bit address is checked. Therefore, 15.255.152.4:H gives the host with the IP address 15.255.152.4 the ability to look up data in the zone.

If we wanted to restrict queries for information in *movie.edu* to hosts on Movie U.'s networks, we could add the following lines to *db.movie* on the *movie.edu* primary:

```
secure_zone    IN    TXT    "192.249.249.0:255.255.255.0"
secure_zone    IN    TXT    "192.253.253.0:255.255.255.0"
secure_zone    IN    TXT    "192.253.254.0:255.255.255.0"
secure_zone    IN    TXT    "127.0.0.1:H"
```

Notice that we included the address 127.0.0.1 in our access list. That's so a resolver can query its local name server. If you forget the :H, you'll see the following syslog message:

```
Aug 17 20:58:22 terminator named[2509]: build_secure_netlist
        (movie.edu): addr (127.0.0.1) is not in mask (0xff000000)
```

Also, note that the secure zones records here apply only to the zone they're in—that is, *movie.edu*. If you wanted to prevent unauthorized queries for data in other zones on this server, you'd have to add secure zones records to that zone on its primary master name server, too.

Preventing Unauthorized Zone Transfers

Even more important than controlling who can query your name server is ensuring that only your real slave name servers can transfer zones from your name server. Users on remote hosts that can query your name server's zone data can only look up data (e.g., addresses) for hosts whose domain names they already know, one at a time. Users who can start zone transfers from your server can list all of the hosts in your zones. It's the difference between letting random folks call your company's switchboard and ask for John Q. Cubicle's phone number and sending them a copy of your corporate phone directory.

BIND 8's *allow-transfer* substatement and 4.9's *xfrnets* directive let administrators apply an access list to zone transfers. *allow-transfer* can restrict transfers of a particular zone as a *zone* substatement or can restrict all zone transfers as an *options* substatement. It takes an address match list as an argument.

Say the slave servers for your *acmebw.com* zone have the IP addresses 192.168.0.1 and 192.168.1.1. The *zone* statement:

```
zone "acmebw.com" {
            type master;
            file "db.acmebw";
            allow-transfer { 192.168.0.1; 192.168.1.1; };
};
```

will allow only those slaves to transfer *acmebw.com* from the primary master name server. Note that since BIND 8's default is to allow any IP address to transfer zones, and because hackers can just as easily transfer the zone from your slaves, you should probably also have a *zone* statement like this on your slaves:

```
zone "acmebw.com" {
            type slave;
            masters { 192.168.0.4; };
            allow-transfer { none; };
};
```

BIND 8 will also let you establish a global access list on zone transfers. This applies to any zones that don't have their own, explicit access lists defined as *zone* substatements. For example, you might want to limit all zone transfers to your internal IP addresses:

```
options {
            allow-transfer { 192.168/16; };
};
```

The BIND 4.9 *xfrnets* directive takes as its arguments the networks or IP addresses you'd like to allow to transfer zones from your name server. Networks are specified by the dotted-octet form of the network number; for example:

```
xfrnets 15.0.0.0 128.32.0.0
```

allows only hosts on the Class A network 15 or the Class B network 128.32 to transfer zones from this name server. Unlike secure zones, this restriction applies to any zones the server is authoritative for.

If you want to specify just a part of the network, down to a single IP address, you can add a network mask. The syntax for including a network mask is *network&netmask*. Note that there are no spaces either between the network and the ampersand or between the ampersand and the netmask: they're not allowed.

To pare down the addresses allowed to transfer zones in the previous example to just the IP address 15.255.152.4 and the subnet 128.32.1.0, you could use the *xfrnets* directive:

```
xfrnets 15.255.152.4&255.255.255.255 128.32.1.0&255.255.255.0
```

For a primary master name server accessible from the Internet, you probably want to limit zone transfers to just your slave name servers. You probably don't need to use *xfrnets* on name servers inside your firewall, unless you're worried about your own employees listing your zone data.

Running BIND as a Non-Root User

Running a network server such as BIND as the root user can be dangerous—and BIND normally runs as root. If a hacker finds a vulnerability in the server through which he can read or write files, he'll have root access to the filesystem. If he can exploit a flaw that allows him to execute commands, he'll execute them as root.

BIND 8.1.2 includes experimental code that allows you to change the user and group the name server runs as. This allows you to run the name server with what's known as "least privilege:" the minimal set of rights it needs to do its job. That way, if someone is able to break into your host through the name server, at least they won't have root privileges.

BIND 8.1.2 also includes an option that allows you to *chroot* the name server: to change its view of the filesystem so that its root directory is actually a particular directory on your host's filesystem. This effectively traps your name server in this directory, along with any attackers who successfully compromise your name server's security.

The command-line options that implement these features are:

-u

Specifies the username or user ID the name server changes to after starting, e.g., `named -u bin`.

-g

Specifies the group or group ID the name server changes to after starting, e.g., `named -g other`. If *-u* is specified without *-g*, the name server will use the user's primary group.

-t

Specifies the directory for the name server to *chroot* to.

If you opt to use the *-u* and *-g* options, you'll have to decide what user and group to use. Your best bet is to create a new user and group for the name server to run as, such as *named*. Since the name server reads *named.conf* before giving up root privileges, you don't have to change that file's permissions. However, you may have to change the permissions and ownership of your zone data files so that the user the name server runs as can read them. If you use dynamic update, you'll have to make the zone data files for dynamically-updated zones writable by the name server.

The name server may have trouble writing the *named.pid* file, too, since it occasionally rewrites it after startup (and after giving up root privileges). On most versions of UNIX, */var/run* (the directory in which the name server saves *named.pid*) isn't writable by non-root users. The easiest way to deal with this is to use the *pid-file* substatement to move *named.pid* to another directory:

```
options {
                pid-file "/var/named/named.pid";
};
```

Then make sure that file is writable by the user *named* runs as.

If your name server is configured to log to files (as opposed to syslog), make sure those files exist and are writable by the name server before starting the server.

The *-t* option takes a little more special configuration. In particular, you need to make sure that all the files *named* uses are present in the directory you're restricting the server to. That includes the following:

named-xfer

Most *named*s expect to find the *named-xfer* executable in */etc/named-xfer*. If you *chroot* the server to */var/named*, that becomes */var/named/etc/named-xfer*.

Shared libraries

If you build the name server with shared libraries, you'll need to put copies of those shared libraries in whatever directory your operating system expects them in. For example, if your OS looks for shared libraries in */lib*, you'll need copies in */var/named/lib*. The alternative is to build your name server as a statically-linked executable.

/dev/null

> The name server needs a */dev/null* in the *chroot*ed directory. You can find out how to make one by reading */dev/MKDEV*, or the manual page for *mknod*.

Finally, the name server may not be able to syslog in a *chroot*ed environment. If that's the case, use the *logging* statement described in Chapter 7, *Maintaining BIND*, to log to files in the *chroot*ed directory.

With any of these options, you'll have to remember to either edit *ndc* to specify the options upon restart or start, or to start and restart *named* manually.

"Delegated" Name Server Configuration

Some of your name servers answer nonrecursive queries from other name servers on the Internet, because your name servers appear in NS records delegating your zones to them. We'll call these name servers "delegated" name servers.

There are special measures you can take to secure your delegated name servers. But first, you should make sure that these servers don't receive any recursive queries (that is, you don't have any resolvers configured to use these servers, and no name servers use them as forwarders). Some of the precautions we'll take—like making the server respond nonrecursively even to recursive queries—preclude your resolvers from using these servers. If you do have resolvers using your delegated name servers, consider establishing another class of name servers to serve just your resolvers, as described in the next section.

Once you know your name server only answers queries from other name servers, you can turn off recursion. This eliminates a major vector of attack: the most common spoofing attacks involve inducing the target name server to query name servers under the hacker's control by sending the target a recursive query for a domain name in a zone served by the hacker's servers. To turn off recursion, you'd use:

```
options {
                recursion no;
};
```

on a BIND 8 server, and:

```
options no-recursion
```

on a BIND 4.9 server.

You should also restrict zone transfers of your zones to known slave servers, as described in "Preventing Unauthorized Zone Transfers," earlier in this chapter.

Finally, you might also want to turn off glue fetching. The name server will automatically try to resolve the names of any name servers in the RDATA of NS records; to prevent this from happening, and keep your name server from sending any queries of its own, use:

```
options {
                fetch-glue no;
};
```

on a BIND 8 server, and:

```
options no-fetch-glue
```

on BIND 4.9.

Resolving Name Server Configuration

We'll call a name server that serves one or more resolvers, or is configured as another name server's forwarder, a "resolving" name server. Unlike a delegated name server, a "resolving" name server can't refuse recursive queries. Consequently, we have to configure it a little differently to secure it. Since we know our name server should only receive queries from our own resolvers, we can configure it to deny queries from any but our resolvers' IP addresses.

Only BIND 8 will allow us to restrict which IP addresses can send our name server arbitrary queries. (BIND 4.9 servers will let us restrict which IP addresses can send the server queries in authoritative zones, via the *secure_zone* TXT record, but we're actually more worried about recursive queries in others' zones.) This *allow-query* substatement will restrict queries to just our internal network:

```
options {
                allow-query { 192.168/16; };
};
```

With this configuration, the only resolvers that can send your server recursive queries, and induce your name servers to query other name servers, are your internal resolvers, which are presumably relatively benevolent.

Two Name Servers in One

What if you only have one name server to advertise your zone and serve your resolvers, and you can't afford the additional expense of buying another computer to run another name server on? There are still a couple of options open to you. One is a single-server solution that takes advantage of BIND 8's flexibility. This configuration allows anyone to query the name server for information in your delegated zones, but only your internal resolvers can query the name server for other information. While this doesn't prevent remote resolvers from sending your name server recursive queries, those queries have to be in your authoritative zones, so they won't induce your name server to send additional queries.

Here's a *named.conf* file to do that:

```
options {
                allow-query { 192.168/16; };
};

zone "acmebw.com" {
                type master;
                file "db.acmebw";
                allow-query { any };
                allow-transfer { 192.168.0.1; 192.168.1.1; };
};

zone "168.192.in-addr.arpa" {
                type master;
                file "db.192.168";
                allow-query { any; };
                allow-transfer { 192.168.0.1; 192.168.1.1; };
};
```

Here, the more permissive zone-specific access lists apply to queries in the server's authoritative zones, but the more restrictive global access list applies to all other queries.

Another option is to run two *named* processes on a single host. One is configured as the delegated server, another as the resolving name server. Since we have no way of telling remote servers or configuring resolvers to query one of our name servers on a port other than 53, the default DNS port, we have to run these servers on different IP addresses.

Of course, if your host already has more than one network interface, that's no problem. Even if it only has one, the operating system may support IP address aliases. These allow you to attach more than one IP address to a single network interface. One *named* process can listen on each. Finally, if the operating system doesn't support IP aliases, you can still bind one *named* against the network interface's IP address, and one against the loopback address. Only the local host will be able to send queries to the *named* listening on the loopback address, but that's fine if the local host's resolver is the only one you need to serve.

First, here's the *named.conf* file for the delegated name server, listening on the network interface's IP address:

```
options {
                directory "/usr/local/named";
                recursion no;
                listen-on { 192.168.0.4; };
                pid-file "delegated.pid";
};
```

```
zone "acmebw.com" {
                type master;
                file "db.acmebw";
                allow-query { any };
                allow-transfer { 192.168.0.1; 192.168.1.1; };
};

zone "168.192.in-addr.arpa" {
                type master;
                file "db.192.168";
                allow-query { any; };
                allow-transfer { 192.168.0.1; 192.168.1.1; };
};

zone "." {
                type hint;
                file "db.cache";
};
```

Next, here's the *named.conf* file for the resolving name server, listening on the loopback address:

```
options {
                directory "/usr/local/named1";
                listen-on { 127.0.0.1; };
                pid-file "resolving.pid";
};

zone "." {
                type hint;
                file "db.cache";
};
```

The *listen-on* substatement tells the server reading the conf file to listen only on network interfaces whose IP addresses match the address match list. We've specified the IP address explicitly, so that there's no chance of mistakes. You can also use *listen-on* to have *named* listen on a port other than 53; for that, use the syntax:

```
options {
                listen-on port <n> { address_match_list };
};
```

Note that we turn recursion off on the delegated name server, but must leave it on on the resolving name server. We also give each name server its own PID file and its own directory, so that they don't try to use the same default filename for their PID files, debug files, and statistics files.

To use the resolving name server, listening on the loopback address, the local host's *resolv.conf* file must include:

```
nameserver 127.0.0.1
```

as the first *nameserver* directive.

Load Sharing Between Mirrored Servers

Name servers released since BIND 4.9 have formalized some load-sharing functionality that has existed in patches to BIND for some time. Bryan Beecher wrote patches to BIND 4.8.3 to implement what he called "shuffle address records." These were address records of a special type that the name server rotated between responses. For example, if the domain name *foo.bar.baz* had three "shuffled" IP addresses, 192.1.1.1, 192.1.1.2, and 192.1.1.3, an appropriately patched name server would give them out first in the order:

```
192.1.1.1 192.1.1.2 192.1.1.3
```

then in the order:

```
192.1.1.2 192.1.1.3 192.1.1.1
```

and then in the order:

```
192.1.1.3 192.1.1.1 192.1.1.2
```

before starting over again with the first order, and repeating the rotation *ad infinitum.*

The functionality is enormously useful if you have a number of equivalent network resources, like mirrored FTP servers, Web servers, or terminal servers, and you'd like to spread the load among them. You establish one domain name that refers to the group of resources, configure clients to access that domain name, and the name server inverse-multiplexes the accesses between the IP addresses you list.

BIND 4.9 and later versions do away with the shuffle address record as a separate record type, subject to special handling. Instead, a modern name server rotates addresses for any domain name that has more than one A record. (In fact, the name server will rotate any type of record, except PTR records, as long as a given domain name has more than one of them.) So the records:

```
foo.bar.baz.    60    IN    A    192.1.1.1
foo.bar.baz.    60    IN    A    192.1.1.2
foo.bar.baz.    60    IN.   A    192.1.1.3
```

accomplish on a 4.9 or later name server just what the shuffle address records did on a patched 4.8.3 server. The BIND documentation calls this process *round robin.*

It's a good idea to reduce the records' time-to-live, too, as we did in this example. This ensures that if the addresses are cached on an intermediate name server that doesn't support round robin, they'll time out of the cache quickly. If the intermediate name server looks up the name again, your authoritative name server can round robin the addresses again.

Note that this is really load sharing, not load balancing, since the name server gives out the addresses in a completely deterministic way, without regard to the actual load or capacity of the servers servicing the requests. In our example, the server at address 192.1.1.3 could be a 486DX33 running Linux, and the other two servers HP9000 K420s, and the Linux box would still get a third of the queries. Listing a higher-capacity server's address multiple times won't help, because BIND eliminates duplicate records.

11

nslookup

> *"Don't stand chattering to yourself like that,"*
> *Humpty Dumpty said, looking at her for the first*
> *time, "but tell me your name and your business."*
>
> *"My name is Alice, but—"*
>
> *"It's a stupid name enough!" Humpty Dumpty*
> *interrupted impatiently. "What does it mean?"*
>
> *"Must a name mean something?" Alice asked*
> *doubtfully.*
>
> *"Of course it must," Humpty Dumpty said with a*
> *short laugh...*

To be proficient at troubleshooting name server problems, you'll need a special tool to make DNS queries, one that gives you complete control. We'll cover *nslookup* in this chapter because it's distributed with BIND and with many vendors' systems. If you're the explorer type, you might also check out *dig*; it provides similar functionality, and some people like its user interface better. You can pick up source for *dig* from the *tools* directory (BIND 4) or *src/bin* directory (BIND 8) of the BIND distribution.

Note that this chapter isn't comprehensive; there are aspects of *nslookup*—mostly obscure and seldom used—that we won't cover. You can always consult the manual pages for those.

Is nslookup a Good Tool?

Much of the time you'll use *nslookup* to make queries, in the same way the resolver makes them. Sometimes, though, you'll use *nslookup* to query other name servers as a name server would, instead. Which one you emulate will depend on the problem you're trying to debug. You might wonder, "How accurately does *nslookup* emulate a resolver or a name server? Does *nslookup* actually use the BIND resolver library routines?" No, *nslookup* uses its own routines for querying name servers, but those routines are based on the resolver routines. Consequently, *nslookup*'s behavior is very similar to the resolver's behavior, but it does differ slightly. We'll point out some of those differences. As for emulating name server behavior, *nslookup* allows us to query another server with the same query packet that a name server would use, but the retransmission scheme is quite different. Like a name server, though, *nslookup* can pull a copy of the zone data. So *nslookup* does not exactly emulate either the resolver or the name server, but it does emulate them well enough to make a good troubleshooting tool. Let's delve into those differences we alluded to.

Multiple Servers

nslookup only talks to one name server at a time. This is the biggest difference between *nslookup*'s behavior and the resolver's behavior. The resolver makes use of each *nameserver* entry in *resolv.conf*. If there are two *nameserver* lines in *resolv.conf*, the resolver tries the first name server, then the second, then the first, then the second, until it receives a response or it gives up. The resolver does this for every query. On the other hand, *nslookup* tries the first name server in *resolv.conf* and keeps retrying until it finally gives up on the first name server and tries the second. Once it gets a response, it locks onto that server and doesn't try the other. But, you *want* your troubleshooting tool to talk only with one name server, so you can reduce the number of variables when analyzing a problem. If *nslookup* used more than one name server, you wouldn't have as much control over your troubleshooting session. So, talking to only one server is the right thing for a troubleshooting tool to do.

Timeouts

The *nslookup* timeouts match the resolver timeouts when the resolver is only querying one name server. A name server's timeouts, however, are based on how quickly the remote server answered the last query, a dynamic measure. *nslookup* will never match name server timeouts, but that's not a problem either. When you're querying remote name servers with *nslookup*, you probably only care *what* the response was, not how long it took.

Domain Searches

nslookup implements the search list just as the resolver code does. Name servers don't implement search lists, so, to act like a name server, the *nslookup* search function must be turned off—more on that later.

Zone Transfers

nslookup will do zone transfers just like a name server. Unlike the name server, *nslookup* does not check SOA serial numbers before pulling the zone data; you'll have to do that manually, if you want to.

Using NIS and /etc/hosts

This last point doesn't compare *nslookup* to the resolver or name server but to ways of looking up names in general. *nslookup*, as distributed from the Internet Software Consortium, only uses DNS; it won't use NIS or */etc/hosts*. Most applications will use DNS, NIS, or */etc/hosts*. Don't look to *nslookup* to help you find your lookup problem unless your host is really configured to use name servers.

Interactive Versus Noninteractive

Let's start our tutorial on *nslookup* by looking at how to start it and how to exit from it. *nslookup* can be run either interactively or noninteractively. If you only want to look up one piece of data, use the noninteractive form. If you plan on doing something more extensive, like changing servers or options, then use an interactive session.

To start an interactive session, just type *nslookup*:

```
% nslookup
Default Server: terminator.movie.edu
Address: 0.0.0.0

> ^D
```

If you need help, type *?* or *help*. When you want to exit, type ∧*D* (control-D). If you try to exit from *nslookup* by interrupting it, with ∧*C* (or whatever your interrupt character is), you won't get very far. *nslookup* catches the interrupt, stops whatever it is doing (like a zone transfer), and gives you the > prompt.

For a noninteractive lookup, include the name you are looking up on the command line:

```
% nslookup carrie
Server: terminator.movie.edu
Address: 0.0.0.0

Name:   carrie.movie.edu
Address: 192.253.253.4
```

Option Settings

nslookup has its own set of dials and knobs, called option settings. All of the option settings can be changed. We'll discuss here what each of the options means. We'll use the rest of the chapter to show you how to use them.

```
% nslookup
Default Server:  bladerunner.fx.movie.edu
Address:  0.0.0.0

> set all
Default Server:  bladerunner.fx.movie.edu
Address:  0.0.0.0

Set options:
  nodebug          defname          search          recurse
  nod2             novc             noignoretc      port=53
  querytype=A      class=IN         timeout=5       retry=4
  root=a.root-servers.net.
  domain=fx.movie.edu
  srchlist=fx.movie.edu


> ^D
```

Before we get into the options, we need to cover the introductory lines. The default name server is *bladerunner.fx.movie.edu*. This means that every query sent by *nslookup* is going to be sent to *bladerunner*. The address 0.0.0.0 means "this host." When *nslookup* is using address 0.0.0.0 or 127.0.0.1 as its server, it is using the name server running on the local system—in this case, *bladerunner*.

The options come in two flavors: *Boolean* and *value*. The options that do not have an equals sign after them are Boolean options. They have the interesting property of being either "on" or "off." The value options can take on different, well, values. How can we tell which Boolean options are on and which are off? The option is *off* when a "no" precedes the option's name. *nodebug* means that debugging is off. As you might guess, the option *search* is on.

How you change Boolean or value options depends on whether you are using *nslookup* interactively or not. In an interactive session, you change an option with the *set* command, as in *set debug* or *set domain=classics.movie.edu*. From the command line, you omit the word *set* and precede the option with a hyphen, as in *nslookup -debug* or *nslookup -domain=classics.movie.edu*. The options can be abbreviated to their shortest unique string—e.g., *nodeb* for *nodebug*. In addition to its abbreviation, the *querytype* option can also be called simply *type*.

Let's go through each of the options:

[no]debug

Debugging is turned off by default. If it is turned on, the name server shows timeouts and displays the response packets. See *[no]d2* for a discussion of debug level 2.

[no]defname

By default, *nslookup* adds the default domain name to names without a dot in them. Before search lists existed, the BIND resolver code would only add the default domain to names without *any* dots in them; this option reflects that behavior. *nslookup* can implement the pre-search list behavior (with *search* off and *defname* on), or it can implement the search list behavior (with *search* on).

[no]search

The search option "overshadows" the default domain name (*defname*) option. That is, *defname* only applies if *search* is turned off. By default, *nslookup* appends the domains in the search list (*srchlist*) to names that don't end in a dot.

[no]recurse

nslookup requests recursive service by default. This turns on the recursion-desired bit in query packets. The BIND resolver sends recursive queries in the same way. Name servers, however, send out nonrecursive queries to other name servers.

[no]d2

Debugging at level 2 is turned off by default. If it is turned on, you see the query packets sent out in addition to the regular debugging output. Turning on *d2* also turns on *debug*. Turning off *d2* turns off *d2* only; *debug* is left on. Turning off *debug* turns off both *debug* and *d2*.

[no]vc

By default, *nslookup* makes queries using UDP packets instead of over a *v*irtual *c*ircuit (TCP). Most BIND resolver queries are made with UDP, so the default *nslookup* behavior matches the resolver. As the resolver can be instructed to use TCP, so can *nslookup*.

[no]ignoretc

By default, *nslookup doesn't* ignore *t*runcated packets. If a packet is received that has the "truncated" bit set—indicating that the name server couldn't fit all the important information in the UDP response packet—*nslookup* doesn't ignore it; it retries the query using a TCP connection instead of UDP. Again, this matches the BIND resolver behavior. The reason for retrying the query using a TCP connection is that TCP responses can be twice as large as UDP responses. TCP responses *could* be many times the size of a UDP response (a TCP connection can carry much more data than a single UDP packet), but the buffers BIND uses for a TCP query are only twice as large as the UDP buffers.

port=53

> The DNS service is on port 53. You can start a name server on another port—for debugging purposes, for example—and *nslookup* can be directed to use that port.

querytype=A

> By default, *nslookup* looks up A (address) resource record types. In addition, if you type in an IP address (and the *nslookup* query type is address or pointer), then *nslookup* will invert the address, append *in-addr.arpa*, and look up PTR (pointer) data instead.

class=IN

> The only class that matters is *Internet*. Well, there is the *Hesiod* (HS) class too, if you are an MITer or run Ultrix.

timeout=5

> If the name server doesn't respond within 5 seconds, *nslookup* resends the query and doubles the timeout (to 10, 20, and then 40 seconds). The BIND resolver uses the same timeouts when querying a single name server.

retry=4

> Send the query four times before giving up. After each retry, the timeout value is doubled. Again, this matches the BIND resolver behavior.

root=a.root-servers.net.

> There is a convenience command called *root*, which switches your default server to the server named here. Executing the *root* command from a modern *nslookup*'s prompt is equivalent to executing *server a.root-servers.net*. Older versions use *nic.ddn.mil* (old) or even *sri-nic.arpa* (ancient) as the default root name server. You can change the default "root" server with *set root=server*.

domain=fx.movie.edu

> This is the default domain appended if the *defname* option is on.

srchlist=fx.movie.edu

> If *search* is on, these are the domains appended to names that do not end in a dot. The domains are listed in the order that they are tried, separated by a slash. (The 4.8.3 search list defaulted to *fx.movie.edu/ movie.edu*. At 4.9.3, you have to explicitly set the search list in */etc/resolv.conf* to get both *fx.movie.edu* and *movie.edu*.)

The .nslookuprc File

You can set up new default *nslookup* options in an *.nslookuprc* file. *nslookup* will look for an *.nslookuprc* file in your home directory when it starts up, in both interactive and noninteractive modes. The *.nslookuprc* file can contain any legal *set* commands, one per line. This is useful, for example, if your old *nslookup* still thinks *sri-nic.arpa* is a root name server. You can set the default root name server to a real root with a line like this in your *.nslookuprc* file:

```
set root=a.root-servers.net.
```

You might also use *.nslookuprc* to set your search list to something other than your host's default search list, or to change the timeouts *nslookup* uses.

Avoiding the Search List

nslookup implements the search list, as the resolver does. When you are debugging, the search list can get in your way. Either you need to turn the search list off completely (*set nosearch*), or you need to add a trailing dot to the fully qualified domain name you are looking up. We prefer the latter, as you'll see in our examples.

Common Tasks

There are little chores you'll come to use *nslookup* for almost every day: finding the IP address or MX records for a given domain name, or querying a particular name server for data. We'll cover these first, before moving on to the more occasional stuff.

Looking Up Different Data Types

By default, *nslookup* looks up the address for a name, or the name for an address. You can look up any data type by changing the *querytype*, as we will show in this example:

```
% nslookup
Default Server:  terminator.movie.edu
Address:  0.0.0.0

> misery                    —Look up address
Server:  terminator.movie.edu
Address:  0.0.0.0

Name:    misery.movie.edu
Address:  192.253.253.2

> 192.253.253.2            —Look up name
Server:  terminator.movie.edu
Address:  0.0.0.0

Name:    misery.movie.edu
Address:  192.253.253.2

> set q=mx                 —Look up MX data
> wormhole
Server:  terminator.movie.edu
Address:  0.0.0.0
```

```
wormhole.movie.edu          preference = 10, mail exchanger = wormhole.movie.edu
wormhole.movie.edu          internet address = 192.249.249.1
wormhole.movie.edu          internet address = 192.253.253.1

> set q=any               —Look up data of any type
> diehard
Server:  terminator.movie.edu
Address:  0.0.0.0

diehard.movie.edu           internet address = 192.249.249.4
diehard.movie.edu           preference = 10, mail exchanger = diehard.movie.edu
diehard.movie.edu           internet address = 192.249.249.4
```

These are only a few of the valid DNS data types, of course. For the complete list, see Appendix A, *DNS Message Format and Resource Records*.

Authoritative Versus Nonauthoritative Answers

If you've used *nslookup* before, you might have noticed something peculiar—the first time you look up a remote name, the answer is authoritative, but the second time you look up the same name it is nonauthoritative. Here's an example:

```
% nslookup
Default Server:  relay.hp.com
Address:  15.255.152.2

> slate.mines.colorado.edu.
Server:  relay.hp.com
Address:  15.255.152.2

Name:     slate.mines.colorado.edu
Address:  138.67.1.3

> slate.mines.colorado.edu.
Server:  relay.hp.com
Address:  15.255.152.2

Non-authoritative answer:
Name:     slate.mines.colorado.edu
Address:  138.67.1.3
```

While this looks odd, it really isn't. What is happening is that the first time the local name server looks up *slate*, it contacts the name server for *mines.colorado.edu*, and the *mines.colorado.edu* server responds with an authoritative answer. The local name server, in effect, passes the authoritative response directly back to *nslookup*. It also caches the response. The second time you look up *slate*, the name server answers out of its cache, which results in the answer "nonauthoritative."

Notice that we ended the domain name with a trailing dot each time we looked it up. The response would have been the same had we left the trailing dot off. There are times when it is critical that you use the trailing dot while debugging, and times when it is not. Rather than stopping to decide if *this* name needs a trailing dot, we always add one if we know the name is fully qualified, except, of course, for the example where we turn off the search list.

Switching Servers

Sometimes you want to query another name server directly—you may think it is misbehaving, for example. You can switch servers with *nslookup* by using the *server* or *lserver* command. The difference between *server* and *lserver* is that *lserver* queries your "local" server—the one you started out with—to get the address of the server you want to switch to; *server* uses the default server instead of the local server. This difference is important to know because the server you just switched to may not be responding, as we'll show in this example:

```
% nslookup
Default Server:  relay.hp.com
Address:  15.255.152.2
```

When we start up, our first server, *relay.hp.com*, becomes our lserver. This will matter later on in this session.

```
> server galt.cs.purdue.edu.
Default Server:  galt.cs.purdue.edu
Address:  128.10.2.39

> cs.purdue.edu.
Server:  galt.cs.purdue.edu
Address:  128.10.2.39

*** galt.cs.purdue.edu can't find cs.purdue.edu.: No response from server
```

At this point we try to switch back to our original name server. But there is no name server running on galt to look up relay's address.

```
> server relay.hp.com.

*** Can't find address for server relay.hp.com.: No response from server
```

Instead of being stuck, though, we use the *lserver* command to have our local server look up *relay*'s address:

```
> lserver relay.hp.com.
Default Server:  relay.hp.com
Address:  15.255.152.2

> ^D
```

Since the server on *galt* did not respond—it's not even running a name server—it wasn't possible to look up the address of *relay* to switch back to using *relay*'s name server. Here's where *lserver* comes to the rescue: the local name server, *relay*, was still responding, so we used it. Instead of using *lserver*, we could have recovered by using *relay*'s IP address directly—*server 15.255.152.2.*

You can even change servers on a per-query basis. To specify that you'd like *nslookup* to query a particular server for information about a given domain name, you can specify the server as the second argument on the line, after the domain name to look up—like so:

```
% nslookup
Default Server:  relay.hp.com
Address:  15.255.152.2

> saturn.sun.com. ns.sun.com.
Name Server:  ns.sun.com
Address:  192.9.9.3

Name:     saturn.sun.com
Addresses: 192.9.25.2

> ^D
```

And, of course, you can change servers from the command line. You can specify the server to query as the argument after the domain name to look up, like this:

```
% nslookup -type=mx fisherking.movie.edu. terminator.movie.edu.
```

This instructs *nslookup* to query *terminator.movie.edu* for MX records for *fisherking.movie.edu.*

Finally, to specify an alternate default server and enter interactive mode, you can use a hyphen in place of the domain name to look up:

```
% nslookup - terminator.movie.edu.
```

Less Common Tasks

These are tricks you'll probably have to use less often, but which are very handy to have in your repertoire. Most of these will be helpful when you're trying to troubleshoot a DNS or BIND problem; they'll enable you to grub around in the packets the resolver sees, and mimic a BIND name server querying another name server or transferring zone data.

Seeing the Query and Response Packets

If you need to, you can direct *nslookup* to show you the queries it sends out and the responses it receives. Turning on *debug* shows you the responses. Turning on *d2* shows you the queries as well. When you want to turn off debugging completely, you have to use *set nodebug*, since *set nod2* only turns off level 2 debugging. After the following trace, we'll explain some parts of the packet output. If you want, you can pull out your copy of RFC 1035, turn to page 25, and read along with our explanation.

```
% nslookup
Default Server:  terminator.movie.edu
Address:  0.0.0.0

> set debug
> wormhole
Server:  terminator.movie.edu
Address:  0.0.0.0

------------
Got answer:
    HEADER:
        opcode = QUERY, id = 6813, rcode = NOERROR
        header flags:  response, auth. answer, want recursion,
        recursion avail.  questions = 1,  answers = 2,
        authority records = 2,  additional = 3

    QUESTIONS:
        wormhole.movie.edu, type = A, class = IN
    ANSWERS:
    -> wormhole.movie.edu
        internet address = 192.253.253.1
        ttl = 86400 (1D)
    -> wormhole.movie.edu
        internet address = 192.249.249.1
        ttl = 86400 (1D)
    AUTHORITY RECORDS:
    -> movie.edu
        nameserver = terminator.movie.edu
        ttl = 86400 (1D)
    -> movie.edu
        nameserver = wormhole.movie.edu
        ttl = 86400 (1D)
    ADDITIONAL RECORDS:
    -> terminator.movie.edu
        internet address = 192.249.249.3
        ttl = 86400 (1D)
    -> wormhole.movie.edu
        internet address = 192.253.253.1
        ttl = 86400 (1D)
    -> wormhole.movie.edu
        internet address = 192.249.249.1
        ttl = 86400 (1D)

------------
Name:    wormhole.movie.edu
Addresses:  192.253.253.1, 192.249.249.1

> set d2
> wormhole
Server:  terminator.movie.edu
```

```
Address:   0.0.0.0
```

This time the query is also shown.

```
------------
SendRequest(), len 36
    HEADER:
        opcode = QUERY, id = 6814, rcode = NOERROR
        header flags:  query, want recursion
        questions = 1,  answers = 0,  authority records = 0,
      additional = 0

    QUESTIONS:
        wormhole.movie.edu, type = A, class = IN

------------
------------
Got answer (164 bytes):
```

The answer is the same as above.

The text between the dashes is the query and response packets. As promised, we will go through the packet contents. DNS packets are composed of five sections:

1. Header section

2. Question section

3. Answer section

4. Authority section

5. Additional section

Header section

The header section is present in every query and response. The operation code is always QUERY. The only other opcodes are inverse query (IQUERY) and status (STATUS), but those aren't used. The id is used to associate a response with a query and to detect duplicate queries or responses. You have to look in the header flags to see which packets are queries and which are responses. The string **want recursion** means that the querier wants the name server to do all the work. The flag is parroted in the response. The string **auth. answer** means that this response is *authoritative.* In other words, the response is from the name server's authoritative data, not from its cache data. The response code, **rcode**, can be one of **no error, server failure, name error** (also known as **nxdomain** or **nonexistent domain**), **not implemented,** or **refused**. The **server failure, name error, not implemented,** and **refused** response codes cause the *nslookup* "Server failed," "Nonexistent domain," "Not implemented," and "Query refused" errors, respectively. The last four entries in the header section are counters—they indicate how many resource records there are in each of the next four sections.

Question section

There is always *one* question in a DNS packet; it includes the name and the requested data type and class. There is never more than one question in a DNS packet. The capability of handling more than one question in a DNS packet would require a redesign of the packet format. For one thing, the single authority bit would have to be changed, because the answer section could contain a mix of authoritative answers and nonauthoritative answers. In the present design, setting the authoritative answer bit means that the name server is an authority for the domain name in the question section.

Answer section

This section contains the resource records that answer the question. There can be more than one resource record in the response. For example, if the host is multihomed, there will be more than one address resource record.

Authority section

The authority section is where name server records are returned. When a response refers the querier to some other name servers, those name servers are listed here.

Additional section

The additional records section adds information that may complete information included in other sections. For instance, if a name server is listed in the authority section, the name server's address is added to the additional records section. After all, to contact the name server, you need to have its address.

For you sticklers for detail, there *is* a time when the number of questions in a query packet isn't one: in an inverse query, when it's zero. In an inverse query, there is one answer in the query packet, and the question section is empty. The name server fills in the question. But, as we said, inverse queries are almost nonexistent.

Querying Like a BIND Name Server

You can make *nslookup* send out the same query packet a name server would. Name server query packets are not much different from resolver packets. The primary difference in the query packets is that resolvers request recursive services, and name servers seldom do. Recursion is the default with *nslookup*, so you have to explicitly turn it off. The difference in *operation* between a resolver and a name server is that the resolver implements the search list, and the name server doesn't. By default, *nslookup* implements the search list, so that, too, has to be turned off. Of course, judicious use of the trailing dot will have the same effect.

In raw *nslookup* terms, this means that to query like a resolver, you use *nslookup*'s default settings. To query like a name server, use *set norecurse* and *set nosearch*. On the command line, that's *nslookup -norecurse -nosearch*.

When a BIND name server gets a query, it looks for the answer in its cache. If it doesn't have the answer, and it is authoritative for the domain, the name server responds that the name doesn't exist or that there is no data for that type. If the name server doesn't have the answer, and it is *not* authoritative for the domain, it starts walking up the domain tree looking for NS records. There will always be NS records somewhere higher in the domain tree. As a last resort, it will use the NS records at the root domain, the highest level.

If the name server received a nonrecursive query, it would respond to the querier by giving the NS records that it had found. On the other hand, if the original query was a recursive query, the name server would then query the remote name servers in the NS records that it found. When the name server receives a response from one of the remote name servers, it caches the response, and repeats this process, if necessary. The remote server's response will either have the answer to the question or it will contain a list of name servers lower in the domain tree and closer to the answer.

Let's assume for our example that we are trying to satisfy a recursive query and that we didn't find any NS records until we checked the *gov* domain. That is, in fact, the case when we ask the name server on *relay.hp.com* about *www.whitehouse.gov*—it doesn't find any NS records until the *gov* domain. From there we switch servers to a *gov* name server and ask the same question. It directs us to the *whitehouse.gov* servers. We then switch to a *whitehouse.gov* name server and ask the same question:

```
% nslookup
Default Server:  relay.hp.com
Address:  15.255.152.2

> set norec              —Query like a name server: turn off recursion
> set nosearch           —turn off the search list
> www.whitehouse.gov     —We don't need to dot-terminate since we've turned
                         —search off
Server:  relay.hp.com
Address:  15.255.152.2

Name: www.whitehouse.gov
Served by:
- H.ROOT-SERVERS.NET
  128.63.2.53
  gov
- B.ROOT-SERVERS.NET
  128.9.0.107
  gov
- C.ROOT-SERVERS.NET
  192.33.4.12
  gov
- D.ROOT-SERVERS.NET
  128.8.10.90
  gov
```

```
- E.ROOT-SERVERS.NET
  192.203.230.10
  gov
- I.ROOT-SERVERS.NET
  192.36.148.17
  gov
- F.ROOT-SERVERS.NET
  192.5.5.241
  gov
- G.ROOT-SERVERS.NET
  192.112.36.4
  gov
- A.ROOT-SERVERS.NET
  198.41.0.4
  gov
```

Switch to a gov name server. You may have to turn recursion back on temporarily, if the name server doesn't have the address already cached.

```
> server e.root-servers.net
Default Server:  e.root-servers.net
Address: 192.203.230.10
```

Ask the same question of the gov name server. It will refer us to name servers closer to our desired answer.

```
> www.whitehouse.gov.
Server:  e.root-servers.net
Address:  192.203.230.10

Name:    www.whitehouse.gov
Served by:
- SEC1.DNS.PSI.NET
          38.8.92.2
          WHITEHOUSE.GOV
- SEC2.DNS.PSI.NET
          38.8.93.2
          WHITEHOUSE.GOV
```

Switch to a whitehouse.gov name server—either of them will do.

```
> server sec1.dns.psi.net.
Default Server:  sec1.dns.psi.net
Address:  38.8.92.2

> www.whitehouse.gov.
Server:  sec1.dns.psi.net
Address:  38.8.92.2

Name:    www.whitehouse.gov
Addresses:  198.137.240.91, 198.137.240.92
```

We hope this example gives you a feeling for how name servers look up names. If you need to refresh your understanding of what this looks like graphically, flip back to Figure 2-10.

Before we move on, notice that we asked each of the servers the very same question: "What's the address for *www.whitehouse.gov*?" What do you think would happen if the *gov* name server had already cached *www.whitehouse.gov*'s address itself? The *gov* name server would have answered the question out of its cache instead of referring you to the *whitehouse.gov* name servers. Why is this significant? Suppose you messed up a particular host's address in your zone. Someone points it out to you, and you clean up the problem. Even though your name server now has the correct data, some remote sites find the old, messed-up data when they look up the name. One of the name servers higher up in the domain tree, such as a root name server, has cached the incorrect data; when it receives a query for that host's address, it returns the incorrect data instead of referring the querier to your name servers. What makes this problem hard to track down is that only one of the "higher up" name servers has cached the incorrect data, so only some of the remote lookups get the wrong answer—the ones that use this server. Fun, huh? Eventually, though, the "higher up" name server will time out the old record. If you're pressed for time, you can contact the administrators of the remote name server and ask them to kill and restart *named* to flush the cache. Of course, if the remote name server is an important, much-used name server, they may tell you where to go with that suggestion.

Zone Transfers

nslookup can be used to transfer a whole zone using the *ls* command. This feature is useful for troubleshooting, for figuring out how to spell a remote host's name, or just for counting how many hosts are in some remote domain. Since the output can be substantial, *nslookup* allows you to redirect the output to a file. If you want to bail out in the middle of a transfer, you can interrupt it by typing your interrupt character.

Beware: some hosts won't let you pull a copy of their zone, either for security reasons or to limit the load on their name server host. The Internet is a friendly place, but administrators have to defend their turf.

Let's look at the *movie.edu* zone. As you will see in the output below, all the zone data is listed—the SOA record is listed twice, which is an artifact of how the data is exchanged during the zone transfer. (BIND 4's *nslookup* only shows you address and name server data, not all the data.)

```
% nslookup
Default Server:  terminator.movie.edu
Address:  0.0.0.0

> ls movie.edu.
@                         4D IN SOA      terminator root.terminator (
                                         1997080605      ; serial
```

```
                                      3H              ; refresh
                                      1H              ; retry
                                      4w2d            ; expiry
                                      1D )            ; minimum

                   4D IN NS           terminator
terminator         4D IN A            192.249.249.3
                   4D IN MX           10 terminator
                   4D IN NS           wormhole
wormhole           4D IN A            192.249.249.1
                   4D IN A            192.253.253.1
                   4D IN MX           10 wormhole
robocop            4D IN A            192.249.249.2
                   4D IN MX           10 robocop
wh249              4D IN A            192.249.249.1
wh253              4D IN A            192.253.253.1
wh                 4D IN CNAME        wormhole
shining            4D IN A            192.253.253.3
                   4D IN MX           10 shining
localhost          4D IN A            127.0.0.1
bitg               4D IN CNAME        terminator
carrie             4D IN A            192.253.253.4
                   4D IN MX           10 carrie
dh                 4D IN CNAME        diehard
diehard            4D IN A            192.249.249.4
                   4D IN MX           10 diehard
misery             4D IN A            192.253.253.2
                   4D IN MX           10 misery
@                  4D IN SOA          terminator root.terminator (
                                      1997080605      ; serial
                                      3H              ; refresh
                                      1H              ; retry
                                      4w2d            ; expiry
                                      1D )            ; minimum
Received 48 answers (0 records).
> ls movie.edu  > /tmp/movie   —List all data into /tmp/movie
[terminator.movie.edu]
Received 48 answers (0 records).
```

Troubleshooting nslookup Problems

The last thing you want is to have problems with your troubleshooting tool. Unfortunately, some types of failures render the troubleshooting tool mostly useless. Other types of *nslookup* failures are, at best, confusing because they don't give you any direct information to work with. While there may be a few problems with *nslookup* itself, most of the problems you encounter will be with name server configuration and operation. We'll cover a few odd problems here.

Looking Up the Right Data

This isn't really a problem, *per se*, but it can be awfully confusing. If you use *nslookup* to look up a type of data for a domain name, and the domain name exists, but no data of the type you're looking for exists, you'll get an error like this:

```
% nslookup
Default Server: terminator.movie.edu
Address:  0.0.0.0

> movie.edu.

*** No address (A) records available for movie.edu.
```

So what types of records *do* exist? Just *set type=any* to find out:

```
> set type=any
> movie.edu.
Server:  terminator.movie.edu
Address:  0.0.0.0

movie.edu
        origin = terminator.movie.edu
        mail addr = al.robocop.movie.edu
        serial = 42
        refresh = 10800 (3H)
        retry   = 3600 (1H)
        expire  = 604800 (7D)
        minimum ttl = 86400 (1D)
movie.edu       nameserver = terminator.movie.edu
movie.edu       nameserver = wormhole.movie.edu
movie.edu       nameserver = zardoz.movie.edu
movie.edu       preference = 10, mail exchanger = postmanrings2x.movie.edu
postmanrings2x.movie.edu        internet address = 192.249.249.66
```

No Response from Server

What could have gone wrong if your server can't look up its own name?

```
% nslookup
Default Server: terminator.movie.edu
Address:  0.0.0.0

> terminator
Server:  terminator.movie.edu
Address:  0.0.0.0

*** terminator.movie.edu can't find terminator: No response from server
```

The "no response from server" error message means exactly that: the name server didn't get back a response. *nslookup* doesn't necessarily look up anything when it starts up. If you see that the address of your server is 0.0.0.0, *nslookup* grabbed the system's host name (what the *hostname* command returns) for the server field and gave you its prompt. It is only when you try to look up something that you find out that there is no server responding. In this case, it is pretty obvious that there is no name server running—a name server ought to be able to look up its own name. If you are looking up some remote information, though, the name server could fail to respond because it is still trying to look up the item and *nslookup* gave up waiting. How can you tell the difference between a name server that isn't running and a name server that is running but didn't respond? Use the *ls* command to point out the difference:

```
% nslookup
Default Server:  terminator.movie.edu
Address:  0.0.0.0

> ls foo.      —Try to list a nonexistent domain
*** Can't list domain foo.: No response from server
```

In this case, no name server is running. If the host couldn't be reached, the error would be "timed out." If a name server is running, you'll see the following error message:

```
% nslookup
Default Server:  terminator.movie.edu
Address:  0.0.0.0

> ls foo.
[terminator.movie.edu]
*** Can't list domain foo.: No information
```

That is, unless there's a top-level *foo* domain in your world.

No PTR Data for Name Server's Address

Here is one of the most annoying problems: something went wrong, and *nslookup* exited on startup:

```
% nslookup

*** Can't find server name for address 192.249.249.3: Non-existent host/domain
*** Default servers are not available
```

The "nonexistent domain" means that the name *3.249.249.192.in-addr.arpa* doesn't exist. In other words, *nslookup* couldn't find the name for 192.249.249.3, its name server host. But didn't we just say that *nslookup* doesn't look up anything when it starts up? In the configuration presented before, *nslookup* didn't look up anything, but that's not a rule. If you create a *resolv.conf* that includes *nameserver* lines, *nslookup* looks up the address in order to get the name server's name. In the preceding example, there *is* a name server running on 192.249.249.3, but it said there is no PTR data for the address 192.249.249.3. Obviously, this name server's data is messed up, at least for the *249.249.192.in-addr.arpa* zone.

The "default servers are not available" message in the example is misleading. After all, there is a name server there to say the address doesn't exist. More often, you'll see the error "no response from server" if the name server isn't running on the host or the host can't be reached. Only then does the "default servers are not available" message makes sense.

Query Refused

Refused queries can cause problems at startup, and they can cause lookup failures during a session. Here's what it looks like when *nslookup* exits on startup because of a refused query:

```
% nslookup
*** Can't find server name for address 192.249.249.3: Query refused
*** Default servers are not available
%
```

This one has two possible causes. Either your name server does not support inverse queries (older *nslookup*s only), or zone security is stopping the lookup.

Old versions of *nslookup* (pre-4.8.3) used an inverse query on startup. Inverse queries were never widely used—*nslookup* was one of the few applications that did use them. At 4.9.3, support for inverse queries was dropped, which broke old *nslookup*s. To accommodate these old clients, a configuration file statement was added.

In BIND 4, the statement looks like this:

```
options fake-iquery
```

In BIND 8, the statement looks like this:

```
options { fake-iquery yes; };
```

This statement causes your name server to respond to the inverse query with a "fake" response that is good enough for *nslookup* to continue.

Zone security features can also cause *nslookup* startup problems. When *nslookup* attempts to find the name of its server (using a PTR query, not an inverse query), the query can be refused. If you think the problem is zone security, make sure your BIND 4 *secure_zone* TXT resource records or BIND 8 *allow-transfer* substatement include the network for the host running *nslookup*, and the address 127.0.0.1 if *nslookup* is running on the host also running the name server.

Zone security is not limited to causing *nslookup* to fail to start up. It can also cause lookups and zone transfers to fail in the middle of a session when you point *nslookup* to a remote name server. This is what you will see:

```
% nslookup
Default Server:  hp.com
```

```
Address:  15.255.152.4

> server terminator.movie.edu
Default Server:  terminator.movie.edu
Address:  192.249.249.3

> carrie.movie.edu.
Server:  terminator.movie.edu
Address:  192.249.249.3

*** terminator.movie.edu can't find carrie.movie.edu.: Query refused

> ls movie.edu                     —This attempts a zone transfer
[terminator.movie.edu]
*** Can't list domain movie.edu: Query refused
>
```

First resolv.conf Name Server Not Responding

Here is another twist on the last problem:

```
% nslookup

*** Can't find server name for address 192.249.249.3: No response from server
Default Server:  wormhole.movie.edu
Address:  192.249.249.1
```

This time the first *nameserver* in *resolv.conf* did not respond. We had put a second *nameserver* line in *resolv.conf*, and the second server did respond. From now on, *nslookup* will send queries only to *wormhole*; it won't try the name server at 192.249.249.3 again.

Finding Out What Is Being Looked Up

We've been waving our hands in the last examples, saying that *nslookup* was looking up the name server's address, but we didn't prove it. Here is our proof. This time, when we started up *nslookup* we turned on *d2* debugging from the command line. This causes *nslookup* to print out the query packets it sent, as well as printing out when the query timed out and was retransmitted:

```
% nslookup -d2
------------
SendRequest(), len 44
    HEADER:
        opcode = QUERY, id = 1, rcode = NOERROR
        header flags:  query, want recursion
        questions = 1,  answers = 0,  authority records = 0,
        additional = 0

    QUESTIONS:
        3.249.249.192.in-addr.arpa, type = PTR, class = IN
```

```
------------
timeout (5 secs)
timeout (10 secs)
timeout (20 secs)
timeout (40 secs)
SendRequest failed

*** Can't find server name for address 192.249.249.3: No response from server
*** Default servers are not available
```

As you can see by the timeouts, it took 75 seconds for *nslookup* to give up. Without the debugging output, you won't see anything printed to your screen for 75 seconds; it'll look as if *nslookup* has hung.

Unspecified Error

You can run into a rather unsettling problem called "unspecified error." We have an example of this error here. We've only included the tail end of the output, since we only want to talk about the error at this point. You'll find the whole *nslookup* session that produced this segment in Chapter 13, *Troubleshooting DNS and BIND*.

```
Authoritative answers can be found from:
(root)   nameserver = NS.NIC.DDN.MIL
(root)   nameserver = B.ROOT-SERVERS.NET
(root)   nameserver = E.ROOT-SERVERS.NET
(root)   nameserver = D.ROOT-SERVERS.NET
(root)   nameserver = F.ROOT-SERVERS.NET
(root)   nameserver = C.ROOT-SERVERS.NET
(root)   nameserver =
*** Error: record size incorrect (1050690 != 65519)

*** relay.hp.com can't find .: Unspecified error
```

What happened here is that there was too much data to fit into a UDP datagram. The name server stopped filling in the response when it ran out of room. The name server *didn't* set the truncation bit in the response packet, or *nslookup* would have retried the query over a TCP connection; the name server must have decided that enough of the "important" information fit. You won't see this kind of error very often. You'll see it if you create too many NS records for a domain, so don't create too many. (Advice like this makes you wonder why you bought this book, right?) How many is too many depends upon how well the names can be "compressed" in the packet, which, in turn, depends upon how many name servers share the same domain in their domain name. The root name servers were renamed to all be in the *root-servers.net* domain for this very reason—more names fit in DNS packets if they share a common domain, which allows more root name servers to support the Internet. As a rule of thumb, don't go over 10 NS records. As for what caused *this* error, you'll have to read Chapter 13. Those of you who just read Chapter 9, *Parenting*, may know already.

Best of the Net

System administrators have a thankless job. There are certain questions, usually quite simple ones, that they are asked over and over again. And sometimes, in a creative mood, they come up with a clever way to help their users. When the rest of us find out about their ingenuity, we can only sit back, smile admiringly, and wish we had thought of it ourselves. Here is one such case, where a system administrator found a way to communicate the solution to the sometimes perplexing puzzle of how to end an *nslookup* session:

```
% nslookup
Default Server:  envy.ugcs.caltech.edu
Address:  131.215.134.135

> quit
Server:  envy.ugcs.caltech.edu
Addresses:  131.215.134.135, 131.215.128.135

Name:    ugcs.caltech.edu
Addresses:  131.215.128.135, 131.215.134.135
Aliases:  quit.ugcs.caltech.edu
          use.exit.to.leave.nslookup.-.-.-.ugcs.caltech.edu

> exit
%
```

12

Reading BIND Debugging Output

"O Tiger-lily!" said Alice, addressing herself to one that was waving gracefully about in the wind, "I wish you could talk!"

"We can talk," said the Tiger-lily, "when there's anybody worth talking to."

One of the tools in your troubleshooting toolchest is the name server's debugging output. As long as your name server has been compiled with DEBUG defined, you can get query-by-query reports of its internal operation. The messages you get are often quite cryptic; they were meant for someone who has the source code to follow. We'll explain some of the debugging output in this chapter. Our goal is to cover enough for you to follow what the name server is doing; we aren't trying to supply an exhaustive compilation of debugging messages.

As you read through the explanations here, think back to material covered in earlier chapters. Seeing this information again, in another context, should help you understand more fully how a name server works.

Debugging Levels

The amount of information the name server provides depends on the debugging level. The lower the debugging level, the less information you get. Higher debugging levels give you more information, but they also fill up your disk faster. After you've read a lot of debugging output, you'll develop a feel for how much information you'll need to solve any particular problem. Of course, if you can easily recreate the problem, you can start at level 1 and increase the debugging level until you have enough information. For the most basic problem—why a name can't be looked up—level 1 will often suffice, so you should start there.

What Information Is at Each Level?

Here is a list of the information that each debugging level will give. The debugging information is cumulative; for example, level 2 includes all level 1's debugging information. The data are divided into the following basic areas: starting up, updating the database, processing queries, and maintaining zones. We won't cover updating the name server's internal database—problems always occur elsewhere. However, *what* the name server adds or deletes from its internal database can be a problem, as you'll see in Chapter 13, *Troubleshooting DNS and BIND*.

Level 1

> The information at this level is necessarily brief. Name servers can process *lots* of queries, which can create *lots* of debugging output. Since the output is condensed, you can collect data over long periods. Use this debugging level for basic startup information and for watching query transactions. You'll see some errors logged at this level, including syntax errors and DNS packet formatting errors. This level will also show referrals.

Level 2

> Level 2 provides lots of useful stuff: it lists the IP addresses of remote name servers that are used during a lookup, along with their round trip time values; it calls out bad responses; and it tags a response as to which type of query it is answering, a SYSTEM (sysquery) or a USER query. When you are tracking down a problem with a secondary server loading a zone, this level shows you the zone values—serial number, refresh time, retry time, expire time, and time left—as the secondary checks if it is up-to-date with its master.

Level 3

> Level 3 debugging becomes much more verbose because it generates lots of messages about updating the name server database. Make sure you have enough disk space if you are going to collect debugging output at level 3 or above. At level 3, you'll also see: duplicate queries called out, system queries generated (sysquery), the names of the remote name servers used during a lookup, and the number of addresses found for each server.

Level 4

> Use level 4 debugging when you want to see the query and response packets *received* by the name server. This level also shows the credibility level for cached data.

Level 5

> There are a variety of messages at level 5, but none of them are particularly useful for general debugging. This level includes some error messages, for example, when a *malloc()* fails, and a message when the name server gives up on a query.

Level 6

Level 6 shows you the response sent to the original query.

Level 7

Level 7 shows you a few configuration and parsing messages.

Level 8

There is no significant debugging information at this level.

Level 9

There is no significant debugging information at this level.

Level 10

Use level 10 debugging when you want to see the query and response packets *sent* by the name server. The format of these packets is the same format used in level 4. You wouldn't use this level very often, since you can see the name server response packet with *nslookup.*

Level 11

There are only a couple of debugging messages at this level, and they are in seldom-traversed code.

With BIND 8, you can configure the name server to print out the debug level with the debug message. Just turn on the logging option *print-severity* as explained in "BIND 8 Logging," in Chapter 7, *Maintaining BIND.*

Keep in mind that this *is* debugging information—it was used by the authors of BIND to debug the code, so it is not as readable as you might like. You can use it, too, to figure out why the name server isn't doing what you think it should be doing, or just to learn how the name server operates—but don't expect nicely designed, carefully formatted output.

Turning On Debugging

Name server debugging can be started either from the command line or with signals. If you need to see the startup information to diagnose your current problem, you'll have to use the command-line option. If you want to start debugging on a name server that is already running, or if you want to turn off debugging, you'll have to use signals. The name server writes its debugging output to *named.run.* A BIND 4 name server will create *named.run* in */usr/tmp* (or */var/tmp*). A BIND 8 name server will create *named.run* in the name server's current directory.

Debugging Command-Line Option

When troubleshooting, you sometimes need to see the sort list, know which interface a file descriptor is bound to, or find out where in the initialization stage the name server was when it exited (if the syslog error message wasn't clear enough). To see this kind of debugging information, you'll have to start debugging with a command-line option; by the time you send a signal, it will be too late. The command-line option for debugging is *-d level.* When you use the command-line option to turn on debugging, a BIND 4 name server will not go into the background as it does normally; you'll have to add the "&" at the end of your command line to get your shell prompt back. Here's how to start the name server at debugging level 1:

```
# /etc/named -d 1 &
```

Changing the Debugging Level with Signals

If you don't need to see the name server initialization, start your name server without the debugging command-line option. You can later turn debugging on and off by sending the USR1 and USR2 signals to the name server process. The first USR1 signal causes *named* to start writing debugging output at level 1. Each subsequent USR1 signal increases the debugging level by 1. Send USR2 to turn off debugging. Here, we set debugging to level 3, then turn debugging off:

```
# kill -USR1 `cat /etc/named.pid`         —Level 1
# kill -USR1 `cat /etc/named.pid`         —Level 2
# kill -USR1 `cat /etc/named.pid`         —Level 3
# kill -USR2 `cat /etc/named.pid`         —Off
```

And, as you might expect, if you turn on debugging from the command line, you can still send USR1 and USR2 signals to the name server.

Reading Debugging Output

We'll cover five examples of debugging output. The first example shows the name server starting up. The next two examples show successful name lookups. The fourth example shows a secondary name server keeping its zone up to date. In the last example, we switch from showing you name server behavior to showing you resolver behavior: the resolver search algorithm. After each trace, except the last one, we killed the name server and started it again so that each trace started with a fresh, nearly empty cache.

You might wonder why we've chosen to show normal name server behavior for all our examples; after all, this chapter is about debugging. We are showing you normal behavior because you have to know what normal operation *is* before you track down abnormal operation. Another reason is to help you *understand* the concepts (retransmissions, round trip times, etc.) we have described in earlier chapters.

Name Server Startup (Debug Level 1)

We'll start the debugging examples by watching the name server initialize. We used
-d 1 on the command line, and this is the *named.run* output that resulted:

```
1)  Debug level 1
2)  Version = named 8.1.1 Sat Jul 19 08:06:36 EDT 1997
3)       pma@terminator:/home/pma/named
4)  conffile = named.conf
5)  starting.  named 8.1.1 Sat Jul 19 08:06:36 EDT 1997
6)       pma@terminator:/home/pma/named
7)  ns_init(named.conf)
8)  update_zone_info('0.0.127.IN-ADDR.ARPA', 1)
9)  source = db.127.0.0
10) purge_zone(0.0.127.IN-ADDR.ARPA,1)
11) reloading zone
12) db_load(db.127.0.0, 0.0.127.IN-ADDR.ARPA, 1, Nil)
13) np_parent(0x0) couldn't find root entry
14) master zone "0.0.127.IN-ADDR.ARPA" (IN) loaded (serial 1)
15) zone[1] type 1: '0.0.127.IN-ADDR.ARPA' z_time 0, z_refresh 0
16) update_zone_info('.', 3)
17) source = db.cache
18) reloading zone
19) db_load(db.cache, , 0, Nil)
20) cache zone "" (IN) loaded (serial 0)
21) zone[0] type 3: '.' z_time 0, z_refresh 0
22) getnetconf(generation 887560796)
23) getnetconf: considering lo [127.0.0.1]
24) ifp->addr [127.0.0.1].53 d_dfd 20
25) evSelectFD(ctx 0x808f0e0, fd 20, mask 0x1, func 0x8056bf0,
    uap 0x80ac350)
26) evSelectFD(ctx 0x808f0e0, fd 21, mask 0x1, func 0x806fb08,
    uap 0x80ac398)
27) listening [127.0.0.1].53 (lo)
28) getnetconf: considering eth0 [192.249.249.3]
29) ifp->addr [192.249.249.3].53 d_dfd 22
30) evSelectFD(ctx 0x808f0e0, fd 22, mask 0x1, func 0x8056bf0,
    uap 0x80ac408)
31) evSelectFD(ctx 0x808f0e0, fd 23, mask 0x1, func 0x806fb08,
    uap 0x80ac450)
32) listening [192.249.249.3].53 (eth0)
33) fwd ds 5 addr [0.0.0.0].1142
34) Forwarding source address is [0.0.0.0].1142
35) evSelectFD(ctx 0x808f0e0, fd 5, mask 0x1, func 0x8056bf0, uap 0)
36) exit ns_init()
37) Ready to answer queries.
38) prime_cache: priming = 0
39) evSetTimer(ctx 0x808f0e0, func 0x8054cf4,
    uap 0, due 887560800.000000000, inter 0.000000000)
40) sysquery: send -> [192.5.5.241].53 dfd=5 nsid=41705 id=0 41)
    retry=887560800
41) evSetTimer(ctx 0x808f0e0, func 0x804ee88,
```

```
        uap 0x80a4a20, due 887560803.377717000, inter 0.000000000)
42) datagram from [192.5.5.241].53, fd 5, len 436
43) 13 root servers
```

We added the line numbers to the debugging output; you won't see them in yours. Lines 2 through 6 give the version of BIND you are running and the name of the configuration file. Version 8.1.1 was released by ISC (Internet Software Consortium) in 1997. We used the configuration file in the current directory, *./named.conf,* for this run.

Lines 7 through 21 show BIND reading the configuration file and the db files. This name server is a caching-only name server—the only files read are *db.127.0.0* (lines 8 through 15) and *db.cache* (lines 16–21). Line 8 lists the zone being updated (*0.0.127.IN-ADDR.ARPA*) and line 9 shows the file containing the zone data (*db.127.0.0*). Line 10 indicates that any old data for the zone is purged before new data is added. Line 11 says the zone is being reloaded, even though the zone is actually being loaded for the first time. The zone data is loaded during lines 12 through 14. Ignore the useless error message on line 13. On lines 15 and 21, *z_time* is the time to check when this zone is up to date; *z_refresh* is the zone refresh time. These values only matter when the server is a secondary server for the zone.

Lines 22 through 35 show the initialization of file descriptors. (In this case, they're really socket descriptors.) File descriptors 20 and 21 (lines 24–26) are bound to 127.0.0.1, the loopback address. Descriptor 20 is a datagram socket and descriptor 21 is a stream socket. File descriptors 22 and 23 (lines 29–31) are bound to the 192.249.249.3 interface. Each interface address was considered and used—they would not be used if the interface had not been initialized, or if the address were already in the list. File descriptor 5 (lines 33–35) is bound to 0.0.0.0, the wildcard address. Most network daemons use only one socket bound to the wildcard address, not sockets bound to individual interfaces. The wildcard address picks up packets sent to any interface on the host. Let's digress for a moment to explain why *named* uses both a socket bound to the wildcard address and sockets bound to specific interfaces.

When *named* receives a request from an application or from another name server, it will receive the request on one of the sockets bound to a specific interface. If *named* did not have sockets bound to specific interfaces, it would receive the requests on the socket bound to the wildcard address. When *named* sends back a response, it uses the same socket descriptor that the request came in on. Why does *named* do this? When responses are sent out via the socket bound to the wildcard address, the kernel fills in the sender's address with the address of the interface the response was actually sent out on. This address may or may not be the same address that the request was sent to. When responses are sent out via the socket bound to a specific address, the kernel fills in the sender's address with that specific address—

the same address the request was sent to. If the name server gets a response from an IP address it didn't know about, the response is tagged a "martian" and discarded. *named* tries to avoid martian responses by sending its responses on descriptors bound to specific interfaces, so the sender's address is the same address the request was sent to. However, when *named* sends out *queries*, it uses the wildcard descriptor, since there is no need to force a specific IP address.

Lines 38 through 43 show the name server sending out a system query to find out which name servers are currently serving the root domain. This is known as "priming the cache." The first server queried sent a response that included 13 name servers.

The name server is now initialized, and it is ready to answer queries.

A Successful Lookup (Debug Level 1)

Suppose you want to watch the name server look up a name. Your name server wasn't started with debugging. Send a USR1 signal to turn on debugging, look up the name, then send a USR2 signal to turn off debugging, like this:

```
# kill -USR1 `cat /etc/named.pid`
# /etc/ping galt.cs.purdue.edu.
# kill -USR2 `cat /etc/named.pid`
```

We did this; here's the resulting *named.run* file:

```
datagram from [192.249.249.3].1162, fd 20, len 36

req: nlookup(galt.cs.purdue.edu) id 29574 type=1 class=1
req: missed 'galt.cs.purdue.edu' as '' (cname=0)
forw: forw -> [198.41.0.10].53 ds=4 nsid=40070 id=29574 2ms retry 4sec
datagram from [198.41.0.10].53, fd 4, len 343

;; ->>HEADER<<- opcode: QUERY, status: NOERROR, id: 40070
;; flags: qr; QUERY: 1, ANSWER: 0, AUTHORITY: 9, ADDITIONAL: 9
;;              galt.cs.purdue.edu, type = A, class = IN
EDU.                    6D IN NS    A.ROOT-SERVERS.NET.
EDU.                    6D IN NS    H.ROOT-SERVERS.NET.
EDU.                    6D IN NS    B.ROOT-SERVERS.NET.
EDU.                    6D IN NS    C.ROOT-SERVERS.NET.
EDU.                    6D IN NS    D.ROOT-SERVERS.NET.
EDU.                    6D IN NS    E.ROOT-SERVERS.NET.
EDU.                    6D IN NS    I.ROOT-SERVERS.NET.
EDU.                    6D IN NS    F.ROOT-SERVERS.NET.
EDU.                    6D IN NS    G.ROOT-SERVERS.NET.
A.ROOT-SERVERS.NET.          5w6d16h IN A    198.41.0.4
H.ROOT-SERVERS.NET.          5w6d16h IN A    128.63.2.53
B.ROOT-SERVERS.NET.          5w6d16h IN A    128.9.0.107
C.ROOT-SERVERS.NET.          5w6d16h IN A    192.33.4.12
D.ROOT-SERVERS.NET.          5w6d16h IN A    128.8.10.90
E.ROOT-SERVERS.NET.          5w6d16h IN A    192.203.230.10
I.ROOT-SERVERS.NET.          5w6d16h IN A    192.36.148.17
```

```
F.ROOT-SERVERS.NET.            5w6d16h IN A    192.5.5.241
G.ROOT-SERVERS.NET.            5w6d16h IN A    192.112.36.4
resp: nlookup(galt.cs.purdue.edu) qtype=1
resp: found 'galt.cs.purdue.edu' as 'edu' (cname=0)
resp: forw -> [192.36.148.17].53 ds=4 nsid=40071 id=29574 1ms
datagram from [192.36.148.17].53, fd 4, len 202

;; ->>HEADER<<- opcode: QUERY, status: NOERROR, id: 40071
;; flags: qr rd; QUERY: 1, ANSWER: 0, AUTHORITY: 4, ADDITIONAL: 4
;;   galt.cs.purdue.edu, type = A, class = IN
PURDUE.EDU.                    2D IN NS    NS.PURDUE.EDU.
PURDUE.EDU.                    2D IN NS    MOE.RICE.EDU.
PURDUE.EDU.                    2D IN NS    PENDRAGON.CS.PURDUE.EDU.
PURDUE.EDU.                    2D IN NS    HARBOR.ECN.PURDUE.EDU.
NS.PURDUE.EDU.                 2D IN A     128.210.11.5
MOE.RICE.EDU.                  2D IN A     128.42.5.4
PENDRAGON.CS.PURDUE.EDU.           2D IN A  128.10.2.5
HARBOR.ECN.PURDUE.EDU.             2D IN A     128.46.199.76
resp: nlookup(galt.cs.purdue.edu) qtype=1
resp: found 'galt.cs.purdue.edu' as 'cs.purdue.edu' (cname=0)
resp: forw -> [128.46.199.76].53 ds=4 nsid=40072 id=29574 8ms
datagram from [128.46.199.76].53, fd 4, len 234

send_msg -> [192.249.249.3].1162 (UDP 20) id=29574
Debug off
```

First, notice that IP addresses are logged, not names—odd for a *name* server, don't you think? It's not that odd, though. If you are trying to debug a problem with looking up names, you don't want the name server looking up additional names just to make the debugging output more readable—the extra queries would interfere with the debugging. None of the debugging levels translate IP addresses into names. You'll have to use a tool (like the one we provide later) to convert them for you.

Let's go through this debugging output line by line. This detailed approach is important if you want to understand what each line means. If you turn on debugging, you're probably trying to find out why some name can't be looked up, and you're going to have to figure out what the trace means.

```
datagram from [192.249.249.3].1162, fd 20, len 36
```

A datagram came from the host with IP address 192.249.249.3 (*terminator*). You may see the datagram come from 127.0.0.1 if the sender is on the same host as the name server. The sending application used port 1162. The name server received the datagram on file descriptor (*fd*) 20. The startup debugging output, like the one shown earlier, will tell you which interface file descriptor 20 is bound to. The length (*len*) of the datagram was 36 bytes.

```
req: nlookup(galt.cs.purdue.edu) id 29574 type=1 class=1
```

Since the next debugging line starts with req, we know that the datagram was a *request*. The name looked up in the request was *galt.cs.purdue.edu*. The request id is 29574. The `type=1` means the request is for *address* information. The `class=1` means the class was IN. You will find a complete list of query types and classes in the header file */usr/include/arpa/nameser.b*.

```
req: missed 'galt.cs.purdue.edu' as '' (cname=0)
```

The name server looked up the requested name and didn't find it. Then it tried to find a remote name server to ask; none was found until the root domain (the empty quotes). The *cname=0* means the name server has not encountered a CNAME record. If it does see a CNAME record, the canonical name is looked up instead of the original name, and *cname* will be nonzero.

```
forw: forw -> [198.41.0.10].53 ds=4 nsid=40070 id=29574 2ms retry 4sec
```

The query was forwarded to the name server (port 53) on host 198.41.0.10 (*j.root-servers.net*). The name server used file descriptor 4 (which is the wildcard address) to send the query. The name server tagged this query with ID number 40070 (*nsid=40070*) so that it could match the response to the original question. The application used ID number 29574 (*id=29574*), as you saw on the *nlookup* line. The name server will wait 4 seconds before trying the next name server.

```
datagram from [198.41.0.10].53, fd 4, len 343
```

The name server on *j.root-servers.net* responded. Since the response was a delegation, it is printed in full in the debug log.

```
resp: nlookup(galt.cs.purdue.edu) qtype=1
```

After the information is cached in the response packet, the name is looked up again. As mentioned earlier, `query type=1` means that the name server is looking for *address* information.

```
resp: found 'galt.cs.purdue.edu' as 'edu' (cname=0)
resp: forw -> [192.36.148.17].53 ds=4 nsid=40071 id=29574 1ms
datagram from [192.36.148.17].53, fd 4, len 202
```

The root server responded with a delegation to the *edu* servers. The same query is sent to 192.36.148.17 (*i.root-servers.net*), one of the *edu* servers. *i.root-servers.net* responds with information about the *purdue.edu* servers.

```
resp: found 'galt.cs.purdue.edu' as 'cs.purdue.edu' (cname=0)
```

This time there is some information at the *cs.purdue.edu* level.

```
resp: forw -> [128.46.199.76].53 ds=4 nsid=40072 id=29574 8ms
```

A query was sent to the name server on 128.46.199.76 (*barbor.ecn.purdue.edu*). This time the name server ID is 40072.

```
datagram from [128.46.199.76].53, fd 4, len 234
```

The name server on *barbor.ecn.purdue.edu* responded. We have to look at what happens next to figure out the contents of this response.

```
send_msg -> [192.249.249.3].1162 (UDP 20) id=29574
```

The last response must have contained the address requested, since the name server responded to the application (which used port 1162, if you look back at the original query). The response was in a UDP packet (as opposed to a TCP connection), and it used file descriptor 20.

This name server was "quiet" when we did this trace; it wasn't handling other queries at the same time. When you do a trace on an active name server you won't be so lucky. You'll have to sift through the output and patch together those pieces that pertain to the lookup in which you are interested. It's not that hard, though. Start up your favorite editor, search for the *nlookup* line with the name you looked up, then trace the entries with the same *nsid*. You'll see how to follow the *nsid* in the next trace.

A Successful Lookup with Retransmissions (Debug Level 1)

Not all lookups are as "clean" as the last one—sometimes the query must be retransmitted. The user doesn't see any difference so long as the lookup succeeds, although the query involving retransmissions will take longer. Following is a trace where there are retransmissions. We converted the IP addresses to names after the trace was done. Notice how much easier it is to read with names!

```
1)  Debug turned ON, Level 1
2)
3)  datagram from terminator.movie.edu port 3397, fd 20, len 35
4)  req: nlookup(ucunix.san.uc.edu) id 1 type=1 class=1
5)  req: found 'ucunix.san.uc.edu' as 'edu' (cname=0)
6)  forw: forw -> i.root-servers.net port 53   ds=4 nsid=2 id=1 0ms
    retry 4 sec
7)
8)  datagram from i.root-servers.net port 53, fd 4, len 240
    <delegation lines removed>
9)  resp: nlookup(ucunix.san.uc.edu) qtype=1
10) resp: found 'ucunix.san.uc.edu' as 'san.uc.edu' (cname=0)
11) resp: forw -> uceng.uc.edu port 53 ds=4 nsid=3 id=1 0ms
12) resend(addr=1 n=0) - > ucbeh.san.uc.edu port 53 ds=4 nsid=3
    id=1 0ms
13)
14) datagram from terminator.movie.edu port 3397, fd 20, len 35
15) req: nlookup(ucunix.san.uc.edu) id 1 type=1 class=1
16) req: found 'ucunix.san.uc.edu' as 'san.uc.edu' (cname=0)
17) resend(addr=2 n=0) - > uccba.uc.edu port 53 ds=4 nsid=3 id=1 0ms
18) resend(addr=3 n=0) - > mail.cis.ohio-state.edu port 53 ds=4 nsid=3
    id=1 0ms
19)
20) datagram from mail.cis.ohio-state.edu port 53, fd 4, len 51
21) send_msg -> terminator.movie.edu (UDP 20 3397) id=1
```

This trace starts out like the last trace (lines 1 through 11): the name server receives a query for *ucunix.san.uc.edu*, sends the query to an *edu* name server (*i.root-servers.net*), receives a response that includes a list of name servers for *uc.edu*, and sends the query to one of the *uc.edu* name servers (*uceng.uc.edu*).

What's new in this trace is the *resend* lines (lines 12, 17, and 18). The *forw* on line 11 counts as "resend(addr=0 n=0)"—CS dweebs always start counting with zero. Since *uceng.uc.edu* didn't respond, the name server went on to try *ucbeh* (line 12), *uccba* (line 17), and *mail* (line 18). The off-site name server on *mail.cis.ohio-state.edu* finally responded (line 20). Notice that you can track all of the retransmissions by searching for *nsid=3*; that's important to know because lots of other queries can be wedged between these.

Also, notice the second datagram from *terminator* (line 14). It has the same port, file descriptor, length, ID, and type as the query on line 3. The application didn't receive a response in time, so it retransmitted its original query. Since the name server is still working on the first query transmitted, this one is a duplicate. It doesn't say so in this output, but the name server detected the duplicate and dropped it. We can tell because there is no *forw:* line after the *req:* lines, as there was on lines 4 through 6.

Can you guess what this output might look like if the name server were having trouble looking up a name? You'd see a lot of retransmissions as the name server kept trying to look up the name (which you could track by matching the *nsid=* lines). You'd see the application send a couple more retransmissions, thinking that the name server hadn't received the application's first query. Eventually the name server would give up, usually after the application itself gave up.

A Slave Name Server Checking Its Zone (Debug Level 1)

In addition to tracking down problems with name server lookups, you may have to track down why a slave server is not loading from its master. Tracking down this problem can often be done by simply comparing the domain's SOA serial numbers on the two servers, using *nslookup* or *dig*, as we'll show in Chapter 13. If your problem is more elusive, you may have to resort to looking at the debugging information. We'll show you what the debugging information should look like if your server is running normally.

This debugging output was generated on a "quiet" name server—one not receiving any queries—to show you exactly which lines pertain to zone maintenance. If you remember, a slave name server uses a child process to transfer the zone data to the local disk before reading it in. While the slave logs its debugging information to *named.run*, the slave's child process logs its debugging information to *xfer.ddt.PID*. The *PID* suffix, by default the process ID of the child process, may be changed to

ensure that the filename is unique. Beware—turning on debugging on a slave name
server will leave *xfer.ddt.PID* files lying around, even if you are only trying to trace
a lookup. Our trace is at debugging level 1 and we turned on the BIND 8 logging
option *print-time*. Debug level 3 gives you more information, more than you may
want if a transfer actually occurs. A debugging level 3 trace of a zone transfer of
several hundred resource records can create an *xfer.ddt.PID* file several megabytes
large:

```
21-Feb 00:13:18.026 do_zone_maint for zone movie.edu (class IN)
21-Feb 00:13:18.034 zone_maint('movie.edu')
21-Feb 00:13:18.035 qserial_query(movie.edu)
21-Feb 00:13:18.043 sysquery: send -> [192.249.249.3].53 dfd=5
                            nsid=29790 id=0 retry=888048802
21-Feb 00:13:18.046 qserial_query(movie.edu) QUEUED
21-Feb 00:13:18.052 next maintenance for zone 'movie.edu' in 2782 sec
21-Feb 00:13:18.056 datagram from [192.249.249.3].53, fd 5, len 380
21-Feb 00:13:18.059 qserial_answer(movie.edu, 26739)
21-Feb 00:13:18.060 qserial_answer: zone is out of date
21-Feb 00:13:18.061 startxfer() movie.edu
21-Feb 00:13:18.063 /usr/etc/named-xfer -z movie.edu -f db.movie
                            -s 26738 -C 1 -P 53 -d 1 -l xfer.ddt 192.249.249.3
21-Feb 00:13:18.131 started xfer child 390
21-Feb 00:13:18.132 next maintenance for zone 'movie.edu' in 7200 sec

21-Feb 00:14:02.089 endxfer: child 390 zone movie.edu returned
                            status=1 termsig=-1
21-Feb 00:14:02.094 loadxfer() "movie.edu"
21-Feb 00:14:02.094 purge_zone(movie.edu,1)

21-Feb 00:14:30.049 db_load(db.movie, movie.edu, 2, Nil)
21-Feb 00:14:30.058 next maintenance for zone 'movie.edu' in 1846 sec

21-Feb 00:17:12.478 slave zone "movie.edu" (IN) loaded (serial 26739)
21-Feb 00:17:12.486 no schedule change for zone 'movie.edu'

21-Feb 00:42:44.817 Cleaned cache of 0 RRs

21-Feb 00:45:16.046 do_zone_maint for zone movie.edu (class IN)
21-Feb 00:45:16.054 zone_maint('movie.edu')
21-Feb 00:45:16.055 qserial_query(movie.edu)
21-Feb 00:45:16.063 sysquery: send -> [192.249.249.3].53 dfd=5
                            nsid=29791 id=0 retry=888050660
21-Feb 00:45:16.066 qserial_query(movie.edu) QUEUED
21-Feb 00:45:16.067 next maintenance for zone 'movie.edu' in 3445 sec
21-Feb 00:45:16.074 datagram from [192.249.249.3].53, fd 5, len 380
21-Feb 00:45:16.077 qserial_answer(movie.edu, 26739)
21-Feb 00:45:16.078 qserial_answer: zone serial is still OK
21-Feb 00:45:16.131 next maintenance for zone 'movie.edu' in 2002 sec
```

Unlike the previous traces, each line in this trace has a timestamp. The timestamp
makes clear which debug statements are grouped together.

This server is a slave for a single zone, *movie.edu*. The line with time 00:13:18.026 shows that it is time to check with the master server. The server queries for the zone's SOA record and compares serial numbers before deciding to load the zone. The lines with times 00:13:18.059 through 00:13:18.131 show you the zone's serial number (26739), tell you the zone is out of date, and start a child process (pid 390) to transfer the zone. At time 00:13:18.132, a timer is set to expire 7200 seconds later. This is the amount of time the server allows for a transfer to complete. At time 00:14:02.089, you see the exit status of the child process. The status of 1 indicates that the zone data was successfully transferred. The old zone data is purged (time 00:14:02.094), and the new data is loaded.

The next maintenance (see time 00:14:30.058) is scheduled for 1846 seconds later. For this zone, the refresh interval is 3600, but the name server chose to check again in 1846 seconds. Why? The name server is trying to avoid having the refresh periods become synchronized. Instead of using 3600 exactly, it uses a random time between half the refresh interval (1800) and the full refresh interval (3600). At 00:45:16.046, the zone is checked again and this time it is up-to-date.

If your trace ran long enough, you'd see more lines like the one at 00:42:44.817—one line each hour. What's happening is that the server is making a pass through its cache, freeing any data that has expired, to reduce the amount of memory used.

The master server for this zone is a BIND 4 name server. If the master were a BIND 8 name server, the slave would be notified when a zone changed rather than waiting for the refresh interval to expire. The slave server's debug output would look almost exactly the same, but the trigger to check the zone status is a NOTIFY:

```
rcvd NOTIFY(movie.edu, IN, SOA) from [192.249.249.3].1059
qserial_query(movie.edu)
sysquery: send -> [192.249.249.3].53 dfd=5
        nsid=29790 id=0 retry=888048802
```

The Resolver Search Algorithm and Negative Caching

In this trace, we'll show you the BIND 4.9 and BIND 8 search algorithm and the impact of negative caching. We could look up *galt.cs.purdue.edu* like the last trace, but it wouldn't show you the search algorithm. Instead, we will look up *foo.bar*, a name that doesn't exist. In fact, we will look it up twice:

```
1)   datagram from cujo.horror.movie.edu 1109, fd 6, len 25
2)   req: nlookup(foo.bar) id 19220 type=1 class=1
3)   req: found 'foo.bar' as '' (cname=0)
4)   forw: forw -> D.ROOT-SERVERS.NET 53 ds=7 nsid=2532 id=19220
                                        0ms retry 4sec
5)
```

```
6)  datagram from D.ROOT-SERVERS.NET 53, fd 5, len 25
7)  ncache: dname foo.bar, type 1, class 1
8)  send_msg -> cujo.horror.movie.edu 1109 (UDP 6) id=19220
9)
10) datagram from cujo.horror.movie.edu 1110, fd 6, len 42
11) req: nlookup(foo.bar.horror.movie.edu) id 19221 type=1 class=1
12) req: found 'foo.bar.horror.movie.edu' as 'horror.movie.edu'
                                                  (cname=0)
13) forw: forw -> carrie.horror.movie.edu 53 ds=7 nsid=2533
                                  id=19221 0ms retry 4sec

14) datagram from carrie.horror.movie.edu 53, fd 5, len 42
15) ncache: dname foo.bar.horror.movie.edu, type 1, class 1
16) send_msg -> cujo.horror.movie.edu 1110 (UDP 6) id=19221
```

Look up *foo.bar* again:

```
17) datagram from cujo.horror.movie.edu 1111, fd 6, len 25
18) req: nlookup(foo.bar) id 15541 type=1 class=1
19) req: found 'foo.bar' as 'foo.bar' (cname=0)
20) ns_req: answer -> cujo.horror.movie.edu 1111 fd=6 id=15541
                                          size=25 Local
21)
22) datagram from cujo.horror.movie.edu 1112, fd 6, len 42
23) req: nlookup(foo.bar.horror.movie.edu) id 15542 type=1 class=1
24) req: found 'foo.bar.horror.movie.edu' as
                     'foo.bar.horror.movie.edu' (cname=0)
25) ns_req: answer -> cujo.horror.movie.edu 1112 fd=6 id=15542
                                          size=42 Local
```

Let's look at the resolver search algorithm. The first name looked up (line 2) is exactly the name we typed in. Since the name had at least one dot, it is looked up without modification. When that name lookup failed, *horror.movie.edu* was appended to the name and looked up. (Resolvers before BIND 4.9 would try appending both *horror.movie.edu* and *movie.edu*.)

Line 7 shows caching the *negative* answer (**ncache**). If the same name is looked up again in the next few minutes (line 19), the name server still has the negative response in its cache, so the server can answer immediately that the name doesn't exist. (If you don't believe this hand waving, compare lines 3 and 19. On line 3, nothing was found for *foo.bar*, but line 19 shows the whole name being found.)

Tools

Let's wrap up a few loose ends. We told you about a tool to convert IP addresses to names so that your debugging output is easier to read. Here is such a tool written in Perl:

```
#!/usr/bin/perl

use "Socket.pm";
```

```
while(< >) {
  if(/\b)([0-9]+\.[0-9]+\.[0-9]+\.[0-9]+)\b/) {
      $addr = pack('C4', split(/\./, $1));
      ($name, $rest) = gethostbyaddr($addr, &AF_INET);
      if($name) {s/$1/$name/; }

   print;
}
```

It's best not to pipe *named.run* output into this script with debugging on, because the script will generate its own queries to the name server.

If you do any significant amount of name server debugging, you'll want a tool to turn debugging on and off. The 4.9 and later BIND distributions include a tool called *ndc*, which can be used for this purpose. The command *ndc trace* will turn on debugging, or increment the debug level if debugging is already on. The command *ndc notrace* will turn debugging off.

13

Troubleshooting DNS and BIND

"Of course not," said the Mock Turtle. "Why, if a fish came to me, and told me he was going a journey, I should say, 'With what porpoise?'"

"Don't you mean 'purpose'?" said Alice.

"I mean what I say," the Mock Turtle replied, in an offended tone. And the Gryphon added, "Come, let's hear some of your adventures."

In the last two chapters, we've demonstrated how to use *nslookup* and how to read the name server's debugging information. In this chapter, we'll show you how to use these tools—plus traditional UNIX networking tools like trusty ol' *ping*—to troubleshoot real-life problems with DNS and BIND.

Troubleshooting, by its nature, is a tough subject to teach. You start with any of a world of symptoms and try to work your way back to the cause. We can't cover the whole gamut of problems you may encounter on the Internet, but we will certainly do our best to show you how to diagnose the most common of them. And along the way, we hope to teach you troubleshooting techniques that will be valuable in tracking down more obscure problems that we don't document.

Is NIS Really Your Problem?

Before we launch into a discussion of how to troubleshoot a DNS or BIND problem, we should make sure you know how to tell whether a problem is caused by DNS, not by NIS. On hosts running NIS, figuring out whether the culprit is DNS or NIS can be difficult. The stock BSD *nslookup*, for example, doesn't pay any attention to NIS. You can run *nslookup* on a Sun and query the name server 'til the cows come home, while all the other services are using NIS.

How do you know where to put the blame? Some vendors have modified *nslookup* to use NIS for name service if NIS is configured. The HP-UX *nslookup*, for example, will report that it's querying an NIS server when it starts up:

```
% nslookup
Default NIS Server:  terminator.movie.edu
Address:  192.249.249.3

>
```

On hosts with vanilla versions of *nslookup*, you can often use *ypmatch* to determine whether you're using DNS or NIS. *ypmatch* will print a blank line after the host information if it received the data from a name server. So in this example, the answer came from NIS:

```
% ypmatch ruby hosts
140.186.65.25   ruby ruby.ora.com
%
```

Whereas in this example the answer came from a name server:

```
% ypmatch harvard.harvard.edu hosts
128.103.1.1       harvard.harvard.edu

%
```

Note that this works now (with SunOS 4.1.1), but is not guaranteed to work on every future version of SunOS. For all we know, this is a bug-*cum*-feature that may disappear in the next release.

A more surefire way to decide whether an answer came from NIS is to use *ypcat* to list the hosts database. For example, to find out whether *andrew.cmu.edu* is in your NIS hosts map, you could execute:

```
% ypcat hosts | grep andrew.cmu.edu
```

If you find the answer in NIS (and you know NIS is being consulted first), you've found the cause of the problem.

Finally, in the versions of UNIX that use the *nsswitch.conf* file, you can determine the order in which the different name services are used by referring to the entry for the *hosts* source in the file. An entry like this, for example, indicates that NIS is being checked first:

```
hosts:    nis dns files
```

while this entry has the name resolver querying DNS first:

```
hosts:    dns nis files
```

For more detailed information on the syntax and semantics of the *nsswitch.conf* file, see Chapter 6, *Configuring Hosts*.

These hints should help you identify the guilty party, or at least exonerate one suspect. If you narrow down the suspects, and DNS is still implicated, you'll just have to read this chapter.

Troubleshooting Tools and Techniques

We went over *nslookup* and the name server's debugging output in the last two chapters. Before we go on, let's introduce two new tools that can be useful in troubleshooting: *named-xfer* and name server database dumps.

How to Use named-xfer

named-xfer is the program *named* starts to perform zone transfers. *named-xfer* checks whether the slave's copy of the zone data is up-to-date, and transfers a new zone, if necessary. (In versions 4.9 and 8, *named* checks first if a zone is up to date in order to avoid starting up child processes when no transfer is necessary.)

In Chapter 12, *Reading BIND Debugging Output*, we showed you the debugging output a slave name server logged as it checked its zone. When the slave server transferred the zone, it started a child process (*named-xfer*) to pull the data to the local file system. We didn't tell you, however, that you can also start *named-xfer* manually, instead of waiting for *named* to start it, and that you can tell it to produce debugging output independently of *named*.

This can be useful if you're tracking down a problem with zone transfers but don't want to wait for *named* to schedule one. To test a zone transfer manually, you need to specify a number of command-line options:

```
% /etc/named-xfer
Usage: xfer
        -z zone_to_transfer
        -f db_file
        -s serial_no
        [-d debug_level]
        [-l debug_log_file]
        [-t trace_file]
        [-p port]
        [-S]
        [-C class]
        servers...
```

When *named* starts *named-xfer*, it specifies the *-z* option (the zone *named* wants to check), the *-f* option (the name of the db file that corresponds to the zone, from *named.boot*), the *-s* option (the zone's serial number on the slave, from the current SOA record), and the addresses of the servers the secondary was instructed to load from (the IP addresses from the *masters* substatement in the *zone* statement in *named.conf,* or from the *secondary* directive in *named.boot).* If *named* is running in debug mode, it also specifies the debug level for *named-xfer* with the *-d* option.

When you run *named-xfer* manually, you can also specify the debug level on the command line with *-d.* (Don't forget, though, that debug levels above three will produce tons of debugging output if the transfer succeeds!) You can also specify an alternate filename for the debug file with the *-l* option. The default log file is */usr/ tmp/xfer.ddt.XXXXXX*, where *XXXXXX* is a suffix appended to preserve uniqueness, or a file by the same name in */var/tmp.* And you can specify the name of the host to load from, instead of its IP address.

For example, you could check to see whether zone transfers from *terminator* were working, with the following command line:

```
% /etc/named-xfer -z movie.edu -f /tmp/db.movie -s 0 terminator
% echo $?
1
```

In this command, we specified a serial number of zero because we wanted to force *named-xfer* to attempt a zone transfer, even if it wasn't needed. Zero is a special serial number—*named-xfer* will transfer the zone regardless of the actual zone serial number. Also, we told *named-xfer* to put the new zone file in */tmp*, rather than overwriting the zone's working data file.

We can tell if the transfer succeeded by looking at *named-xfer*'s return value, which has four possible values:

0

The zone data is up-to-date and no transfer was needed

1

Indicates a successful transfer

2

The host(s) *named-xfer* queried can't be reached, or an error occurred and *named-xfer* may have logged an error message

3

An error occurred and *named-xfer* logged an error message

How to Read a Database Dump

Poring over a dump of the name server's internal database—including cached information—can also help you track down problems. The INT signal causes *named* to dump its authoritative data, cache data, and hints data to *named_dump.db* in BIND's running directory (or in */usr/tmp/named_dump.db* or */var/tmp/ named_dump.db*, for BIND 4). An example of a *named_dump.db* file follows. The authoritative data and cache entries, mixed together, appear first in the file. At the end of the file are the hints data:

```
; Dumped at Tue Jan  6 10:49:08 1998
;; ++zone table++
; 0.0.127.in-addr.arpa (type 1, class 1, source db.127.0.0)
;    time=0, lastupdate=0, serial=1,
;    refresh=0, retry=3600, expire=608400, minimum=86400
;    ftime=884015430, xaddr=[0.0.0.0], state=0041, pid=0
;; --zone table--
; Note: Cr=(auth,answer,addtnl,cache) tag only shown for non-auth RR's
; Note: NT=milliseconds for any A RR which we've used as a nameserver
; --- Cache & Data ---
$ORIGIN .
.    518375  IN      NS   G.ROOT-SERVERS.NET.    ;Cr=auth [128.8.10.90]
     518375  IN      NS   J.ROOT-SERVERS.NET.    ;Cr=auth [128.8.10.90]
     518375  IN      NS   K.ROOT-SERVERS.NET.    ;Cr=auth [128.8.10.90]
     518375  IN      NS   L.ROOT-SERVERS.NET.    ;Cr=auth [128.8.10.90]
     518375  IN      NS   M.ROOT-SERVERS.NET.    ;Cr=auth [128.8.10.90]
     518375  IN      NS   A.ROOT-SERVERS.NET.    ;Cr=auth [128.8.10.90]
     518375  IN      NS   H.ROOT-SERVERS.NET.    ;Cr=auth [128.8.10.90]
     518375  IN      NS   B.ROOT-SERVERS.NET.    ;Cr=auth [128.8.10.90]
     518375  IN      NS   C.ROOT-SERVERS.NET.    ;Cr=auth [128.8.10.90]
     518375  IN      NS   D.ROOT-SERVERS.NET.    ;Cr=auth [128.8.10.90]
     518375  IN      NS   E.ROOT-SERVERS.NET.    ;Cr=auth [128.8.10.90]
     518375  IN      NS   I.ROOT-SERVERS.NET.    ;Cr=auth [128.8.10.90]
     518375  IN      NS   F.ROOT-SERVERS.NET.    ;Cr=auth [128.8.10.90]
EDU 86393    IN      SOA A.ROOT-SERVERS.NET.  hostmaster.INTERNIC.NET. (
        1998010500 1800 900 604800 86400 )   ;Cr=addtnl [128.63.2.53]
$ORIGIN  0.127.in-addr.arpa.
0        IN    SOA cujo.movie.edu. root.cujo.movie.edu. (
         1998010600 10800 3600 608400 86400 )        ;Cl=5
         IN    NS cujo.movie.edu.   ;Cl=5
$ORIGIN  0.0.127.in-addr.arpa.
1        IN    PTR localhost.    ;Cl=5
$ORIGIN EDU.
PURDUE   172787  IN NS  NS.PURDUE.EDU.             ;Cr=addtnl [192.36.148.17]
         172787  IN NS  MOE.RICE.EDU.             ;Cr=addtnl [192.36.148.17]
         172787  IN NS  PENDRAGON.CS.PURDUE.EDU.  ;Cr=addtnl [192.36.148.17]
         172787  IN NS  HARBOR.ECN.PURDUE.EDU.    ;Cr=addtnl [192.36.148.17]
$ORIGIN  movie.EDU.
;cujo    593     IN  SOA  A.ROOT-SERVERS.NET. hostmaster.INTERNIC. NET. (
;           1998010500 1800 900 604800 86400 );EDU.; NXDOMAIN  ;-$
   ;Cr=auth [128.63.2.53]
$ORIGIN   RICE.EDU.
MOE      172787  IN  A   128.42.5.4       ;NT=84 Cr=addtnl [192.36.148.17]
$ORIGIN   PURDUE.EDU.
CS       86387   IN NS  pendragon.cs.PURDUE.edu.   ;Cr=addtnl [128.42.5.4]
         86387   IN NS  ns.PURDUE.edu.             ;Cr=addtnl [128.42.5.4]
         86387   IN NS  harbor.ecn.PURDUE.edu.     ;Cr=addtnl [128.42.5.4]
         86387   IN NS  moe.rice.edu.              ;Cr=addtnl [128.42.5.4]
NS       172787  IN  A  128.210.11.5      ;NT=4 Cr=addtnl [192.36.148.17]
$ORIGIN   ECN.PURDUE.EDU.
HARBOR   172787  IN  A  128.46.199.76     ;NT=6 Cr=addtnl [192.36.148.17]
```

```
$ORIGIN    CS.PURDUE.EDU.
galt       86387    IN   A   128.10.2.39                    ;Cr=auth [128.42.5.4]
PENDRAGON  172787   IN   A   128.10.2.5        ;NT=20 Cr=addtnl [192.36.148.17]
$ORIGIN    ROOT-SERVERS.NET.
K          604775   IN   A   193.0.14.129      ;NT=10 Cr=answer [128.8.10.90]
A          604775   IN   A   198.41.0.4        ;NT=20 Cr=answer [128.8.10.90]
L          604775   IN   A   198.32.64.12      ;NT=8 Cr=answer [128.8.10.90]
B          604775   IN   A   128.9.0.107       ;NT=9 Cr=answer [128.8.10.90]
M          604775   IN   A   202.12.27.33      ;NT=20 Cr=answer [128.8.10.90]
C          604775   IN   A   192.33.4.12       ;NT=17 Cr=answer [128.8.10.90]
D          604775   IN   A   128.8.10.90       ;NT=11 Cr=answer [128.8.10.90]
E          604775   IN   A   192.203.230.10    ;NT=9 Cr=answer [128.8.10.90]
F          604775   IN   A   192.5.5.241       ;NT=73 Cr=answer [128.8.10.90]
G          604775   IN   A   192.112.36.4      ;NT=14 Cr=answer [128.8.10.90]
H          604775   IN   A   128.63.2.53       ;NT=160 Cr=answer [128.8.10.90]
I          604775   IN   A   192.36.148.17     ;NT=102 Cr=answer [128.8.10.90]
J          604775   IN   A   198.41.0.10       ;NT=21 Cr=answer [128.8.10.90]
; --- Hints ---
$ORIGIN .
.          3600              IN   NS   A.ROOT-SERVERS.NET.      ;Cl=0
           3600              IN   NS   B.ROOT-SERVERS.NET.      ;Cl=0
           3600              IN   NS   C.ROOT-SERVERS.NET.      ;Cl=0
           3600              IN   NS   D.ROOT-SERVERS.NET.      ;Cl=0
           3600              IN   NS   E.ROOT-SERVERS.NET.      ;Cl=0
           3600              IN   NS   F.ROOT-SERVERS.NET.      ;Cl=0
           3600              IN   NS   G.ROOT-SERVERS.NET.      ;Cl=0
           3600              IN   NS   H.ROOT-SERVERS.NET.      ;Cl=0
           3600              IN   NS   I.ROOT-SERVERS.NET.      ;Cl=0
           3600              IN   NS   J.ROOT-SERVERS.NET.      ;Cl=0
           3600              IN   NS   K.ROOT-SERVERS.NET.      ;Cl=0
           3600              IN   NS   L.ROOT-SERVERS.NET.      ;Cl=0
           3600              IN   NS   M.ROOT-SERVERS.NET.      ;Cl=0
$ORIGIN    ROOT-SERVERS.NET.
K          3600    IN   A   193.0.14.129      ;NT=11 Cl=0
L          3600    IN   A   198.32.64.12      ;NT=9 Cl=0
A          3600    IN   A   198.41.0.4        ;NT=10 Cl=0
M          3600    IN   A   202.12.27.33      ;NT=11 Cl=0
B          3600    IN   A   128.9.0.107       ;NT=1288 Cl=0
C          3600    IN   A   192.33.4.12       ;NT=21 Cl=0
D          3600    IN   A   128.8.10.90       ;NT=1288 Cl=0
E          3600    IN   A   192.203.230.10    ;NT=19 Cl=0
F          3600    IN   A   192.5.5.241       ;NT=23 Cl=0
G          3600    IN   A   192.112.36.4      ;NT=18 Cl=0
H          3600    IN   A   128.63.2.53       ;NT=11 Cl=0
I          3600    IN   A   192.36.148.17     ;NT=21 Cl=0
J          3600    IN   A   198.41.0.10       ;NT=13 Cl=0
```

The name server that created this *named_dump.db* file was authoritative only for *0.0.127.in-addr.arpa*. Only two names have been looked up by this server: *galt.cs.purdue.edu* and *cujo.movie.edu*. In the process of looking up *galt*, this server cached not only the address of *galt*, but also the list of name servers for *purdue.edu* and the addresses for those servers. The name *cujo.movie.edu*, however, doesn't really exist (nor does the domain *movie.edu*, except in our examples), so the server cached the negative response. In the dump file, the negative response is commented out (the line starts with a semicolon), and the reason is listed (NXDOMAIN) instead of real data. You'll notice the TTL is quite low (593). Negative responses are only cached for 10 minutes (600 seconds).

The hints section at the bottom of the file contains the data from the *db.cache* file. The TTL of the hints data is decremented, and it may go to zero, but the hints are never discarded.

Note that some of the resource records are followed by a semicolon and NT=. You will only see these on the *address* records of *name servers*. The number is a round-trip time calculation that the name server keeps so that it knows which name servers have responded most quickly in the past; the name server with the lowest round-trip time will be tried first the next time.

The cache data is easy to pick out—those entries have a *credibility* tag (Cr=) and the IP address of the server the data came from. The zone data and hint data are tagged with (Cl=), which is just a count of the level in the domain tree. (*root* is level 0, *foo* is level 1, *foo.foo* is level 2, etc.) Let's digress a moment to explain the concept of credibility.

One of the advances between version 4.8.3 and 4.9 is the addition of a credibility measure. This allows a name server to make more intelligent decisions about what to do with new data from a remote server.

A 4.8.3 name server only had two credibility levels—locally authoritative data, and everything else. The locally authoritative data were data from your zone files—your name server knew better than to update its internal copy of what came from your zone file. But, all data from remote name servers were considered equal.

Here is a situation that could happen, and the way a 4.8.3 server would deal with it. Suppose that your server looked up an address for *terminator.movie.edu* and received an authoritative answer from the *movie.edu* name server. (Remember, an authoritative answer is the best you can get.) Sometime later while looking up *foo.ora.com*, your server receives another address record for *terminator.movie.edu*, but this time as part of the delegation info for *ora.com* (which *terminator.movie.edu* backs up). The 4.8.3 name server would update the cached address record for *terminator.movie.edu*, even though the data came from the *com* name server instead of the authoritative *movie.edu* name server. Of course, the *com* and *movie.edu* name servers will have exactly the same data for *terminator*, so this won't be a problem, right? Yeah, and it never rains in southern California, either.

A 4.9 or 8 name server is more intelligent. Like a 4.8.3 name server, it still considers your zone data beyond any doubt. But a 4.9 name server distinguishes among the different data from remote name servers. Here is the hierarchy of remote data credibility from most credible to least:

auth

These records are data from authoritative answers—the answer section of a response packet with the authoritative answer bit set.

answer

These records are data from nonauthoritative, or cached, answers—the answer section of a response packet without the authoritative answer bit set.

addtnl ·

These records are data from the rest of the response packet—the *authority* and *additional*. The *authority* section of the response contains NS records that delegate a domain to an authoritative name server. The *additional* section contains address records that may complete information in other sections (i.e., address records that go with NS records in the authority section).

There is one exception to this rule: when the server is priming its root name server cache, the records that would be at credibility *addtnl* are bumped up to *answer* credibility, to make them harder to change accidentally. Notice in the dump that the address records for root name servers are at credibility *answer*, but the address records for the *purdue.edu* name servers are at credibility *addtnl*.

In the situation just described, a 4.9 or 8 name server would not replace the authoritative data (credibility = *auth*) for *terminator.movie.edu* with the delegation data (credibility = *addtnl*) because the authoritative answer has higher credibility.

Logging Queries

BIND version 4.9 added a feature, query logging, which can be used to help diagnose certain problems. When query logging is turned on, a running name server will log every query with syslog. This feature could help you find resolver configuration errors, because you can check that the name you think is being looked up really is the name being looked up.

First you must make sure that LOG_INFO messages are being logged by syslog for the facility *daemon*. Next you need to turn on query logging. This can be done three ways: for BIND 4.9, set *options query-log* in your name server boot file; for BIND 4.9 or BIND 8, start the name server with *-q* on the command line, or send a WINCH signal to a running name server. You'll start seeing syslog messages like this:

```
Feb 20 21:43:25 terminator named[3830]:
                    XX /192.253.253.2/carrie.movie.edu/A
Feb 20 21:43:32 terminator named[3830]:
                    XX /192.253.253.2/4.253.253.192.in-addr.arpa/PTR
```

These messages include the IP address of the host that made the query and the query itself. Inverse queries will have a dash before the query type (i.e., an inverse query for an address record would be logged as "-A" instead of just "A"). After enough queries have been logged, you can turn off query logging by sending a WINCH signal to your name server.

Potential Problem List

Now that we've given you a nice set of tools, let's talk about how you can use them to diagnose real problems. There are some problems that are easy to recognize and correct. We should cover these as a matter of course—they're some of the most common problems because they're caused by some of the most common mistakes. Here are the contestants, in no particular order. We call 'em our "Unlucky Thirteen."

1. Forgot to Increment Serial Number

The main symptom of this problem is that slave name servers don't pick up any changes you make to the zone's db file on the primary. The slaves think the zone data hasn't changed, since the serial number is still the same.

How do you check whether or not you remembered to increment the serial number? Unfortunately, that's not so easy. If you don't remember what the old serial number was, and your serial number gives you no indication of when it was updated, there's no direct way to tell whether it's changed.* When you signal the primary, it will load the updated zone file regardless of whether you've changed the serial number. It will check the file's timestamp, see that it's been modified since it last loaded the data, and read the file. About the best you can do is to use *nslookup* to compare the data returned by the primary and by a slave. If they return different data, you probably forgot to increment the serial number. If you can remember a recent change you made, you can look for that data. If you can't remember a recent change, you could try transferring the zone from a primary and from a slave, sorting the results, and using *diff* to compare them.

The good news is that, although determining whether the zone was transferred is tricky, making sure the zone is transferred is simple. Just increment the serial number on the primary's copy of the db file and signal the primary to reload. The slaves should pick up the new data within their refresh interval, or sooner if they use NOTIFY. If you want to make sure the slaves can transfer the new data, you can execute *named-xfer* by hand (on the slaves, naturally):

---

* On the other hand, if you encode the date into the serial number, as many people do (e.g., 1998010500 is the first rev of data on January 5, 1998), you may be able to tell at a glance whether you updated the serial number when you made the change.

```
# /etc/named-xfer -z movie.edu -f db.movie -s 0 terminator
# echo $?
```

If *named-xfer* returns 1, the zone was transferred successfully. Other return values indicate that no zone was transferred, either because of an error or because the slave thought the zone was up-to-date. (See "How to Use named-xfer," earlier in this chapter, for more details.)

There's another variation on the "forgot to increment the serial number" line. We see it in environments where administrators use tools like *h2n* to create db files from the host table. With scripts like *h2n*, it's temptingly easy to delete old db files and create new ones from scratch. Some administrators do this occasionally because they mistakenly believe that data in the old db files can creep into the new ones. The problem with deleting the db files is that, without the old db file to read for the current serial number, *h2n* starts over at serial number 1. If your primary's serial number rolls all the way back to 1 from 598 or what-have-you, the slaves (versions 4.8.3 and earlier) don't complain; they just figure they're all caught up and don't need zone transfers. A 4.9 or later slave server, however, is ever watchful, and will emit a syslog error message warning you that something might be wrong:

```
Jun  7 20:14:26 wormhole named[29618]: Zone "movie.edu"
                (class 1) SOA serial# (1) rcvd from [192.249.249.3]
                is < ours (112)
```

So if the serial number on the primary looks suspiciously low, check the serial number on the slaves, too, and compare them:

```
% nslookup
Default Server:  terminator.movie.edu
Address:  192.249.249.3

> set q=soa
> movie.edu.
Server:  terminator.movie.edu
Address:  192.249.249.3

movie.edu
        origin = terminator.movie.edu
        mail addr = al.robocop.movie.edu
        serial = 1
        refresh = 10800 (3 hours)
        retry   = 3600 (1 hour)
        expire  = 604800 (7 days)
        minimum ttl = 86400 (1 day)
> server wormhole.movie.edu.
Default Server:  wormhole.movie.edu
Addresses:  192.249.249.1, 192.253.253.1

> movie.edu.
Server:  wormhole.movie.edu
Addresses:  192.249.249.1, 192.253.253.1
```

```
movie.edu
        origin = terminator.movie.edu
        mail addr = al.robocop.movie.edu
        serial = 112
        refresh = 10800 (3 hours)
        retry  = 3600 (1 hour)
        expire = 604800 (7 days)
        minimum ttl = 86400 (1 day)
```

wormhole, as a *movie.edu* slave, should never have a larger serial number than the primary master, so clearly something's amiss.

This problem is really easy to spot, by the way, with the tool we'll write in Chapter 14, *Programming with the Resolver and Name Server Library Routines*, coming up next.

2. Forgot to Signal Primary Master Server

Occasionally, you may forget to signal your primary master name server after making a change to the conf file or to the db file. The name server won't know to load the new data—it doesn't automatically check the timestamp of the file and notice that it changed. Consequently, any changes you've made won't be reflected in the name server's data: new zones won't be loaded, and new records won't percolate out to the slaves.

To check when you last signaled the name server to reload, scan the *syslog* output for the last entry like this:

```
Mar  8 17:22:08 terminator named[22317]: reloading nameserver
```

This is the last time you sent a HUP signal to the name server. If you killed and then restarted the name server, you'll see an entry like this:

```
Mar  8 17:22:08 terminator named[22317]: restarted
```

or, on a 4.9 name server:

```
Mar  8 17:22:08 terminator named[22317]: starting
```

If the time of the restart doesn't correlate with the time you made the last change, signal the name server to reload its data again. And check that you incremented the serial numbers on db files you changed, too.

3. Slave Server Can't Load Zone Data

If a slave name server can't get the current serial number for a zone from its master name server, it'll log a message like the following via *syslog*:

```
Jan  6 11:55:25 wormhole named[544]: Err/TO getting serial# for "movie.edu"
```

On a BIND 4 name server, that looks like this:

```
Mar  3 8:19:34 wormhole named[22261]: zoneref: Masters for secondary
       zone movie.edu unreachable
```

If you let this problem fester, the slave will expire the zone:

```
Mar  8 17:12:43 wormhole named[22261]: secondary zone
       "movie.edu" expired
```

Once the zone has expired, you'll start getting SERVFAIL errors when you query the name server for data in the zone:

```
% nslookup robocop wormhole.movie.edu.
Server:  wormhole.movie.edu
Addresses:  192.249.249.1, 192.253.253.1

*** wormhole.movie.edu can't find robocop.movie.edu: Server failed
```

There are three leading causes of this problem: a loss in connectivity to the master server due to network failure, an incorrect IP address for the master server in the conf file, and a syntax error in the zone data file on the master server. First check the conf file's entry for the zone and see what IP address the slave is attempting to load from:

```
zone "movie.edu" {
               type slave;
               file "db.movie";
               masters { 192.249.249.3; };
};
```

On a BIND 4 server, the directive would look like this:

```
secondary       movie.edu       192.249.249.3       db.movie
```

Make sure that's really the IP address of the master name server. If it is, check connectivity to that IP address:

```
% ping 192.249.249.3 -n 10
PING 192.249.249.3: 64 byte packets

----192.249.249.3 PING Statistics----
10 packets transmitted, 0 packets received, 100% packet loss
```

If the master server isn't reachable, make sure that the server's host is really running (e.g., is powered on, etc.), or look for a network problem. If the server is reachable, make sure *named* is running on the host, and that you can manually transfer the zone:

```
# named-xfer -z movie.edu -f /tmp/db.movie -s 0 192.249.249.3
# echo $?
2
```

A return code of 2 means that an error occurred. Check to see if there is a *syslog* message. In this case there was a message:

```
Jan  6 14:56:07 zardoz named-xfer[695]: record too short from [192.249.249.3],
```

```
zone movie.edu
```

At first glance, this error looks like a truncation problem. The real problem is easier to see if you use *nslookup*:

```
% nslookup - terminator.movie.edu
Default Server:  terminator.movie.edu
Address:  192.249.249.3

> ls movie.edu                        —This attempts a zone transfer
[terminator.movie.edu]
*** Can't list domain movie.edu: Query refused
```

What has happened here is that *named* is refusing to allow you to transfer its zone data. The remote server has secured its zone data with the *allow-transfer* substatement, the *secure_zone* resource record, or *xfrnets* boot file directive.

If the master server is responding as not authoritative for the zone, you'll see a message like this:

```
Jan  6 11:58:36 zardoz named[544]: Err/TO getting serial# for "movie.edu"
Jan  6 11:58:36 zardoz named-xfer[793]: [192.249.249.3] not authoritative for
    movie.edu, SOA query got rcode 0, aa 0, ancount 0, aucount 0
```

If this is the correct master server, the server *should* be authoritative for the zone. This probably indicates that the master had a problem loading the zone, usually because of a syntax error in the zone data file. Contact the administrator of the master server and have him check his syslog output for indications of a syntax error (see problem 5, later in this chapter).

4. Added Name to Database File, but Forgot to Add PTR Record

Because the mappings from host names to IP addresses are disjointed from the mappings from IP addresses to host names in DNS, it's easy to forget to add a PTR record for a new host. Adding the A record is intuitive, but many people who are used to host tables assume that adding an address record takes care of the reverse mapping, too. That's not true—you need to add a PTR record for the host to the appropriate *in-addr.arpa* domain.

Forgetting to add the PTR record for a host usually causes that host to fail authentication checks. For example, users on the host won't be able to *rlogin* to other hosts without specifying a password, and *rsh* or *rcp* to other hosts simply won't work. The servers these commands talk to need to be able to map the connection's IP address to a domain name to check *.rhosts* and *hosts.equiv.* These users' connections will cause entries like this to be *syslog*ged:

```
Aug 15 17:32:36 terminator inetd[23194]: login/tcp:
    Connection from unknown (192.249.249.23)
```

Also, many large *ftp* archives, including *ftp.uu.net*, refuse anonymous *ftp* access to hosts whose IP addresses don't map back to domain names. *ftp.uu.net*'s *ftp* server emits a message that reads, in part:

```
530- Sorry, we're unable to map your IP address 140.186.66.1 to a hostname
530- in the DNS.  This is probably because your nameserver does not have a
530- PTR record for your address in its tables, or because your reverse
530- nameservers are not registered.  We refuse service to hosts whose
530- names we cannot resolve.
```

That makes the reason you can't use anonymous *ftp* pretty evident. Other *ftp* sites, however, don't bother printing informative messages; they simply deny service.

nslookup is handy for checking whether you've forgotten the PTR record or not:

```
% nslookup
Default Server:  terminator.movie.edu
Address:  192.249.249.3

> beetlejuice        —Check for a hostname-to-address mapping
Server:  terminator.movie.edu
Address:  192.249.249.3

Name:     beetlejuice.movie.edu
Address:  192.249.249.23

> 192.249.249.23    —Now check for a corresponding address-to-hostname mapping
Server:  terminator.movie.edu
Address:  192.249.249.3

*** terminator.movie.edu can't find 192.249.249.23: Non-existent domain
```

On the primary for *249.249.192.in-addr.arpa*, a quick check of the *db.192.249.249* file will tell you if the PTR record hasn't been added to the db file yet, or if the name server hasn't been signaled to load the file. If the name server having trouble is a slave for the zone, check that the serial number was incremented on the primary and that the slave has had enough time to load the zone.

5. Syntax Error in the Conf File or DNS Database File

Syntax errors in the conf file and in zone database files are also relatively common (more or less, depending on the experience of the administrator). Generally, an error in the conf file will cause the name server to fail to load one or more zones. Some typos in the *options* statement will cause the name server to fail to start at all, and to log an error like this via *syslog*:

```
Jan  6 11:59:29 terminator named[544]: can't change directory to /var/name: No
    such file or directory
```

Note that you won't see an error message when you try to start *named* on the command line, but *named* won't stay running for long.

If the syntax error is in a less important line in the boot file—say, in *zone* statement—only that zone will be affected. Usually, the name server will not be able to load the zone at all (say, you misspell "master" or the name of the data file, or you forget to put quotes around the file name or domain name). This would produce *syslog* output like:

```
Jan  6 12:01:36 terminator named[841]: /etc/named.conf:10: syntax error near
    'movie.edu'
```

If a db file contains a syntax error, yet the name server succeeds in loading the zone, it will either answer as "non-authoritative" for *all* data in the zone or will return a SERVFAIL error for lookups in the zone:

```
% nslookup carrie
Server:  terminator.movie.edu
Address:  192.249.249.3

Non-authoritative answer:
Name:    carrie.movie.edu
Address:  192.253.253.4
```

Here's the *syslog* message produced by the syntax error that caused this problem:

```
Jan  6 15:07:46 huskymo named[693]: db.movie:11: Priority error
    (postmanrings2x.movie.edu.)
Jan  6 15:07:46 huskymo named[693]: master zone "movie.edu" (IN) rejected due
    to errors (serial 1997010600)
Jan  6 15:07:46 huskymo named[693]: slave zone "movie.edu" (IN) removed
```

If you looked in the db file for the problem, you'd find this record:

```
postmanrings2x    IN    MX    postmanrings2x.movie.edu.
```

The MX record is missing the preference field, which causes the error.

Note that unless you correlate the lack of authority (when you expect the name server to be authoritative) with a problem, or scan your *syslog* file assiduously, you might never notice the syntax error!

Starting with BIND 4.9.4, an "invalid" host name can be a syntax error:

```
Jan  6 12:04:10 terminator named[841]: owner name "ID_4.movie.edu" IN (primary)
    is invalid - rejecting
Jan  6 12:04:10 terminator named[841]: db.movie:11: owner name error
Jan  6 12:04:10 terminator named[841]: db.movie:11: Database error (a)
Jan  6 12:04:10 terminator named[841]: master zone "movie.edu" (IN) rejected
    due to errors (serial 1997010600)
```

6. Missing Dot at the End of a Name in a DNS Database File

It's *very* easy to leave off trailing dots when editing a db file. Since the rules for when to use them change so often (*don't* use them in the boot file, *don't* use them in *resolv.conf*, *do* use them in db files to override $ORIGIN...), it's hard to keep them straight. These resource records:

```
zorba           IN    MX    10 zelig.movie.edu
movie.edu       IN    NS    terminator.movie.edu
```

really don't look that odd to the untrained eye, but they probably don't do what they're intended to. In the *db.movie* file, they'd be equivalent to:

```
zorba.movie.edu.        IN    MX    10 zelig.movie.edu.movie.edu.
movie.edu.movie.edu.    IN    NS    terminator.movie.edu.movie.edu.
```

unless the origin were explicitly changed.

If you omit a trailing dot after a domain name in the resource record's data (as opposed to leaving off a trailing dot in the resource record's *name*), you usually end up with wacky NS or MX records:

```
% nslookup -type=mx zorba.movie.edu.
Server:  terminator.movie.edu
Address:  192.249.249.3

zorba.movie.edu        preference = 10, mail exchanger
                       = zelig.movie.edu.movie.edu
zorba.movie.edu        preference = 50, mail exchanger
                       = postmanrings2x.movie.edu.movie.edu
```

The cause of this should be fairly clear from the *nslookup* output. But if you forget the trailing dot on the domain name field in a record (as in the *movie.edu* NS record above), spotting your mistake might not be as easy. If you try to look up the record with *nslookup*, you won't find it under the name you thought you used. Dumping your name server's database may help you root it out:

```
$ORIGIN edu.movie.edu.
movie   IN    NS    terminator.movie.edu.movie.edu.
```

The $ORIGIN line looks odd enough to stand out.

7. Missing Cache Data

If, for some reason, you forget to install a cache file on your host, or if you accidentally delete it, your name server will be unable to resolve names outside of its authoritative data. This behavior is easy to recognize using *nslookup*, but be careful to use full, dot-terminated domain names, or else the search list may cause misleading failures.

```
% nslookup
Default Server:  terminator.movie.edu
Address:  192.249.249.3

> ftp.uu.net.    —A lookup of a name outside your name server's authoritative data
                                     —causes a SERVFAIL error...
Server:  terminator.movie.edu
Address:  192.249.249.3

*** terminator.movie.edu can't find ftp.uu.net.: Server failed
```

A lookup of a name in your name server's authoritative data returns a response:

```
> wormhole.movie.edu.
Server:  terminator.movie.edu
Address:  192.249.249.3

Name:    wormhole.movie.edu
Addresses:  192.249.249.1, 192.253.253.1

> ^D
```

To confirm your suspicion that the cache data are missing, check the *syslog* output for an error like this:

```
Jan  6 15:10:22 terminator named[764]: No root nameservers for class IN
```

Class 1, you'll remember, is the IN, or Internet, class. This error indicates that because no cache data were available, no root name servers were found.

8. Loss of Network Connectivity

Though the Internet is more reliable today than it was back in the wild and woolly days of the ARPAnet, network outages are still relatively common. Without "lifting the hood" and poking around in debugging output, these failures usually look like poor performance:

```
% nslookup nisc.sri.com.
Server:  terminator.movie.edu
Address:  192.249.249.3

*** Request to terminator.movie.edu timed out ***
```

If you turn on name server debugging, though, you'll see that your name server, anyway, is healthy. It received the query from the resolver, sent the necessary queries, and waited patiently for a response. It just didn't get one. Here's what the debugging output might look like:

```
Debug turned ON, Level 1
```

Here *nslookup* sends the first query to our local name server, for the IP address of *nisc.sri.com*. You can tell it's not another name server because the query is received from a port other than 53, the name server's port. Notice that the query is forwarded to another name server, and when no answer is received, it is resent to a different name server:

```
datagram from [192.249.249.3].1051, fd 5, len 30
req: nlookup(nisc.sri.com) id 18470 type=1 class=1
req: missed 'nisc.sri.com' as 'com' (cname=0)
forw: forw -> [198.41.0.4].53 ds=7 nsid=58732 id=18470 0ms retry 4 sec
resend(addr=1 n=0) -> [128.9.0.107].53 ds=7 nsid=58732 id=18470 0ms
```

Now *nslookup* is getting impatient, and it queries our local name server again. Notice that it uses the same port. The local name server ignores the duplicate query and tries forwarding the query two more times:

```
datagram from [192.249.249.3].1051, fd 5, len 30
req: nlookup(nisc.sri.com) id 18470 type=1 class=1
req: missed 'nisc.sri.com' as 'com' (cname=0)
resend(addr=2 n=0) -> [192.33.4.12].53 ds=7 nsid=58732 id=18470 0ms
resend(addr=3 n=0) -> [128.8.10.90].53 ds=7 nsid=58732 id=18470 0ms
```

nslookup queries the local name server again, and the name server fires off more queries:

```
datagram from [192.249.249.3].1051, fd 5, len 30
req: nlookup(nisc.sri.com) id 18470 type=1 class=1
req: missed 'nisc.sri.com' as 'com' (cname=0)
resend(addr=4 n=0) -> [192.203.230.10].53 ds=7 nsid=58732 id=18470 0ms
resend(addr=0 n=1) -> [198.41.0.4].53 ds=7 nsid=58732 id=18470 0ms
resend(addr=1 n=1) -> [128.9.0.107].53 ds=7 nsid=58732 id=18470 0ms
resend(addr=2 n=1) -> [192.33.4.12].53 ds=7 nsid=58732 id=18470 0ms
resend(addr=3 n=1) -> [128.8.10.90].53 ds=7 nsid=58732 id=18470 0ms
resend(addr=4 n=1) -> [192.203.230.10].53 ds=7 nsid=58732 id=18470 0ms
resend(addr=0 n=2) -> [198.41.0.4].53 ds=7 nsid=58732 id=18470 0ms
Debug turned OFF
```

From the debugging output, you can extract a list of the IP addresses of the name servers that your name server tried to query, and then check your connectivity to them. Odds are, *ping* won't have much better luck than your name server did:

```
% ping 198.41.0.4 -n 10     –ping first name server queried
PING 198.41.0.4: 64 byte packets

----198.41.0.4 PING Statistics----
10 packets transmitted, 0 packets received, 100% packet loss
% ping 128.9.0.107 -n 10     –ping second name server queried
PING 128.9.0.107: 64 byte packets

----128.9.0.107 PING Statistics----
10 packets transmitted, 0 packets received, 100% packet loss
```

If it does, you should check that the remote name servers are really running. You might also check whether your Internet firewall is inadvertently blocking your name server's queries. If you've upgraded to BIND 8 recently, see "A Gotcha with BIND 8 and Packet Filtering Firewalls," in Chapter 15, *Miscellaneous*, and see if it applies to you.

If *ping* can't get through, either, all that's left to do is to locate the break in the network. Utilities like *traceroute* and *ping*'s record route option can be very helpful in determining whether the problem is on your network, the destination network, or somewhere in the middle.

You should also use your own common sense when tracking down the break. In this trace, for example, the remote name servers your name server tried to query are all root name servers. (You might have had their PTR records cached somewhere, so you could find out their domain names.) Now it's not very likely that each root's local network went down, nor is it likely that the Internet's commercial backbone networks collapsed entirely. Occam's razor says that the simplest condition that could cause this behavior—namely, the loss of *your* network's link to the Internet— is the most likely cause.

9. Missing Subdomain Delegation

Even though the InterNIC does its best to process your requests as quickly as possible, it may take a day or two for your domain's delegation to appear in the root name servers. If the InterNIC doesn't manage your parent domain, your mileage may vary. Some parents are quick and responsible, others are slow and inconsistent. Just like in real life, though, you're stuck with them.*

Until your delegation data appear in your parent domain's name servers, your name servers will be able to look up data in the Internet domain name space, but no one else on the Internet (outside of your domain) will know how to look up data in *your* name space.

That means that even though you can send mail outside of your domain, the recipients won't be able to reply to it. Furthermore, no one will be able to *telnet* to, *ftp* to, or even *ping* your hosts by name.

Remember that this applies equally to any *in-addr.arpa* subdomains you may run. Until the parent delegates those subdomains to your servers, name servers on the Internet won't be able to reverse map addresses on your networks.

To determine whether or not your zone's delegation has made it into your parent zone's name servers, query a parent name server for the NS records for your zone. If the parent name server has the data, any name server on the Internet can find it:

```
% nslookup
Default Server: terminator.movie.edu
```

---

* Until the GTLD Memorandum of Understanding is adopted, that is. See *http://www.gtld-mou.org/*.

```
Address:  192.249.249.3

> server a.root-servers.net.   –Query a root name server
Default Server:  a.root-servers.net
Address:  198.41.0.4

> set norecurse              —Instruct the server to answer out of its own data
> set type=ns                —and to look for NS records
> 249.249.192.in-addr.arpa.  —for 249.249.192.in-addr.arpa
Server:  a.root-servers.net
Address:  198.41.0.4

*** a.root-servers.net can't find 249.249.192.in-addr.arpa.: Non-existent
domain
```

Here, the delegation clearly hasn't been added yet. You can either wait patiently, or if an unreasonable amount of time has passed since you requested delegation from your parent, contact your parent and ask what's up.

10. Incorrect Subdomain Delegation

Incorrect subdomain delegation is another familiar problem on the Internet. Keeping delegation up to date requires human intervention—informing your parent zone's administrator of changes to your set of authoritative name servers. Consequently, delegation information often becomes inaccurate as administrators make changes without letting their parents know. Far too many administrators believe that setting up delegation is a one-shot deal: they let their parents know which name servers are authoritative once, when they set up their zone, and then they never talk to them again. They don't even call on Mother's Day.

An administrator may add a new name server, decommission another, and change the IP address of a third, all without telling the parent zone's administrator. Gradually, the number of name servers correctly delegated to by the parent zone dwindles. In the best case, this leads to long resolution times, as querying name servers struggle to find an authoritative name server for the zone. If the delegation information becomes badly out of date, and the last authoritative name server host is brought down for maintenance, the information within the zone will be inaccessible.

If you suspect bad delegation from your parent to your zone, from your zone to one of your children, or from a remote zone to one of its children, you can check with *nslookup*:

```
% nslookup
Default Server:  terminator.movie.edu
Address:  192.249.249.3

> server a.root-servers.net.     —Set server to the parent name server you suspect
                                            has bad delegation
```

```
Default Server:  a.root-servers.net
Address:  198.41.0.4

> set type=ns              —Look for NS records
> hp.com.                  —for the zone in question
Server:  a.root-servers.net
Address:  198.41.0.4

Non-authoritative answer:
hp.com          nameserver = RELAY.HP.COM
hp.com          nameserver = HPLABS.HPL.HP.COM
hp.com          nameserver = NNSC.NSF.NET
hp.com          nameserver = HPSDLO.SDD.HP.COM

Authoritative answers can be found from:
hp.com          nameserver = RELAY.HP.COM
hp.com          nameserver = HPLABS.HPL.HP.COM
hp.com          nameserver = NNSC.NSF.NET
hp.com          nameserver = HPSDLO.SDD.HP.COM
RELAY.HP.COM    internet address = 15.255.152.2
HPLABS.HPL.HP.COM       internet address = 15.255.176.47
NNSC.NSF.NET    internet address = 128.89.1.178
HPSDLO.SDD.HP.COM       internet address = 15.255.160.64
HPSDLO.SDD.HP.COM       internet address = 15.26.112.11
```

Let's say you suspect that the delegation to *hpsdlo.sdd.hp.com* is incorrect. You now query *hpsdlo* for data in the *hp.com* zone and check the answer:

```
> server hpsdlo.sdd.hp.com.
Default Server:  hpsdlo.sdd.hp.com
Addresses:  15.255.160.64, 15.26.112.11

> set norecurse
> set type=soa
> hp.com.
Server:  hpsdlo.sdd.hp.com
Addresses:  15.255.160.64, 15.26.112.11

Non-authoritative answer:
hp.com
        origin = relay.hp.com
        mail addr = hostmaster.hp.com
        serial = 1001462
        refresh = 21600 (6 hours)
        retry  = 3600 (1 hour)
        expire = 604800 (7 days)
        minimum ttl = 86400 (1 day)

Authoritative answers can be found from:
hp.com          nameserver = RELAY.HP.COM
hp.com          nameserver = HPLABS.HPL.HP.COM
hp.com          nameserver = NNSC.NSF.NET
RELAY.HP.COM    internet address = 15.255.152.2
HPLABS.HPL.HP.COM       internet address = 15.255.176.47
```

```
NNSC.NSF.NET      internet address = 128.89.1.178
```

If *hpsdlo* really were authoritative, it would have responded with an authoritative answer. The administrator of the *hp.com* zone can tell you whether *hpsdlo* should be an authoritative name server for *hp.com*, so that's who you should contact.

Another common symptom of this is a "lame server" error message:

```
Oct 1 04:43:38 terminator named[146]: Lame server on '40.234.23.210.in-
addr.arpa' (in '210.in-addr.arpa'?): [198.41.0.5].53 'RS0.INTERNIC.NET':
learnt(A=198.41.0.21,NS=128.63.2.53)
```

Here's how to read that: your name server was referred by the name server at 128.63.2.53 to the name server at 198.41.0.5 for a name in the domain *210.in-addr.arpa* specifically *40.234.23.210.in-addr.arpa*. The server at 198.41.0.5's response indicated that it wasn't, in fact, authoritative for *210.in-addr.arpa*, and therefore either the delegation that 128.63.2.53 gave you is wrong or the server at 198.41.0.5 is misconfigured.

11. Syntax Error in resolv.conf

Despite the *resolv.conf* file's simple syntax, people do occasionally make mistakes when editing it. And, unfortunately, lines with syntax errors in *resolv.conf* are silently ignored by the resolver. The result is usually that some part of your intended configuration doesn't take effect: either your domain or search list isn't set correctly, or the resolver won't query one of the name servers you configured it to query. Commands that rely on the search list won't work, your resolver won't query the right name server(s), or it won't query a name server at all.

The easiest way to check whether your *resolv.conf* file is having the intended effect is to run *nslookup*. *nslookup* will kindly report the default domain and search list it derives from *resolv.conf*, plus the name server it's querying, when you type **set all**, as we showed you in Chapter 11, *nslookup*:

```
% nslookup
Default Server:  terminator.movie.edu
Address:  192.249.249.3

> set all
Default Server:  terminator.movie.edu
Address:  192.249.249.3

Set options:
  nodebug          defname          search           recurse
  nod2             novc             noignoretc       port=53
  querytype=A      class=IN         timeout=5        retry=4
  root=ns.nic.ddn.mil.
  domain=movie.edu
  srchlist=movie.edu

>
```

Check that the output of *set all* is what you expect, given your *resolv.conf* file. For example, if you'd set search *fx.movie.edu movie.edu* in *resolv.conf,* you'd expect to see:

```
domain=fx.movie.edu
srchlist=fx.movie.edu/movie.edu
```

in the output. If you don't see what you're expecting, look carefully at *resolv.conf.* If you don't see anything obvious, look for nonprinting characters (with *vi*'s *set list* command, for example). Watch out for trailing spaces, especially; a trailing space after the domain name will set the default domain to include a space. No real domain names actually end with spaces, so all of your non-dot-terminated lookups will fail.

12. Default Domain Not Set

Failing to set your default domain is another old standby gaffe. You can set it implicitly, by setting your *hostname* to your host's fully qualified domain name, or explicitly, in *resolv.conf.* The characteristics of an unset default domain are straightforward: folks who use single-label names (or abbreviated domain names) in commands get no joy:

```
% telnet br
br: No address associated with name
% telnet br.fx
br.fx: No address associated with name
% telnet br.fx.movie.edu
Trying...
Connected to bladerunner.fx.movie.edu.
Escape character is '^]'.

HP-UX bladerunner.fx.movie.edu A.08.07 A 9000/730 (ttys1)
login:
```

You can use *nslookup* to check this one, much as you do when you suspect a syntax error in *resolv.conf:*

```
% nslookup
Default Server:  terminator.movie.edu
Address:  192.249.249.3

> set all
Default Server:  terminator.movie.edu
Address:  192.249.249.3

Set options:
  nodebug         defname         search          recurse
  nod2            novc            noignoretc      port=53
  querytype=A     class=IN        timeout=5       retry=4
  root=ns.nic.ddn.mil.
  domain=
  srchlist=
```

Notice that neither the local domain nor the search list is set. You can also track this down by enabling debugging on the name server. (This, of course, requires access to the name server, which may not be running on the host the problem's affecting.) Here's how the debugging output might look after trying those *telnet* commands:

```
Debug turned ON, Level 1

datagram from [192.249.249.3].1057, fd 5, len 20
req: nlookup(br) id 27974 type=1 class=1
req: missed 'br' as '' (cname=0)
forw: forw -> [198.41.0.4].53 ds=7 nsid=61691 id=27974 0ms retry 4 sec

datagram from [198.41.0.4].53, fd 5, len 20
ncache: dname br, type 1, class 1
send_msg -> [192.249.249.3].1057 (UDP 5) id=27974

datagram from [192.249.249.3].1059, fd 5, len 23
req: nlookup(br.fx) id 27975 type=1 class=1
req: missed 'br.fx' as '' (cname=0)
forw: forw -> [128.9.0.107].53 ds=7 nsid=61692 id=27975 0ms retry 4 sec

datagram from [128.9.0.107].53, fd 5, len 23
ncache: dname br.fx, type 1, class 1
send_msg -> [192.249.249.3].1059 (UDP 5) id=27975

datagram from [192.249.249.3].1060, fd 5, len 33
req: nlookup(br.fx.movie.edu) id 27976 type=1 class=1
req: found 'br.fx.movie.edu' as 'br.fx.movie.edu' (cname=0)
req: nlookup(bladerunner.fx.movie.edu) id 27976 type=1 class=1
req: found 'bladerunner.fx.movie.edu' as 'bladerunner.fx.movie.edu'
    (cname=1)
ns_req: answer -> [192.249.249.3].1060 fd=5 id=27976 size=183 Local
Debug turned OFF
```

Contrast this with the debugging output produced by the application of the search list in Chapter 12. The only names looked up here are exactly what the user typed, with no domains appended at all. Clearly the search list isn't being applied.

13. Response from Unexpected Source

One problem we've seen increasingly often in the DNS newsgroups is the "response from unexpected source." This was once called a Martian response: it's a response that comes from an IP address other than the one your server sent a query to. When a BIND name server sends a query to a remote server, BIND conscientiously makes sure that answers come only from the IP addresses on that server. This helps minimize the possibility of accepting spoofed responses. BIND is equally demanding of itself: a BIND server makes every effort to reply via the same network interface that it received a query on.

Here's the error message you'd see upon receiving a possibly unsolicited response:

```
Mar  8 17:21:04 terminator named[235]: Response from unexpected source
([205.199.4.131].53)
```

This can mean one of two things: either someone is trying to spoof your name server, or—more likely—you sent a query to an older BIND server or a different make of name server that's not as assiduous about replying from the same interface it receives queries on.

Transition Problems

With the release of BIND 4.9, many UNIX operating systems are updating their resolver and name servers to include 4.9's new functionality. Some of 4.9's features, however, may seem like errors to you after you upgrade to a new version of your operating system. We'll try to give you an idea of some changes you may notice in your name service after making the jump.

Resolver Behavior

The changes to the resolver's default search list that we described in Chapter 6 may seem like a problem to your users. Recall that with a domain setting of *fx.movie.edu*, your default search list will no longer include *movie.edu*. Therefore, users accustomed to using commands like *telnet db.personnel* and having the partial domain name expanded to *db.personnel.movie.edu* will have their commands fail. To solve this problem, you can use the *search* directive to define an explicit search list that includes your default domain's parent domain.

Name Server Behavior

Before version 4.9, a BIND name server would gladly load data describing any zone from a data file the name server read as a primary master. If you declared the name server primary for *movie.edu* and told it that the *movie.edu* data was in *db.movie*, you could stick data about *hp.com* in *db.movie*, and your name server would load the *hp.com* resource records. Some books even suggested putting the data for all of your *in-addr.arpa* zones in one file.

With BIND 4.9, the name server ignores any "out of zone" resource records in a zone data file. So if you cram PTR records for all your *in-addr.arpa* domains into one file and load it with a single *zone* statement or *primary* directive, the name server will ignore all the records not in the named zone. And that, of course, will mean loads of missing PTR records and failed *gethostbyaddr()* calls.

BIND does log that it's ignoring the records in syslog. The messages look like this:

```
Jan  7 13:58:01 terminator named[231]: db.movie:16: data "hp.com" outside zone
"movie.edu" (ignored)
```

```
Jan  7 13:58:01 terminator named[231]: db.movie:17: data "hp.com" outside zone
    "movie.edu" (ignored)
```

The solution is to use one zone data file and one *zone* statement or *primary* directive per zone.

Interoperability and Version Problems

With the move to BIND 8 and the introduction of Microsoft Windows DNS Server, more interoperability problems are cropping up between name servers. There are also a handful of problems that are unique to one version or another of BIND or the underlying operating system. Many of these are easy to spot and correct, and we would be remiss if we didn't cover them.

Zone Transfer Fails Because of Proprietary WINS Record

When a Microsoft Windows DNS Server is configured to consult a WINS server for names it can't find in a given zone, it inserts a special record into the zone data file. The record looks like this:

```
@               IN    WINS          &IP address of WINS server
```

Unfortunately, WINS is not a standard record type in the IN class. Consequently, if there are BIND slaves that transfer this zone, they'll choke on the WINS record and refuse to load the zone:

```
May 23 15:58:43 terminator named-xfer[386]: "fx.movie.edu IN 65281" - unknown
    type (65281)
```

The workaround for this is to configure the Microsoft DNS Server to filter out the proprietary record before transferring the zone. You do this by selecting the zone in the left-hand side of the DNS Manager screen, right clicking on it and selecting Properties. Click on the WINS Lookup tab in the resulting Zone Properties window, shown in Figure 13-1.

Checking "Settings only affect local server" will filter out the WINS record for that zone. However, any Microsoft DNS Server slaves won't see the record, even though they could use it.

Name Server Reports "No NS Record for SOA MNAME"

You'll only see this error on BIND 8.1 servers:

```
May 8 03:44:38 terminator named[11680]: no NS RR for SOA MNAME "movie.edu" in
    zone "movie.edu"
```

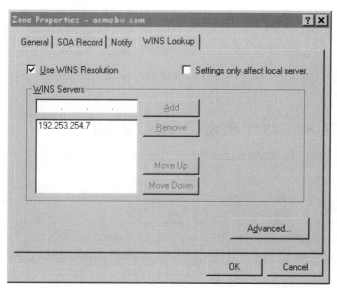

Figure 13-1. "Settings only affect local server" checkbox

The 8.1 server was a real stickler about the first field in the SOA record. Remember that one? In Chapter 4, *Setting Up BIND*, we said that it was, by convention, the domain name of the primary master name server for the zone. BIND 8.1 assumes it is, and checks for a corresponding NS record pointing the zone's domain name to the server in that field. If there's no such NS record, BIND emits that error message. It will also prevent NOTIFY messages from working correctly. The solution is either to change your MNAME field to the domain name of a name server listed in an NS record or upgrade to a newer version of BIND 8. The check was removed at BIND 8.1.1.

Name Server Reports "Too Many Open Files"

On hosts with many IP addresses, or a low limit on the maximum number of files a user can open, BIND will report:

```
Dec 12 11:52:06 terminator named[7770]: socket(SOCK_RAW): Too many open files
```

and die.

Since BIND tries to *bind()* to and listen on every network interface on the host, it may run out of file descriptors. This is especially common on hosts that use lots of virtual interfaces, often in support of web hosting. The two possible solutions are:

- Configure BIND to listen on only one or a few of the host's network interfaces using the *listen-on* substatement. If *terminator* is the host we're having this problem with:

```
options {
                listen-on { 192.249.249.3; };
};
```

will tell *named* on *terminator* to *bind()* only to the IP address 192.249.249.3.

* Reconfigure your operating system to allow a process to open more file descriptors concurrently.

Resolver Reports "Looked for PTR, Found CNAME"

This is another problem related to BIND's strictness. On some lookups, the resolver will log:

```
Sep 24 10:40:11 terminator syslog: gethostby*.getanswer: asked for
      "37.103.74.204.in-addr.arpa IN PTR", got type "CNAME"
Sep 24 10:40:11 terminator syslog: gethostby*.getanswer: asked for
      "37.103.74.204.in-addr.arpa", got "37.32/27.103.74.204.in-addr.arpa"
```

What happened here is that the resolver asked the name server to reverse map the IP address 204.74.103.37 to a domain name. The server did, but in the process found that *37.103.74.204.in-addr.arpa* was actually an alias for *37.32/27.103.74.204.in-addr.arpa*. That's almost certainly because the folks who run *103.74.204.in-addr.arpa* are using the scheme we described in Chapter 9, *Parenting*, to delegate part of their name space. The BIND 4.9.3-BETA resolver, however, doesn't understand that, and flags it as an error, thinking it didn't get the domain name or the type it was after.

The only solution to this problem is to upgrade to a newer version of the BIND resolver.

Name Server Startup Fails Because UDP Checksums Disabled

On some hosts running SunOS 4.1.X, you'll see this error:

```
Sep 24 10:40:11 terminator named[7770]: ns_udp checksums NOT turned on: exiting
```

named checked to make sure UDP checksumming was on on this system, and it wasn't, so *named* exited. *named* is so insistent on UDP checksumming being on for good reason: it makes copious use of UDP, and needs those UDP datagrams to arrive unmolested.

The solution to this problem is to enable UDP checksums on your system. The BIND distribution has documentation on that in *shres/sunos/INSTALL* and *shres/sunos/ISSUES* (in the BIND 4 distribution) or *src/port/sunos/shres/ISSUES* (in the BIND 8 distribution).

SunOS Resolver Is Configured, but Host Doesn't Use DNS

The last of these problems is implementation-specific. Some administrators on SunOS 4 hosts configure their resolvers with *resolv.conf* and naively assume that *ping*, *telnet*, and their brethren should work right away. However, in Chapter 7, *Maintaining BIND*, we discussed how SunOS 4 implements the resolver (in *ypserv*, if you recall). If the host isn't running NIS, configuring the resolver won't do it. The administrator will either have to set up at least an empty *hosts* map or replace the resolver routines. For details on both of these options, see Chapter 7.

Other Name Servers Don't Cache Your Negative Answers

You'd need a keen eye to notice this problem, and you'd also have to have turned off an important BIND 8 feature to have caused the problem. If you're running a BIND 8 name server and other resolvers and servers seem to ignore your server's cached negative responses, you just might have turned off *auth-nxdomain*.

auth-nxdomain is an options substatement that tells the BIND 8 server to flag cached negative responses as authoritative, even though they're not. That is, if your name server has cached the fact that *titanic.movie.edu* does not exist from the authoritative *movie.edu* name servers, *auth-nxdomain* tells your server to pass along that cached response to resolvers and servers that query it as though it were the authoritative name server for *movie.edu*.

The reason this is necessary is because some name servers check to make sure that negative responses, like NXDOMAIN and no records with a NOERROR return code, are marked authoritative. In the days before negative caching, negative responses had to be authoritative, so this was a sensible sanity check. With the advent of negative caching, however, a negative response may come from the cache. To make sure that older servers don't ignore such answers, though, or consider them errors, BIND 8 lets you falsely flag those responses as authoritative. In fact, that's the default behavior, so you shouldn't see remote queriers ignoring your server's negative responses unless you turn off *auth-nxdomain*.

Problem Symptoms

Some problems, unfortunately, aren't as easy to identify as the ones we listed. You'll experience some misbehavior but won't be able to attribute it directly to its cause, often because any of a number of problems may cause the symptoms you see. For cases like this, we'll suggest some of the common causes of these symptoms and ways to isolate them.

Local Name Can't Be Looked Up

The first thing to do when a program like *telnet* or *ftp* can't look up a local name is to use *nslookup* to try to look up the same name. When we say "the same name," we mean *literally* the same name—don't add a domain and a trailing dot if the user didn't type either one. Don't query a different name server than the user did.

As often as not, the user mistyped the name, or doesn't understand how the search list works, and just needs direction. Occasionally, you'll turn up real host configuration errors:

- Syntax errors in *resolv.conf* (problem 11 in the "Potential Problem List" mentioned earlier in this chapter)

- An unset default domain (problem 12)

You can check for either of these using *nslookup*'s *set all* command.

If *nslookup* points to a problem with the name server, rather than with the host configuration, check for the problems associated with the type of name server. If the name server is the primary master for the zone, but it doesn't respond with data you think it should:

- Check that the db file contains the data in question, and that the name server has been signaled to reload it (problem 2).

- Check the conf or boot file and the pertinent db file for syntax errors (problem 5).

- Ensure that the records have trailing dots, if they require them (problem 6).

If the name server is a slave server, you should first check whether or not its master has the correct data. If it does, and the slave doesn't:

- Make sure you've incremented the serial number on the primary (problem 1).

- Look for a problem on the slave in updating the zone (problem 3).

If the primary *doesn't* have the correct data, of course, diagnose the problem on the primary.

If the problem server is a caching-only name server:

- Make sure it has its cache data (problem 7).

- Check that your parent zone's delegation to your zone exists and is correct (problems 9 and 10). Remember that to a caching-only server, your zone looks just like any other remote zone. Even though the host it runs on may be inside your zone, the caching-only name server must be able to locate an authoritative server for your zone from your parent zone's servers.

Remote Names Can't Be Looked Up

If your local lookups succeed, but you can't look up names outside your local zones, there is a different set of problems to check:

- First, did you just set up your servers? You might have omitted the cache data (problem 7).

- Can you *ping* the remote zone's name servers? Maybe you can't reach the remote zone's servers because of connectivity loss (problem 8).

- Is the remote zone new? Maybe its delegation hasn't yet appeared (problem 9). Or the delegation information for the remote zone may be wrong or out of date, due to neglect (problem 10).

- Does the domain name actually exist on the remote zone's servers (problem 2)? On all of them (problems 1 and 3)?

Wrong or Inconsistent Answer

If you get the wrong answer when looking up a local name, or an inconsistent answer, depending on which name server you ask or when you ask, first check the synchronization between your name servers:

- Are they all holding the same serial number for the zone? Did you forget to increment the serial number on the primary after you made a change (problem 1)? If you did, the name servers may all have the same serial number, but they will answer differently out of their authoritative data.

- Did you roll the serial number back to one (problem 1 again)? Then the primary's serial number will appear much lower than the slaves' serial numbers.

- Did you forget to signal the primary (problem 2)? Then the primary will return (via *nslookup,* for example) a different serial number than the serial number in the data file.

- Are the slaves having trouble updating from the primary (problem 3)? If so, they should have *syslog*ged appropriate error messages.

- Is the name server's round robin feature rotating the addresses of the domain name you're looking up?

If you get these results when looking up a name in a remote zone, you should check whether the remote zone's name servers have lost synchronization. You can use tools like *nslookup* to determine whether the remote zone's administrator has forgotten to increment the serial number, for example. If the name servers answer differently from their authoritative data but show the same serial number, the serial number probably wasn't incremented. If the primary's serial number is much lower than the slaves', the primary's serial number was probably accidentally reset. We usually assume a zone's primary name server is running on the host listed as the origin in the SOA record.

You probably can't determine conclusively that the primary hasn't been signaled, though. It's also difficult to pin down updating problems between remote name servers. In cases like this, if you've determined that the remote name servers are giving out incorrect data, contact the zone administrator and (gently) relay what you've found. This will help the administrator track down the problem on the remote end.

If you can determine that a parent server—a remote zone's parent, your zone's parent, or even your zone—is giving out a bad answer, check whether this is coming from old delegation information. Sometimes this will require contacting both the administrator of the remote zone and the administrator of its parent to compare the delegation and the current, correct list of authoritative name servers.

If you can't induce the administrator to fix his data, and it's causing your name server problems, or if you can't track down the administrator, you can always use the *bogus* substatement or *bogusns* directive to instruct your name server not to query that particular server.

Lookups Take a Long Time

Long name resolution is usually due to one of two problems:

- Connectivity loss (problem 8), which you can diagnose with name server debugging output and tools like *ping*

- Incorrect delegation information (problem 10), which points to the wrong name servers or the wrong IP addresses

Usually, going over the debugging output and sending a few *ping*s will point to one or the other. Either you can't reach the name servers at all, or you can reach the hosts, but the name servers aren't responding.

Sometimes, though, the results are inconclusive. For example, the parent name servers delegate to a set of name servers that don't respond to *ping*s or queries, but connectivity to the remote network seems all right (a *traceroute*, for example, will get you to the remote network's "doorstep"—the last router between you and the host). Is the delegation information so badly out of date that the name servers have long since moved to other addresses? Are the hosts simply down? Or is there really a remote network problem? Usually, finding out will require a call or a message to the administrator of the remote zone. (And remember, *whois* gives you phone numbers!)

rlogin and rsh to Host Fails Access Check

This is a problem you expect to see right after you set up your name servers. Users unaware of the change from the host table to domain name service won't know to update their *.rhosts* files. (We covered what needs to be updated in Chapter 6.) Consequently, *rlogin*'s or *rsh*'s access check will fail and deny the user access.

Other causes of this problem are missing or incorrect *in-addr.arpa* delegation (problems 9 and 10), and forgetting to add a PTR record for the client host (problem 4). If you've recently upgraded to BIND 4.9 or 8 and have PTR data for more than one *in-addr.arpa* subdomain in a single file, your name server may be ignoring the out-of-zone data. Any of these situations will result in the same behavior:

```
% rlogin wormhole
Password:
```

In other words, the user is prompted for a password despite having set up passwordless access with *.rhosts* or *hosts.equiv*. If you were to look at the *syslog* file on the destination host (*wormhole*, in this case), you'd probably see something like this:

```
May  4 18:06:22 wormhole inetd[22514]: login/tcp: Connection
        from unknown (192.249.249.213)
```

You can tell which problem it is by stepping through the resolution process with *nslookup*. First query one of your *in-addr.arpa* domain's parent name servers for NS records for your *in-addr* subdomain. If these are correct, query the name servers listed for the PTR record corresponding to the IP address of the *rlogin* or *rsh* client. Make sure they all have the PTR record, and that the record maps to the right domain name. If not all the name servers have the record, check for a loss of synchronization between the primary and the slaves (problems 1 and 3).

Access to Services Denied

Sometimes *rlogin* and *rsh* aren't the only services to go. Occasionally you'll install DNS on your server and your diskless hosts won't boot, and hosts won't be able to mount disks from the server, either.

If this happens, make sure the case of the names your name servers return agrees with the case your previous name service returned. For example, if you were running NIS, and your NIS host's maps contained only lowercase names, you should make sure your name servers also return lowercase names. Some programs are case-sensitive and won't recognize names in a different case in a data file, such as */etc/bootparams* or */etc/exports*.

Name Server Is Infected with Bogus Root Server Data

NOTE   BIND name servers version 4.9 and newer are resistant to this
             problem.

Here's a problem that will be familiar to anyone who's run a name server on the
Internet for any length of time:

```
% nslookup
Default Server:  terminator.movie.edu
Address:  192.249.249.3

> set type=ns
> .
Server:  terminator.movie.edu
Address:  192.249.249.3

Non-authoritative answer:
(root)   nameserver = NS.NIC.DDN.MIL
(root)   nameserver = B.ROOT-SERVERS.NET
(root)   nameserver = E.ROOT-SERVERS.NET
(root)   nameserver = D.ROOT-SERVERS.NET
(root)   nameserver = F.ROOT-SERVERS.NET
(root)   nameserver = C.ROOT-SERVERS.NET
(root)   nameserver = G.ROOT-SERVERS.NET
(root)   nameserver = hpfcsx.fc.hp.com
(root)   nameserver = hp-pcd.cv.hp.com
(root)   nameserver = hp-ses.sde.hp.com
(root)   nameserver = hpsatc1.gva.hp.com
(root)   nameserver = named_master.ch.apollo.hp.com
(root)   nameserver = A.ISI.EDU
(root)   nameserver = SRI-NIC.ARPA
(root)   nameserver = GUNTER-ADAM.ARPA

Authoritative answers can be found from:
(root)   nameserver = NS.NIC.DDN.MIL
(root)   nameserver = B.ROOT-SERVERS.NET
(root)   nameserver = E.ROOT-SERVERS.NET
(root)   nameserver = D.ROOT-SERVERS.NET
(root)   nameserver = F.ROOT-SERVERS.NET
(root)   nameserver = C.ROOT-SERVERS.NET
(root)   nameserver =

*** Error: record size incorrect (1050690 != 65519)

*** terminator.movie.edu can't find .: Unspecified error
```

Whoa! Where in the heck did all those root name servers come from? And why is
the record size messed up?

If you look carefully, you'll notice that most of those records are bogus. SRI-NIC.ARPA, for example, is the original name of *nic.ddn.mil*, from the days when all ARPAnet hosts lived under the top-level ARPA domain. Moreover, even the name server on *nic.ddn.mil* was decommissioned as a root some time ago, replaced by a new root on *ns.nic.ddn.mil* (and *that* name server moved from the old NIC at SRI to the new one at NSI...).

The name servers in *hp.com* aren't Internet roots, and haven't *ever* been. So how did these get into our cache? Here's how.

Remember when we described what a name server does when queried for a name it isn't authoritative for? It does its best to provide information that will be helpful to the querier: NS records that are as close as possible to the domain name the querier is after. Sometimes the queried name server can only get as close as the root name servers. And sometimes the name server has the *wrong* list of roots, either accidentally (because of incorrect configuration) or because no one went to the effort to keep the cache file up-to-date.

So what does that have to do with caching? Well, say your name server queries what it thinks is a *10.in-addr.arpa* name server, and the name server turns out to know nothing about *10.in-addr.arpa*. The name server, trying to be helpful, sends along its current list of root name servers in a response packet, but the list is wrong. BIND (versions 4.8.3 and earlier), trusting as a newborn, gratefully caches all this useless information. Later versions, older and wiser, flag this as a lame delegation and toss the bad data.

Why did *nslookup* return a record size error when we looked up your name server's list of root servers? The list of roots exceeded the size of a UDP response packet, but it was truncated to fit into a response. The length field in the response indicated that more data was included, though, so *nslookup* complained.

This infection can spread if the bogus NS records point to real—but nonroot—name servers. If these name servers give out more bogus data, your name server's cache may become polluted by more and more erroneous records.

The only ways to track down the source of these bogus roots are to turn name server debugging way up (to level four or above) and watch for the receipt of these records, or to patch your name server so that it reports receiving bad root information. With BIND 4.9 and BIND 8, you can see the source of the bad data in a database dump. Even when you think you've found the culprit, though, you may have only discovered another name server that was corrupted before yours, not the original source of the corruption. To uncover the original sinner, you'd have to work backwards, together with other administrators, to discover who made the first gaffe. If you don't have the tenacity to suffer through that process, it's probably easier just to upgrade to a BIND 4.9 or BIND 8 server.

Name Server Keeps Loading Old Data

Here's a weird class of problems related to the previous cache corruption problem. Sometimes, after decommissioning a name server, or changing a name server's IP address, you'll find the old address record lingering around. An old record may show up in a name server's cache or in a zone data file weeks, or even months, later. The record clearly should have timed out of any caches by now. So why's it still there? Well, there are a few reasons this happens. We'll describe the simpler cases first.

Old delegation information

The first (and simplest) case occurs if a parent zone doesn't keep up with its children, or if the children don't inform the parent of changes to the authoritative name servers for the zone. If the *edu* administrators have this old delegation information for *movie.edu*:

```
$ORIGIN movie.edu.
@       86400   in    ns    terminator
        86400   in    ns    wormhole
terminator      86400   in    a    192.249.249.3
wormhole        86400   in    a    192.249.249.254 ; wormhole's former
                                                   ; IP address
```

then the *edu* name servers will give out the bogus old address for *wormhole*.

This is easily corrected once it's isolated to the parent name servers: just contact the parent zone's administrator and ask to have the delegation information updated. If any of the child zone's servers have cached the bad data, kill them (to clear out their caches), delete any data files that contain the bad data, then restart them.

Unnecessary glue data

When *named-xfer* pulls zone data over from a master server, it transfers more than it strictly needs. This is a bug in BIND 4.8.3 and earlier. The main excess baggage *named-xfer* retrieves is the addresses of name servers for the zone, when those servers are outside of the zone. If the name servers are in the zone, their addresses are necessary as glue data. But if they're not in the zone, they don't belong in the zone's data file. So, for example, in a backup file for *movie.edu*, you'd find these partial contents of file *db.movie*:

```
$ORIGIN edu.
movie           IN    NS    terminator.movie.edu.
$ORIGIN movie.edu.
terminator      IN    A     192.249.249.3
$ORIGIN edu.
movie           IN    NS    wormhole.movie.edu.
$ORIGIN movie.edu.
wormhole        IN    A     192.249.249.1
                IN    A     192.253.253.1
                IN    A     192.249.249.254
```

But you'd also find similar records in *db.192.249.249* and *db.192.253.253*:

```
$ORIGIN 249.192.in-addr.arpa.
249             IN      NS      terminator.movie.edu.
$ORIGIN movie.edu.
terminator      56422   IN      A       192.249.249.3
$ORIGIN 249.192.in-addr.arpa.
249             IN      NS      wormhole.movie.edu.
$ORIGIN movie.edu.
wormhole        56422   IN      A       192.249.249.1
                56422   IN      A       192.253.253.1
                56422   IN      A       192.249.249.254
```

The last of *wormhole*'s addresses is *wormhole*'s former address.

NOTE   BIND name servers version 4.9 and newer do not have this problem.

There's no reason to include the address records for *terminator* or *wormhole* in either *in-addr.arpa* backup file. They *should* be listed in *db.movie*, but since they're not necessary as glue in either *in-addr.arpa* subdomain, they shouldn't appear in *db.192.249.249* or *db.192.253.253*.

When the slave loads the *in-addr.arpa* backup file, it also loads the address records for *terminator* and *wormhole*. If the address is old, then the name server loads—and gives out—the wrong address:

```
% nslookup wormhole
Server:   wormhole.movie.edu
Address:  192.249.249.1

Name:     wormhole.movie.edu
Address:  192.249.249.1, 192.253.253.1, 192.249.249.254
```

You might think, "If I clean the old address out of *db.movie*," (you can think in italics), "the slaves will time it out of the *in-addr.arpa* subdomains. After all, there's a TTL on the address records."

Unfortunately, the slave servers don't age those records. They're given out with the TTL in the data file, but the slave never decrements the TTL or times out the record. So the old address could linger as long as the *in-addr.arpa* backup files remain unchanged. And *in-addr.arpa* zones are very stable if no one's adding new hosts to the network or shuffling IP addresses. There's no need to increment their serial numbers and have them reloaded by the slaves.

The secret is to increment *all* of the zones' serial numbers at once when you make a change affecting the zones' authoritative name servers. That way, you flush out any old, stale records and ensure that the slaves all load up-to-date glue.

Mutual infection

There's one more scenario we're familiar with that can cause these symptoms. This one doesn't require old data in files at all—just two slave name servers. BIND can run into problems when two name servers act as slave for each other, and when one zone is the child of the other; for example, when name server A loads *movie.edu* from name server B, and B loads *fx.movie.edu* from A.

NOTE   BIND name servers version 4.9 and newer are resistant to this
              problem.

In these cases, certain data can float back and forth between the two name servers indefinitely. In particular, the name servers can pass delegation data, which is really part of the "child" zone, back and forth.

How does this work? Say *terminator.movie.edu* is the primary master *movie.edu* server and it backs up *fx.movie.edu* from *bladerunner. bladerunner* is the primary master *fx.movie.edu* name server and backs up *movie.edu* from *terminator.* Then suppose you change *bladerunner*'s IP address. You remember to change *named.conf* on *terminator* to load *fx.movie.edu* from *bladerunner*'s new IP address, and you change the IP address in *db.fx.* You even update the *fx* subdomain's delegation data in *db.movie* on the primary to reflect the address change. Isn't that enough?

Nope. Here's why: *terminator* still has *bladerunner*'s old IP address in the backup file *db.fx,* and *bladerunner* still has its own old address in its backup copy of *db.movie* (a glue record in the *fx* delegation).

Now let's say you delete *db.fx* on *terminator* and kill and restart its name server. Won't that suffice? No, because *bladerunner* still has the old address and will pass it along to *terminator* in the next *fx.movie.edu* zone transfer. If you delete *db.movie* on *bladerunner* and kill and restart the name server, something similar will happen: *bladerunner* will get the old record back with the next *movie.edu* zone transfer.

That's a little complicated to follow—for us, too—so Figure 13-2 will help you picture what's going on.

You need to rid both name servers of the old record simultaneously. Our solution to this problem is to bring both name servers down at the same time, clean out any backup files, and then start them both up again. That way, the caches can't re-infect each other.

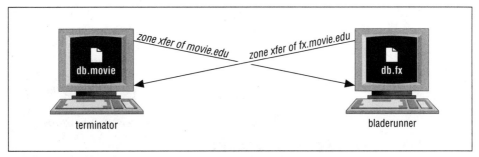

Figure 13-2. Infection through zone transfer

What have I got?

How do you determine which of these problems is plaguing you? Pay attention to which name servers are distributing the old data, and which domains the data relate to:

- Is the name server your parent name server? Check the parent for either old delegation information or parent-child infection.

- Are both a name server and its parent affected? Then check for parent-child infection.

- Are slaves affected, but not the primary? Check for stale data in backup files.

That's about all we can think to cover. It's certainly less than a comprehensive list, but we hope it'll help you solve the more common problems you encounter with DNS, and give you ideas about how to approach the rest. Boy, if we'd only had a troubleshooting guide when *we* started!

14

Programming with the Resolver and Name Server Library Routines

"I know what you're thinking about," said Tweedledum; "but it isn't so, nohow."

"Contrariwise," continued Tweedledee, "if it was so, it might be; and if it were so, it would be; but as it isn't, it ain't. That's logic."

I bet you think resolver programming is hard. Contrariwise! It isn't very hard, really. The format of DNS packets is quite straightforward—you don't have to deal with ASN.1[*] at all, as you have to do with SNMP. And you have nifty library routines to make parsing DNS packets easy. We've included portions of RFC 1035 in Appendix A, *DNS Message Format and Resource Records*. However, you might find it handy to have a copy of RFC 1035 to look at while we are going through this chapter; at least have a copy of it nearby when you write your own DNS program.

Shell Script Programming with nslookup

Before you go off and write a C program to do your DNS chore, you should write the program as a shell script using *nslookup*. There are good reasons to start with a shell script:

- You'll write the shell script much faster than you'll write the C program.

- If you are not comfortable with DNS, you can work out the muck in your program's logic with a quick shell script prototype. When you finally write the

---

[*] ASN.1 stands for Abstract Syntax Notation. ASN.1 is a language for encoding object types, accepted as an international standard by the International Organization for Standardization.

C program, you can focus on the additional control you have with C, rather than spending your time reworking the basic functionality.

- You might find out that the shell script version does your task well enough so that you don't have to write the C program after all. Not only is the coding time shorter, but shell scripts are easier to maintain if you stick with them for the long run.

If you prefer Perl over plain old shell programming, you can do that too. At the end of this chapter, we'll show you how to use the Perl Net::DNS module written by Michael Fuhr.

A Typical Problem

Before you write a program, you have to have a problem to solve. Let's suppose you want your network management system to watch over your primary and secondary name servers. You want it to notify you of several problems: a name server that is not running (it might have died), a name server that is not authoritative for a domain that it is supposed to be authoritative for (the boot file might have been messed up), or a name server that has fallen behind in updating its data (the primary's serial number might have been decreased accidentally).

Each of these problems is easily detectable. If a name server is not running on a host, the host will send back an ICMP *port unreachable* message. You can find this out with both *nslookup* and the resolver routines. Checking if a name server is authoritative for a domain is easy: ask it for the domain's SOA record. If the answer is nonauthoritative, or the name server does not have the SOA record, there is a problem. You'll have to ask for the SOA record in a *nonrecursive* query so that the name server doesn't go off and look up the SOA record from another server. Once you have the SOA record, you can extract the serial number.

Solving This Problem with a Script

This problem requires a program that takes the domain name of a zone as an argument, looks up the name servers for that zone, and then queries each of those name servers for the SOA record for the zone. The response will show if the server is authoritative, and it will show the zone's serial number. If there is no response, the program needs to determine if a name server is even running on the host. Once this program is written, it needs to be called for every zone you want to watch over. Since this program looks up the name servers (by looking up the NS records for the zone), we assume that you have listed all your name servers in NS records in your zone data. If that is not the case, then you will have to change this program to take a list of name servers from the command line.

Let's write the basic program as a shell script that uses *nslookup*. First, we must figure out what the output of *nslookup* looks like, so that we can parse it with UNIX tools. We'll look up NS records to find out which servers are supposed to be authoritative for a zone, both when the server is authoritative for the NS records and when it isn't:

```
% nslookup
Default Server:  relay.hp.com
Address:  15.255.152.2

> set type=ns
```

Find out what the response looks like when the server is not authoritative for the NS records:

```
> mit.edu.
Server:  relay.hp.com
Address:  15.255.152.2

Non-authoritative answer:
mit.edu nameserver = STRAWB.MIT.EDU
mit.edu nameserver = W20NS.MIT.EDU
mit.edu nameserver = BITSY.MIT.EDU

Authoritative answers can be found from:
MIT.EDU nameserver = STRAWB.MIT.EDU
MIT.EDU nameserver = W20NS.MIT.EDU
MIT.EDU nameserver = BITSY.MIT.EDU
STRAWB.MIT.EDU  internet address = 18.71.0.151
W20NS.MIT.EDU   internet address = 18.70.0.160
BITSY.MIT.EDU   internet address = 18.72.0.3
```

Find out what the response looks like when the server is authoritative for the NS records:

```
> server strawb.mit.edu.
Default Server:  strawb.mit.edu
Address:  18.71.0.151

> mit.edu.
Server:  strawb.mit.edu
Address:  18.71.0.151

mit.edu nameserver = BITSY.MIT.EDU
mit.edu nameserver = STRAWB.MIT.EDU
mit.edu nameserver = W20NS.MIT.EDU
BITSY.MIT.EDU   internet address = 18.72.0.3
STRAWB.MIT.EDU  internet address = 18.71.0.151
W20NS.MIT.EDU   internet address = 18.70.0.160
```

You can see from this output that we can grab the name server names by looking for the lines that contain *nameserver* and saving the last field. When the server was not authoritative for the NS records, it printed them twice, so we'll have to weed out duplicates.

Next, we look up the SOA record for the zone, both when the server is authoritative for the SOA record and when it isn't. We turn off *recurse* so the name server doesn't go off and query an authoritative name server for the SOA:

```
% nslookup
Default Server:  relay.hp.com
Address:  15.255.152.2

> set type=soa
> set norecurse
```

Find out what the response looks like when the server does not have the SOA record:

```
> mit.edu.
Server:  relay.hp.com
Address:  15.255.152.2

Authoritative answers can be found from:
MIT.EDU nameserver = STRAWB.MIT.EDU
MIT.EDU nameserver = W20NS.MIT.EDU
MIT.EDU nameserver = BITSY.MIT.EDU
STRAWB.MIT.EDU  internet address = 18.71.0.151
W20NS.MIT.EDU   internet address = 18.70.0.160
BITSY.MIT.EDU   internet address = 18.72.0.3
```

Find out what the response looks like when the server is authoritative for the zone:

```
> server strawb.mit.edu.
Default Server:  strawb.mit.edu
Address:  18.71.0.151

> mit.edu.
Server:  strawb.mit.edu
Address:  18.71.0.151

mit.edu
        origin = BITSY.MIT.EDU
        mail addr = NETWORK-REQUEST.BITSY.MIT.EDU
        serial = 378
        refresh = 3600 (1 hour)
        retry   = 300 (5 mins)
        expire  = 3600000 (41 days 16 hours)
        minimum ttl = 21600 (6 hours)
```

When the name server was not authoritative for the zone, it returned references to other name servers. If the name server had previously looked up the SOA record and cached it, the name server would have returned the SOA record and said it was "non-authoritative." We need to check for both cases. When the name server returns the SOA record and it is authoritative, we can grab the serial number from the line that contains *serial.*

Now, we need to see what *nslookup* returns when no name server is running on a host. We'll change servers to a host that does not normally run a name server and look up an SOA record:

```
% nslookup
Default Server:  relay.hp.com
Address:  15.255.152.2

> server galt.cs.purdue.edu.
Default Server:  galt.cs.purdue.edu
Address:  128.10.2.39

> set type=soa
> mit.edu.
Server:  galt.cs.purdue.edu
Address:  128.10.2.39

*** galt.cs.purdue.edu can't find mit.edu.: No response from server
```

Last, we need to see what *nslookup* returns if a host is not responding. We can test this by switching servers to an unused IP address on our LAN:

```
% nslookup
Default Server:  relay.hp.com
Address:  15.255.152.2

> server 15.255.152.100
Default Server:  [15.255.152.100]
Address:  15.255.152.100

> set type=soa
> mit.edu.
Server:  [15.255.152.100]
Address:  15.255.152.100

*** Request to [15.255.152.100] timed-out
```

In the last two error cases, the error message was written to *stderr*. We can make use of that fact when writing our shell script. Now we are ready to compose the shell script. We'll call it *check_soa*:

```
#!/bin/sh
if test "$1" = ""
then
    echo usage: $0 domain
    exit 1
fi
DOMAIN=$1
#
# Use nslookup to discover the nameservers for this domain ($1).
# Use awk to grab the name server names from the nameserver lines.
# (The names are always in the last field.)  Use sort -u to weed out
# duplicates; we don't actually care about collation.
#
```

```
SERVERS=`nslookup -type=ns $DOMAIN |\
                 awk '/nameserver/ {print $NF}' | sort -u`
if test "$SERVERS" = ""
then
    #
    # Didn't find any servers.  Just quit silently; nslookup will
    # have detected this error and printed a message.  That will
    # suffice.
    #
    exit 1
fi
#
# Check each server's SOA serial number.  The output from
# nslookup is saved in two tmp files: nso.$$ (standard output)
# and nse.$$ (standard error).  These files are rewritten on
# every iteration.  Turn off defname and search since we
# should be dealing with fully qualified names.
#
# NOTE: this loop is rather long; don't be fooled.
#
for i in $SERVERS
do
  nslookup >/tmp/nso.$$ 2>/tmp/nse.$$ <<-EOF
    server $i
    set nosearch
    set nodefname
    set norecurse
    set q=soa
    $DOMAIN
EOF
  #
  # Does this response indicate that the current server ($i) is
  # authoritative?  The server is NOT authoritative if (a) the
  # response says so, or (b) the response tells you to find
  # authoritative info elsewhere.
  #
  if egrep "Non-authoritative|Authoritative answers can be" \
                             /tmp/nso.$$ >/dev/null
  then
    echo $i is not authoritative for $DOMAIN
    continue
  fi
  #
  # We know the server is authoritative; extract the serial number.
  #
  SERIAL=`cat /tmp/nso.$$ | grep serial | sed -e "s/.*= //"`
  if test "$SERIAL" = ""
  then
    #
    # We get here if SERIAL is null.  In this case, there should
    # be an error message from nslookup; so cat the "standard
    # error" file.
    #
    cat /tmp/nse.$$
```

```
    else
      #
      # Report the server's name and its serial number.
      #
      echo $i has serial number $SERIAL
    fi
done  # end of the "for" loop
#
# Delete the temporary files.
#
rm -f /tmp/nso.$$ /tmp/nse.$$
```

Here is what the output looks like:

```
% check_soa mit.edu
BITSY.MIT.EDU has serial number 378
STRAWB.MIT.EDU has serial number 378
W20NS.MIT.EDU has serial number 378
```

If you are pressed for time, this short tool will solve your problem, and you can go on to other work. If you find that you are checking lots of zones and that this tool is too slow, you'll want to convert it to a C program. Also, if you want more control over the error messages—rather than relying on *nslookup* for error messages—then you'll have to write a C program. We'll do just that, later on in this chapter.

C Programming with the Resolver Library Routines

Before writing any code, though, you need to be familiar with the DNS packet format and the resolver library routines. In the shell script we just wrote, *nslookup* parsed the DNS packet. In a C program, you have to do the parsing. Let's start this section on programming by looking at the DNS packet format.

DNS Packet Format

You've seen the DNS packet format before, in Chapter 11, *nslookup*. It looks like this:

1. Header section

2. Question section

3. Answer section

4. Authority section

5. Additional section

The format of the header section is described in RFC 1035 on pages 26–28 and in Appendix A. It looks like this:

```
query identification number (2 octets)
query response (1 bit)
opcode (4 bits)
authoritative answer (1 bit)
truncation (1 bit)
recursion desired (1 bit)
recursion available (1 bit)
reserved (3 bits)
response code (4 bits)
question count (2 octets)
answer record count (2 octets)
name server record count (2 octets)
additional record count (2 octets)
```

You'll also find opcode, response code, type, and class values defined in *arpa/ nameser.h* as well as routines to extract this information from a response. We'll discuss these routines, the *name server library*, shortly.

The question section is described on pages 28–29 of RFC 1035. It looks like this:

```
domain name (variable length)
query type (2 octets)
query class (2 octets)
```

The answer, authority, and additional sections are described on pages 29–30 of RFC 1035. These sections comprise some number of resource records that look like this:

```
domain name (variable length)
type (2 octets)
class (2 octets)
TTL (4 octets)
resource data length (2 octets)
resource data (variable length)
```

The header section contains a count of how many of these resource records are in each section.

Domain Name Storage

As you can see, the names stored in the DNS packet are of variable length. Unlike C, DNS does not store the names as null-terminated strings. Domain names are stored as a series of length/value pairs ending with an octet of zero. Each label in a domain name is composed of a length octet and a label. A name like *venera.isi.edu* is stored as:

```
6 venera  3  isi  3 edu 0
```

You can imagine how much of a DNS packet could be devoted to storing names. The DNS authors recognized this, and came up with a simple way to compress domain names.

Domain Name Compression

Often an entire domain name or, at least, the trailing labels of a domain name match a name already stored in the response. Domain name compression eliminates the repetition of domain names by storing a pointer to the earlier occurrence of the name instead of inserting the name again. Here is how it works. Suppose a response packet already contains the name *venera.isi.edu*. If the name *vaxa.isi.edu* is added to the response, the label *vaxa* is stored, and then a pointer to the earlier occurrence of *isi.edu* is added. So how are pointers implemented?

The first two bits of the length octet indicate whether a length/label pair or a pointer to a length/label pair follows. If the first two bits are zero, then the length and label follow. As you may have read elsewhere, a label is limited to 63 characters. That's because the length field has only the remaining six bits for the length of the label—enough to represent the lengths 0–63. If the first two bits of the length octet are ones, then what follows is not a length, but a pointer. The pointer is the last six bits of the length octet *and* the next octet—14 bits total. The pointer is an offset from the start of the DNS packet. Now, when *vaxa.isi.edu* is compressed into a buffer containing only *venera.isi.edu*, this is what results:

```
byte offset: 0 123456 7 890 1 234 5 6 7890 1    2
             -------------+--------------+--------
pkt contents: 6 venera 3 isi 3 edu 0 4 vaxa 0xC0 7
```

The 0xC0 is a byte with the high two bits ones and the rest of the bits zeros. Since the high two bits are ones, this is a pointer instead of a length. The pointer value is seven—the last six bits of the first octet are zeros and the second octet is seven. At offset seven in this buffer, you find the rest of the *vaxa* domain name: *isi.edu*.

In this example, we only showed compressing two names in a buffer, not a whole DNS packet. A DNS packet would have had a header as well as other fields. This example is intended to give you only an idea of how the domain name compression works. Now the good news: you don't have to care how names are compressed, as long as the library routines do it properly. What you need to know is how parsing a DNS response can get messed up if you are off by one byte. For example, try to expand the name starting with byte two instead of byte one. You'll discover that "*v*" doesn't make a very good length octet or pointer.

The Resolver Library Routines

The resolver library contains the routines that you need to write your application. You'll use these routines to generate queries. You'll use the *name server library* routines, explained next, to parse the response.

Here are the header files you must include:

```
#include <sys/types.h>
#include <netinet/in.h>
#include <arpa/nameser.h>
#include <resolv.h>
```

These are the resolver library routines:

```
int res_search(const char *dname,
               int class,
               int type,
               u_char *answer,
               int anslen)
```

res_search is the "highest" level resolver routine. It is called by *gethostbyname*. *res_search* implements the search algorithm on the domain name passed to it. That is, it takes the domain name it receives (*dname*), "completes" the name (if it's not fully qualified) by adding the various "extensions" from the resolver search list, and calls *res_query* until it receives a successful response, indicating that it found a valid, fully qualified name. In addition to implementing the search algorithm, *res_search* looks in the file referenced by your HOSTALIASES environment variable. (The HOSTALIASES variable was described in Chapter 6, *Configuring Hosts.*) So it also takes care of any "private" host aliases you might have. *res_search* returns the size of the response, or it fills in *h_errno* and returns –1 if there was an error or the answer count is zero. (*h_errno* is like *errno*, but for DNS lookups.)

Therefore, the only parameter that's really of interest to *res_search* is *dname*; the others are just passed to *res_query* and the other resolver routines. The other arguments are:

class
> The "address type" of the data you're looking up. This is almost always the constant C_IN, which requests an "internet class" address. These constants are defined in *arpa/nameser.h*.

type
> The type of request that you're making. Again, this is a constant defined in *arpa/nameser.h*. A typical value would be T_NS, to retrieve a name server record; or T_MX, to retrieve an MX record.

answer
> A buffer in which *res_search* will place the response packet. Its size should be at least PACKETSZ (from *arpa/nameser.h*) bytes.

anslen
> The size of the *answer* buffer (e.g., PACKETSZ).

res_search returns the size of the response, or –1 if there was an error.

```
int res_query(const char *dname,
              int class,
```

```
            int type,
            u_char *answer,
            int anslen)
```

res_query is one of the "midlevel" resolver routines. It does all the real work in looking up the domain name; it makes a query packet by calling *res_mkquery*, sends the query by calling *res_send*, and looks at enough of the response to determine if your question was answered. In many cases, *res_query* is called by *res_search*, which just feeds it the different domain names to look up. As you'd expect, these two functions have the same arguments. *res_query* returns the size of the response, or it fills in *h_errno* and returns –1 if there was an error or the answer count was zero.

```
int res_mkquery(int op,
            const char *dname,
            int class,
            int type,
            const u_char *data,
            int datalen,
            const u_char *newrr,
            u_char *buf,
            int buflen)
```

res_mkquery creates the query packet. It fills in all the header fields, compresses the domain name into the question section, and fills in the other question fields.

The *dname*, *class*, and *type* arguments are the same as for *res_search* and *res_query*. The remaining arguments are:

op

The "operation" to be performed. This is normally QUERY, but it can be IQUERY (inverse query). However, as we've explained before, IQUERY is seldom used. BIND versions 4.9.4 and later, by default, do not even support IQUERY anymore.

data

A buffer containing the data for inverse queries. It is NULL when *op* is QUERY.

datalen

The size of the *data* buffer. If *data* is NULL, then *datalen* is zero.

newrr

A buffer used for the dynamic update code (covered in Chapter 10, *Advanced Features and Security*). Unless you are playing with this feature, it is always NULL.

buf

A buffer in which *res_mkquery* makes the query packet. It should be PACKETSZ or larger, just like the answer buffer in *res_search* and *res_query*.

buflen

The size of the *buf* buffer (e.g., PACKETSZ).

res_mkquery returns the size of the query packet, or −1 if there was an error.

```
int res_send(const u_char *msg,
             int msglen,
             u_char *answer,
             int anslen)
```

res_send implements the retry algorithm. It sends the query packet, *msg*, in a UDP packet, but it can also send it over a TCP stream. The response packet is stored in *answer*. This routine, of all the resolver routines, is the only one to use black magic (unless you know all about connected datagram sockets). You've seen these arguments before in the other resolver routines:

msg
>   The buffer containing the DNS query packet

msglen
>   The size of the *msg*

answer
>   The buffer in which to store the DNS response packet

anslen
>   The size of the *answer* buffer

res_send returns the size of the response, or −1 if there was an error. If this routine returns −1 and *errno* is ECONNREFUSED, then there is no name server running on the target name server host.

You can look at *errno* to see if it is ECONNREFUSED after calling *res_search* or *res_query*. (*res_search* calls *res_query*, which calls *res_send*.) If you want to check *errno* after calling *res_query*, then clear *errno* first. That way, you know the current call to *res_send* was the one that set *errno*. However, you don't have to clear *errno* before calling *res_search*. *res_search* clears *errno* itself before calling *res_query*.

```
int res_init(void)
```

res_init reads *resolv.conf* and initializes a data structure called *_res* (more about that later). All of the previously discussed routines will call *res_init* if they detect that it hasn't been called previously. Or you can call it on your own; this is useful if you want to change some of the defaults before calling the first resolver library routine. If there are any lines in *resolv.conf* that *res_init* doesn't understand, it ignores them. *res_init* always returns zero, even if the manpage reserves the right to return −1.

```
extern int h_errno;
int herror(const char *s)
```

herror is a routine like *perror*, except that it prints out a string based on the value of the external variable *h_errno* instead of *errno*. The only argument is:

s

A string used to identify the error message. If a string *s* is supplied, it is printed first, followed by ": " and then a string based on the value of *h_errno*.

Here are the possible values of *h_errno*:

HOST_NOT_FOUND

The domain name does not exist. The return code in the name server response was NXDOMAIN.

TRY_AGAIN

Either the name server is not running, or the name server returned SERVFAIL.

NO_RECOVERY

Either the domain name could not be compressed because it was an invalid domain name (e.g., a name missing a label—*movie.edu*) or the name server returned FORMERR, NOTIMP, or REFUSED.

NO_DATA

The domain name exists, but there are no data of the requested type.

NETDB_INTERNAL

There was a library error unrelated to the network or name service. Instead, see *errno* for the problem description.

The _res Structure

Each of the resolver routines (i.e., each routine whose name starts with *res_*) makes use of a common data structure called *_res*. You can change the behavior of the resolver routines by changing *_res*. If you want to change the number of times *res_send* retries a query, you can change the value of the *retry* field. If you want to turn off the resolver search algorithm, you turn off the RES_DNSRCH bit from the *options* mask. You'll find the all-important *_res* structure in *resolv.h*:

```
struct __res_state {
    int       retrans;    /* retransmission time interval */
    int       retry;      /* number of times to retransmit */
    u_long    options;    /* option flags - see below. */
    int       nscount;    /* number of name servers */
    struct sockaddr_in
              nsaddr_list[MAXNS];  /* address of name server */
#define nsaddr nsaddr_list[0]      /* for backward compatibility */
    u_short id;                    /* current packet id */
    char     *dnsrch[MAXDNSRCH+1]; /* components of domain to search */
    char     defdname[MAXDNAME];   /* default domain */
    u_long   pfcode;               /* RES_PRF_ flags - see below. */
    unsigned ndots:4;              /* threshold for initial abs. query */
    unsigned nsort:4;              /* number of elements in sort_list[] */
    char     unused[3];
    struct {
```

```
                struct in_addr   addr;    /* address to sort on */
                u_int32_t        mask;
        } sort_list[MAXRESOLVSORT];
};
```

The *options* field is a simple bit mask of the enabled options. To turn on a feature, turn on the corresponding bit in the options field. Bit masks for each of the options are defined in *resolv.h*; the options are:

RES_INIT

If this bit is on, then *res_init* has been called.

RES_DEBUG

This bit causes resolver debugging messages to be printed, if the resolver routines were compiled with DEBUG, that is. Off is the default.

RES_AAONLY

Requires the answer to be authoritative, not from a name server's cache. It's too bad this isn't implemented; it would be a useful feature. With the BIND resolver's design, this feature would have to be implemented in the name server, and it's not.

RES_PRIMARY

Query the primary server only—again, it's not implemented.

RES_USEVC

Turn this bit on if you'd like the resolver to make its queries over a virtual circuit (TCP) connection instead of with UDP packets. As you might guess, there is a performance penalty for setting up and tearing down a TCP connection. Off is the default.

RES_STAYOPEN

If you are making your queries over a TCP connection, turning this bit on causes the connection to be left open. Otherwise, the connection is torn down after the query has been answered. Off is the default.

RES_IGNTC

If the name server response has the truncation bit set, then the default resolver behavior is to retry the query using TCP. If this bit is turned on, then the truncation bit in the response packet is ignored and the query is not retried using TCP. Off is the default.

RES_RECURSE

The default behavior for the BIND resolver is to make recursive queries. Turning this bit off turns off the "recursion desired" bit in the query packet. On is the default.

RES_DEFNAMES

> The default behavior for the BIND resolver is to append the default domain to names that do not have a dot in them. Turning this bit off turns off appending the default domain. On is the default.

RES_DNSRCH

> The default behavior for the BIND resolver is to append each entry in the search list to a name that does not end in a dot. Turning this bit off turns off the search list function. On is the default.

RES_INSECURE1

> The default behavior for a 4.9.3 or later BIND resolver is to ignore answers from servers that were not queried. Turning this bit on disables this security check. Off (i.e., security check on) is the default.

RES_INSECURE2

> The default behavior for a 4.9.3 or later BIND resolver is to ignore answers where the question section of the response does not match the question section of the original query. Turning this bit on disables this security check. Off (i.e., security check on) is the default.

RES_NOALIASES

> The default behavior for the BIND resolver is to use aliases defined in the file specified by the user's HOSTALIASES environment variable. Turning this bit on disables the HOSTALIASES feature for 4.9.3 and later BIND resolvers. Previous resolvers did not allow this feature to be disabled. Off is the default.

The Name Server Library Routines

The name server library contains routines you need to parse response packets. Here are the header files you must include:

```
#include <sys/types.h>
#include <netinet/in.h>
#include <netdb.h>
#include <arpa/nameser.h>
#include <resolv.h>
```

Here are the name server library routines:

```
int ns_init_parse(const u_char *msg,
                  int msglen,
                  ns_msg *handle)
```

ns_init_parse is the first routine you must call before you use the other name server library routines. *ns_init_parse* fills in the data structure pointed to by *handle*, which is a parameter passed to other routines. The arguments are:

msg

A pointer to the beginning of the response buffer

msglen

The size of the response buffer

handle

A pointer to a data structure filled in by *ns_init_parse*

ns_init_parse returns zero on success and –1 when it fails to parse the response buffer.

```
const u_char *ns_msg_base(ns_msg handle)
const u_char *ns_msg_end(ns_msg handle)
int ns_msg_size(ns_msg handle)
```

These routines return a pointer to the start of the response, a pointer to the end of the response, and the size of the response. They are returning data you passed into *ns_init_parse*. The only argument is:

handle

A data structure filled in by *ns_init_parse*

```
u_int16_t ns_msg_id(ns_msg handle)
```

ns_msg_id returns the identification from the header section (described earlier) of the response packet. The only argument is:

handle

A data structure filled in by *ns_init_parse*.

```
u_int16_t ns_msg_get_flag(ns_msg handle, ns_flag flag)
```

ns_msg_get_flag returns the "flag" fields from the header section of the response packet. Its arguments are:

handle

A data structure filled in by *ns_init_parse*.

flag

An enumerated type that can have the following values:

```
ns_f_qr     /* Question/Response */
ns_f_opcode /* Operation Code */
ns_f_aa     /* Authoritative Answer */
ns_f_tc     /* Truncation Occurred */
ns_f_rd     /* Recursion Desired */
ns_f_ra     /* recursion Available */
ns_f_rcode  /* Response Code */
u_int16_t ns_msg_count(ns_msg handle, ns_sect section)
```

ns_msg_count returns a counter from the header section of the response packet. Its arguments are:

handle

A data structure filled in by *ns_init_parse.*

section

An enumerated type that can have the following values:

```
ns_s_qd  /* Question section */
ns_s_an  /* Answer section */
ns_s_ns  /* Name Server section */
ns_s_ar  /* Additional records sectiona */

int ns_parserr(ns_msg *handle,
               ns_sect section,
               int rrnum,
               ns_rr *rr)
```

ns_parserr extracts information about a response record and stores it in *rr*. *rr* is a parameter passed to other name server libarary routines. The arguments are:

handle

A pointer to a data structure filled in by *ns_init_parse.*

section

The same parameter described in *ns_msg_count.*

rrnum

A resource record number for the resource records in this section. Resource records start numbering at 0. *ns_msg_count* tells you how many resource records are in this section.

rr

A pointer to a data structure to be initialized.

ns_parserr returns zero on success and –1 when it fails to parse the response buffer.

```
char *ns_rr_name(ns_rr rr)
u_int16_t ns_rr_type(ns_rr rr)
u_int16_t ns_rr_class(ns_rr rr)
u_int32_t ns_rr_ttl(ns_rr rr)
u_int16_t ns_rr_rdlen(ns_rr rr)
const u_char *ns_rr_rdata(ns_rr rr)
```

These routines return individual fields from a response record. Their only argument is:

rr

A data structure filled in by *ns_parserr.*

```
int ns_name_compress(const char *exp_dn,
                     u_char *comp_dn,
                     size_t length,
                     const u_char **dnptrs,
                     const u_char **lastdnptr)
```

ns_name_compress compresses a domain name. You won't normally call this routine yourself—you'll let *res_mkquery* do it for you. However, if you need to compress a name for some reason, this is the tool to do it. The arguments are:

exp_dn

The "expanded" domain name that you supply; i.e., a normal null-terminated string containing a fully qualified domain name.

comp_dn

The place where *ns_name_compress* will store the compressed domain name.

length

The size of the *comp_dn* buffer.

dnptrs

An array of pointers to previously compressed domain names. *dnptrs[0]* points to the beginning of the message; the list ends with a NULL pointer. After you've initialized *dnptrs[0]* to the beginning of the message and *dnptrs[1]* to NULL, *dn_comp* updates the list each time you call it.

lastdnptr

A pointer to the end of the *dnptrs* array. *ns_name_compress* needs to know where the end of the array is, so it doesn't overrun it.

If you want to use this routine, look at how it is used in *res/res_mkquery.c* from the BIND source. It's often easier to see how to use a routine from an example than from an explanation. *ns_name_compress* returns the size of the compressed name, or –1 if there was an error.

```
int ns_name_uncompress(const u_char *msg,
                       const u_char *eomorig,
                       const u_char *comp_dn,
                       char *exp_dn,
                       size_t length)
```

ns_name_uncompress expands a "compressed" domain name. You will use this routine if you parse a name server response, as we do in the example that follows. The arguments are:

msg

A pointer to the beginning of your response packet (message).

eomorig

A pointer to the first byte after the message. It is used to make sure that *ns_name_uncompress* doesn't go past the end of the message.

comp_dn

A pointer to the compressed domain name within the message.

exp_dn

> The place where *ns_name_uncompress* will store the expanded name. You should always allocate an array of MAXDNAME characters for the expanded name.

length

> The size of the *exp_dn* buffer.

ns_name_uncompress returns the size of the compressed name, or –1 if there was an error. You might wonder why *ns_name_uncompress* returns the size of the *compressed* name, not the size of the *expanded* name. It does this because when you call *ns_name_uncompress*, you are parsing a DNS packet and need to know how much space the compressed name took in the packet so that you can skip over it.

```
int ns_name_skip(const u_char **ptrptr, const u_char *eom)
```

ns_name_skip is like *ns_name_uncompress*, but instead of uncompressing the name, it just skips over it. The arguments are:

ptrptr

> A pointer to a pointer to the name to skip over. The original pointer is advanced past the name.

eom

> A pointer to the first byte after the message. It is used to make sure that *ns_name_skip* doesn't go past the end of the message.

ns_name_skip returns zero if successful. It returns –1 when it fails to uncompress the name.

```
u_int ns_get16(const u_char *cp)
void  ns_put16(u_int s, u_char *cp)
```

The DNS packets have fields that are unsigned short integer (type, class, and data length, to name a few). *ns_get16* returns a 16-bit integer pointed to by *cp*. *ns_put16* assigns the 16-bit value of *s* to the location pointed to by *cp*.

```
u_long ns_get32(const u_char *cp)
void   ns_put32(u_long l, u_char *cp)
```

These routines are like their 16-bit counterparts, except that they deal with a 32-bit integer instead of a 16-bit integer. The TTL field (time to live) of a resource record is a 32-bit integer.

Parsing DNS Responses

The easiest way to learn how to parse a DNS packet is to look at code that already does it. Assuming that you have the DNS source code, the best file to look through is *res/res_debug.c* (BIND 4) or *src/lib/resolv/res_debug.c* (BIND 8). This file has *fp_query*, the routine that prints out the DNS packets in the name server debugging output. Our sample program traces its parentage to code from this file.

You won't always want to parse the DNS response manually. An "intermediate" way to parse the response is to call *p_query*, which calls *fp_query*, to print out the DNS packet. Then use basic UNIX tools, like *Perl* or *awk*, to grab what you need. Cricket has been known to wimp out this way.

A Sample Program: check_soa

Here is a C program to solve the same problem that we wrote a shell script for earlier:

```
/****************************************************************
 * check_soa -- Retrieve the SOA record from each name server   *
 *     for a given domain and print out the serial number.      *
 *                                                              *
 * usage: check_soa domain                                      *
 *                                                              *
 * The following errors are reported:                           *
 *     o There is no address for a server.                      *
 *     o There is no server running on this host.               *
 *     o There was no response from a server.                   *
 *     o The server is not authoritative for the domain.        *
 *     o The response had an error response code.               *
 *     o The response had more than one answer.                 *
 *     o The response answer did not contain an SOA record.     *
 *     o The expansion of a compressed domain name failed.      *
 ****************************************************************/

/* Various header files */
#include <sys/types.h>
#include <netinet/in.h>
#include <netdb.h>
#include <stdio.h>
#include <errno.h>
#include <arpa/nameser.h>
#include <resolv.h>

/* Error variables */
extern int h_errno;  /* for resolver errors */
extern int errno;    /* general system errors */

/* Our own routines; code included later in this chapter */
void nsError();            /* report resolver errors */
void findNameServers();    /* find a domain's name servers */
void addNameServers();     /* add name servers to our list */
void queryNameServers();   /* grab SOA records from servers */
void returnCodeError();    /* report response packet errors */

/* Maximum number of name servers we will check */
#define MAX_NS 20
```

Here are the header files that are needed, the declarations for external variables, and the declarations of functions. Notice that we use both *h_errno* (for the resolver routines) and *errno*. We've set a limit of 20 name servers that this program will check. You will rarely see a zone with more than ten name servers, so an upper limit of 20 should suffice:

```
main(argc, argv)
int argc;
char *argv[];
{
    char *nsList[MAX_NS];  /* list of name servers */
    int  nsNum = 0;        /* number of name servers in list */

    /* sanity check: one (and only one) argument? */
    if(argc != 2){
        (void) fprintf(stderr, "usage: %s domain\n", argv[0]);
        exit(1);
    }

    (void) res_init();

    /*
     * Find the name servers for the domain.
     * The name servers are written into nsList.
     */
    findNameServers(argv[1], nsList, &nsNum);

    /*
     * Query each name server for the domain's SOA record.
     * The name servers are read from nsList.
     */
    queryNameServers(argv[1], nsList, nsNum);

    exit(0);
}
```

The main body of the program is small. We have an array of string pointers, *nsList*, to store the names of the name servers for the zone. We call the resolver function *res_init* to initialize the *_res* structure. It wasn't necessary for this program to call *res_init* explicitly, since it would have been called by the first resolver routine that used the *_res* structure. However, if we had wanted to modify the value of any of the *_res* fields before calling the first resolver routine, we would have made the modifications right after calling *res_init*. Next, the program calls *findNameServers* to find all the name servers for the zone referenced in *argv[1]* and to store them in *nsList*. Last, the program calls *queryNameServers* to query each of the name servers in *nsList* for the SOA record for the zone.

The routine *findNameServers* follows. This routine queries the local name server for the NS records for the zone. It then calls *addNameServers* to parse the response packet and store away all the name servers it finds. The header files, *arpa/nameser.h* and *resolv.h*, contain declarations we make extensive use of:

```
/****************************************************************
 * findNameServers -- find all of the name servers for the     *
 *     given domain and store their names in nsList.  nsNum is  *
 *     the number of servers in the nsList array.               *
 ****************************************************************/
void
findNameServers(domain, nsList, nsNum)
char *domain;
char *nsList[];
int  *nsNum;
{
    union {
        HEADER hdr;               /* defined in resolv.h */
        u_char buf[NS_PACKETSZ]; /* defined in arpa/nameser.h */
    } response;                   /* response buffers */
    int responseLen;              /* buffer length */

    ns_msg handle;  /* handle for response packet */

    /*
     * Look up the NS records for the given domain name.
     * We expect the domain to be a fully qualified name, so
     * we use res_query().  If we wanted the resolver search
     * algorithm, we would have used res_search() instead.
     */
    if((responseLen =
            res_query(domain,        /* the domain we care about   */
                    ns_c_in,         /* Internet class records     */
                    ns_t_ns,         /* Look up name server records*/
                    (u_char *)&response,       /*response buffer*/
                    sizeof(response)))         /*buffer size    */
                            < 0){  /*If negative    */
        nsError(h_errno, domain); /* report the error           */
        exit(1);                  /* and quit                   */
    }

    /*
     * Initialize a handle to this response.  The handle will
     * be used later to extract information from the response.
     */
    if (ns_initparse(response.buf, responseLen, &handle) < 0) {
        fprintf(stderr, "ns_initparse: %s\n", strerror(errno));
        return;
    }

    /*
     * Create a list of name servers from the response.
     * NS records may be in the answer section and/or in the
     * authority section depending on the DNS implementation.
     * Walk through both.  The name server addresses may be in
```

```
     * the additional records section, but we will ignore them
     * since it is much easier to call gethostbyname() later
     * than to parse and store the addresses here.
     */

    /*
     * Add the name servers from the answer section.
     */
    addNameServers(nsList, nsNum, handle, ns_s_an);

    /*
     * Add the name servers from the authority section.
     */
    addNameServers(nsList, nsNum, handle, ns_s_ns);
}

/****************************************************************
 * addNameServers -- Look at the resource records from a       *
 *      section.  Save the names of all name servers.          *
 ****************************************************************/

void
addNameServers(nsList, nsNum, handle, section)
char *nsList[];
int  *nsNum;
ns_msg handle;
ns_sect section;
{
    int rrnum;  /* resource record number */
    ns_rr rr;   /* expanded resource record */

    int i, dup; /* misc variables */

    /*
     * Look at all the resource records in this section.
     */
    for(rrnum = 0; rrnum < ns_msg_count(handle, section); rrnum++)
    {
        /*
         * Expand the resource record number rrnum into rr.
         */
        if (ns_parserr(&handle, section, rrnum, &rr)) {
            fprintf(stderr, "ns_parserr: %s\n", strerror(errno));
        }

        /*
         * If the record type is NS, save the name of the
         * name server.
         */
        if (ns_rr_type(rr) == ns_t_ns) {

            /*
             * Allocate storage for the name.  Like any good
             * programmer should, we test malloc's return value,
```

```
             * and quit if it fails.
             */
            nsList[*nsNum] = (char *) malloc (MAXDNAME);
            if(nsList[*nsNum] == NULL){
                (void) fprintf(stderr, "malloc failed\n");
                exit(1);
            }

            /* Expand the name server's name */
            if (ns_name_uncompress(
                        ns_msg_base(handle),/* Start of the packet   */
                        ns_msg_end(handle), /* End of the packet      */
                        ns_rr_rdata(rr),    /* Position in the packet*/
                        nsList[*nsNum],     /* Result                */
                        MAXDNAME)           /* Size of nsList buffer */
                                < 0) {      /* Negative: error       */
                (void) fprintf(stderr, "ns_name_uncompress failed\n");
                exit(1);
            }

            /*
             * Check the name we've just unpacked and add it to
             * the list of servers if it is not a duplicate.
             * If it is a duplicate, just ignore it.
             */
            for(i = 0, dup=0; (i < *nsNum) && !dup; i++)
                dup = !strcasecmp(nsList[i], nsList[*nsNum]);
            if(dup)
                free(nsList[*nsNum]);
            else
                (*nsNum)++;
        }
    }
}
```

Notice that we don't explicitly check for finding zero name server records. We don't need to check because *res_query* flags that case as an error; it returns −1 and sets *herrno* to *NO_DATA*. If *res_query* returns −1, we call our own routine, *nsError*, to print out an error string from *h_errno* instead of using *herror*. The *herror* routine isn't a good fit for our program because its messages assume you are looking up address data (e.g., if *h_errno* is *NO_DATA*, the error message is "No address associated with name").

The next routine queries each name server that we've found for an SOA record. In this routine, we change the value of several of the *_res* structure fields. By changing the *nsaddr_list* field, we change which server *res_send* queries. We disable the search list by turning off bits in the *options* field—all the names that this program handles are fully qualified:

```
/****************************************************************
 * queryNameServers -- Query each of the name servers in nsList *
 *      for the SOA record of the given domain.  Report any     *
 *      errors encountered.  (e.g., a name server not running or *
 *      the response not being an authoritative response.)  If  *
 *      there are no errors, print out the serial number for the *
 *      domain.                                                 *
 ****************************************************************/
void
queryNameServers(domain, nsList, nsNum)
char *domain;
char *nsList[];
int nsNum;
{
    union {
        HEADER hdr;                 /* defined in resolv.h */
        u_char buf[NS_PACKETSZ];    /* defined in arpa/nameser.h */
    } query, response;              /* query and response buffers */
    int responseLen, queryLen;      /* buffer lengths */

    u_char      *cp;        /* character pointer to parse DNS packet */

    struct in_addr saveNsAddr[MAXNS];   /* addrs saved from _res */
    int nsCount;                /* count of addresses saved from _res */
    struct hostent *host;   /* structure for looking up ns addr */
    int i;                  /* counter variable */

    ns_msg handle;  /* handle for response packet */
    ns_rr rr;       /* expanded resource record */

    /*
     * Save the _res name server list since
     * we will need to restore it later.
     */
    nsCount = _res.nscount;
    for(i = 0; i < nsCount; i++)
      saveNsAddr[i] = _res.nsaddr_list[i].sin_addr;

    /*
     * Turn off the search algorithm and turn off appending
     * the default domain before we call gethostbyname(); the
     * name server names will be fully qualified.
     */
    _res.options &= ~(RES_DNSRCH | RES_DEFNAMES);

    /*
     * Query each name server for an SOA record.
     */
    for(nsNum-- ; nsNum >= 0; nsNum--){

        /*
         * First, we have to get the IP address of every server.
         * So far, all we have are names.  We use gethostbyname
         * to get the addresses, rather than anything fancy.
```

```
 * But first, we have to restore certain values in _res
 * because _res affects gethostbyname().  (We altered
 * _res in the previous iteration through the loop.)
 *
 * We can't just call res_init() again to restore
 * these values since some of the _res fields are
 * initialized when the variable is declared, not when
 * res_init() is called.
 */
_res.options |= RES_RECURSE;   /* recursion on (default) */
_res.retry = 4;                /* 4 retries (default)    */
_res.nscount = nsCount;        /* original name servers  */
for(i = 0; i < nsCount; i++)
    _res.nsaddr_list[i].sin_addr = saveNsAddr[i];

/* Look up the name server's address */
host = gethostbyname(nsList[nsNum]);
if (host == NULL) {
    (void) fprintf(stderr,"There is no address for %s\n",
                                    nsList[nsNum]);
    continue; /* nsNum for-loop */
}

/*
 * Now get ready for the real fun.  host contains IP
 * addresses for the name server we're testing.
 * Store the first address for host in the _res
 * structure.  Soon, we'll look up the SOA record...
 */
(void) memcpy((void *)&_res.nsaddr_list[0].sin_addr,
    (void *)host->h_addr_list[0], (size_t)host->h_length);
_res.nscount = 1;

/*
 * Turn off recursion.  We don't want the name server
 * querying another server for the SOA record; this name
 * server ought to be authoritative for this data.
 */
_res.options &= ~RES_RECURSE;

/*
 * Reduce the number of retries.  We may be checking
 * several name servers, so we don't want to wait too
 * long for any one server.  With two retries and only
 * one address to query, we'll wait at most 15 seconds.
 */
_res.retry = 2;

/*
 * We want to see the response code in the next
 * response, so we must make the query packet and
 * send it ourselves instead of having res_query()
 * do it for us.  If res_query() returned -1, there
 * might not be a response to look at.
```

```
 *
 * There is no need to check for res_mkquery()
 * returning -1.  If the compression was going to
 * fail, it would have failed when we called
 * res_query() earlier with this domain name.
 */
queryLen = res_mkquery(
            ns_o_query,     /* regular query       */
            domain,         /* the domain to look up */
            ns_c_in,        /* Internet type       */
            ns_t_soa,       /* Look up an SOA record */
            (u_char *)NULL, /* always NULL       */
            0,              /* length of NULL      */
            (u_char *)NULL, /* always NULL       */
            (u_char *)&query,/* buffer for the query  */
            sizeof(query)); /* size of the buffer    */


/*
 * Send the query packet.  If there is no name server
 * running on the target host, res_send() returns -1
 * and errno is ECONNREFUSED.  First, clear out errno.
 */
errno = 0;
if((responseLen = res_send((u_char *)&query,/* the query  */
                      queryLen,          /* true length*/
                      (u_char *)&response,/*buffer   */
                      sizeof(response)))  /*buf size*/
                          < 0){           /* error  */
    if(errno == ECONNREFUSED) { /* no server on the host */
        (void) fprintf(stderr,
            "There is no name server running on %s\n",
            nsList[nsNum]);
    } else {                    /* anything else: no response */
        (void) fprintf(stderr,
            "There was no response from %s\n",
            nsList[nsNum]);
    }
    continue; /* nsNum for-loop */
}


/*
 * Initialize a handle to this response.  The handle will
 * be used later to extract information from the response.
 */
if (ns_initparse(response.buf, responseLen, &handle) < 0) {
    fprintf(stderr, "ns_initparse: %s\n", strerror(errno));
    return;
}


/*
 * If the response reports an error, issue a message
 * and proceed to the next server in the list.
 */
if(ns_msg_getflag(handle, ns_f_rcode) != ns_r_noerror){
```

```
                    returnCodeError(ns_msg_getflag(handle, ns_f_rcode),
                                                    nsList[nsNum]);
            continue; /* nsNum for-loop */
        }

        /*
         * Did we receive an authoritative response?  Check the
         * authoritative answer bit.  If the server isn't
         * authoritative, report it, and go on to the next server.
         */
        if(!ns_msg_getflag(handle, ns_f_aa)){
            (void) fprintf(stderr,
                "%s is not authoritative for %s\n",
                nsList[nsNum], domain);
            continue; /* nsNum for-loop */
        }

        /*
         * The response should only contain one answer; if more,
         * report the error, and proceed to the next server.
         */
        if(ns_msg_count(handle, ns_s_an) != 1){
            (void) fprintf(stderr,
                "%s: expected 1 answer, got %d\n",
                nsList[nsNum], ns_msg_count(handle, ns_s_an));
            continue; /* nsNum for-loop */
        }

        /*
         * Expand the answer section record number 0 into rr.
         */
        if (ns_parserr(&handle, ns_s_an, 0, &rr)) {
                if (errno != ENODEV){
                        fprintf(stderr, "ns_parserr: %s\n",
                                strerror(errno));
                }
        }

        /*
         * We asked for an SOA record; if we got something else,
         * report the error and proceed to the next server.
         */
        if (ns_rr_type(rr) != ns_t_soa) {
            (void) fprintf(stderr,
                "%s: expected answer type %d, got %d\n",
                nsList[nsNum], ns_t_soa, ns_rr_type(rr));
            continue; /* nsNum for-loop */
        }

        /*
         * Set cp to point the the SOA record.
         */
        cp = (u_char *)ns_rr_rdata(rr);
```

```
                    /*
                     * Skip the SOA origin and mail address, which we don't
                     * care about.  Both are standard "compressed names."
                     */
                    ns_name_skip(&cp, ns_msg_end(handle));
                    ns_name_skip(&cp, ns_msg_end(handle));

                    /* cp now points to the serial number; print it. */
                    (void) printf("%s has serial number %d\n",
                        nsList[nsNum], ns_get32(cp));

            } /* end of nsNum for-loop */
    }
```

Notice that we use recursive queries when we call *gethostbyname*, but use
nonrecursive queries when we look up the SOA record. *gethostbyname* may need
to query other servers to find the host's address. But we don't want the name server
querying another server when we ask it for the SOA record—it's *supposed* to be
authoritative for this zone, after all. Allowing the name server to ask another server
for the SOA record would defeat the error check.

The next two routines print out error messages:

```
/*****************************************************************
 * nsError -- Print an error message from h_errno for a failure *
 *      looking up NS records.  res_query() converts the DNS    *
 *      packet return code to a smaller list of errors and      *
 *      places the error value in h_errno.  There is a routine  *
 *      called herror() for printing out strings from h_errno   *
 *      like perror() does for errno.  Unfortunately, the       *
 *      herror() messages assume you are looking up address     *
 *      records for hosts.  In this program, we are looking up  *
 *      NS records for domains, so we need our own list of error *
 *      strings.                                                *
 *****************************************************************/
void
nsError(error, domain)
int error;
char *domain;
{
    switch(error){
        case HOST_NOT_FOUND:
            (void) fprintf(stderr, "Unknown domain: %s\n", domain);
            break;
        case NO_DATA:
            (void) fprintf(stderr, "No NS records for %s\n", domain);
            break;
        case TRY_AGAIN:
            (void) fprintf(stderr, "No response for NS query\n");
            break;
        default:
            (void) fprintf(stderr, "Unexpected error\n");
            break;
```

```
        }
    }

    /*****************************************************************
     * returnCodeError -- print out an error message from a DNS      *
     *      response return code.                                    *
     *****************************************************************/
    void
    returnCodeError(rcode, nameserver)
    ns_rcode rcode;
    char *nameserver;
    {
        (void) fprintf(stderr, "%s: ", nameserver);
        switch(rcode){
            case ns_r_formerr:
                (void) fprintf(stderr, "FORMERR response\n");
                break;
            case ns_r_servfail:
                (void) fprintf(stderr, "SERVFAIL response\n");
                break;
            case ns_r_nxdomain:
                (void) fprintf(stderr, "NXDOMAIN response\n");
                break;
            case ns_r_notimpl:
                (void) fprintf(stderr, "NOTIMP response\n");
                break;
            case ns_r_refused:
                (void) fprintf(stderr, "REFUSED response\n");
                break;
            default:
                (void) fprintf(stderr, "unexpected return code\n");
                break;
        }
    }
```

To compile this program using the resolver and name server routines in *libc*:

```
% cc -o check_soa check_soa.c
```

Or, if you've newly ported the BIND code as we describe in Appendix B, *Compiling and Installing* BIND *on a Sun,* and want to use the latest header files and resolver library:

```
% cc -o check_soa \    -I/tmp/src/include \    -I/tmp/src/include/port/solaris/
include \    check_soa.c \    /tmp/src/lib/libbind.a
```

Here is what the output looks like:

```
% check_soa mit.edu
BITSY.MIT.EDU has serial number 378
W20NS.MIT.EDU has serial number 378
STRAWB.MIT.EDU has serial number 378
```

If you look back at the shell script output, it looks the same, except that the shell script's output is sorted by the name server's name. What you can't see is that the C program ran much faster.

Perl Programming with Net::DNS

If using the shell to parse *nslookup*'s output seems too awkward and writing a C program seems too complicated, consider writing your program in Perl using the Net::DNS module written by Michael Fuhr. You'll find the package at *http://www.perl.com/CPAN-local/modules/by-module/Net/*.

Net::DNS treats resolvers, DNS packets, sections of DNS packets, and individual resource records as objects and provides methods for setting or querying each object's attributes. We'll examine each object type first, then give a Perl version of our *check_soa* program.

Resolver Objects

Before making any queries, you must first create a resolver object:

```
$res = new Net::DNS::Resolver;
```

Resolver objects are initialized from your *resolv.conf* file, but you can change the default settings by making calls to the object's methods. Many of the methods described in the Net::DNS::Resolver manual page correspond to fields and options of the *_res* structure described earlier in the C programming section. For example, if you want to set the number of times the resolver tries each query before timing out, you can call the *$res->retry* method:

```
$res->retry(2);
```

To make a query, call one of the following methods:

```
$res->search
$res->query
$res->send
```

These methods behave like the *res_search*, *res_query*, and *res_send* library functions described in the C programming section, though they take fewer arguments. You must provide a name, and you can optionally provide a DNS record type and class (the default behavior is to query for A records in the IN class). These methods return Net::DNS::Packet objects, which we'll describe shortly. Here are a few examples:

```
$packet = $res->search("terminator");
$packet = $res->query("movie.edu", "MX");
$packet = $res->send("version.bind", "TXT", "CH");
```

Packet Objects

Resolver queries return Net::DNS::Packet objects, whose methods you can use to access the header, question, answer, authority, and additional sections of a DNS packet:

```
$header     = $packet->header;
@question   = $packet->question;
@answer     = $packet->answer;
@authority  = $packet->authority;
@additional = $packet->additional;
```

Header Objects

DNS packet headers are returned as Net::DNS::Header objects. The methods described in the Net::DNS::Header manual page correspond to the header fields described in RFC 1035 and in the *HEADER* structure used in C programs. For example, if you want to find out if this is an authoritative answer, you would call the *$header->aa* method:

```
if ($header->aa) {
    print "answer is authoritative\n";
} else {
    print "answer is not authoritative\n";
}
```

Question Objects

The question section of a DNS packet is returned as a list of Net::DNS::Question objects. You can find the name, type, and class of a question object with the following methods:

```
$question->qname
$question->qtype
$question->qclass
```

Resource Record Objects

The answer, authority, and additional sections of a DNS packet are returned as lists of Net::DNS::RR objects. You can find the name, type, class, and TTL of an RR object with the following methods:

```
$rr->name
$rr->type
$rr->class
$rr->ttl
```

Each record type is a subclass of Net::DNS::RR and has its own type-specific methods. Here's an example that shows how to get the preference and mail exchange out of an MX record:

```
$preference = $rr->preference;
$exchange   = $rr->exchange;
```

A Perl Version of check_soa

Now that we've described the objects Net::DNS uses, let's look at how to use them in a complete program. We've rewritten *check_soa* in Perl:

```perl
#!/usr/local/bin/perl -w

use Net::DNS;

#----------------------------------------------------------------------
# Get the domain from the command line.
#----------------------------------------------------------------------

die "Usage:  check_soa domain\n" unless @ARGV == 1;
$domain = $ARGV[0];

#----------------------------------------------------------------------
# Find all the nameservers for the domain.
#----------------------------------------------------------------------

$res = new Net::DNS::Resolver;

$res->defnames(0);
$res->retry(2);

$ns_req = $res->query($domain, "NS");
die "No nameservers found for $domain: ", $res->errorstring, "\n"
    unless defined($ns_req) and ($ns_req->header->ancount > 0);

@nameservers = grep { $_->type eq "NS" } $ns_req->answer;

#----------------------------------------------------------------------
# Check the SOA record on each nameserver.
#----------------------------------------------------------------------

$| = 1;
$res->recurse(0);

foreach $nsrr (@nameservers) {

    #--------------------------------------------------------------
    # Set the resolver to query this nameserver.
    #--------------------------------------------------------------

    $ns = $nsrr->nsdname;
    print "$ns ";
```

```perl
    unless ($res->nameservers($ns)) {
        warn ": can't find address: ", $res->errorstring, "\n";
        next;
    }

    #--------------------------------------------------------------------
    # Get the SOA record.
    #--------------------------------------------------------------------

    $soa_req = $res->send($domain, "SOA");
    unless (defined($soa_req)) {
        warn ": ", $res->errorstring, "\n";
        next;
    }

    #--------------------------------------------------------------------
    # Is this nameserver authoritative for the domain?
    #--------------------------------------------------------------------

    unless ($soa_req->header->aa) {
        warn "is not authoritative for $domain\n";
        next;
    }

    #--------------------------------------------------------------------
    # We should have received exactly one answer.
    #--------------------------------------------------------------------

    unless ($soa_req->header->ancount == 1) {
        warn ": expected 1 answer, got ",
                $soa_req->header->ancount, "\n";
        next;
    }

    #--------------------------------------------------------------------
    # Did we receive an SOA record?
    #--------------------------------------------------------------------

     unless (($soa_req->answer)[0]->type eq "SOA") {
        warn ": expected SOA, got ",
                ($soa_req->answer)[0]->type, "\n";
        next;
    }

    #--------------------------------------------------------------------
    # Print the serial number.
    #--------------------------------------------------------------------

    print "has serial number ", ($soa_req->answer)[0]->serial, "\n";
}
```

Now that you've seen how to write a DNS program using a shell script, a Perl script, and C code, you should be able to write one on your own using the language that best fits your situation.

15

Miscellaneous

> *"The time has come," the Walrus said, "To talk of many things: Of shoes—and ships—and sealing-wax—Of cabbages—and kings—And why the sea is boiling hot—And whether pigs have wings."*

It's time we tied up loose ends. We've already covered the mainstream of DNS and BIND, but there's a handful of interesting niches we haven't explored. Some of these may actually be useful to you, like instructions on how to set up DNS on a network without Internet connectivity; others may just be interesting. We can't in good conscience send you out into the world without completing your education!

Using CNAME Records

We talked about CNAME resource records in Chapter 4, *Setting Up BIND*. We didn't tell you all about CNAME records, though; we saved that for this chapter. When you set up your first name servers, you didn't care about the subtle nuances of the magical CNAME record. Maybe you didn't realize there was more than we explained; maybe you didn't care. Some of this trivia is interesting, some is arcane. We'll let you decide which is which.

CNAMEs Attached to Interior Nodes

If you've ever renamed your zone because of a company re-org, you may have considered creating a single CNAME record that pointed from the zone's old domain name to the new domain name. For instance, if the *fx.movie.edu* zone were renamed to *magic.movie.edu*, we'd be tempted to create a single CNAME record to map all the old names to the new names:

```
fx.movie.edu.  IN  CNAME  magic.movie.edu.
```

With this in place, you'd expect a lookup of *empire.fx.movie.edu* to result in a lookup of *empire.magic.movie.edu*. Unfortunately, this doesn't work—you *can't* have a CNAME record attached to an interior node like *fx.movie.edu* if it owns other records. Remember that *fx.movie.edu* has an SOA record and NS records, so attaching a CNAME record to it violates the rule that a domain name be either an alias or a canonical name, not both. So, instead of a single CNAME record to rename a complete zone, you'll have to do it the old-fashioned way—a CNAME record for each individual host within the zone:

```
empire.fx.movie.edu.        IN  CNAME  empire.magic.movie.edu.
bladerunner.fx.movie.edu.   IN  CNAME  bladerunner.magic.movie.edu.
```

If the subdomain isn't delegated, and consequently doesn't have an SOA record and NS records attached, you can create an alias for *fx.movie.edu*, but it will apply only to the domain name *fx.movie.edu*, and not to domain names in *fx.movie.edu*.

Hopefully, the tool you use to manage your DNS database files will handle creating CNAME records for you. (*h2n*, which was introduced in Chapter 4, does.)

CNAMEs Pointing to CNAMEs

You may have wondered whether it was possible to have an alias (CNAME record) pointing to another alias. This might be useful in situations where an alias points from a domain name outside of your zone to a domain name inside your zone. You may not have any control over the alias outside of your zone. What if you want to change the domain name it points to? Can you simply add another CNAME record?

The answer is yes: you can chain together CNAME records. The BIND implementation supports it, and the RFCs don't expressly forbid it. But, while you *can* chain CNAME records, is it a wise thing to do? The RFCs recommend against it, because of the possibility of creating a CNAME loop, and because it slows resolution. You may be able to do it in a pinch, but you probably won't find much sympathy on the Net if something breaks. And all bets are off if a new (non-BIND-based) name server implementation emerges.[*]

CNAMEs in the Resource Record Data

For any other record besides a CNAME record, you must have the canonical name in the resource record data. Applications and name servers won't operate correctly otherwise. As we mentioned back in Chapter 5, *DNS and Electronic Mail*, for example, *sendmail* only recognizes the canonical name of the local host on the right side of an MX record. If *sendmail* doesn't recognize the local host name, it won't

---

[*] And one has (the Micrsoft DNS Server, shipped with Windows NT). It permits CNAMEs that point to CNAMEs, too, though.

strip the right MX records out when paring down the MX list, and may deliver mail to itself or less-preferred hosts, causing mail to loop.

Multiple CNAME Records

One pathological configuration that honestly hadn't occurred to us—and many pathological configurations *have* occurred to us—before we saw an option to allow it is multiple CNAME records attached to the same name. Some administrators use this with round robin to rotate between RRsets. For example, the records:

```
fullmonty   IN  CNAME  fullmonty1
fullmonty   IN  CNAME  fullmonty2
fullmonty   IN  CNAME  fullmonty3
```

could be used to return all of the addresses attached to *fullmonty1*, then all the addresses of *fullmonty2*, then all the addresses of *fullmonty3*, on a name server that didn't recognize this as the abomination it is. (It violates the "CNAME and other data" rule, for one.)

BIND 4, for one, doesn't recognize this as a misconfiguration. BIND 8 does, but will let you permit it if you want to with:

```
options {
                multiple-cnames yes;
};
```

The default, naturally, is to disallow it.

Looking Up CNAMEs

At times you may want to look up a CNAME record itself, not data for the canonical name. With *nslookup*, this is easy to do. You can either set the query type to *cname*, or you can set query type to *any* and then look up the name:

```
% nslookup
Default Server:  wormhole
Address:  0.0.0.0

> set query=cname
> bigt
Server:  wormhole
Address:  0.0.0.0

bigt.movie.edu  canonical name = terminator.movie.edu
> set query=any
> bigt
Server:  wormhole
Address:  0.0.0.0

bigt.movie.edu  canonical name = terminator.movie.edu
```

Finding Out a Host's Aliases

One thing you can't easily do with DNS is find out a host's aliases. With the host table, it's easy to find both the canonical name of a host and any aliases: no matter which you look up; they're all there, together, on the same line:

```
% grep terminator /etc/hosts
192.249.249.3  terminator.movie.edu terminator bigt
```

With DNS, however, if you look up the canonical name, all you get is the canonical name. There's no easy way for the name server or the application to know whether aliases exist for that canonical name:

```
% nslookup
Default Server:  wormhole
Address:  0.0.0.0

> terminator
Server:  wormhole
Address:  0.0.0.0

Name:    terminator.movie.edu
Address:  192.249.249.3
```

If you use *nslookup* to look up an alias, you'll see that alias and the canonical name. *nslookup* reports both the alias and the canonical name in the packet. But you won't see any other aliases that might point to that canonical name:

```
% nslookup
Default Server:  wormhole
Address:  0.0.0.0

> bigt
Server:  wormhole
Address:  0.0.0.0

Name:    terminator.movie.edu
Address:  192.249.249.3
Aliases:  bigt.movie.edu
```

About the only way to find out all the CNAMEs for a host is to transfer the whole zone and pick out the CNAME records where that host is the canonical name:

```
% nslookup
Default Server:  wormhole
Address:  0.0.0.0

> ls -t cname movie.edu
 [wormhole.movie.edu]
         1D IN SOA     terminator.movie.edu. al.robocop.movie.edu. (
                 25                  ; serial
                 3H                  ; refresh
                 1H                  ; retry
```

```
                1W                      ; expire
                1D )                    ; minimum

            1D IN NS      terminator.movie.edu.
            1D IN NS      wormhole.movie.edu.
            1D IN NS      zardoz.movie.edu.
            1D IN A      1.1.1.1
localhost.movie.edu.        1D IN A       127.0.0.1
awakenings.movie.edu.       1W IN A       192.253.253.254
classics.movie.edu.         1D IN NS      gwtw.classics.movie.edu.
gwtw.classics.movie.edu.    1D IN A  1.1.1.1
dh.movie.edu.               1D IN CNAME   diehard.movie.edu.
wormhole.movie.edu.         1D IN A       192.249.249.1
            1D IN A          192.253.253.1
web.movie.edu.              1D IN CNAME    www.movie.edu.
misery.movie.edu.           1D IN A       192.253.253.2
robocop.movie.edu.          1D IN A       192.249.249.2
carrie.movie.edu.           1D IN A       192.253.253.4
diehard.movie.edu.          1D IN A       192.249.249.4
fx.movie.edu.               1D IN NS      bladerunner.fx.movie.edu.
bladerunner.fx.movie.edu.  1D IN A  192.253.254.2
fx.movie.edu.               1D IN NS      outland.fx.movie.edu.
outland.fx.movie.edu.       1D IN A       192.253.254.3
rainman.movie.edu.          1W IN A       192.249.249.254
wh.movie.edu.               1D IN CNAME    wormhole.movie.edu.
wh249.movie.edu.            1D IN A       192.249.249.1
wh253.movie.edu.            1D IN A       192.253.253.1
bigt.movie.edu.             1D IN CNAME    terminator.movie.edu.
www.movie.edu.              1D IN CNAME    movie.edu.
zardoz.movie.edu.           1D IN A       192.249.249.9
            1D IN A          192.253.253.9
terminator.movie.edu.       1D IN A       192.249.249.3
            1H IN MX         10 terminator.movie.edu.
ftp.movie.edu.              1D IN A       192.249.249.1
            1D IN A             198.105.232.1
shining.movie.edu.          1D IN A       192.253.253.3
pma.movie.edu.              30S IN A      1.2.3.4
postmanrings2x.movie.edu.  1D IN A  1.1.1.1
            1D IN MX             10 postmanrings2x.movie.edu.
movie.edu.  1D IN SOA            terminator.movie.edu. al.robocop.movie.edu. (
                25             ; serial
                3H             ; refresh
                1H             ; retry
                1W             ; expire
                1D )                    ; minimum
```

Even this method will only show you the aliases within that zone—there could be aliases in a different zone, pointing to canonical names in this zone.

Wildcards

Something else we haven't covered yet is DNS *wildcards*. There are times when you want a single resource record to cover any possible name, rather than creating zillions of resource records that are all the same except for the domain name to which they apply. DNS reserves a special character, the asterisk ("*"), to be used in a DNS database file as a wildcard name. It will match any number of labels in a name, as long as there isn't an exact match with a name already in the DNS database.

Most often, you'd use wildcards to forward mail to non-Internet-connected networks. Suppose your site is not connected to the Internet, but you have a host that will relay mail between the Internet and your network. You could add a wildcard MX record to the *movie.edu* zone for Internet consumption that points all your mail to the relay. Here is an example:

```
*.movie.edu.  IN  MX  10 movie-relay.nea.gov.
```

Since the wildcard matches one or more labels, this resource record would apply to names like *terminator.movie.edu*, *empire.fx.movie.edu*, or *casablanca.bogart. classics.movie.edu*. The danger with wildcards is that they clash with search lists. This wildcard also matches *cujo.movie.edu.movie.edu*, making wildcards dangerous to use in your internal zone data. Remember that some versions of *sendmail* apply the search list when looking up MX records:

```
% nslookup
Default Server:  wormhole
Address:  0.0.0.0

> set type=mx                                —Look up MX records
> cujo.movie.edu                             —for cujo
Server:  wormhole
Address:  0.0.0.0

cujo.movie.edu.movie.edu     —This isn't a real host's name!
        preference = 10, mail exchanger = movie-relay.nea.gov
```

What are the limitations of wildcards? Wildcards do not match names for which there is already data. Suppose you *did* use wildcards within your zone data, as in these partial contents of *db.movie:*

```
*      IN  MX  10 mail-hub.movie.edu.
et     IN  MX  10 et.movie.edu.
jaws   IN  A   192.253.253.113
fx     IN  NS  bladerunner.fx.movie.edu.
fx     IN  NS  outland.fx.movie.edu.
```

Mail to *terminator.movie.edu* will be sent to *mail-hub*, but mail to *et.movie.edu* will be sent directly to *et*. An MX lookup of *jaws.movie.edu* would result in a response that said there was no MX data for that name. The wildcard doesn't apply because an A record exists. The wildcard also doesn't apply to domain names in *fx.movie.edu*, because they don't apply across delegation.

Can you use wildcards safely within your zone data? Yes. We'll cover that case a little later in this chapter.

A Limitation of MX Records

While we are on the topic of MX records, let's talk about how they can result in mail taking a longer path than necessary. The MX records are a list of data returned when a name is looked up. The list is not ordered according to which exchanger is closest to the sender. Here is an example of this problem. Your non-Internet-connected network has two hosts capable of relaying Internet mail to your network. One host is in the U.S., and one host is in France. Your network is in Greece. Most of your mail comes from the U.S., so you have someone maintain your zone and install two wildcard MX records—the highest preference to the U.S. relay, and a lower preference to the France relay. Since the U.S. relay is at a higher preference, *all* mail will go through that relay (as long as it is reachable). If someone in France sends you a letter, it will travel across the Atlantic to the U.S. and back, because there is nothing in the MX list to indicate that the French relay is closer to that sender.

DNS and Internet Firewalls

The Domain Name System wasn't designed to work with Internet firewalls. It's a testimony to the flexibility of DNS and of the BIND implementation that you can configure DNS to work with, or even through, an Internet firewall.

That said, configuring BIND to work in a firewalled environment, although not difficult, takes a good, complete understanding of DNS and a few of BIND's more obscure features. Describing it also requires a large portion of this chapter, so here's a roadmap.

We start by describing the two major families of Internet firewall software—packet filters and application gateways. The capabilities of each family have a bearing on how you'll need to configure BIND to work through the firewall. The next section details the two most common DNS architectures used with firewalls, forwarders and internal roots, and describes the advantages and disadvantages of each. Then we introduce a new feature, conditional forwarding, which combines the best of internal roots and forwarders. Finally, we discuss shadow namespaces and the configuration of the bastion host, the host at the core of your firewall system.

Types of Firewall Software

Before you start configuring BIND to work with your firewall, it's important you understand what your firewall is capable of. Your firewall's capabilities may influence your choice of DNS architecture and will determine how you implement it. If you don't know the answers to the questions in this section, track down someone in your organization who does know and ask. Better yet, work with your firewall's administrator when designing your architecture to ensure it will coexist with the firewall.

Note that this is far from a complete explanation of Internet firewalls. These few paragraphs only describe the two most common types of Internet firewalls, and only in enough detail to show how the differences in their capabilities impact name servers. For a comprehensive treatment of Internet firewalls, see Brent Chapman and Elizabeth Zwicky's *Building Internet Firewalls* (O'Reilly & Associates).

Packet filters

The first type of firewall we'll cover is the packet filtering firewall. Packet filtering firewalls operate largely at the transport and network levels of the TCP/IP stack (layers three and four of the OSI reference model, if you dig that). They decide whether to route a packet based upon packet-level criteria like the transport protocol (i.e., whether it's TCP or UDP), the source and destination IP address, and the destination port (see Figure 15-1).

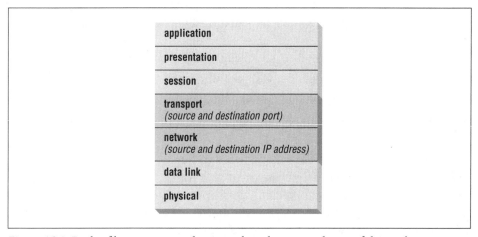

Figure 15-1. Packet filters operate at the network and transport layers of the stack

What's most important to us about packet filtering firewalls is that you can typically configure them to allow DNS traffic selectively between hosts on the Internet and your internal hosts. That is, you can let an arbitrary set of internal hosts communicate with Internet name servers. Some packet filtering firewalls can even permit your name servers to query name servers on the Internet, but not vice versa. All router-based Internet firewalls are packet filtering firewalls. Checkpoint's FireWall-1, Cisco's PIX, and Sun's SunScreen are popular commercial packet filtering firewalls.

A Gotcha with BIND 8 and Packet Filtering Firewalls

BIND 4 name servers always send queries from port 53, the well-known port for DNS servers, to port 53. Resolvers, on the other hand, usually send queries from high-numbered ports (above 1023) to port 53. Though name servers clearly have to send their queries to the DNS port on a remote host, there's no reason they have to send the queries *from* the DNS port. And, wouldn't you know it, BIND 8 name servers don't send queries from port 53 by default. Instead, they send queries from high-numbered ports, same as resolvers do.

This can cause problems with packet filtering firewalls that have been configured to allow server-to-server traffic but not resolver-to-server traffic, because they typically expect server-to-server traffic to originate from port 53 and terminate at port 53.

There are two solutions to this problem:

1. Reconfigure the firewall to allow name server queries from ports other than 53 (assuming this doesn't compromise the security of the firewall by allowing packets from Internet hosts to high-numbered ports on internal name servers).

2. Configure BIND to revert to its old behavior with the *query-source* substatement.

query-source takes as arguments an address specification and an optional port number. For example:

```
options { query-source address * port 53;};
```

tells BIND to use port 53 as the source port for queries sent from all interfaces. You can use a non-wildcard address specification to limit the addresses that BIND will send queries from. For example, on *wormhole*:

```
options { query-source 192.249.249.1 port *;};
```

would tell BIND to send all queries from the 192.249.249.1 address (i.e., not from 192.253.253.1), and to use dynamic, high-numbered ports.

Application gateways

Application gateways operate at the application protocol level, several layers higher in the OSI reference model than most packet filters (Figure 15-2). In a sense, they "understand" the application protocol in the same way a server for that particular application would. An FTP application gateway, for example, can make the decision to allow or deny a particular FTP operation, like a *RETR* (a *get*) or a *STOR* (a *put*).

The bad news, and what's important for our purposes, is that most application gateway firewalls handle only TCP-based application protocols. DNS, of course, is

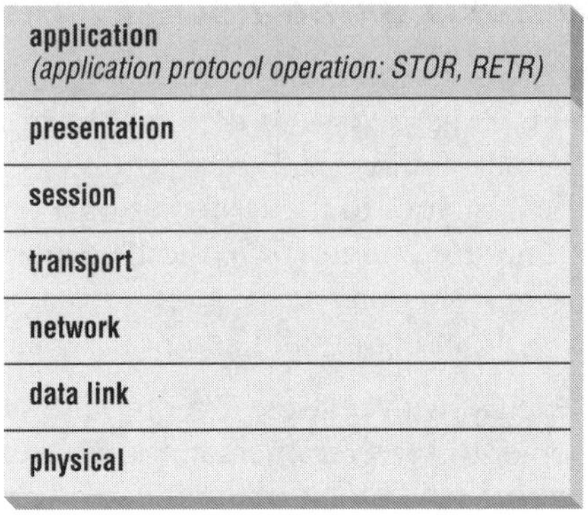

| application
(application protocol operation: STOR, RETR) |
| presentation |
| session |
| transport |
| network |
| data link |
| physical |

Figure 15-2. Application gateways operate at the application layer of the stack

largely UDP-based, and we know of no application gateways for DNS. This implies that if you run an application gateway firewall, your internal hosts will likely not be able to communicate directly with name servers on the Internet.

The popular Firewall Toolkit from Trusted Information Systems (TIS) is a suite of application gateways for common Internet protocols like Telnet, FTP, and HTTP. TIS's Gauntlet product is also based on application gateways, as is Raptor's Eagle Firewall.

Note that these two categories of firewall are really just generalizations. The state of the art in firewalls changes very quickly, and by the time you read this, you may have a firewall that includes an application gateway for DNS. Which family your firewall falls into is only important because it *suggests* what that firewall is capable of; what's more important is whether your particular firewall will let you permit DNS traffic between arbitrary internal hosts and the Internet.

A Bad Example

The simplest configuration is to allow DNS traffic to pass freely through your firewall (assuming you can configure your firewall to do that). That way, any internal name server can query any name server on the Internet, and any Internet name server can query any of your internal name servers. You don't need any special configuration.

Unfortunately, this is a really bad idea, for a number of reasons:

Version control

    The developers of BIND are constantly finding and fixing security-related bugs in the BIND code. Consequently, it's important to run the latest released version of BIND, especially on name servers that are directly exposed to the Internet. If one or just a few of your name servers communicate directly with name servers on the Internet, upgrading to a new version is easy. If any of the name servers on your network can, it's another story.

Possible vector for attack

Even if you're not running a name server on a particular host, a hacker might be able to take advantage of the fact that you allow DNS traffic through your firewall to attack that host. For example, a co-conspirator working on the inside could set up a Telnet daemon listening on the host's DNS port, allowing the hacker to *telnet* right in.

For the rest of this chapter, we'll try to set a good example.

Internet Forwarders

Given the dangers of allowing bidirectional DNS traffic through the firewall unrestricted, most organizations elect to limit the internal hosts that can "talk DNS" to the Internet. In an application gateway firewall, or any firewall without the ability to pass DNS traffic, the only host that can communicate with Internet name servers is the bastion host (see Figure 15-3).

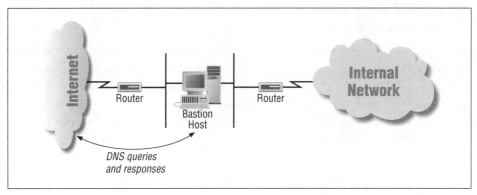

Figure 15-3. Diagram of a small network, showing the bastion host

In a packet-filtering firewall, the firewall's administrator can configure the firewall to let any set of internal name servers communicate with Internet name servers. Often, this is a small set of hosts that run name servers under the direct control of the domain administrator (see Figure 15-4).

Servers that can query name servers on the Internet directly don't require any special configuration. Their hints files contain the Internet's root name servers, which enables them to resolve Internet domain names. Internal name servers that *can't* query name servers on the Internet, however, need to know to forward queries they can't resolve to one of the name servers that can. This is done with the *forwarders*

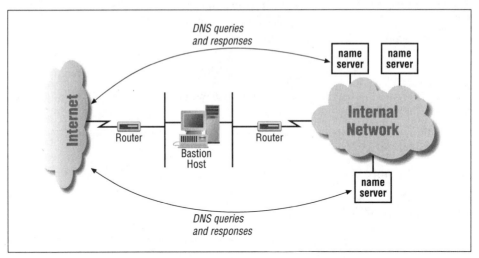

Figure 15-4. Diagram of a small network, showing select internal name servers

directive or substatement, introduced in Chapter 10, *Advanced Features and Security*.

Figure 15-5 illustrates a common forwarding setup, with internal name servers forwarding queries to a name server running on a bastion host.

At Movie U., we put in a firewall to protect ourselves from the Big Bad Internet several years ago. Ours is a packet-filtering firewall, and we negotiated with our firewall administrator to allow DNS traffic between Internet name servers and two of our name servers, *terminator.movie.edu* and *wormhole.movie.edu*. Here's how we configured the other internal name servers at the university. For our BIND 8 name servers:

```
options {
                forwarders { 192.249.249.1; 192.249.249.3; };
                forward only;
};
```

and for our BIND 4 name servers:

```
forwarders 192.249.249.3 192.249.249.1
options forward-only
```

(We vary the order in which the forwarders appear to help spread the load between them.)

When an internal name server receives a query for a name it can't resolve locally, like an Internet domain name, it forwards that query to one of our forwarders, which can resolve the name using name servers on the Internet. Simple!

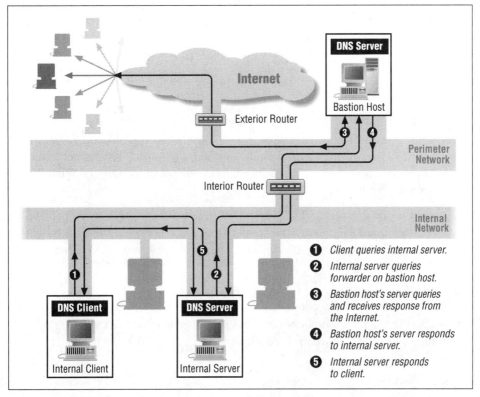

Figure 15-5. Using forwarders

The trouble with forwarding

Unfortunately, it's a little too simple. Forwarding starts to get in the way once you implement subdomains or build an extensive network. To explain what we mean, take a look at part of the configuration file on *zardoz.movie.edu*:

```
options {
                directory "/usr/local/named";
                forwarders { 192.249.249.1; 192.253.253.3; };
};

zone "movie.edu" {
                type slave;
                file "db.movie";
                masters { 192.249.249.3; };
};
```

zardoz.movie.edu is a slave for *movie.edu* and uses our two forwarders. What happens when *zardoz* receives a query for a name in *fx.movie.edu? zardoz*, as an authoritative *movie.edu* name server, has the NS records that delegate *fx.movie.edu* to its authoritative name servers. But it's also been configured to forward queries it can't resolve locally to *terminator* and *wormhole*. Which will it do?

It turns out that *zardoz* will ignore the delegation information and forward the query to *terminator*. That'll work, since *terminator* will receive the recursive query and ask an *fx.movie.edu* name server on *zardoz*'s behalf. But it's not particularly efficient, since *zardoz* could easily have sent the query directly.

Now imagine the scale of the network is much larger: a corporate network that spans many continents, with tens of thousands of hosts and hundreds or thousands of name servers. All of the internal name servers that don't have direct Internet connectivity—the vast majority of them—use a small set of forwarders. What are the problems with this picture?

Single point of failure

> If the forwarders fail, your name servers lose the ability to resolve both Internet domain names and internal domain names that they don't have cached or in authoritative data.

Concentration of load

> The forwarders will have an enormous query load placed on them. This is both because of the large number of internal name servers that use them and because the queries are recursive and require a good deal of work to answer.

Inefficient resolution

> Imagine two internal name servers, authoritative for *west.acmebw.com* and *east.acmebw.com*, respectively, both on the same network segment in Boulder, Colorado. Both are configured to use the company's forwarder in Bethesda, Maryland. For the *west.acmebw.com* name server to resolve a name in *east.acmebw.com*, it sends a query to the forwarder in Bethesda. The forwarder in Bethesda then sends a query back to Boulder to the *east.acmebw.com* name server, the original querier's neighbor. The *east.acmebw.com* name server replies by sending a response back to Bethesda, which the forwarder sends back to Boulder.

> In a traditional configuration with root name servers, the *west.acmebw.com* name server would quickly have learned that an *east.acmebw.com* name server was next door, and would favor it (because of its low round-trip time). Using forwarders "short-circuits" the normally efficient resolution process.

The upshot is that forwarding is fine for small networks and simple namespaces, but probably inadequate for large networks and complex namespaces. We found this out the hard way at Movie U. as our network grew, and were forced to implement internal roots.

Internal Roots

If you want to avoid the scalability problems of forwarding, you can set up your own root name servers. These internal roots will serve only the name servers in your organization. They'll only know about the portions of the namespace relevant to your organization.

What good are they? By using an architecture based on root name servers, you gain the scalability of the Internet's namespace (which should be good enough for most companies), plus redundancy, distributed load, and efficient resolution. You can have as many internal roots as the Internet has roots—thirteen or so—whereas having that many forwarders may be an undue security exposure and a configuration burden. Most of all, the internal roots don't get used frivolously. Name servers only need to consult an internal root when they time out the NS records for your top-level zones. Using forwarders, name servers may have to query a forwarder once *per resolution*.

The moral of our story is that if you have, or intend to have, a large name space and lots of internal name servers, internal root name servers will scale better than any other solution.

Where to put internal root name servers

Since name servers "lock on" to the closest root name server by favoring the one with the lowest roundtrip time, it pays to pepper your network with internal root name servers. If your organization's network spans the U.S., Europe, and the Pacific Rim, consider locating at least one internal root name server on each continent. If you have three major sites in Europe, give each of them an internal root.

Forward mapping delegation

Here's how an internal root name server is configured. An internal root delegates directly to any domains you administer. For example, on the *movie.edu* network, the root zone's data file would contain:

```
movie.edu.    86400   IN   NS   terminator.movie.edu.
              86400   IN   NS   wormhole.movie.edu.
              86400   IN   NS   zardoz.movie.edu.
terminator.movie.edu.    86400   IN   A   192.249.249.3
wormhole.movie.edu.      86400   IN   A   192.249.249.1
                         86400   IN   A   192.253.253.1
zardoz.movie.edu.        86400   IN   A   192.249.249.9
                         86400   IN   A   192.253.253.9
```

On the Internet, this information would appear in the *edu* name servers' databases. On the *movie.edu* network, of course, there aren't any *edu* name servers, so you delegate directly to *movie.edu* from the root.

Notice that this doesn't contain delegation to *fx.movie.edu* or any other subdomain of *movie.edu*. The *movie.edu* name servers know which name servers are authoritative for all *movie.edu* subdomains, and all queries for information in those subdomains will pass through the *movie.edu* name servers, so there's no need to delegate them here.

in-addr.arpa delegation

We also need to delegate from the internal roots to the *in-addr.arpa* domains that correspond to the networks *movie.edu* uses:

```
249.249.192.in-addr.arpa.   86400   IN   NS   terminator.movie.edu.
                            86400   IN   NS   wormhole.movie.edu.
                            86400   IN   NS   zardoz.movie.edu.
253.253.192.in-addr.arpa.   86400   IN   NS   terminator.movie.edu.
                            86400   IN   NS   wormhole.movie.edu.
                            86400   IN   NS   zardoz.movie.edu.
254.253.192.in-addr.arpa.   86400   IN   NS   bladerunner.fx.movie.edu.
                            86400   IN   NS   outland.fx.movie.edu.
                            86400   IN   NS   alien.fx.movie.edu.
20.254.192.in-addr.arpa.    86400   IN   NS   bladerunner.fx.movie.edu.
                            86400   IN   NS   outland.fx.movie.edu.
                            86400   IN   NS   alien.fx.movie.edu.
```

Notice that we *did* include delegation for the *254.253.192.in-addr.arpa* and *20.254.192.in-addr.arpa* zones, even though they correspond to the *fx.movie.edu* zone. We didn't need to delegate to *fx.movie.edu*, because we'd already delegated to its parent. The *movie.edu* name servers delegate to *fx.movie.edu*, so by transitivity the roots delegate to *fx.movie.edu*. Since neither of the other *in-addr.arpa* zones is a parent of *254.253.192.in-addr.arpa* or *20.254.192.in-addr.arpa*, we needed to delegate both zones from the root. As we've covered earlier, we don't need to add address records for the three Special Effects name servers, *bladerunner, outland,* and *alien*, because a remote name server can already find their addresses by following delegation from *movie.edu*.

The db.root file

All that's left is to add an SOA record for the root zone and NS records for this internal root name server and any others:

```
.   IN   SOA   rainman.movie.edu.   hostmaster.movie.edu.   (
                1        ; serial
                86400    ; refresh
                3600     ; retry
                608400   ; expire
                86400 )  ; minimum

    IN   NS   rainman.movie.edu.
    IN   NS   awakenings.movie.edu.
```

```
rainman.movie.edu.     86400   IN  A  192.249.249.254
awakenings.movie.edu.  86400   IN  A  192.253.253.254
```

rainman.movie.edu and *awakenings.movie.edu* are the hosts running internal root name servers. We shouldn't run an internal root on a bastion host, because if a name server on the Internet accidentally queries it for data it's not authoritative for, the internal root will respond with its list of roots—all internal!

So the whole *db.root* file (by convention, we call the root zone's data file *db.root*) looks like this:

```
.  IN  SOA  rainman.movie.edu.  hostmaster.movie.edu.  (
                1        ; serial
                86400    ; refresh
                3600     ; retry
                608400   ; expire
                86400 )  ; minimum


        IN  NS  rainman.movie.edu.
        IN  NS  awakenings.movie.edu.

rainman.movie.edu.     604800  IN  A  192.249.249.254
awakenings.movie.edu.  604800  IN  A  192.253.253.254

movie.edu.  86400  IN  NS  terminator.movie.edu.
            86400  IN  NS  wormhole.movie.edu.
            86400  IN  NS  zardoz.movie.edu.

terminator.movie.edu.  86400  IN  A  192.249.249.3
wormhole.movie.edu.    86400  IN  A  192.249.249.1
                       86400  IN  A  192.253.253.1
zardoz.movie.edu.      86400  IN  A  192.249.249.9
                       86400  IN  A  192.253.253.9

249.249.192.in-addr.arpa.  86400  IN  NS  terminator.movie.edu.
                           86400  IN  NS  wormhole.movie.edu.
                           86400  IN  NS  zardoz.movie.edu.
253.253.192.in-addr.arpa.  86400  IN  NS  terminator.movie.edu.
                           86400  IN  NS  wormhole.movie.edu.
                           86400  IN  NS  zardoz.movie.edu.
254.253.192.in-addr.arpa.  86400  IN  NS  bladerunner.fx.movie.edu.
                           86400  IN  NS  outland.fx.movie.edu.
                           86400  IN  NS  alien.fx.movie.edu.
20.254.192.in-addr.arpa.   86400  IN  NS  bladerunner.fx.movie.edu.
                           86400  IN  NS  outland.fx.movie.edu.
                           86400  IN  NS  alien.fx.movie.edu.
```

The *named.conf* file on both of the internal root name servers, *rainman* and *awakenings*, contains the lines:

```
zone "." {
                type master;
                file "db.root";
};
```

Or, for a BIND 4 server's *named.boot* file:

```
primary    .    db.root
```

This replaces a *zone* statement of type *hint* or a *cache* directive—a root name server doesn't need a cache file to tell it where the other roots are; it can find that in *db.root.* Did we really mean that *each* root name server is a primary for the root domain? Actually, that depends on the version of BIND you're running. BIND versions after 4.9 will let you declare a server a slave for the root domain, but BIND 4.8.3 and earlier insist that all root name servers load *db.root* as primaries.

If you don't have a lot of idle hosts sitting around that you can turn into internal roots, don't despair! Any internal name server (i.e., one that's not running on a bastion host or outside your firewall) can serve double duty as an internal root *and* as an authoritative name server for whatever other zones you need it to load. Remember, a single name server can be authoritative for many, many zones, including the root.

Configuring other internal name servers

Once you've set up internal root name servers, configure all your name servers on hosts anywhere on your internal network to use them. Any name server running on a host without direct Internet connectivity should list the internal roots in its hints file:

```
; Internal db.cache file, for movie.edu hosts without direct
; Internet connectivity
;
; Don't use this cache file on a host with Internet connectivity!
;

.   99999999   IN   NS   rainman.movie.edu.
    99999999   IN   NS   awakenings.movie.edu.

rainman.movie.edu.      99999999   IN   A   192.249.249.254
awakenings.movie.edu.   99999999   IN   A   192.253.253.254
```

Name servers running on hosts using this cache file will be able to resolve names in *movie.edu* and in Movie U.'s *in-addr.arpa* domains, but not outside of those domains.

How internal name servers use internal roots

To tie together how this whole scheme works, let's go through an example of name resolution on an internal caching-only name server using these internal root name servers. First, the internal name server receives a query for a domain name in *movie.edu*, say the address of *gump.fx.movie.edu.* If the internal name server doesn't have any "better" information cached, it starts by querying an internal root name server. If it has communicated with the internal roots before, it has a round-trip time associated with each, which tells it which of the internal roots is responding to it most quickly. It sends a *nonrecursive* query to that internal root for *gump.fx.movie.edu*'s address. The internal root answers with a referral to the *movie.edu* name servers on *terminator.movie.edu*, *wormhole.movie.edu*, and *zardoz.movie.edu*. The caching-only name server follows up by sending another nonrecursive query to one of the *movie.edu* name servers for *gump*'s address. The *movie.edu* name server responds with a referral to the *fx.movie.edu* name servers. The caching-only name server sends the same nonrecursive query for *gump*'s address to one of the *fx.movie.edu* name servers, and finally receives a response.

Contrast this with the way a forwarding setup would have worked. Let's imagine that instead of using internal root name servers, our caching-only name server were configured to forward queries to first *terminator* and then *wormhole*. In that case, the caching-only name server would have checked its cache for the address of *gump.fx.movie.edu* and, not finding it, would have forwarded the query to *terminator*. *terminator* would have queried an *fx.movie.edu* name server on the caching-only name server's behalf and returned the answer. Should the caching-only name server need to look up another name in *fx.movie.edu*, it would still ask the forwarder, even though the forwarder's response to the query for *gump.fx.movie.edu*'s address may have contained the names and addresses of the *fx.movie.edu* name servers.

Mail from internal hosts to the Internet

But wait! That's not all internal roots will do for you. We talked about getting mail to the Internet without changing *sendmail*'s configuration all over the network.

Wildcard records are the key to getting mail to work—specifically, wildcard MX records. Let's say we'd like mail to the Internet to be forwarded through *postmanrings2x.movie.edu*, the Movie U. bastion host, which has direct Internet connectivity. Then adding these records to *db.root*:

```
*         IN    MX     5 postmanrings2x.movie.edu.
*.edu.    IN    MX     10 postmanrings2x.movie.edu.
```

will get the job done. We need the *.edu* MX record in addition to the * record because of the DNS wildcard production rules we described in the wildcards section in Chapter 10. Since there are explicit data for *movie.edu* in the zone, the first wildcard won't match *movie.edu* or any other subdomains of *edu*. We need another, explicit wildcard record for *edu* to match these domains.

Now mailers on our internal *movie.edu* hosts will send mail addressed to Internet domains to *postmanrings2x* for forwarding. For example, mail addressed to *nic.ddn.mil* will match the first wildcard MX record:

```
% nslookup -type=mx nic.ddn.mil.   —Matches the MX record for *
Server:  rainman.movie.edu
```

```
Address:  192.249.249.19

nic.ddn.mil
     preference = 5, mail exchanger = postmanrings2x.movie.edu
postmanrings2x.movie.edu     internet address = 192.249.249.20
```

while mail addressed to *vangogh.cs.berkeley.edu* will match the second MX record:

```
% nslookup -type=mx vangogh.cs.berkeley.edu.  —Matches theMX record for *.edu
Server:  rainman.movie.edu
Address:  192.249.249.19

vangogh.cs.berkeley.edu
     preference = 10, mail exchanger = postmanrings2x.movie.edu
postmanrings2x.movie.edu     internet address = 192.249.249.20
```

Once the mail reaches *postmanrings2x*, our bastion host, *postmanrings2x*'s mailer will look up the MX records for these addresses itself. Since *postmanrings2x* will resolve the name using the Internet's name space instead of the internal name space, it will find the real MX records for the destination domain and deliver the mail. No changes to *sendmail*'s configuration are necessary.

Mail to specific Internet domains

Another nice perk of this internal root scheme is that it gives you the ability to forward mail addressed to certain Internet domains through particular bastion hosts, if you have more than one. We can choose, for example, to send all mail addressed to *uk* domain recipients to our bastion host in London first, and then out onto the Internet. This can be very useful if our internal network's connectivity or reliability is better than the U.K.'s section of the Internet.

Movie U. has a private network connection to our sister university in London near Pinewood Studios. As it turns out, sending mail across our private link, and then through the Pinewood host to correspondents in the U.K., is more reliable than sending it directly across the Internet. So we add the following wildcard records to *db.root*:

```
; holygrail is at the other end of the U.K. Internet link
*.uk.    IN    MX    10 holygrail.movie.ac.uk.
holygrail.movie.ac.uk.    IN    A    192.168.76.4
```

Now, mail addressed to users in subdomains of *uk* will be forwarded to the host *holygrail.movie.ac.uk* at our sister university, which presumably has facilities to forward that mail to other domains in the U.K.

The trouble with internal roots

Unfortunately, just as forwarding has its problems, internal roots have their limitations. Chief among these is the fact that your internal hosts can't see the Internet namespace. On some networks, this isn't an issue, because most internal hosts don't have any direct Internet connectivity. On others, however, the Internet firewall or other software may require that all internal hosts have the ability to resolve names in the Internet's namespace. For these networks, an internal root architecture won't work.

Views

The solution to this problem may be views, which the ISC hopes to introduce to BIND sometime soon in the version 8 release stream.[*] Views would allow you to specify when during resolution a name server tries its forwarders and under what conditions.[†]

By default, a BIND name server configured to use forwarders consults them *before* attempting normal resolution, or instead of normal iterative resolution. Also, when a BIND name server is configured to use forwarders, it will consult those forwarders for queries about *any* domain name. A view lets you specify whose queries are forwarded and what those queries have to be about (which domain names) in order to be forwarded.

The syntax of the *view* statement might look something like this:

```
view viewname {
                [ interface ip_list; ]
                [ domain domain_list; ]
                [ client ip_list; ]
                forward on reasons [ to ip_list ];
      };
```

Here's how the statement works: *domain* specifies the domains to which the view applies. *domain* takes a list of domain names as an argument. The *client* substatement determines which addresses this view applies to. *client* takes an address match list as an argument (as described in Chapter 10). *interface* specifies the interfaces on the local host to which the view applies. If the server receives a query on one of the interfaces specified, from a client whose address matches an address in the *client* substatement, *and* about a domain name specified in *domain*, the view applies. The default for *interface* is the built-in address match list *localhost*, the default for *client* is *any*, and the default for *domain* is ".", the root, meaning that by default, the view applies to queries from any IP address looking up any name.

forward would replace and extend the *forwarders* substatement of the *options* statement. It lists the IP addresses of the forwarders to use for queries that match the

---

[*] Views haven't been implemented yet, but we were granted a peek at how they may work and are documenting them in the hope that they'll beat this book to production.

[†] Todd Aven's *noforward* patch for BIND 4.9 was a precursor to this functionality. It's still available from *ftp://ftp.isc.org/isc/bind/src/4.9.3/contrib/noforward.tar.gz*.

specifications of this view. The forwarders are listed in the order in which you want them queried. What's new is the *reasons* clause. *reasons* might include *no-domain* and *no-answer.* These are the conditions under which the forwarders are used:

- *no-domain* corresponds to an NXDOMAIN (no such domain) response.

- *no-answer* corresponds to a NOERROR/no records response (that is, the domain name exists but the record type doesn't).

If we were to implement views in our internal root environment at Movie U., here's how our internal name server's *view* statements might look:

```
view {
    client { 192.249.249/24; 192.253.253/24; 192.253.254/24 };
    domain { "!movie.edu"; "!249.249.192.in-addr.arpa";
        "!253.253.192.in-addr.arpa"; "!254.253.192.in-addr.arpa"; };
    forward on no-domain to { 192.249.249.3; 192.249.249.1; };
};
```

This tells our internal name servers (all except *terminator* and *wormhole*, which can resolve Internet domain names directly) to forward queries *from* our internal IP addresses and *about* domain names that are not (note the negation operator) in *movie.edu* or our *in-addr.arpa* subdomains to *terminator* and *wormhole*, in that order.

Please note that we've described just one possible implementation of views. The actual implementation the ISC decides upon may differ, both in features and in syntax.

A Shadow Namespace

Many organizations would like to advertise different zone data to the Internet than they do internally. In most cases, much of the internal zone data is irrelevant to the Internet because of the organization's Internet firewall. The firewall may not allow direct access to most internal hosts, and may also translate internal, unregistered IP addresses into a range of IP addresses registered to the organization. Therefore, the organization may need to trim out irrelevant information from the external view of the zone, or change internal addresses to their external equivalents.

Unfortunately, BIND doesn't support automatic filtering and translation of zone data. Consequently, many organizations manually create what have become known as "split namespaces." In a split namespace, the real namespace is available only internally, while a pared-down, translated version of it, called "the shadow namespace," is visible to the Internet.

The shadow namespace contains the name-to-address and address-to-name mappings of only those hosts that are accessible from the Internet, through the firewall. The addresses advertised may be the translated equivalents of real internal addresses. The shadow namespace may also contain one or more MX records to direct email from the Internet through the firewall to a mail server.

Since Movie U. has an Internet firewall that greatly limits access from the Internet to the internal network, we elected to create a shadow namespace. For *movie.edu*, the only information we need to give out is about the zone (an SOA and a few NS records), the bastion host (*postmanrings2x*), and the new external name server, *ns.movie.edu*, which also functions as an external web server, *www.movie.edu*. The address of the external interface on the bastion host is 200.1.4.2, while the address of the name/web server is 200.1.4.3. The shadow *movie.edu* zone data file looks like this:

```
@    IN    SOA    ns.movie.edu.        hostmaster.movie.edu. (
                            1        ; Serial
                            86400    ; Refresh
                            3600     ; Retry
                            608400   ; Expire
                            86400 )  ; Default TTL

     IN    NS     ns.movie.edu.
     IN    NS     ns.isp.net.         ; our ISP's name server

     IN    A      200.1.4.3
     IN    MX     10 postmanrings2x.movie.edu.
     IN    MX     100 mail.isp.net.

www             IN    CNAME movie.edu.

postmanrings2x  IN    A     200.1.4.2
                IN    MX    10 postmanrings2x.movie.edu.
                IN    MX    100 mail.isp.net.

;postmanrings2x handles mail addressed to ns
ns              IN    A     200.1.4.3
                IN    MX    10 postmanrings2x.movie.edu.
                IN    MX    100 mail.isp.net.

*               IN    MX    10 postmanrings2x.movie.edu.
                IN    MX    100 mail.isp.net.
```

Note that there's no mention of any of the subdomains of *movie.edu*, including any delegation to the servers for those subdomains. The information simply isn't necessary, since there's nothing in any of the subdomains that you can get to from the Internet, and inbound mail addressed to hosts in the subdomains is caught by the wildcard.

The *db.200.1.4* file, which we need to reverse map the two Movie U. IP addresses that hosts on the Internet might see, looks like this:

```
@    IN    SOA    ns.movie.edu.        hostmaster.movie.edu. (
                            1        ; Serial
```

```
                      86400   ; Refresh
                      3600    ; Retry
                      608400  ; Expire
                      86400 ) ; Default TTL

      IN    NS    ns.movie.edu.
      IN    NS    ns.isp.net.

2     IN    PTR   postmanrings2x.movie.edu.
3     IN    PTR   ns.movie.edu.
```

One precaution that we need to take is to make sure that the resolver on our bastion host isn't configured to use the server on *ns.movie.edu*. Since that server can't see the real *movie.edu*, using it would render *postmanrings2x* unable to map internal names to addresses or addresses to names.

The bastion host

The bastion host is a special case in a split namespace. The bastion host has a foot in each environment: one network interface connects it to the Internet, and another connects it to the internal network. Now that we have split our name space in two, how can our bastion host see both the Internet name space and our real internal name space? If we configure it with the Internet root name servers in its hints file, it will follow delegation from the Internet's *edu* name servers to an external *movie.edu* name server with shadow zone data. It would be blind to our internal name space, which it needs to see to log connections, deliver inbound mail, and more. On the other hand, if we configure it with our internal roots, then it won't see the Internet's name space, which it clearly needs to do in order to function as a bastion host. What to do?

If we have internal name servers that support conditional forwarding, we can simply configure the bastion host's resolver to query those servers, since they can already see both the internal and Internet namespaces. If we use forwarding internally, depending on the type of firewall we're running, we may also need to run a name server on the bastion host itself. If the firewall won't pass DNS traffic, we'll need to run at least a caching-only name server, configured with the Internet roots, on the bastion host, so that our internal name servers will have somewhere to forward their unresolved queries.

Without conditional forwarding, the simplest solution is to run a name server on the bastion host (if you aren't already doing so). The name server must be configured as a slave for *movie.edu* and any *in-addr.arpa* subdomains in which it needs to resolve addresses. This way, if it receives a query for a name in *movie.edu*, it'll use its local authoritative data to resolve the name. If the name is in a subdomain of *movie.edu*, it'll follow NS records in the zone data to query an internal name server for the name. Therefore, it doesn't need to be configured as a slave for any *movie.edu* subdomains, such as *fx.movie.edu,* just the "top" domain (see Figure 15-6).

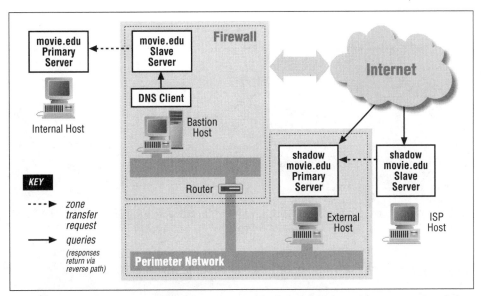

Figure 15-6. A split DNS solution

The *named.conf* file on our bastion host looks like this:

```
options {
                directory "/var/named";
};

zone "movie.edu" {
                type slave;
                file "db.movie";
                masters { 192.249.249.3; };
};

zone "249.249.192.in-addr.arpa" {
                type slave;
                file "db.192.249.249";
                masters { 192.249.249.3; };
};

zone "253.253.192.in-addr.arpa" {
                type slave;
                file "db.192.253.253.in-addr.arpa";
                masters { 192.249.249.3; };
};

zone "254.253.192.in-addr.arpa" {
                type slave;
                file "db.192.253.254";
```

```
                     masters { 192.253.254.2; };
    };

    zone "20.254.192.in-addr.arpa" {
                     type slave;
                     file "db.192.254.20";
                     masters { 192.253.254.2; };
    };

    zone "." {
                     type hint;
                     file "db.cache";
    };
```

An equivalent *named.boot* file would look like this:

```
    directory     /var/named
    secondary     movie.edu      192.249.249.3     db.movie
    secondary     249.249.192.in-addr.arpa     192.249.249.3     db.192.249.249
    secondary     253.253.192.in-addr.arpa     192.249.249.3     db.192.253.253
    secondary     254.253.192.in-addr.arpa     192.253.254.2     db.192.253.254
    secondary     20.254.192.in-addr.arpa      192.253.254.2     db.192.254.20
    cache     .     db.cache     ; lists Internet roots
```

Protecting zone data on the bastion host

Unfortunately, loading these zones on the bastion host also exposes them to the possibility of disclosure on the Internet, which we were trying to avoid by splitting the name space. But as long as we're running BIND 4.9 or better, we can protect the zone data using the *secure_zone* TXT record or the *allow-query* substatement. With *allow-query*, we can place a global access list on our zone data. Here's the new *options* statement from our *named.conf* file:

```
    options {
                     directory "/var/named";
                     allow-query { 127/8; 192.249.249/24; 192.253.253/24;
                                     192.253.254/24; 192.254.20/24; };
    };
```

With BIND 4.9's *secure_zone*, we can turn off all external access to our zone data by including these TXT records in each db file:

```
    secure_zone     IN     TXT     "192.249.249.0:255.255.255.0"
                    IN     TXT     "192.253.253.0:255.255.255.0"
                    IN     TXT     "192.253.254.0:255.255.255.0"
                    IN     TXT     "192.254.20.0:255.255.255.0"
                    IN     TXT     "127.0.0.1:H"
```

Don't forget to include the loopback address in the list, or the bastion host's own resolver may not get answers from the name server!

Dialup Connections

Another relatively recent development in networking that presents a challenge to DNS is the dialup Internet connection. When the Internet was young, and DNS was born, there was no such thing as a dialup connection. With the enormous explosion in the Internet's popularity, and the propagation of Internet service providers who offer dialup Internet connectivity to the masses, a whole new breed of problems with name service has been introduced.

We'll separate dialup connections into two categories: simple dialup, by which we mean a single computer that connects to the Internet occasionally, when a user manually initiates a connection, and dial-on-demand, which means one or more computers that connect to the Internet automatically whenever they generate traffic bound for the Internet. Often, the device that makes this dial-on-demand connectivity possible is a small dialup router with an analog modem or ISDN interface, like an Ascend Pipeline 25.

Simple Dialup

The easiest way to deal with simple dialup is to configure your dialup computer's resolver to use a name server provided by your Internet service provider (ISP). Most ISPs run name servers for their subscribers' use. If you're not sure whether your ISP provides name servers for your use, or if you don't know what their IP addresses are, check their web site, send them email, or give them a call.

Some operating systems, like Windows 95 and NT, will let you define a set of name servers for a particular dialup provider. So, for example, you can configure one set of name servers to use when you dial up Netcom, and another to use when you dial up your office. Unfortunately, defining name servers for your LAN connection under Windows 95 currently overrides all your precious dialup settings. See Chapter 6, *Configuring Hosts*, for details.

This configuration is usually adequate for most casual dialup users. Name resolution will fail unless the dialup connection is up, but that's not likely to be a problem, since there's no use for Internet name service without Internet connectivity. If you have special needs that aren't addressed by this configuration, take a look at the recommendations in the dial-on-demand section.

Dial-on-Demand

A more sophisticated dialup solution is dial-on-demand. Dial-on-demand Internet connections often use dedicated hardware, like a small dialup router, to provide connectivity whenever it's needed. If you initiate a connection to the Internet from the "remote" end of a dial-on-demand router, bingo, it dials up another router on the Internet and routes your packets across. If the connection is idle for more than a specified amount of time, the router drops the connection.

The challenge with DNS is to keep a local name server from continuously bringing the demand dial connection up and down like a yo-yo. This could be costly for you, since you sometimes pay a premium for connection setup with technologies like ISDN.

The most important strategy for minimizing this off-net traffic is to configure your resolvers to use a minimal search list. Default search lists with resolvers based on BIND 4.8.3 or earlier search the ancestors of your local domain, which can cause unnecessary remote traffic. For instance, say your local domain is *tinyoffice. majorcorp.com*, and you have a dial-on-demand connection to Majorcorp's enterprise network. On your older (pre-4.9) hosts, your default search list is:

```
tinyoffice.majorcorp.com
majorcorp.com
```

A user typing *telnet foo.tinyoffice.majorcorp.com* to log in to the workstation next to him will inadvertently cause lookups of:

```
foo.tinyoffice.majorcorp.com.tinyoffice.majorcorp.com and
foo.tinyoffice.majorcorp.com.majorcorp.com
```

before the correct domain name, *foo.tinyoffice.majorcorp.com*, is looked up. Since your local name server is probably authoritative for *tinyoffice.majorcorp.com*, it can tell that the first domain name, *foo.tinyoffice.majorcorp.com.tinyoffice.major-corp.com*, is bogus. (It ends in *com.tinyoffice.majorcorp.com*, so it would require the existence of a *com* subdomain of your local domain, and there isn't one.) But it can't tell about the second domain name without talking to a *majorcorp.com* name server first. If there isn't one locally, it'll have to bring up that dial-on-demand connection.

The easiest way to prevent these unnecessary queries is to trim the parent domain out of your search list explicitly, using the *search* directive. Or, if you can, upgrade your resolver to BIND 4.9 or later, which will check the domain name as is first if it has at least *ndots* dots in it, and which doesn't put any ancestor domains into the search list by default.

If your name server continues to bring up the link, try turning on query logging (with *options query-log* on a 4.9 name server, or *ndc query* with a BIND 4.9 or 8 name server, or by turning on debugging on an older name server) and look for the domain names that bring up the link. If many of them are in your parent zone, you might consider configuring your local name server as a slave for your parent zone. At least that way you'll only bring up the link at most once per refresh interval to resolve names in your parent zone. The same logic could be applied to nearly any zone your local name server queries often.

Network Names and Numbers

The original DNS definitions didn't provide the ability to look up network names based on a network number—a feature that was provided by the original *HOSTS.TXT* file. More recently, a procedure for storing network names has been defined; this procedure also works for subnets and subnet masks, so it goes significantly beyond *HOSTS.TXT*. Moreover, it doesn't require any modification to the DNS server software at all; it's based entirely on the clever use of pointer and address records.

If you remember, to map an IP address to a name in DNS, you reverse the IP address, append *in-addr.arpa*, and look up PTR data. This same technique is used to map a network number to a network name; for example, to map network 15.0.0.0 to "HP Internet." To look up the network number, include the trailing zeros to make it four bytes, and look up PTR data just as you did with a host's IP address. For example, to find the network name for the old ARPAnet, network 10.0.0.0, look up PTR data for *0.0.0.10.in-addr.arpa.* You'd get back an answer like *ARPAnet.ARPA.*

If the ARPAnet were subnetted, you'd also find an address record at *0.0.0.10.in-addr.arpa.* The address would be the subnet mask, 255.255.0.0, for instance. If you were interested in the subnet name instead of the network name, you'd apply the mask to the IP address and look up the subnet number.

This technique allows you to map the network number to a name. To provide a complete solution, there must be a way to map a network name to its network number. This, again, is accomplished with PTR records. The network name has PTR data that point to the network number (reversed with *in-addr.arpa* appended).

Let's see what the data might look like in HP's zone data files (the HP Internet has network number 15.0.0.0), and step through mapping a network number to a network name.

Partial contents of the file *db.hp*:

```
;
; Map HP's network name to 15.0.0.0.
;
hp-net.hp.com.          IN  PTR 0.0.0.15.in-addr.arpa.
```

Partial contents of the file *db.corp*:

```
;
; Map corp's subnet name to 15.1.0.0.
;
corp-subnet.corp.hp.com.  IN  PTR 0.0.1.15.in-addr.arpa.
```

Partial contents of the file *db.15*:

```
;
; Map 15.0.0.0 to hp-net.hp.com.
; HP's subnet mask is 255.255.248.0.
```

```
;
0.0.0.15.in-addr.arpa.     IN  PTR hp-net.hp.com.
                           IN  A   255.255.248.0
```

Partial contents of the file *db.15.1*:

```
;
; Map the 15.1.0.0 back to its subnet name.
;
0.0.1.15.in-addr.arpa.     IN  PTR corp-subnet.corp.hp.com.
```

Here's the procedure to look up the subnet name for the IP address 15.1.0.1:

1. Apply the default network mask for the address's class. Address 15.1.0.1 is a class A address, so the mask is 255.0.0.0. Applying the mask to the IP address makes the network number 15.

2. Send a query (*type=a* or *type=any*) for *0.0.0.15.in-addr.arpa*.

3. The query response contains address data. Since there is address data at *0.0.0.15.in- addr.arpa* (the subnet mask-255.255.248.0), apply the subnet mask to the IP address. This yields 15.1.0.0.

4. Send a query (*type=a* or *type=any*) for *0.0.1.15.in-addr.arpa*.

5. The query response does not contain address data, so 15.1.0.0 is not further subnetted.

6. Send a PTR query for *0.0.1.15.in-addr.arpa*.

7. The query response contains the network name for 15.1.0.1: *corp-subnet.corp.hp.com*.

In addition to mapping between network names and numbers, you can also list all the networks for your domain with PTR records:

```
movie.edu.   IN  PTR  0.249.249.192.in-addr.arpa.
             IN  PTR  0.253.253.192.in-addr.arpa.
```

Now for the bad news: despite the fact that RFC 1101 contains everything you need to know to set this up, there's no software we know of (yet) that actually *uses* this type of network name encoding, and very few administrators go to the trouble of adding this information. Until software actually makes use of DNS-encoded network names, about the only reason for setting this up is to show off. But that's a good enough reason for many of us.

Additional Resource Records

There are a couple of resource records that we haven't covered yet in this book. The first of these has been around since the beginning, HINFO, but hasn't been widely used. The others were defined in RFC 1183 and several successive RFCs. Most are experimental, but some are on the standards track and are coming into more prevalent use. We'll describe them here to give you a little head start in getting used to them.

Host Information

HINFO stands for *Host INFOrmation*. The data are a pair of strings identifying the host's hardware type and operating system. The strings should come from the MACHINE NAMES and OPERATING SYSTEM NAMES listed in the "Assigned Numbers" RFC (currently RFC 1700), but this requirement is not enforced; you can use your own abbreviations. The RFC isn't at all comprehensive, so it is quite possible you won't find your system in the list anyway. Originally, host information records were designed to let services like FTP determine how to interact with the remote system. This would have made it possible to negotiate data type transformations automatically. Unfortunately, this didn't happen—few sites supply accurate HINFO values for all their systems. Some network administrators use HINFO records to help them keep track of the machine types, instead of recording the machine types in a database or a notebook. Here are two examples of HINFO records; note that the hardware type or operating system must be surrounded with quotes if it includes any whitespace:

```
;
; These machine names and system names did not come from RFC 1340
;
wormhole   IN   HINFO   ACME-HW   ACME-GW
cujo       IN   HINFO   "Watch Dog Hardware"   "Rabid OS"
```

As we pointed out, HINFO records are a security risk—by providing easily accessible information about a system, you are making it easier for a hacker to break in.

AFSDB

AFSDB has a syntax like that of the MX record, and semantics a bit like that of the NS record. An AFSDB record gives either the location of an AFS cell database server or of a DCE cell's authenticated name server. The type of server the record points to, and the name of the host running the server, are contained in the record-specific data portion of the record.

So what's an AFS cell database server? Or AFS, for that matter? AFS originally stood for the Andrew File System, designed by the good folks at Carnegie-Mellon University as part of the Andrew Project. (It's now a registered trademark of Transarc Corporation, which sells AFS as a product.) AFS is a network filesystem, like NFS, but one that handles the latency of wide area networks much better than NFS does and provides local caching of files to enhance performance. An AFS cell database server runs the process responsible for tracking the location of filesets (groups of files) on various AFS fileservers within a cell (a logical group of hosts). So being able to find the AFS cell database server is the key to finding any file in the cell.

And what's an authenticated name server? It holds location information about all sorts of services available within a DCE cell. A DCE cell? That's a logical group of hosts that share services offered by the Open Group's Distributed Computing Environment (DCE).

And now, back to our story. To access another cell's AFS or DCE services across a network, you must first find out where that cell's cell database servers or authenticated name servers are. Hence the new record type. The domain name the record is attached to gives the name of the cell the server knows about. Cells are often named after DNS domains, so this usually doesn't look at all odd.

As we said, the AFSDB record's syntax is like the MX record's syntax. In place of the preference value, you specify the number 1 for an AFS cell database server or 2 for a DCE authenticated name server.

In place of the mail exchanger host, you specify the name of the host running the server. Simple!

Say an *fx.movie.edu* systems administrator sets up a DCE cell (which includes AFS services) because she wants to experiment with distributed processing to speed up graphics rendering. She runs both an AFS cell database server and a DCE name server on *bladerunner.fx.movie.edu*, another cell database server on *empire*, and another DCE name server on *aliens*. She should set up the AFSDB records as follows:

```
; Our DCE cell is called fx.movie.edu, same as the domain
fx.movie.edu.   IN  AFSDB  1 bladerunner.fx.movie.edu.
                IN  AFSDB  2 bladerunner.fx.movie.edu.
                IN  AFSDB  1 empire.fx.movie.edu.
                IN  AFSDB  2 aliens.fx.movie.edu.
```

X25, ISDN, and RT

These three record types were created specifically in support of research on next-generation internets. Two of the records, X25 and ISDN, are simply address records specific to X.25 and ISDN networks, respectively. Both take arguments (record-specific data) appropriate to the type of network. The X25 record type uses an X.121 address (X.121 is the ITU-T recommendation that specifies the format of addresses used in X.25 networks). The ISDN record type uses an ISDN address.

ISDN stands for Integrated Services Digital Network. Telephone companies around the world have proposed using ISDN protocols to allow their telephone networks to carry both voice and data, creating an integrated network. Although ISDN's availability is spotty throughout the U.S., it has been widely adopted in some international markets. Since ISDN uses the telephone companies' networks, an ISDN address is just a phone number, and in fact consists of a country code, followed by an area code or city code, then by a local phone number. Sometimes there are a few extra digits you wouldn't see in a phone number at the end, called a subaddress. The subaddress is specified in a separate field in the record-specific data.

Examples of the X25 and ISDN record types are:

```
relay.pink.com.   IN   X25   31105060845

delay.hp.com.    IN   ISDN   141555514539488
hep.hp.com.      IN   ISDN   141555514539488 004
```

These records are intended for use in conjunction with the Route Through (RT) record type. RT is syntactically and semantically similar to the MX record type: it specifies an intermediate host that will route *packets* (instead of mail) to a destination host. So now, instead of only being able to route mail to a host that isn't directly connected to the Internet, you can route any kind of IP packet to that host by using another host as a forwarder. The packet could be part of a *telnet* or *ftp* session, or perhaps even a DNS query!

Like MX, RT includes a preference value, which indicates how desirable delivery to a particular host is. For example, the records:

```
housesitter.movie.edu.   IN   RT   10 relay.pink.com.
                         IN   RT   20 delay.hp.com.
```

instruct hosts to route packets bound for *housesitter* through *relay.pink.com* (the first choice) or through *delay.hp.com* (the second choice).

The way RT works with X25 and ISDN (and even A) records is like this:

1. Internet host A wants to send a packet to host B, which is not connected to the Internet.

2. Host A looks up host B's RT records. This search also returns all address records (A, X25, *and* ISDN) for each intermediate host.

3. Host A sorts the list of intermediate hosts and looks for its own domain name. If it finds it, it removes it and all intermediate hosts at higher preference values. This is analogous to *sendmail*'s "paring down" a list of mail exchangers.

4. Host A examines the address record(s) for the most preferred intermediate host that remains. If host A is attached to a network that corresponds to the type of address record indicated, it uses that network to send the packet to the intermediate host. For example, if host A were trying to send a packet through *relay.pink.com*, it would need connectivity to an X.25 network.

5. If host A lacks appropriate connectivity, it tries the next intermediate host specified by the RT records. For example, if host A lacked X.25 connectivity, it might fall back to delivering via ISDN to *delay.hp.com*.

This process continues until the packet is routed to the most preferred intermediate host. The most preferred intermediate host may then deliver the packet directly to the destination host's address (which may be A, X25, or ISDN).

Location

RFC 1876 defines an experimental record type, LOC, that allows domain administrators to encode the location of their computers, subnets and networks. In this case, location means latitude, longitude and altitude. Future applications could use this information to produce network maps, assess routing efficiency, and more.

In its basic form, the LOC record takes latitude, longitude and altitude (in that order) as its record-specific data. Latitude and longitude are expressed in the format:

```
<degrees> [minutes [seconds.<fractional seconds>]] (N|S|E|W)
```

Altitude is expressed in meters.

If you're wondering how in the world you're going to get that data, check out "RFC 1876 Resources," at *http://www.ckdbr.com/dns-loc/*. This site, created by Christopher Davis, one of the authors of RFC 1876, is an indispensable collection of information and useful links and utilities for people creating LOC records.

If you don't have your own Global Positioning System receiver to carry around to all of your computers, two sites that may come in handy are Etak's Eagle Geocoder, at *http://www.geocode.com/eagle.html-ssi*, which you can use to find the latitude and longitude of most addresses in the United States; and AirNav's Airport Information, at *http://www.airnav.com/airports/*, which will let you find the elevation of the closest airport to you. If you don't have a major airport near you, don't worry: the database even includes the helipad at my neighborhood hospital!

Here's a LOC record for one of our hosts:

```
huskymo.acmebw.com.        IN    LOC    40 2 0.373 N 105 17 23.528 W 1638m
```

Optional fields in the record-specific data allow you to specify how large the entity you're describing is, in meters (LOC records can describe networks, after all, which can be quite large), as well as the horizontal and vertical precision. The size defaults to one meter, which is perfect for a single host. Horizontal precision defaults to 10,000 meters, and vertical precision to ten meters. These defaults represent the size of a typical ZIP or postal code, the idea being that you can fairly easily find a latitude and longitude given a ZIP code.

You can also attach LOC records to the names of subnets and networks. If you've taken the time to enter information about the names and addresses of your networks in the format described in RFC 1101 (covered earlier in this chapter), you can attach LOC records to the network names:

```
;
; Map HP's network name to 15.0.0.0.
;
hp-net.hp.com.    IN    PTR 0.0.0.15.in-addr.arpa.
                  IN    LOC 37 24 55.393 N 122 8 37 W 26m
```

IPv6 Addresses

If you're to believe the hype, IPv6 is coming soon to a network near you. Clearly, the existing A record won't accommodate IPv6's 128-bit addresses: BIND expects an A record's record-specific data to be a 32-bit address in dotted-octet format.

RFC 1886 introduces a new address record, AAAA, used to store a 128-bit IPv6 address. AAAA takes as its record-specific data the textual format of an IPv6 record described in RFC 1884. This format expresses the 128 bits of the address as eight sets of four hexadecimal digits, separated by colons (":"). The first set of four digits encodes the high-order 16 bits of the address. Every set of four bits are compressed into the equivalent hexadecimal digit (e.g., 1111 becomes f). You can omit leading zeroes in a set of hexadecimal digits.

So, for example, you'd see AAAA records like this:

```
ipv6         IN       AAAA           4321:0:1:2:3:4:567:89ab
```

RFC 1886 also extends the additional processing that BIND and other name servers do, so that name servers include AAAA records for mail exchangers and name servers that speak IPv6, for example.

Finally, RFC 1886 establishes a new reverse mapping namespace for IPv6 addresses, called *ip6.int.* Each level of subdomain under *ip6.int* represents a nibble (a 4-bit quantity) in the 128-bit address, with the low-order nibble encoded first (appearing at the far left of the domain name). Unlike the format of addresses in AAAA records, omitting leading zeroes is not allowed, so there are always 32 nibbles and 32 levels of subdomain below *ip6.int* in a domain name corresponding to a full IPv6 address. The domain name that corresponds to the address in the example above is:

```
b.a.9.8.7.6.5.0.4.0.0.0.3.0.0.0.2.0.0.0.1.0.0.0.0.0.0.0.1.2.3.4.IP6.INT.
```

These domain names have PTR records attached, just as domain names under *in-addr.arpa* do.

SRV

Locating a service or server within a zone, if you don't know which host it runs on, is a difficult problem. Some domain administrators have attempted to solve this problem by using service-specific aliases in their zones. For example, at Movie U. we created the alias *ftp.movie.edu* and point it to the domain name of our FTP archive:

```
ftp.movie.edu.    IN    CNAME       plan9.fx.movie.edu.
```

This makes it easy for people to guess a domain name that will get them to our FTP archive, and separates the name people use to access to archive from the domain name of the host it runs on. If we were to move the archive to a different host, we could simply change the CNAME record.

The experimental SRV record, introduced in RFC 2052, is a general mechanism for locating services. SRV also provides powerful features that allow domain administrators to distribute load and provide backup services, similar to the MX record.

A unique aspect of the SRV record is the format of the domain name it's attached to. Like service-specific aliases, the domain name to which an SRV record is attached gives the name of the service sought, as well as the protocol it runs over, concatenated with a domain name. So, for example:

```
ftp.tcp.movie.edu
```

would represent the SRV records someone *ftp*ing to *movie.edu* should retrieve in order to find the *movie.edu* FTP servers, while:

```
http.tcp.www.movie.edu
```

represents the SRV records someone accessing the URL *http://www.movie.edu/* should look up in order to find the *www.movie.edu* web servers.

The names of the service and protocol should appear in the latest Assigned Numbers RFC (the most recent as of this writing is RFC 1700), or be unique names used only locally. Don't use the port or protocol *numbers*, just the names.

The SRV record has four resource record-specific fields:

```
priority   weight   port   target
```

priority, weight, and *port* are unsigned 16-bit numbers (between 0 and 65535). *target* is a domain name.

Priority works very similarly to the preference in an MX record: the lower the number in the priority field, the more desirable the associated target. When searching for the hosts offering a given service, clients should try targets at the same priority before trying those at a higher priority value.

Weight allows domain administrators to distribute load to multiple targets. Clients should query targets at the same priority in proportion to their weight. For example, if one target has a priority of zero and a weight of one, and another target also has a priority of zero but a weight of two, the second target should receive twice as much load (in queries, connections, whatever) as the first.

Port specifies the port on which the service being sought is running. This allows domain administrators to run servers on non-standard ports. For example, a domain administrator could use SRV records to point web browsers at a web server running on port 8000 instead of the standard HTTP port (80).

Target, finally, specifies the domain name of a host on which the service is running (on the port specified in the *port* field). *Target* must be the canonical name of the host (not an alias), with address records attached to it.

So, for the *movie.edu* FTP server, we added these records to *db.movie*:

```
ftp.tcp              IN     SRV    1        0        21       plan9.fx.movie.edu.
                     IN     SRV    2        0        21        thing.fx.movie.edu.
```

This instructs SRV-capable FTP clients to try the FTP server on *plan9.fx.movie.edu*'s port 21 first when connecting to *movie.edu,* and then to try the FTP server on *thing.fx.movie.edu*'s port 21 if *plan9*'s FTP server isn't available.

The records:

```
http.tcp.www  IN SRV 0 2 80    www.movie.edu.
              IN SRV 0 1 80    www2.movie.edu.
              IN SRV 1 1 8000 postmanrings2x.movie.edu.
```

direct web queries for *www.movie.edu* to *www.movie.edu*'s port 80 and *www2.movie.edu*'s port 80, with *www.movie.edu* getting twice the queries that *www2.movie.edu* does. If neither is available, queries go to *postmanrings2x*, on port 8000.

Unfortunately, we don't know of any clients that support the SRV record yet. That's really too bad, given how useful SRV could be. Since SRV isn't widely supported, don't use SRV records in lieu of address records. It's prudent to include at least one address record for the "base" domain name to which your SRV records are attached, and more if you'd like the load spread between addresses. If you only list a host as a backup in the SRV records, don't include its IP address. Also, if a host runs a service on a non-standard port, don't include an address record for it, since there's no way to redirect clients to a non-standard port with an A record.

So, for *www.movie.edu,* we include all of these records:

```
http.tcp.www IN SRV 0 2 80    www.movie.edu.
             IN SRV 0 1 80    www2.movie.edu.
             IN SRV 1 1 8000 postmanrings2x.movie.edu.
www          IN A 200.1.4.3
             IN A 200.1.4.4
```

Browsers that can handle SRV records (whenever they come out) will send twice as many requests to *www.movie.edu* as to *www2.movie.edu,* and will only use *postmanrings2x.movie.edu* if both of the main web servers are unavailable. Browsers that don't use SRV records will have their requests round-robinned between *www* and *www2*.

DNS Versus X.500

X.500 is an ISO (International Standards Organization) standard distributed directory system that's sometimes seen as a "competitor" to DNS. X.500 does, indeed, include some of the same functionality DNS does. For example, you can use X.500 to retrieve address information for a particular host. And in some ways, the two are similar: X.500 directories store data in hierarchical name spaces, and use recursion and iteration (well, ISO calls them "chaining" and "referral"). While we can hardly claim to be experts on X.500, we can make some general comparisons between DNS and X.500:

- X.500, as a directory service, supports many types of searching. Whereas DNS servers simply look up data attached to a given domain name, you can search the X.500 Directory Information Tree for soundalike matches, or specify incomplete information ("I know his last name is Buttle and he works in the Ministry of Information") and still turn up data.

- X.500 is a full-blown distributed database meant to be used for a wide variety of applications. You can store the phone book in an X.500 database. You can store location data in an X.500 database. You can store information about all sorts of network devices and their attributes. DNS, on the other hand, is a relatively simple distributed database meant to solve a particular problem—an intractable *HOSTS.TXT* database.

- X.500 has security features involving credentials and the support of multiple encryption types; DNS is not secure.[*]

Anyway, you get the idea. X.500 is rich in capabilities and will be extremely useful when it is completely defined, implemented, and optimized. DNS provides a few, critical functions. It is, for the most part, fully implemented, and it will continue to evolve and improve.

Don't let this turn you off to DNS, though. The Domain Name System really is admirably good at its job, and it does it much faster than X.500 does. True, X.500 offers richer functionality, but it may never usurp DNS's position as the Internet's directory system of choice.

DNS and WINS

In our first edition, we mentioned the close alignment between NetBIOS names and DNS domain names, but noted that, alas, there was no way for DNS to function as

---

[*] Yet. The DNS Security Extensions described in RFC 2065 will allow cryptographic authentication of the source of zone data as well as data integrity checking, and more.

a NetBIOS name server. Basically, a DNS name server would need to support dynamic updates to function as a NetBIOS name server.

Of course, BIND 8 supports dynamic updates. Unfortunately, Microsoft's DHCP server doesn't yet send dynamic updates to DNS server. It only talks to Microsoft's WINS servers. WINS servers handle dynamic updates, though only for NetBIOS clients. In other words, a WINS name server doesn't speak DNS.

However, Microsoft provides a DNS server in Windows NT 4.0, which in turn can talk to WINS servers. The Microsoft DNS Server has a nice graphical administration tool, as you would expect from Microsoft, and provides a handy hook into WINS: you can configure the server to query a WINS server for address data if it doesn't find the data in a DNS zone.

This is done with a new WINS record in the zone data file. The WINS record is attached to the zone's domain name, like the SOA record. It acts as a flag, to tell the Microsoft DNS Server to query a WINS server if it doesn't find an address for the name it's looking up. The record:

```
@        0       IN      WINS            192.249.249.39 192.253.253.39
```

tells the Microsoft DNS Server to query the WINS servers running at 192.249.249.39 and 192.253.253.39 (in that order) for the name. The zero TTL is a precaution against the record being looked up and cached.

There's also a companion WINS-R record that allows a Microsoft DNS Server to reverse map IP addresses using a NetBIOS NBSTAT request. If the data file for an *in-addr.arpa* zone contains a WINS-R record, like:

```
@        0       IN      WINS-R          movie.edu
```

and the IP address sought doesn't appear in the file, the name server will attempt to send a NetBIOS NBSTAT request to the IP address being reverse mapped. This amounts to calling a phone number and asking the person on the end, "What's your name?" The result has a dot and the domain name in the record-specific data appended, in this case ".movie.edu".

These records provide valuable glue between the two name spaces. Unfortunately, the integration isn't perfect. As they say, the devil is in the details.

The main problem, as we see it, is that only the Microsoft DNS Servers support WINS and WINS-R.[*] Therefore, if you want lookups in the *fx.movie.edu* zone to be tried on the Special Effects Department's WINS server, then all *fx.movie.edu* name servers must be Microsoft DNS Servers. Why? Imagine that the DNS servers for *fx.movie.edu*

---

[*] And a few commercial products, like MetaInfo's Meta IP/DNS, which is a port of BIND 8.1.1 with WINS capabilities added on. Stock BIND, however, can't talk to WINS servers.

were mixed, some Microsoft DNS Servers and some BIND. If a remote DNS server needed to look up a NetBIOS name in *fx.movie.edu*, it would choose which of the *fx.movie.edu* DNS servers to query according to round trip time. If the server it happened to choose were a Microsoft DNS Server, it would be able to resolve the name to a dynamically assigned address. But if it happened to choose a BIND server, it wouldn't be able to resolve the name.

The best DNS-WINS configuration we've heard of so far puts all WINS-mapped data in its own DNS zone, say *mobile.movie.edu*. All the name servers for *mobile.movie.edu* are Microsoft DNS Servers, and the zone *mobile.movie.edu* contains just SOA records, NS records, and a WINS record pointing to the WINS servers for *mobile.movie.edu*. This way, there's no chance of inconsistent answers between authoritative servers for the zone.

Another problem is that WINS and WINS-R are proprietary. BIND name servers don't understand them, and in fact a BIND slave that transfers a WINS record from a Microsoft DNS Server primary master will fail to load the zone because WINS is an unknown type. (We discussed this, and how to work around it, in greater detail in Chapter 13, *Troubleshooting DNS and BIND*.)

The answer to these problems is the DNS standard dynamic update functionality introduced in BIND 8, described in Chapter 10. Dynamic update will allow authorized addition, modification, and deletion of records in a BIND name server, which in turn gives the folks at Microsoft the functionality they need to use DNS as a name service for NetBIOS. Microsoft has promised to do away with WINS and use standard DNS dynamic update with Windows NT 5.0. Whether they make good on their promise remains to be seen. We hope they do. It's hard enough to administer one naming service well.

DNS Message Format and Resource Records

This appendix outlines the format of DNS messages and enumerates all the resource record types. The resource records are shown in their textual format, as you would specify them in a DNS database file, and in their binary format, as they appear in DNS messages. You'll find a few resource records here that we didn't cover in the book because they are experimental or obsolete.

We've included here the portions of RFC 1035, written by Paul Mockapetris, that deal with the textual format of master files (what we called *db files* or *DNS database files* in the book) or with the DNS message format (for those of you who need to parse DNS packets).

Master File Format

(From RFC 1035, pages 33–35)

The format of these files is a sequence of entries. Entries are predominantly line-oriented, though parentheses can be used to continue a list of items across a line boundary, and text literals can contain CRLF within the text. Any combination of tabs and spaces acts as a delimiter between the separate items that make up an entry. The end of any line in the master file can end with a comment. The comment starts with a ";".

The following entries are defined:

    blank[comment]

    $ORIGIN domain-name [comment]

    $INCLUDE file-name [domain-name] [comment]

```
domain-namerr [comment]
```

```
blankrr [comment]
```

Blank lines, with or without comments, are allowed anywhere in the file.

Two control entries are defined: `$ORIGIN` and `$INCLUDE`. `$ORIGIN` is followed by a domain name, and resets the current origin for relative domain names to the stated name. `$INCLUDE` inserts the named file into the current file, and may optionally specify a domain name that sets the relative domain name origin for the included file. `$INCLUDE` may also have a comment. Note that an `$INCLUDE` entry never changes the relative origin of the parent file, regardless of changes to the relative origin made within the included file.

The last two forms represent RRs. If an entry for an RR begins with a blank, then the RR is assumed to be owned by the last stated owner. If an RR entry begins with a *domain-name*, then the owner name is reset.

rr contents take one of the following forms:

```
[TTL] [class] type RDATA
[class] [TTL] type RDATA
```

The RR begins with optional TTL and class fields, followed by a type and RDATA field appropriate to the type and class. Class and type use the standard mnemonics; TTL is a decimal integer. Omitted class and TTL values are default to the last explicitly stated values. Since type and class mnemonics are disjoint, the parse is unique.

domain-names make up a large share of the data in the master file. The labels in the domain name are expressed as character strings and separated by dots. Quoting conventions allow arbitrary characters to be stored in domain names. Domain names that end in a dot are called absolute, and are taken as complete. Domain names which do not end in a dot are called relative; the actual domain name is the concatenation of the relative part with an origin specified in an `$ORIGIN`, `$INCLUDE`, or as an argument to the master file-loading routine. A relative name is an error when no origin is available.

character-string is expressed in one of two ways: as a contiguous set of characters without interior spaces, or as a string beginning with a " and ending with a ". Inside a "-delimited string any character can occur, except for a " itself, which must be quoted using a backslash ("\").

Because these files are text files, several special encodings are necessary to allow arbitrary data to be loaded. In particular:

Of the root.

@

> A free-standing @ is used to denote the current origin.

\X

> Where X is any character other than a digit (0–9), is used to quote that character so that its special meaning does not apply. For example, "\." can be used to place a dot character in a label.[*]

\DDD

> Where each D is a digit is the octet corresponding to the decimal number described by DDD. The resulting octet is assumed to be text and is not checked for special meaning.[†]

( )

> Parentheses are used to group data that crosses a line boundary. In effect, line terminations are not recognized within parentheses.[‡]

;

> Semicolon is used to start a comment; the remainder of the line is ignored.

Character Case

(From RFC 1035, page 9)

For all parts of the DNS that are part of the official protocol, all comparisons between character strings (e.g., labels, domain names, etc.) are done in a case-insensitive manner. At present, this rule is in force throughout the domain system without exception. However, future additions beyond current usage may need to use the full binary octet capabilities in names, so attempts to store domain names in 7-bit ASCII or use of special bytes to terminate labels, etc., should be avoided.

Types

Here is a complete list of resource record types. The textual representation is used in master files. The binary representation is used in DNS queries and responses. These resource records are described on pages 13–21 of RFC 1035.

A address

(From RFC 1035, page 20)

Textual Representation:

```
owner class ttl A address
```

---

[*] Not implemented by BIND 4.8.3.

[†] Not implemented by BIND 4.8.3.

[‡] BIND 4.8.3 allows parentheses only on SOA and WKS resource records.

Example:

```
localhost.movie.edu.   IN A 127.0.0.1
```

Binary Representation:

```
Address type code: 1
    +--+--+--+--+--+--+--+--+--+--+--+--+--+--+--+--+
    |                    ADDRESS                    |
    +--+--+--+--+--+--+--+--+--+--+--+--+--+--+--+--+
where:
ADDRESS         A 32 bit Internet address.
```

CNAME canonical name

(From RFC 1035, page 14)

Textual Representation:

```
owner class ttl CNAME canonical-dname
```

Example:

```
wh.movie.edu.  IN  CNAME  wormhole.movie.edu.
```

Binary Representation:

```
CNAME type code: 5
    +--+--+--+--+--+--+--+--+--+--+--+--+--+--+--+--+
    /                     CNAME                     /
    /                                               /
    +--+--+--+--+--+--+--+--+--+--+--+--+--+--+--+--+
where:
CNAME           A domain-name which specifies the canonical
                or primary name for the owner.  The owner name is
                an alias.
```

HINFO host information

(From RFC 1035, page 14)

Textual Representation:

```
owner class ttl HINFO cpu os
```

Example:

```
grizzly.movie.edu.  IN  HINFO  VAX-11/780 UNIX
```

Binary Representation:

```
HINFO type code: 13
    +--+--+--+--+--+--+--+--+--+--+--+--+--+--+--+--+
    /                      CPU                      /
    +--+--+--+--+--+--+--+--+--+--+--+--+--+--+--+--+
    /                      OS                       /
    +--+--+--+--+--+--+--+--+--+--+--+--+--+--+--+--+
```

```
where:
CPU                 A character-string which specifies the CPU type.
OS                  A character-string which specifies the
                    operating system type.
```

MB mailbox domain name — experimental

(From RFC 1035, page 14)

Textual Representation:

```
owner class ttl MB mbox-dname
```

Example:

```
al.movie.edu.  IN  MB  robocop.movie.edu.
```

Binary Representation:

```
MB type code: 7
    +--+--+--+--+--+--+--+--+--+--+--+--+--+--+--+--+
    /                    MADNAME                    /
    /                                               /
    +--+--+--+--+--+--+--+--+--+--+--+--+--+--+--+--+
where:
MADNAME             A domain-name which specifies a host which has
                    the specified mailbox.
```

MD mail destination — obsolete

MD has been replaced with MX.

MF mail forwarder — obsolete

MF has been replaced with MX.

MG mail group member — experimental

(From RFC 1035, page 16)

Textual Representation:

```
owner class ttl MG mgroup-dname
```

Example:

```
admin.movie.edu.  IN  MG  al.movie.edu.
                  IN  MG  ed.movie.edu.
                  IN  MG  jc.movie.edu.
```

Binary Representation:

```
MG type code: 8
    +--+--+--+--+--+--+--+--+--+--+--+--+--+--+--+--+
    /                    MGMNAME                    /
    /                                               /
    +--+--+--+--+--+--+--+--+--+--+--+--+--+--+--+--+
```

```
where:
MGMNAME          A domain-name which specifies a mailbox which
                 is a member of the mail group specified by the
                 domain name.
```

MINFO mailbox or mail list information — experimental

(From RFC 1035, page 16)

Textual Representation:

```
owner class ttl MINFO resp-mbox error-mbox
```

Example:

```
admin.movie.edu.  IN  MINFO  al.movie.edu. al.movie.edu.
```

Binary Representation:

```
MINFO type code: 14
    +--+--+--+--+--+--+--+--+--+--+--+--+--+--+--+--+
    /                    RMAILBX                    /
    +--+--+--+--+--+--+--+--+--+--+--+--+--+--+--+--+
    /                    EMAILBX                    /
    +--+--+--+--+--+--+--+--+--+--+--+--+--+--+--+--+
where:
RMAILBX          A domain-name which specifies a mailbox which
                 is responsible for the mailing list or mailbox.
                 If this domain name names the root, the owner of
                 the MINFO RR is responsible for itself.  Note
                 that many existing mailing lists use a mailbox
                 X-request for the RMAILBX field of mailing list
                 X, e.g., Msgroup-request for Msgroup.  This field
                 provides a more general mechanism.
EMAILBX          A domain-name which specifies a mailbox which is
                 to receive error messages related to the mailing
                 list or mailbox specified by the owner of the
                 MINFO RR (similar to the ERRORS-TO: field which has
                 been proposed). If this domain name names the root,
                 errors should be returned to the sender of the
                 message.
```

MR mail rename — experimental

(From RFC 1035, page 17)

Textual Representation:

```
owner class ttl MR new-mbox
```

Example:

```
eddie.movie.edu.  IN  MR  eddie.bornagain.edu.
```

Binary Representation:

```
MR type code: 9
```

```
+--+--+--+--+--+--+--+--+--+--+--+--+--+--+--+--+
/                        NEWNAME                  /
/                                                 /
+--+--+--+--+--+--+--+--+--+--+--+--+--+--+--+--+
```

where:

NEWNAME   A *domain-name* which specifies a mailbox which
is the proper rename of the specified mailbox.

MX mail exchanger

(From RFC 1035, page 17)

Textual Representation:

owner class ttl MX *preference exchange-dname*

Example:

```
ora.com.  IN  MX  0  ora.ora.com.
          IN  MX  10 ruby.ora.com.
          IN  MX  10 opal.ora.com.
```

Binary Representation:

MX type code: 15

```
+--+--+--+--+--+--+--+--+--+--+--+--+--+--+--+--+
|                      PREFERENCE                |
+--+--+--+--+--+--+--+--+--+--+--+--+--+--+--+--+
/                       EXCHANGE                  /
/                                                 /
+--+--+--+--+--+--+--+--+--+--+--+--+--+--+--+--+
```

where:

PREFERENCE   A 16 bit integer which specifies the preference
given to this RR among others at the same owner.
Lower values are preferred.

EXCHANGE   A *domain-name* which specifies a host willing
to act as a mail exchange for the owner name.

NS name server

(From RFC 1035, page 18)

Textual Representation:

owner class ttl NS *name-server-dname*

Example:

```
movie.edu.    IN NS terminator.movie.edu
```

Binary Representation:

NS type code: 2

```
+--+--+--+--+--+--+--+--+--+--+--+--+--+--+--+--+
/                       NSDNAME                   /
/                                                 /
+--+--+--+--+--+--+--+--+--+--+--+--+--+--+--+--+
```

```
where:
NSDNAME              A domain-name which specifies a host which
                     should be authoritative for the specified
                     class and domain.
```

NULL null—experimental

(From RFC 1035, page 17)

Binary Representation:

```
NULL type code: 10
    +--+--+--+--+--+--+--+--+--+--+--+--+--+--+--+--+
    /                   anything                    /
    /                                              /
    +--+--+--+--+--+--+--+--+--+--+--+--+--+--+--+--+
Anything at all may be in the RDATA field so long as it is 65535
octets or less.
```

NULL is not implemented by BIND.

PTR pointer

(From RFC 1035, page 18)

Textual Representation:

```
owner class ttl PTR dname
```

Example:

```
1.249.249.192.in-addr.arpa.  IN PTR wormhole.movie.edu.
```

Binary Representation:

```
PTR type code: 12
    +--+--+--+--+--+--+--+--+--+--+--+--+--+--+--+--+
    /                   PTRDNAME                    /
    +--+--+--+--+--+--+--+--+--+--+--+--+--+--+--+--+
where:
PTRDNAME             A domain-name which points to some location in
                     the domain name space.
```

SOA start of authority

(From RFC 1035, pages 19–20)

Textual Representation:

```
owner class ttl SOA source-dname mbox (
        serial refresh retry expire minimum )
```

Example:

```
movie.edu. IN SOA terminator.movie.edu. al.robocop.movie.edu. (
                        1        ; Serial
                        10800    ; Refresh after 3 hours
```

```
            3600     ; Retry after 1 hour
            604800   ; Expire after 1 week
            86400 )  ; Minimum TTL of 1 day
```

Binary Representation:

```
SOA type code: 6
    +--+--+--+--+--+--+--+--+--+--+--+--+--+--+--+--+
    /                      MNAME                     /
    /                                                /
    +--+--+--+--+--+--+--+--+--+--+--+--+--+--+--+--+
    /                      RNAME                     /
    +--+--+--+--+--+--+--+--+--+--+--+--+--+--+--+--+
    |                      SERIAL                    |
    |                                                |
    +--+--+--+--+--+--+--+--+--+--+--+--+--+--+--+--+
    |                      REFRESH                   |
    |                                                |
    +--+--+--+--+--+--+--+--+--+--+--+--+--+--+--+--+
    |                      RETRY                     |
    |                                                |
    +--+--+--+--+--+--+--+--+--+--+--+--+--+--+--+--+
    |                      EXPIRE                    |
    |                                                |
    +--+--+--+--+--+--+--+--+--+--+--+--+--+--+--+--+
    |                      MINIMUM                   |
    |                                                |
    +--+--+--+--+--+--+--+--+--+--+--+--+--+--+--+--+
```

where:

MNAME	The *domain-name* of the name server that was the original or primary source of data for this zone.
RNAME	A *domain-name* which specifies the mailbox of the person responsible for this zone.
SERIAL	The unsigned 32 bit version number of the original copy of the zone. Zone transfers preserve this value. This value wraps and should be compared using sequence space arithmetic.
REFRESH	A 32 bit time interval before the zone should be refreshed.
RETRY	A 32 bit time interval that should elapse before a failed refresh should be retried.
EXPIRE	A 32 bit time value that specifies the upper limit on the time interval that can elapse before the zone is no longer authoritative.
MINIMUM	The unsigned 32 bit minimum TTL field that should be exported with any RR from this zone.

TXT text

(From RFC 1035, page 20)

Textual Representation:

owner class ttl TXT *txt-strings*

Example:

```
cujo.movie.edu.   IN  TXT  "Location: machine room dog house"
```

Binary Representation:

```
TXT type code: 16
    +--+--+--+--+--+--+--+--+--+--+--+--+--+--+--+--+
    /                     TXT-DATA                  /
    +--+--+--+--+--+--+--+--+--+--+--+--+--+--+--+--+
where:
TXT-DATA        One or more character-strings.
```

WKS well-known services

(From RFC 1035, page 21)

Textual Representation:

```
owner class ttl WKS address protocol service-list
```

Example:

```
terminator.movie.edu.  IN  WKS 192.249.249.3  TCP ( telnet smtp
                                              ftp shell domain )
```

Binary Representation:

```
WKS type code: 11
    +--+--+--+--+--+--+--+--+--+--+--+--+--+--+--+--+
    |                     ADDRESS                   |
    +--+--+--+--+--+--+--+--+--+--+--+--+--+--+--+--+
    |      PROTOCOL         |                       |
    +--+--+--+--+--+--+--+--+                        |
    |                                               |
    /                     BIT MAP                /
    /                                            /
    +--+--+--+--+--+--+--+--+--+--+--+--+--+--+--+--+
where:
ADDRESS         An 32 bit Internet address
PROTOCOL        An 8 bit IP protocol number
BIT MAP         A variable length bit map.  The bit map must
                be a multiple of 8 bits long.
```

New Types from RFC 1183

AFSDB Andrew File System Data Base — experimental

Textual Representation:

```
owner ttl class AFSDB subtype hostname
```

Example:

```
fx.movie.edu.  IN  AFSDB  1 bladerunner.fx.movie.edu.
               IN  AFSDB  2 bladerunner.fx.movie.edu.
```

```
              IN  AFSDB   1 empire.fx.movie.edu.
              IN  AFSDB   2 aliens.fx.movie.edu.
```

Binary Representation:

```
AFSDB type code: 18
     +--+--+--+--+--+--+--+--+--+--+--+--+--+--+--+--+
     |                    SUBTYPE                    |
     +--+--+--+--+--+--+--+--+--+--+--+--+--+--+--+--+
     /                    HOSTNAME                   /
     /                                               /
     +--+--+--+--+--+--+--+--+--+--+--+--+--+--+--+--+
where:
SUBTYPE            Subtype 1 is an AFS cell database server. Subtype 2
                   is a DCE authenticated name server.
HOSTNAME           A *domain-name* which specifies a host that has a
                   server for the cell named by the owner of the RR.
```

ISDN Integrated Services Digital Network address — experimental

Textual Representation:

```
owner ttl class ISDN ISDN-address sa
```

Example:

```
delay.hp.com.    IN  ISDN  141555514539488
hep.hp.com.      IN  ISDN  141555514539488 004
```

Binary Representation:

```
ISDN type code: 20
     +--+--+--+--+--+--+--+--+--+--+--+--+--+--+--+--+
     /                  ISDN ADDRESS                 /
     +--+--+--+--+--+--+--+--+--+--+--+--+--+--+--+--+
     /                  SUBADDRESS                   /
     +--+--+--+--+--+--+--+--+--+--+--+--+--+--+--+--+
where:
ISDN ADDRESS      A *character-string* which identifies the ISDN number
                  of *owner* and DDI (Direct Dial In) if any.
SUBADDRESS        An optional *character-string* specifying the
                  subaddress.
```

RP Responsible Person — experimental

Textual Representation:

```
owner ttl class RP mbox-dname txt-dname
```

Example:

```
; The current origin is fx.movie.edu
@            IN  RP   ajs.fx.movie.edu.   ajs.fx.movie.edu.
bladerunner  IN  RP   root.fx.movie.edu.   hotline.fx.movie.edu.
             IN  RP   richard.fx.movie.edu.   rb.fx.movie.edu.
ajs          IN  TXT  "Arty Segue, (415) 555-3610"
```

```
hotline     IN  TXT  "Movie U. Network Hotline, (415) 555-4111"
rb          IN  TXT  "Richard Boisclair, (415) 555-9612"
```

Binary Representation:

```
RP type code: 17
    +--+--+--+--+--+--+--+--+--+--+--+--+--+--+--+--+
    /                     MAILBOX                   /
    /                                               /
    +--+--+--+--+--+--+--+--+--+--+--+--+--+--+--+--+
    /                     TXTDNAME                  /
    /                                               /
    +--+--+--+--+--+--+--+--+--+--+--+--+--+--+--+--+
```
where:

MAILBOX	A *domain-name* that specifies the mailbox for the responsible person.
TXTDNAME	A *domain-name* for which TXT RR's exist. A subsequent query can be performed to retrieve the associated TXT resource records at *txt-dname*

RT Route Through — experimental

Textual Representation:

> *owner ttl class* RT *preference intermediate-host*

Example:

```
sh.prime.com.  IN  RT  2   Relay.Prime.COM.
               IN  RT  10  NET.Prime.COM.
```

Binary Representation:

```
RT type code: 21
    +--+--+--+--+--+--+--+--+--+--+--+--+--+--+--+--+
    |                    PREFERENCE                 |
    +--+--+--+--+--+--+--+--+--+--+--+--+--+--+--+--+
    /                    INTERMEDIATE               /
    /                                               /
    +--+--+--+--+--+--+--+--+--+--+--+--+--+--+--+--+
```
where:

PREFERENCE	A 16 bit integer which specifies the preference given to this RR among others at the same owner. Lower values are preferred.
EXCHANGE	A *domain-name* which specifies a host which will serve as an intermediate in reaching the host specified by *owner*.

X25 X.25 address — experimental

Textual Representation:

> *owner ttl class* X25 *PSDN-address*

Example:

```
relay.pink.com.   IN   X25    31105060845
```

Binary Representation:

```
X25 type code: 19
    +--+--+--+--+--+--+--+--+--+--+--+--+--+--+--+--+
    /                  PSDN ADDRESS                 /
    +--+--+--+--+--+--+--+--+--+--+--+--+--+--+--+--+
where:
PSDN ADDRESS    A character-string which identifies the PSDN
                (Public Switched Data Network) address in the
                X.121 numbering plan associated with owner.
```

New Types from RFC 1664

PX pointer to X.400/RFC 822 mapping information

Textual Representation:

```
owner ttl class PX preference RFC822 address X.400 address
```

Example:

```
ab.net2.it.   IN   PX   10    ab.net2.it.   O-ab.PRMD-net2.ADMDb.C-it.
```

Binary Representation:

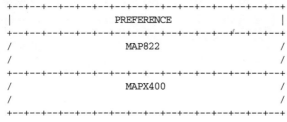

```
PX type code: 26
    +--+--+--+--+--+--+--+--+--+--+--+--+--+--+--+--+
    |                  PREFERENCE                   |
    +--+--+--+--+--+--+--+--+--+--+--+--+--+--+--+--+
    /                    MAP822                     /
    /                                               /
    +--+--+--+--+--+--+--+--+--+--+--+--+--+--+--+--+
    /                    MAPX400                    /
    /                                               /
    +--+--+--+--+--+--+--+--+--+--+--+--+--+--+--+--+
where:
PREFERENCE   A 16 bit integer which specifies the preference given to
             this RR among others at the same owner.  Lower values
             are preferred.
MAP822       A domain-name element containing rfc822-domain, the
             RFC 822 part of the RFC 1327 mapping information.
MAPX400      A domain-name element containing the value of
             x400-in-domain-syntax derived from the X.400 part of
             the RFC 1327 mapping information.
```

Classes

(From RFC 1035, page 13)

CLASS fields appear in resource records. The following CLASS mnemonics and values are defined:

IN

    1 the Internet

CS

    2 the CSNET class (obsolete—used only for examples in some obsolete RFCs)

CH

    3 the CHAOS class

HS

    4 the Hesiod class

DNS Message

In order to write programs that parse DNS packets, you need to understand the message format. DNS queries and responses are most often contained within UDP packets. Each message is fully contained within a UDP packet. If the query and response are sent over TCP, then they are prefixed with a two-byte value indicating the length of the query or response, excluding the two-byte length. The format and content of the DNS packet are as follows.

Format

(From RFC 1035, page 25)

All communications inside of the domain protocol are carried in a single format called a message. The top level format of message is divided into 5 sections (some of which are empty in certain cases) shown below:

```
+---------------------+
|       Header        |
+---------------------+
|      Question       |  the question for the name server
+---------------------+
|       Answer        |  RRs answering the question
+---------------------+
|      Authority      |  RRs pointing toward an authority
+---------------------+
|      Additional     |  RRs holding additional information
+---------------------+
```

The header section is always present. The header includes fields that specify which of the remaining sections are present, and also specify whether the message is a query or a response, a standard query or some other opcode, etc.

The names of the sections after the header are derived from their use in standard queries. The question section contains fields that describe a question to a name server. These fields are a query type (QTYPE), a query class (QCLASS), and a query domain name (QNAME). The last three sections have the same format: a possibly empty list of concatenated resource records (RRs). The answer section contains RRs that answer the question; the authority section contains RRs that point toward an authoritative name server; the additional records section contains RRs which relate to the query, but are not strictly answers for the question.

Header Section Format

(From RFC 1035, pages 26–28)

```
                                    1  1  1  1  1  1
      0  1  2  3  4  5  6  7  8  9  0  1  2  3  4  5
    +--+--+--+--+--+--+--+--+--+--+--+--+--+--+--+--+
    |                      ID                       |
    +--+--+--+--+--+--+--+--+--+--+--+--+--+--+--+--+
    |QR|   Opcode  |AA|TC|RD|RA|    Z   |   RCODE   |
    +--+--+--+--+--+--+--+--+--+--+--+--+--+--+--+--+
    |                    QDCOUNT                    |
    +--+--+--+--+--+--+--+--+--+--+--+--+--+--+--+--+
    |                    ANCOUNT                    |
    +--+--+--+--+--+--+--+--+--+--+--+--+--+--+--+--+
    |                    NSCOUNT                    |
    +--+--+--+--+--+--+--+--+--+--+--+--+--+--+--+--+
    |                    ARCOUNT                    |
    +--+--+--+--+--+--+--+--+--+--+--+--+--+--+--+--+
```

where:

ID
A 16 bit identifier assigned by the program that generates any kind of query. This identifier is copied the corresponding reply and can be used by the requester to match up replies to outstanding queries.

QR
A one bit field that specifies whether this message is a query (0), or a response (1).

OPCODE
A four bit field that specifies kind of query in this message. This value is set by the originator of a query and copied into the response. The values are:

0   a standard query (QUERY)

1   an inverse query (IQUERY)

2   a server status request (STATUS)

3-15   reserved for future use

AA
Authoritative Answer - this bit is valid in responses, and specifies that the responding name server is an authority for the domain name in question section. Note that the contents of the answer section may have multiple owner names because of aliases. The AA bit corresponds to the name which matches the query name, or the first owner name in the answer section.

TC
TrunCation - specifies that this message was truncated due to length greater than that permitted on the transmission channel.

RD
Recursion Desired - this bit may be set in a query and is copied into the response. If RD is set, it directs the name server to pursue the query recursively. Recursive query support is optional.

RA	Recursion Available - this bit is set or cleared in a response, and denotes whether recursive query support is available in the name server.
Z	Reserved for future use. Must be zero in all queries and responses.
RCODE	Response code - this 4 bit field is set as part of responses. The values have the following interpretation:

0	No error condition
1	Format error - The name server was unable to interpret the query.
2	Server failure - The name server was unable to process this query due to a problem with the name server.
3	Name Error - Meaningful only for responses from an authoritative name server, this code signifies that the domain name referenced in the query does not exist.
4	Not Implemented - The name server does not support the requested kind of query.
5	Refused - The name server refuses to perform the specified operation for policy reasons. For example, a name server may not wish to provide the information to the particular requester, or a name server may not wish to perform a particular operation (e.g., zone transfer) for particular data.
6-15	Reserved for future use.

QDCOUNT	an unsigned 16 bit integer specifying the number of entries in the question section.
ANCOUNT	an unsigned 16 bit integer specifying the number of resource records in the answer section.
NSCOUNT	an unsigned 16 bit integer specifying the number of name server resource records in the authority records section.
ARCOUNT	an unsigned 16 bit integer specifying the number of resource records in the additional records section.

Question Section Format

(From RFC 1035, pages 28–29)

The question section is used to carry the "question" in most queries, i.e., the parameters that define what is being asked. The section contains QDCOUNT (usually 1) entries, each of the following format:

```
+--+--+--+--+--+--+--+--+--+--+--+--+--+--+--+--+
|                    QTYPE                       |
+--+--+--+--+--+--+--+--+--+--+--+--+--+--+--+--+
|                    QCLASS                      |
+--+--+--+--+--+--+--+--+--+--+--+--+--+--+--+--+
```

where:

QNAME   a domain name represented as a sequence of labels, where each label consists of a length octet followed by that number of octets. The domain name terminates with the zero length octet for the null label of the root. Note that this field may be an odd number of octets; no padding is used.

QTYPE   a two octet code which specifies the type of the query. The values for this field include all codes valid for a TYPE field, together with some more general codes which can match more than one type of RR.

QCLASS   a two octet code that specifies the class of the query. For example, the QCLASS field is IN for the Internet.

QCLASS values

(From RFC 1035, page 13)

QCLASS fields appear in the question section of a query. QCLASS values are a superset of CLASS values; every CLASS is a valid QCLASS. In addition to CLASS values, the following QCLASSes are defined:

*

    255 any class.

QTYPE values

(From RFC 1035, pages 12–13)

QTYPE fields appear in the question part of a query. QTYPES are a superset of TYPEs, hence all TYPEs are valid QTYPEs. In addition, the following QTYPEs are defined:

AXFR

    252 A request for a transfer of an entire zone

MAILB

    253 A request for mailbox-related records (MB, MG or MR)

MAILA

    254 A request for mail agent RRs (Obsolete—see MX)

*

    255 A request for all records

Answer, Authority, and Additional Section Format

(From RFC 1035, pages 29–30)

The answer, authority, and additional sections all share the same format: a variable number of resource records, where the number of records is specified in the corresponding count field in the header. Each resource record has the following format:

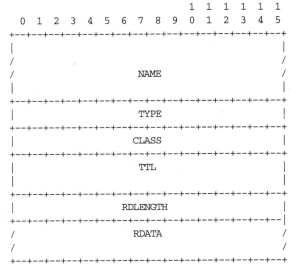

```
                                     1 1 1 1 1 1
          0  1  2  3  4  5  6  7  8  9  0  1  2  3  4  5
        +--+--+--+--+--+--+--+--+--+--+--+--+--+--+--+--+
        |                                              |
        /                                              /
        /                     NAME                     /
        |                                              |
        +--+--+--+--+--+--+--+--+--+--+--+--+--+--+--+--+
        |                     TYPE                     |
        +--+--+--+--+--+--+--+--+--+--+--+--+--+--+--+--+
        |                    CLASS                     |
        +--+--+--+--+--+--+--+--+--+--+--+--+--+--+--+--+
        |                     TTL                      |
        |                                              |
        +--+--+--+--+--+--+--+--+--+--+--+--+--+--+--+--+
        |                   RDLENGTH                   |
        +--+--+--+--+--+--+--+--+--+--+--+--+--+--+--+--|
        /                    RDATA                     /
        /                                              /
        +--+--+--+--+--+--+--+--+--+--+--+--+--+--+--+--+
```

```
where:
NAME            a domain name to which this resource record pertains.
TYPE            two octets containing one of the RR type codes.  This
                field specifies the meaning of the data in the RDATA
                field.
CLASS           two octets which specify the class of the data in the
                RDATA field.
TTL             a 32 bit unsigned integer that specifies the time
                interval (in seconds) that the resource record may be
                cached before it should be discarded.  Zero values are
                interpreted to mean that the RR can only be used for the
                transaction in progress, and should not be cached.
RDLENGTH        an unsigned 16 bit integer that specifies the length in
                octets of the RDATA field.
RDATA           a variable length string of octets that describes the
                resource.  The format of this information varies
                according to the TYPE and CLASS of the resource record.
                For example, if the TYPE is A and the CLASS is IN,
                the RDATA field is a 4 octet ARPA Internet address.
```

Data Transmission Order

(From RFC 1035, pages 8–9)

The order of transmission of the header and data described in this document is resolved to the octet level. Whenever a diagram shows a group of octets, the order of transmission of those octets is the normal order in which they are read in English. For example, in the following diagram, the octets are transmitted in the order they are numbered.

```
    0                   1
    0 1 2 3 4 5 6 7 8 9 0 1 2 3 4 5
   +-+-+-+-+-+-+-+-+-+-+-+-+-+-+-+-+
   |       1       |       2       |
   +-+-+-+-+-+-+-+-+-+-+-+-+-+-+-+-+
   |       3       |       4       |
   +-+-+-+-+-+-+-+-+-+-+-+-+-+-+-+-+
   |       5       |       6       |
   +-+-+-+-+-+-+-+-+-+-+-+-+-+-+-+-+
```

Whenever an octet represents a numeric quantity, the left most bit in the diagram is the high order or most significant bit. That is, the bit labeled 0 is the most significant bit. For example, the following diagram represents the value 170 (decimal).

```
    0 1 2 3 4 5 6 7
   +-+-+-+-+-+-+-+-+
   |1 0 1 0 1 0 1 0|
   +-+-+-+-+-+-+-+-+
```

Similarly, whenever a multi-octet field represents a numeric quantity the left most bit of the whole field is the most significant bit. When a multi-octet quantity is transmitted, the most significant octet is transmitted first.

Resource Record Data

Data Format

In addition to two- and four-octet integer values, resource record data can contain *domain names* or *character strings.*

Domain name

(From RFC 1035, page 10)

Domain names in messages are expressed in terms of a sequence of labels. Each label is represented as a one octet length field followed by that number of octets. Since every domain name ends with the null label of the root, a domain name is terminated by a length byte of zero. The high order two bits of every length octet must be zero, and the remaining six bits of the length field limit the label to 63 octets or less.

Message compression

(From RFC 1035, page 30)

In order to reduce the size of messages, the domain system utilizes a compression scheme which eliminates the repetition of domain names in a message. In this scheme, an entire domain name or a list of labels at the end of a domain name is replaced with a pointer to a prior occurrence of the same name.

The pointer takes the form of a two octet sequence:

```
+--+--+--+--+--+--+--+--+--+--+--+--+--+--+--+--+
| 1  1|                OFFSET                   |
+--+--+--+--+--+--+--+--+--+--+--+--+--+--+--+--+
```

The first two bits are ones. This allows a pointer to be distinguished from a label, since the label must begin with two zero bits because labels are restricted to 63 octets or less. (The 10 and 01 combinations are reserved for future use.) The OFFSET field specifies an offset from the start of the message (i.e., the first octet of the ID field in the domain header). A zero offset specifies the first byte of the ID field, etc.

Character string

(From RFC 1035, page 13)

Character string is a single length octet followed by that number of characters. *Character string* is treated as binary information, and can be up to 256 characters in length (including the length octet).

B

Compiling and Installing BIND on a Sun

The version of BIND shipped with Solaris 2.6 is based on the 4.9.3 release of BIND—a tad stale. Earlier versions of Solaris 2 include a BIND based on 4.8.3, which is downright ripe. For those of you who can't wait until Solaris ships with a version of BIND 8, compiling BIND from the sources on a Sun is relatively easy, because Solaris is based on BSD UNIX, and BIND was originally written for BSD UNIX. Here are instructions on how to compile and install 8.1.2 BIND on your Solaris 2.X host.

Get the Source Code

First, you've got to get the source code. There's a copy on *ftp.isc.org*, available for anonymous *ftp*:

```
% cd /tmp
% ftp ftp.isc.org.
Connected to pub1.pa.vix.com.
220 pub1.pa.vix.com FTP server (Version wu-2.4(1) Fri Dec 29 06:15:49 GMT 1995)
ready.
Name (ftp.isc.org.:user): ftp
331 Guest login ok, send e-mail address as password.
Password:
```

Now you need to find the right file:

```
ftp > cd /isc/bind/src/cur/bind-8
250 CWD command successful.
ftp > binary
200 Type set to I.
ftp > get bind-8.1.2-src.tar.gz
200 PORT command successful.
150 Opening BINARY mode data connection for bind-8.1.2-src.tar.gz (675801
bytes).
226 Transfer complete.
675801 bytes received in 89.5 seconds (7.4 Kbytes/s)
```

```
ftp > quit
221 Goodbye.
```

Unpack the Source Code

Now you've got the compressed *tar* file that contains the BIND source. Just use *zcat* to uncompress it, then un*tar* it:

```
% zcat bind-8.1.2-src.tar.gz | tar -xvf -
```

(This assumes you've got a version of *zcat* that can handle *gzip*ped files; if you don't, go get one via anonymous *ftp* from *alpha.gnu.ai.mit.edu* in */gnu/fileutils-3.16p.tar.gz.*) This will create a *src* directory with several subdirectories, including *bin*, *include*, *lib*, and *port*. They contain:

bin

Source code for all BIND binaries, including *named*.

include

Copies of include files referenced by the BIND code. You should use these to build your name server instead of the ones shipped with your system, since they have been updated.

lib

Source code for libraries used by BIND.

port

Information BIND uses to customize compilation settings and compile-time options for various operating systems.

Use the Proper Compiler Settings

Before you can build everything, you'll need an ANSI/ISO C compiler. If your version of Solaris came with one, great. Otherwise, get *gcc*, the GNU C compiler. You can find information on how to get *gcc* from *http://www.fsf.org/order/ftp.html*.

By default, BIND assumes you're using the GNU C compiler and various other GNUish utilities, like *flex* and *byacc*. If your operating system came with a full complement of development tools, including *cc*, *lex* and *yacc*, you'll need to copy *port/solaris/Makefile.set.sun* to *port/solaris/Makefile.set*. This lets BIND know that you're using the stock tools.

Build Everything

Next, you compile everything from the top-level directory. First, run:

```
% make stdlinks
```

Then run:

```
% make clean
% make depend
```

This will remove any old object files you might have sitting around from previous compilation attempts, and will update the *Makefile* dependencies. Then, compile the source code by running

```
% make
```

The source code should compile without any errors. Next, install the new *named* and *named-xfer* into */usr/sbin*. You'll need to become root to do this. On Solaris, they're called *in.named* and *in.named-xfer*, respectively. Use the command:

```
# make install
```

That's all there is!

C

Top-Level Domains

This table lists all of the two-letter country codes and all of the top-level domains that aren't countries. Not all of the countries are registered in the Internet's name space at the time of this writing, but there aren't many missing.

Domain	Country or Organization
AD	Andorra
AE	United Arab Emirates
AF	Afghanistan
AG	Antigua and Barbuda
AI	Anguilla
AL	Albania
AM	Armenia
AN	Netherlands Antilles
AO	Angola
AQ	Antarctica
AR	Argentina
ARPA	ARPA Internet
AS	American Samoa
AT	Austria
AU	Australia
AW	Aruba
AZ	Azerbaijan
BA	Bosnia and Herzegovina
BB	Barbados
BD	Bangladesh

Domain	Country or Organization
BE	Belgium
BF	Burkina Faso
BG	Bulgaria
BH	Bahrain
BI	Burundi
BJ	Benin
BM	Bermuda
BN	Brunei Darussalam
BO	Bolivia
BR	Brazil
BS	Bahamas
BT	Bhutan
BV	Bouvet Island
BW	Botswana
BY	Belarus
BZ	Belize
CA	Canada
CC	Cocos (Keeling) Islands
CD	Congo, Democratic Republic of the
CF	Central African Republic
CG	Congo
CH	Switzerland
CI	Cote d'Ivoire
CK	Cook Islands
CL	Chile
CM	Cameroon
CN	China
CO	Colombia
COM	commercial
CR	Costa Rica
CU	Cuba
CV	Cape Verde
CX	Christmas Island
CY	Cyprus
CZ	Czech Republic
DE	Germany
DJ	Djibouti

Domain	Country or Organization
DK	Denmark
DM	Dominica
DO	Dominican Republic
DZ	Algeria
EC	Ecuador
EDU	education
EE	Estonia
EG	Egypt
EH	Western Sahara
ER	Eritrea
ES	Spain
ET	Ethiopia
FI	Finland
FJ	Fiji
FK	Falkland Islands (Malvinas)
FM	Micronesia, Federated States of
FO	Faroe Islands
FR	France
FX	France, Metropolitan
GA	Gabon
GB	United Kingdom[a]
GOV	government
GD	Grenada
GE	Georgia
GF	French Guiana
GH	Ghana
GI	Gibraltar
GL	Greenland
GM	Gambia
GN	Guinea
GP	Guadeloupe
GQ	Equatorial Guinea
GR	Greece
GS	South Georgia and the South Sandwich Islands
GT	Guatemala
GU	Guam
GW	Guinea-Bissau

Domain	Country or Organization
GY	Guyana
HK	Hong Kong
HM	Heard and McDonald Islands
HN	Honduras
HR	Croatia
HT	Haiti
HU	Hungary
ID	Indonesia
IE	Ireland
IL	Israel
IN	India
INT	international entities
IO	British Indian Ocean Territory
IQ	Iraq
IR	Iran
IS	Iceland
IT	Italy
JM	Jamaica
JO	Jordan
JP	Japan
KE	Kenya
KG	Kyrgyzstan
KH	Cambodia
KI	Kiribati
KM	Comoros
KN	Saint Kitts and Nevis
KP	Korea, Democratic People's Republic of
KR	Korea, Republic of
KW	Kuwait
KY	Cayman Islands
KZ	Kazakhstan
LA	Lao People's Democratic Republic
LB	Lebanon
LC	Saint Lucia
LI	Liechtenstein
LK	Sri Lanka
LR	Liberia

Domain	Country or Organization
LS	Lesotho
LT	Lithuania
LU	Luxembourg
LV	Latvia
LY	Libyan Arab Jamahiriya
MA	Morocco
MC	Monaco
MD	Moldova, Republic of
MG	Madagascar
MH	Marshall Islands
MIL	military
MK	Macedonia, the Former Yugoslav Republic of
ML	Mali
MM	Myanmar
MN	Mongolia
MO	Macau
MP	Northern Mariana Islands
MQ	Martinique
MR	Mauritania
MS	Montserrat
MT	Malta
MU	Mauritius
MV	Maldives
MW	Malawi
MX	Mexico
MY	Malaysia
MZ	Mozambique
NA	Namibia
NATO	North Atlantic Treaty Organization
NC	New Caledonia
NE	Niger
NET	networking organizations
NF	Norfolk Island
NG	Nigeria
NI	Nicaragua
NL	Netherlands
NO	Norway

Domain	Country or Organization
NP	Nepal
NR	Nauru
NU	Niue
NZ	New Zealand
OM	Oman
ORG	organizations
PA	Panama
PE	Peru
PF	French Polynesia
PG	Papua New Guinea
PH	Philippines
PK	Pakistan
PL	Poland
PM	St. Pierre and Miquelon
PN	Pitcairn
PR	Puerto Rico
PT	Portugal
PW	Palau
PY	Paraguay
QA	Qatar
RE	Reunion
RO	Romania
RU	Russian Federation
RW	Rwanda
SA	Saudi Arabia
SB	Solomon Islands
SC	Seychelles
SD	Sudan
SE	Sweden
SG	Singapore
SH	St. Helena
SI	Slovenia
SJ	Svalbard and Jan Mayen Islands
SK	Slovakia
SL	Sierra Leone
SM	San Marino
SN	Senegal

Domain	Country or Organization
SO	Somalia
SR	Suriname
ST	Sao Tome and Principe
SV	El Salvador
SY	Syrian Arab Republic
SZ	Swaziland
TC	Turks and Caicos Islands
TD	Chad
TF	French Southern Territories
TG	Togo
TH	Thailand
TJ	Tajikistan
TK	Tokelau
TM	Turkmenistan
TN	Tunisia
TO	Tonga
TP	East Timor
TR	Turkey
TT	Trinidad and Tobago
TV	Tuvalu
TW	Taiwan, Province of China
TZ	Tanzania, United Republic of
UA	Ukraine
UG	Uganda
UK	United Kingdom
UM	United States Minor Outlying Islands
US	United States
UY	Uruguay
UZ	Uzbekistan
VA	Holy See (Vatican City State)
VC	Saint Vincent and The Grenadines
VE	Venezuela
VG	Virgin Islands (British)
VI	Virgin Islands (U.S.)
VN	Vietnam
VU	Vanuatu
WF	Wallis and Futuna Islands

Domain	Country or Organization
WS	Samoa
YE	Yemen
YT	Mayotte
YU	Yugoslavia
ZA	South Africa
ZM	Zambia
ZW	Zimbabwe

[a] In practice, the United Kingdom uses "UK" for its top-level domain.

D

Domain Registration Form

This appendix contains the form used to register the name of your domain with the InterNIC. For the most current version of this form, or for the InterNIC's online, HTML-based interface for completing the form, see *http://www.rs.internic.net/rs-internic.html*.

```
[ URL ftp://rs.internic.net/templates/domain-template.txt ] [ 03/98 ]

******* Please DO NOT REMOVE Version Number or Sections A-Q ********

Domain Version Number: 4.0

******* Email completed agreement to hostmaster@internic.net *******

        NETWORK SOLUTIONS, INC.

        DOMAIN NAME REGISTRATION AGREEMENT


A.      Introduction. This domain name registration agreement
("Registration Agreement") is submitted to NETWORK SOLUTIONS, INC.
("NSI") for the purpose of applying for and registering a domain name
on the Internet. If this Registration Agreement is accepted by NSI,
and a domain name is registered in NSI's domain name database and
assigned to the Registrant, Registrant ("Registrant") agrees to be
bound by the terms of this Registration Agreement and the terms of
NSI's Domain Name Dispute Policy ("Dispute Policy") which is
incorporated herein by reference and made a part of this Registration
Agreement. This Registration Agreement shall be accepted at the
offices of NSI.

B. Fees and Payments.

1) Registration or renewal (re-registration) date through March 31, 1998:
Registrant agrees to pay a registration fee of One Hundred United States
```

Dollars (US$100) as consideration for the registration of each new domain name or Fifty United States Dollars (US$50) to renew (re-register) an existing registration.

2) Registration or renewal date on and after April 1, 1998: Registrant agrees to pay a registration fee of Seventy United States Dollars (US$70) as consideration for the registration of each new domain name or the applicable renewal (re-registration) fee (currently Thirty-Five United States Dollars (US$35)) at the time of renewal (re-registration).

3) Period of Service: The non-refundable fee covers a period of two (2) years for each new registration, and one (1) year for each renewal, and includes any permitted modification(s) to the domain name record during the covered period.

4) Payment: Payment is due to Network Solutions within thirty (30) days from the date of the invoice.

C.   Dispute Policy. Registrant agrees, as a condition to submitting this Registration Agreement, and if the Registration Agreement is accepted by NSI, that the Registrant shall be bound by NSI's current Dispute Policy. The current version of the Dispute Policy may be found at the InterNIC Registration Services web site: "http://www.netsol.com/rs/dispute-policy.html".

D.   Dispute Policy Changes or Modifications. Registrant agrees that NSI, in its sole discretion, may change or modify the Dispute Policy, incorporated by reference herein, at any time. Registrant agrees that Registrant's maintaining the registration of a domain name after changes or modifications to the Dispute Policy become effective constitutes Registrant's continued acceptance of these changes or modifications. Registrant agrees that if Registrant considers any such changes or modifications to be unacceptable, Registrant may request that the domain name be deleted from the domain name database.

E.   Disputes. Registrant agrees that, if the registration of its domain name is challenged by any third party, the Registrant will be subject to the provisions specified in the Dispute Policy.

F.   Agents. Registrant agrees that if this Registration Agreement is completed by an agent for the Registrant, such as an ISP or Administrative Contact/Agent, the Registrant is nonetheless bound as a principal by all terms and conditions herein, including the Dispute Policy.

G.   Limitation of Liability. Registrant agrees that NSI shall have no liability to the Registrant for any loss Registrant may incur in connection with NSI's processing of this Registration Agreement, in connection with NSI's processing of any authorized modification to the domain name's record during the covered period, as a result of the Registrant's ISP's failure to pay either the initial registration fee or renewal fee, or as a result of the application of the provisions of the Dispute Policy. Registrant agrees that in no event shall the maximum liability of NSI under this Agreement for any matter exceed Five Hundred United States Dollars (US$500).

H.   Indemnity. Registrant agrees, in the event the Registration Agreement is accepted by NSI and a subsequent dispute arises with any third party, to indemnify and hold NSI harmless pursuant to the terms and conditions contained in the Dispute Policy.

I.   Breach. Registrant agrees that failure to abide by any provision of this Registration Agreement or the Dispute Policy may be considered by NSI to be a material breach and that NSI may provide a written notice, describing the breach, to the Registrant. If, within thirty (30) days of the date of mailing such notice, the Registrant fails to provide evidence, which is reasonably satisfactory to NSI, that it has not breached its obligations, then NSI may delete Registrant's registration of the domain name. Any such breach by a Registrant shall not be deemed to be excused simply because NSI did not act earlier in response to that, or any other, breach by the Registrant.

J.   No Guaranty. Registrant agrees that, by registration of a domain name, such registration does not confer immunity from objection to either the registration or use of the domain name.

K.   Warranty. Registrant warrants by submitting this Registration Agreement that, to the best of Registrant's knowledge and belief, the information submitted herein is true and correct, and that any future changes to this information will be provided to NSI in a timely manner according to the domain name modification procedures in place at that time. Breach of this warranty will constitute a material breach.

L.   Revocation. Registrant agrees that NSI may delete a Registrant's domain name if this Registration Agreement, or subsequent modification(s) thereto, contains false or misleading information, or conceals or omits any information NSI would likely consider material to its decision to approve this Registration Agreement.

M.   Right of Refusal. NSI, in its sole discretion, reserves the right to refuse to approve the Registration Agreement for any Registrant. Registrant agrees that the submission of this Registration Agreement does not obligate NSI to accept this Registration Agreement. Registrant agrees that NSI shall not be liable for loss or damages that may result from NSI's refusal to accept this Registration Agreement.

N.   Severability. Registrant agrees that the terms of this Registration Agreement are severable. If any term or provision is declared invalid, it shall not affect the remaining terms or provisions which shall continue to be binding.

O.   Entirety. Registrant agrees that this Registration Agreement and the Dispute Policy is the complete and exclusive agreement between Registrant and NSI regarding the registration of Registrant's domain name. This Registration Agreement and the Dispute Policy supersede all prior agreements and understandings, whether established by custom, practice, policy, or precedent.

P.   Governing Law. Registrant agrees that this Registration
Agreement shall be governed in all respects by and construed in
accordance with the laws of the Commonwealth of Virginia, United
States of America. By submitting this Registration Agreement,
Registrant consents to the exclusive jurisdiction and venue of the
United States District Court for the Eastern District of Virginia,
Alexandria Division. If there is no jurisdiction in the United States
District Court for the Eastern District of Virginia, Alexandria
Division, then jurisdiction shall be in the Circuit Court of Fairfax
County, Fairfax, Virginia.

Q.   This is Domain Name Registration Agreement Version
Number 4.0. This Registration Agreement is only for registrations
under top-level domains: COM, ORG, NET, and EDU. By completing
and submitting this Registration Agreement for consideration and
acceptance by NSI, the Registrant agrees that he/she has read and
agrees to be bound by A through P above.


```
Authorization
0a.   (N)ew (M)odify (D)elete....:
0b.   Auth Scheme...............:
0c.   Auth Info.................:

1.    Comments..................:

2.    Complete Domain Name......:

Organization Using Domain Name

3a.   Organization Name.........:
3b.   Street Address............:
3c.   City......................:
3d.   State.....................:
3e.   Postal Code...............:
3f.   Country...................:

Administrative Contact
4a.   NIC Handle (if known).....:
4b.   (I)ndividual (R)ole.......:
4c.   Name (Last, First)........:
4d.   Organization Name.........:
4e.   Street Address............:
4f.   City......................:
4g.   State.....................:
4h.   Postal Code...............:
4i.   Country...................:
4j.   Phone Number..............:
4k.   Fax Number................:
4l.   E-Mailbox.................:

Technical Contact
5a.   NIC Handle (if known).....:
5b.   (I)ndividual (R)ole.......:
```

```
5c.  Name (Last, First).........:
5d.  Organization Name..........:
5e.  Street Address.............:
5f.  City.......................:
5g.  State......................:
5h.  Postal Code................:
5i.  Country....................:
5j.  Phone Number...............:
5k.  Fax Number.................:
5l.  E-Mailbox..................:


Billing Contact
6a.  NIC Handle (if known)......:
6b.  (I)ndividual (R)ole........:
6c.  Name (Last, First).........:
6d.  Organization Name..........:
6e.  Street Address.............:
6f.  City.......................:
6g.  State......................:
6h.  Postal Code................:
6i.  Country....................:
6j.  Phone Number...............:
6k.  Fax Number.................:
6l.  E-Mailbox..................:


Prime Name Server
7a.  Primary Server Hostname....:
7b.  Primary Server Netaddress..:

Secondary Name Server(s)
8a.  Secondary Server Hostname..:
8b.  Secondary Server Netaddress:


END OF AGREEMENT


For instructions, please refer to:
"http://rs.internic.net/help/instructions.txt"
```

E

in-addr.arpa Registration Form

This appendix contains the form used to register your *in-addr.arpa* domain with ARIN, the American Registry for Internet Numbers. For the most current version of this form, see *http://www.arin.net/templates/inaddrtemplate.txt*.

03/98

```
*************** Please DO NOT REMOVE Version Number ******************

IN-ADDR Version Number: 1.0

************* Please see attached detailed instructions ***************

Registration Action Type
0.   (N)ew (M)odify (D)elete:

Network Information
1a.   Network Name.................:
1b.   Start of Network Block.......:
1c.   End of Network Block.........:

2a.   Name of Organization.........:
2b.   Postal address of Organization:

Technical Contact
3a.   ARIN-Handle (if known).......:
3b.   Name (Last, First)...........:
3c.   Organization.................:
3d.   Postal Address...............:

3e.   Phone Number.................:
3f.   E-Mail Address...............:

Primary Name Server
```

```
4a.   Primary Server Hostname.......:
4b.   Primary Server Netaddress.....:

Secondary Name Server(s)
5a.   Secondary Server Hostname.....:
5b.   Secondary Server Netaddress...:

6.    Comments.....................:
```

---------------------------- cut here ----------------------------

GENERAL INSTRUCTIONS: REGISTERING INVERSE ADDRESSING (NAME MAPPING) WITH ARIN

The Internet uses a special domain to support gateway location and Internet address to host mapping called In-ADDR.ARPA. The intent of this domain is to provide a guaranteed method to perform host address to host name mapping, and to facilitate queries to locate all gateways on a particular network in the Internet. Whenever an application is used that requires user identification, i.e., ftp, or remote login, the domain must be registered in the IN-ADDR.ARPA zone or the application will be unable to determine the origin of the IP.

IN-ADDR domains are represented using the network number in reverse.

    EXAMPLE: The IN-ADDR domain for network 123.45.67.0 is represented as

                    67.45.123.IN-ADDR.ARPA.

    NOTE: Please do not list your network number in reverse on your template.

Use the above template for registering new IN-ADDR entries, making changes to existing IN-ADDR records, and removing inverse-address mapping from the ARIN database and root servers.

The IN-ADDR template should be submitted via E-mail to ARIN at:

                    hostmaster@arin.net

In order to ensure prompt and accurate processing of IN-ADDR requests, follow precisely the instructions below. Please do not modify the template nor remove the version number. IN-ADDR templates are automatically parsed. Errors in a template result in the template being returned for correction.

Please send only one template per message. In the Subject of the message, use the words: NEW IN-ADDR, MODIFY IN-ADDR, or REMOVE IN-ADDR, as appropriate.

Please do not send hardcopy registrations to ARIN. If you do not have an E-mail connection, you should arrange for your Internet Service Provider (ISP) to send E-mail applications to ARIN on your behalf.

When you submit a template, you will receive an auto-reply from ARIN with a ticket number. The ticket number format is:

                    ARIN -<year><month><day>.<queue position>.

Use the ticket number in the Subject of any message you send regarding a
registration action. When the registration has been completed, you will be
notified via E-mail.

All ISPs receiving from ARIN /16 CIDR blocks (Class B) which are greater than
or equal to (>=)256 Class C's) will be responsible for maintaining all IN-
ADDR.ARPA domain records for their respective customers. The ISP is
responsible for the maintenance of IN-ADDR.ARPA domain records of all longer
prefixes that have been delegated out of that block.

DETAILED INSTRUCTIONS FOR COMPLETING EACH IN-ADDR TEMPLATE FIELD

Section 0.   Registration Action Type

N) New (M) Modify (D) Delete:

(N)   New:
      For new IN-ADDR registration, place an N after the colon.

(M)   Modify:
      To modify/change an EXISTING record IN-ADDR registration, place an M after
      the colon. When "M" is selected, the current records will be replaced with
      the information listed in the template. Please provide a complete list of
      name servers in the order in which they should appear on the record.

      If the modification involves first registering a person or name server(s)
      not entered in the database, the instructions for completing Sections 2,
      3, 4 and 5 apply. Search the WHOIS database for more information if you
      are unsure of the current information for the technical POC or name
      server(s).

      The requested changes will be made if ARIN registry personnel determine
      that the modification request was issued by an authorized source. The
      issuing source may be a listed contact for the domain, others in the same
      organization, the current provider, or a new provider initiating network
      support.

(D)   Delete.
      To delete an existing IN-ADDR from your network record, place a D after
      the colon. List the IN-ADDR server and IP number and it will be deleted.
      The host entry will still exist in the global host tables.

Section 1. Network Record Information.

1a.   Network Name.
      Please supply the network name.

          NOTE: The network name is not the domain name.

      To verify an existing Network Name, use the searchable WHOIS database.

The Network Name is used as an identifier in Internet name and address tables. To create a network name, supply a short name consisting of a combination of up to 12 numbers and letters for the network. You may use a dash (-) as part of the Network Name, but no other special characters. Please do not use periods or underscores.

1b./1c.   Start/End of Network Block.

1b.   Start of Network Block.

If the network record is for a single network, enter the IP address of the single network here. Item 1c is then left blank. If the record is a block of IP addresses, enter the IP address of the start of the network block.

1c.   End of Network Block.

If the network record is a block of IP addresses, Item 1c will be the last IP address of the network block.

If you received a block of IP addresses from your ISP, there may already be IN-ADDR servers on the parent block held by that provider. Please query your ISP before submitting an IN-ADDR request.

Section 2.   Name and Postal Address of Organization.

2a.   Name of Organization.

The network is considered to be registered to an organization, even if the "organization" is an individual. If you are an ISP submitting this request on behalf of your customer, please provide here the name and postal address of the organization that uses the IP address(es).

2b.   Postal Address of Organization.

This is the physical address of the organization. Place the city, state, and zip code together on the same line below the Street Address or Post Office Box. Use a comma to separate the city and state. Do not insert a period following the state abbreviation. To change an address, please provide the new address information in this item, and flag the change in Section 6: Comments.

    EXAMPLE:

                    111 Town Center Drive
                    Herndon, VA 22070

If the organization is located in a country other than the United States, please include the two-letter country code on the last line by itself.

    EXAMPLE:
                    161 James Street
                    Montreal, QC H2S 2C8
                    CA

For the country entry, please use the two-letter country code found at:

      URL: [ftp://rs.arin.net/netinfo/iso3166-countrycodes]

NOTE: If you wish to make a change to an existing registered physical
           address of an organization, please note the change you want in
           Section 6: Comments.

Section 3.   Technical Contact

The technical point of contact (POC) is the person responsible for
the technical aspects of maintaining the network's name servers.
The POC should be able to answer any utilization questions ARIN may have.

3a.   User Handle (if known)

Each person in the ARIN database is assigned a user handle, which is a
unique tag consisting of the user's initials and a serial number. This
tag is used in database records indicate a POC for a domain name, network,
name server or other entity. Each user should have only one handle.

If the user handle is known, insert the handle in Item 3a and leave the
rest of Section 3 blank. If the user's handle is unknown or the user has
never been registered, leave Item 3a blank. The user's database record
will be updated with any new information on the template.

3b.   Name (Last, First)
      Enter the name of the Technical Contact in the format:

           Last Name, First Name.

Separate first and last names by a comma.

3c.   Organization.

Provide the name of the organization with which the Technical Contact
is affiliated. Refer to the instructions for Item 2a.

3d.   Postal Address.

Refer to the instructions for Item 2b.

Section 4.   Primary Name Server.

Networks are required to provide at least two independent servers for
translating address to name mapping for hosts in the domain. The servers should
be in physically separate locations and on different networks, if possible. The
servers should be active and responsive to domain name server (DNS) queries
prior to submission of this application.

ARIN requires that you provide complete information on your primary and
secondary servers in order to process your registration request. Incomplete
information in sections 4 and 5, or inactive servers will result in the return
of the registration request.

NOTE: To change the name or the number of a registered name server, submit
        a separate IN-ADDR template requesting a modification of your IN-ADDR
        registration. Do this by placing an M after the Modify command in
        Section 0: Registration Action Type. New IN-ADDR registrations cannot
        be used to change the name or the number of a registered name server.

4a.   Primary Name Server Hostname.
      Please provide the fully-qualified name of the machine that is to be
      the name server.

         EXAMPLE:
             Use "machine.domainame.com" not just "machine" or just
"domainame.com"
             Many reverse-authentication programs will not search for the
nameserver if only the domain name is listed.

4b.   Primary Name Server Netaddress.

      It is suggested that the fourth octet of an IP address of a server
      should be neither 0 nor 255. The remaining 254 numbers in the fourth
      octet of the IP address are valid.

Section 5.   Secondary Name Server(s)

5a./5b.   Secondary Name Server Hostname/Secondary Name Server Netaddress.

      Please refer to the instructions and examples in Items 4a./4b. above.

      Copy Section 5 as needed to include all Secondary Name Servers.
      Do not renumber or change the copied section. A maximum of six domain
      name servers may be added to a network record.

Section 6.   Comments.

Please use Section 6 to provide ARIN with all comments and any additional
detailed updates relevant to your IN-ADDR registration not provided in Sections
0 through 5. Please provide a brief explanation for
changing an organization name or point of contact information.

F

BIND Name Server and Resolver Statements

BIND Name Server Boot File Statements

Here's a handy list of all the boot file statements for the BIND name server. Some of the statements only exist in later versions, so your server may not support them yet. The version 4 statements are labeled with a specific version number (4.9.3), or if they've been around a long time, they are labeled with a generic version number (4.X.X). The version 8 statements are labeled 8.X.X.

directory (4.X.X)

Function:
Changes the current working directory

Syntax:
directory *new-directory*
Example:
directory /var/named
See also:
8.X.X options statement, directory

Covered in:
Chapter 4, *Setting Up BIND*

primary

Function:
Declares a name server as the primary master for a zone

Syntax:
primary *domain-name-of-zone file*

Example:
```
primary movie.edu   db.movie
```
See also:

8.X.X zone statement, `type master`

Covered in:

Chapter 4, *Setting Up BIND*

secondary

Function:

Declares a name server as a slave for a zone

Syntax:
```
secondary domain-name-of-zone ip-address-list [backup-file]
```
Example:
```
secondary movie.edu   192.249.249.3 db.movie
```
See also:

8.X.X zone statement, `type slave`

Covered in:

Chapter 4, *Setting Up BIND*

cache

Function:

Defines the name of the file from which to load the root hints (the names and addresses of the root name servers)

Syntax:
```
cache domain-name file
```
Example:
```
cache    .    db.cache
```
See also:

8.X.X zone statement, `type hint`

Covered in:

Chapter 4, *Setting Up BIND*

forwarders

Function:

Defines name server(s) to send unresolved queries to

Syntax:
```
forwarders ip-address-list
```
Example:
```
forwarders 192.249.249.1 192.249.249.3
```

See also:
    8.X.X `options` statement, `forwarders`

Covered in:
    Chapter 10, *Advanced Features and Security*

sortlist

Function:
    Specifies network numbers to prefer over others

Syntax:
    `sortlist` `network-list`
Example:
    `sortlist 10.0.0.0`
See also:
    This feature is not supported in version 8.X.X

Covered in:
    Chapter 10, *Advanced Features and Security*

slave

This statement is the same as the 4.9.3 statement `options forward-only` and the 8.X.X `options` statement `forward`.

include (4.9.3)

Function:
    Includes the contents of another file in *named.boot*

Syntax:
    `include` `file`
Example:
    `include bootfile.primary`
See also:
    8.X.X `include` statement

Covered in:
    Chapter 7, *Maintaining BIND*

stub (4.9.3)

Function:
    Specifies a child zone that your server should periodically get delegation information for

Syntax:

```
stub domain ip-address-list [backup-file]
```

Example:

```
stub movie.edu 192.249.249.3 stub.movie
```

See also:

8.X.X zone statement, type stub

Covered in:

Chapter 9, *Parenting*

options (4.9.3)

options forward-only

Function:

Prevents your name server from resolving domain names independently of a forwarder

See also:

8.X.X option statement, forward

Covered in:

Chapter 10, *Advanced Features and Security*

options no-recursion

Function:

Prevents your name server from performing recursive resolution of domain names

See also:

8.X.X options statement, recursion

Covered in:

Chapter 10, *Advanced Features and Security*

options no-fetch-glue

Function:

Prevents your name server from fetching missing glue when constructing a response

See also:

8.X.X options statement, fetch-glue

Covered in:

Chapter 10, *Advanced Features and Security*

`options query-log`

Function:

Logs all queries received by your name server

See also:

8.X.X `logging` statement, `category queries`

Covered in:

Chapter 7, *Maintaining BIND* and Chapter 13, *Troubleshooting DNS and BIND*

`options fake-iquery`

Function:

Tells your name server to respond to old-fashioned inverse queries with a fake answer instead of an error

See also:

8.X.X `options` statement, `fake-iquery`

Covered in:

Chapter 11, *nslookup*

limit (4.9.3)

`limit transfers-in`

Function:

Restricts the total number of zone transfers your name server will attempt at any one time

See also:

8.X.X `options` statement, `transfers-in`

`limit transfers-per-ns`

Function:

Restricts the number of zone transfers your name server will request from any one server simultaneously

See also:

8.X.X `options` statement, `transfers-per-ns`

`limit datasize`

Function:

Increases the size of the data segment *named* uses (only works on some operating systems)

See also:

8.X.X options statement, `datasize`

All covered in:

Chapter 10, *Advanced Features and Security*

xfrnets (4.9.3)

Function:

Restricts zone transfers from your name server to a list of IP addresses or networks

Syntax:

    xfrnets *ip-address-or-network-list*
Example:

    xfrnets 15.0.0.0 128.32.0.0
See also:

8.X.X options statement, `allow-transfer`

Covered in:

Chapter 10, *Advanced Features and Security*

bogusns (4.9.3)

Function:

Tells your name server not to query a list of name servers that are known to give bad answers

Syntax:

    bogusns *ip-address-list*
Example:

    bogusns 15.255.152.4
See also:

8.X.X server statement, `bogus`

Covered in:

Chapter 10, *Advanced Features and Security*

check-names (4.9.4)

Function:

Modifies the name-checking feature

Syntax:

    check-names *primary/secondary/response fail/warn/ignore*
Example:

    check-names primary ignore

See also:

8.X.X `options` statement, `check-names`

Covered in:

Chapter 4, *Setting Up BIND*

acl (8.X.X)

Function:

Creates a named address match list

Syntax:

```
acl name {
    address_match_list
};
```

Covered in:

Chapter 10, *Advanced Features and Security*

include (8.X.X)

Function:

Inserts the specified file at the point that the `include` statement is encountered

Syntax:

```
include path_name;
```

Covered in:

Chapter 7, *Maintaining BIND*

key (8.1.1)

Function:

Defines a key ID which can be used in a `server` statement to associate an authentication method with a particular name server. The `key` statement is intended for future use by the server. In version 8.1.1, it is checked for syntax but is otherwise ignored

Syntax:

```
key key_id {
  algorithm algorithm_id;
  secret secret_string;
};
```

logging (8.X.X)

Function:

Defines the logging behavior

Syntax:

```
logging {
  [ channel channel_name {
    ( file path_name
       [ versions ( number | unlimited ) ]
       [ size size_spec ]
     | syslog ( kern | user | mail | daemon | auth | syslog | lpr |
                news | uucp | cron | authpriv | ftp |
                local0 | local1 | local2 | local3 |
                local4 | local5 | local6 | local7 )
     | null );

    [ severity ( critical | error | warning | notice |
                 info | debug [ level ] | dynamic ); ]
    [ print-category yes_or_no; ]
    [ print-severity yes_or_no; ]
    [ print-time yes_or_no; ]
  }; ]

  [ category category_name {
    channel_name; [ channel_name; ... ]
  }; ]
  ...
};
```

Covered in:

Chapter 7, *Maintaining BIND*

options (8.X.X)

Function:

Sets up global options

Syntax:

```
options {
  [ directory path_name; ]
  [ named-xfer path_name; ]
  [ dump-file path_name; ]
  [ pid-file path_name; ]
  [ statistics-file path_name; ]
  [ auth-nxdomain yes_or_no; ]
  [ fake-iquery yes_or_no; ]
  [ fetch-glue yes_or_no; ]
  [ multiple-cnames yes_or_no; ]
  [ notify yes_or_no; ]
  [ recursion yes_or_no; ]
  [ forward ( only | first ); ]
  [ forwarders { [ in_addr ; [ in_addr ; ... ] ] }; ]
  [ check-names ( master | slave | response ) ( warn | fail | ignore);]
  [ allow-query { address_match_list }; ]
  [ allow-transfer { address_match_list }; ]
  [ listen-on [ port ip_port ] { address_match_list }; ]
  [ query-source [ address ( ip_addr | * ) ] [ port ( ip_port | * ) ];]
```

```
      [ max-transfer-time-in number; ]
      [ transfer-format ( one-answer | many-answers ); ]
      [ transfers-in  number; ]
      [ transfers-out number; ]
      [ transfers-per-ns number; ]
      [ coresize size_spec ; ]
      [ datasize size_spec ; ]
      [ files size_spec ; ]
      [ stacksize size_spec ; ]
      [ cleaning-interval number; ]
      [ interface-interval number; ]
      [ statistics-interval number; ]
      [ topology { address_match_list }; ]
    };
```

Covered in:

> Chapter 4, *Setting Up BIND*
>
> Chapter 10, *Advanced Features and Security*
>
> Chapter 15, *Miscellaneous*

server (8.X.X)

Function:

> Defines the characteristics to be associated with a remote name server

Syntax:

```
    server ip_addr {
      [ bogus yes_or_no; ]
      [ transfers number; ]
      [ transfer-format ( one-answer | many-answers
    ); ]
      [ keys { key_id [key_id ... ] }; ]
    };
```

Covered in:

> Chapter 10, *Advanced Features and Security*

zone (8.X.X)

Function:

> Defines the zones maintained by the name server

Syntax:

```
    zone domain_name [ ( in | hs | hesiod | chaos )
    ] {
      type master;
      file path_name;
      [ check-names ( warn | fail | ignore ); ]
      [ allow-update { address_match_list }; ]
      [ allow-query { address_match_list }; ]
      [ allow-transfer { address_match_list }; ]
      [ notify yes_or_no; ]
```

```
    [ also-notify { ip_addr; [ ip_addr; ... ] };
  };

  zone domain_name [ ( in | hs | hesiod | chaos )
  ] {
    type ( slave | stub );
    [ file path_name; ]
    masters { ip_addr; [ ip_addr; ... ] };
    [ check-names ( warn | fail | ignore ); ]
    [ allow-update { address_match_list }; ]
    [ allow-query { address_match_list }; ]
    [ allow-transfer { address_match_list }; ]
    [ max-transfer-time-in number; ]
    [ notify yes_or_no; ]
    [ also-notify { ip_addr; [ ip_addr; ... ] };
  };

  zone "." [ ( in | hs | hesiod | chaos ) ] {
    type hint;
    file path_name;
    [ check-names ( warn | fail | ignore ); ]
  };
```

Covered in:

Chapter 4, *Setting Up BIND*

Chapter 10, *Advanced Features and Security*

BIND Resolver Statements

The following statements are for the resolver configuration file, */etc/resolv.conf.*

domain

Function:

Defines your resolver's default domain

Syntax:

```
domain domain-name
```
Example:
```
domain corp.hp.com
```
Covered in:

Chapter 6, *Configuring Hosts*

search (4.8.3 and later versions)

Function:

Defines your resolver's default domain and search list

Syntax:

```
search default-domain next-domain-in-search-list
... last-domain- in-search-list
```

Example:
```
search corp.hp.com pa.itc.hp.com hp.com
```
Covered in:
Chapter 6, *Configuring Hosts*

nameserver

Function:
Tells your resolver to query a particular name server

Syntax:
```
nameserver IP-address
```
Example:
```
nameserver 15.255.152.4
```
Covered in:
Chapter 6, *Configuring Hosts*

; and # (4.9.3 and later versions)

Function:
Adds a comment to the resolver configuration file

Syntax:
```
; free-format-comment
```
or
```
# free-format-comment
```
Example:
```
# Added parent domain to search list for compatibility
with 4.8.3
```
Covered in:
Chapter 6, *Configuring Hosts*

sortlist (4.9.3 and later versions)

Function:
Specifies network numbers for your resolver to prefer

Syntax:
```
sortlist network-list
```
Example:
```
sortlist 128.32.4.0/255.255.255.0 15.0.0.0
```
Covered in:
Chapter 6, *Configuring Hosts*

options ndots (4.9.3 and later versions)

Function:

Specifies the number of dots an argument must have in it so that the resolver will look it up before applying the search list

Syntax:

```
options ndots:number-of-dots
```

Example:

```
options ndots:1
```

Covered in:

Chapter 6, *Configuring Hosts*

options debug (4.9.3 and later versions)

Function:

Turns on debugging output in the resolver

Syntax:

```
options debug
```

Example:

```
options debug
```

Covered in:

Chapter 6, *Configuring Hosts*

Index

Symbols

* wildcard, 378
@ notation, 73, 415
. (dot)
    default domain and, 101
    ndots option, 109, 466
    root domain, 4, 11, 68–70
    trailing in domain names, 12, 62, 73,
        314, 414
(hash mark) for comments, 70, 110
( ) (parentheses), 62, 415
; (semicolon) for comments, 110, 415, 465
/* */ comments, 70
// comments, 70

Numbers

/8, /16, /24 networks, subnetting, 215–218

A

A records, 64, 415
    queries statistic, 167
aa (authoritative answer) bit, 219
AAAA records, 407
abbreviations in db files, 73–76
ABRT signal, 165
access
    to name servers (see resolvers)
    rlogin and rsh fail access check, 331
    to services, denied, 331
acl statement, 227
ACLs (access control lists), 227

adding
    domains, 91
    hosts, 134, 311
    name servers, 181–186
    slave name servers, 213–214
    subdomains, 204–214
additional section, DNS packet, 273, 306,
        345, 430
addresses
    A records, 64, 415
    address match lists, 227–228
    address type, 17
    administrators', 62
    IPv6, 407
    ISDN, 404, 423
    local, 83
    loopback, 67, 106
    mapping names to, 63–65
    mapping to names, 30–33, 65
    in MX records, 97
    no PTR data for, 279, 311
    queries statistic, 167
    registering network numbers, 53–57
    searching for, 40
    shuffle address records, 259
    sorting, 63, 240, 243
    X.121, 404
    zero address, 106
administration, xiv
    avoiding bogus name servers, 249
    capacity planning, 176–181
    checking delegation, 218, 222–223, 318

About the Authors

Paul Albitz is a software engineer at Hewlett-Packard. Paul earned a Bachelor of Science degree from the University of Wisconsin, LaCrosse, and a Master of Science degree from Purdue University.

Paul worked on BIND for the HP-UX 7.0 and 8.0 releases. During this time he developed the tools used to run the *hp.com* domain. Since then Paul has worked on networking HP's DesignJet plotter and on the fax subsystem of HP's OfficeJet multifunction peripheral. Before joining HP, Paul was a system administrator in the CS Department of Purdue University. As system administrator, he ran versions of BIND before BIND's initial release with 4.3 BSD. Paul and his wife Katherine live in San Diego, CA.

Cricket Liu matriculated at the University of California's Berkeley campus, that great bastion of free speech, unencumbered UNIX, and cheap pizza. He joined Hewlett-Packard after graduation and worked for HP for nine years.

Cricket began managing the *hp.com* domain after the Loma Prieta earthquake forcibly moved the domain's management from HP Labs to HP's Corporate Offices. He was *hostmaster@hp.com* for over three years, and then joined HP's Professional Services Organization to found HP's Internet consulting program.

Cricket currently runs his own Internet consulting and training company, Acme Byte and Wire, with his friend (and now co-author) Matt Larson.

Cricket, his wife, Paige, and their son, Walt, live in Colorado with two Siberian Huskies, Annie and Dakota. On warm weekend afternoons, you'll probably find them on the flying trapeze.

Colophon

Our look is the result of reader comments, our own experimentation, and feedback from distribution channels. Distinctive covers complement our distinctive approach to technical topics, breathing personality and life into potentially dry subjects. UNIX and its attendant programs can be unruly beasts. Nutshell Handbooks help you tame them.

The insects featured on the cover of *DNS and BIND* are grasshoppers. Grasshoppers are found all over the globe. Of over 5000 species, 100 different grasshopper species are found in North America. Grasshoppers are greenish-brown, and range in length from a half inch to four inches, with wingspans of up to six inches. Their bodies are divided into three sections: the head, thorax, and abdomen, with three pairs of legs and two pairs of wings.

Male grasshoppers use their hind legs and forewings to produce a "chirping" sound. Their hind legs have a ridge of small pegs that are rubbed across a hardened vein in the forewing, causing an audible vibration much like a bow being drawn across a string.

Grasshoppers are major crop pests, particularly when they collect in swarms. A single grasshopper can consume 30mg of food a day. In collections of 50 or more grasshoppers per square yard—a density often reached during grasshopper outbreaks—grasshoppers consume as much as a cow would per acre. In addition to consuming foliage, grasshoppers damage plants by attacking them at vulnerable points and causing the stems to break off.

Ellie Fountain Maden was the production editor and copy editor for *DNS & BIND, Third Edition*; Sheryl Avruch was the production manager. Melanie Wang performed the proofread, and Madeleine Newell and Nicole Gipson Arigo provided quality control. The content was formatted from SGML into FrameMaker 5.5 with Jade, using a DSSSL conversion stylesheet written by Chris Maden. The inside layout uses ITC Garamond Light and ITC Garamond Book fonts, and was designed by Nancy Priest and Edie Freedman. Additional tools support was provided by Mike Sierra and Don Ohl. The figures were created in Adobe Photoshop 5 and Macromedia Freehand 7 by Robert Romano. Seth Maislin wrote the index. This colophon was written by Clairemarie Fisher O'Leary.

Edie Freedman designed the cover of this book, using a 19th-century engraving from the Dover Pictorial Archive. The cover layout was produced with Quark XPress 3.3 using the ITC Garamond font. Whenever possible, our books use Rep-Kover™, a durable and flexible lay-flat binding. If the page count exceeds Rep-Kover's limit, perfect binding is used.

More Titles from O'Reilly

Network Administration

Virtual Private Networks

By *Charlie Scott, Paul Wolfe &
Mike Erwin*
1st Edition February 1998
184 pages, ISBN 1-56592-319-7

This book tells you how to plan and
build a Virtual Private Network (VPN),
a collection of technologies that creates
secure connections or "tunnels" over
regular Internet lines. It starts with general
concerns like costs and configuration and continues with detailed
descriptions of how to install and use VPN technologies that are
available for Windows NT and UNIX, such as PPTP and L2TP, the
AltaVista Tunnel, and the Cisco PIX Firewall.

TCP/IP Network Administration, 2nd Edition

By *Craig Hunt*
2nd Edition December 1997
630 pages, ISBN 1-56592-322-7

A complete guide to setting up and
running a TCP/IP network for practicing
system administrators. Beyond basic
setup, this new second edition discusses
the Internet routing protocols and
provides a tutorial on how to configure
important network services. It now also includes Linux in
addition to BSD and System V TCP/IP implementations.

Networking Personal Computers with TCP/IP

By *Craig Hunt*
1st Edition July 1995
408 pages, ISBN 1-56592-123-2

This book offers practical information as
well as detailed instructions for attaching
PCs to a TCP/IP network and its UNIX
servers. It discusses the challenges you'll
face and offers general advice on how to
deal with them, provides basic TCP/IP
configuration information for some of the popular PC operating
systems, covers advanced configuration topics and configuration
of specific applications such as email, and includes a chapter on
on integrating Netware with TCP/IP.

sendmail, 2nd Edition

By *Bryan Costales & Eric Allman*
2nd Edition January 1997
1050 pages, ISBN 1-56592-222-0

sendmail, 2nd Edition, covers sendmail
Version 8.8 from Berkeley and the standard
versions available on most systems. This
cross-referenced edition offers an expanded
tutorial, solution-oriented examples, and
new topics such as the #error delivery
agent, sendmail's exit values, MIME headers, and how to set up
and use the user database, *mailertable*, and *smrsh*.

Cracking DES

By *Electronic Frontier Foundation*
1st Edition July 1998
272 pages, ISBN 1-56592-520-3

The Data Encryption Standard withstood
the test of time for twenty years. *Cracking
DES: Secrets of Encryption Research, Wiretap
Politics & Chip Design* shows exactly how
it was brought down. Every cryptographer,
security designer, and student of cryptogra-
phy policy should read this book to understand how the world
changed as it fell.

The Networking CD Bookshelf

By *O'Reilly & Associates, Inc.*
1st Edition March 1999
Features CD-ROM
ISBN 1-56592-523-8

Network administrator alert! Six bestselling
O'Reilly Animal Guides are now available
on CD-ROM, easily accessible with your
favorite Web browser: *TCP/IP Network
Administration, 2nd Edition*; *sendmail,
2nd Edition*; *sendmail Desktop Reference*; *DNS and BIND, 3rd
Edition*; *Practical UNIX & Internet Security, 2nd Edition*; and
Building Internet Firewalls. As a bonus, the new hardcopy version
of *DNS and BIND* is also included.

Network Administration

Using & Managing PPP

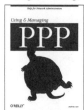

By Andrew Sun
1st Edition March 1999
444 pages, ISBN 1-56592-321-9

This book is for network administrators and others who have to set up computer systems to use PPP. It covers all aspects of the protocol, including how to set up dial-in servers, authentication, debugging, and PPP options. In addition, it contains overviews of related areas, like serial communications, DNS setup, and routing.

Managing IP Networks with Cisco Routers

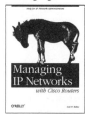

By Scott M. Ballew
1st Edition October 1997
352 pages, ISBN 1-56592-320-0

This practical guide to setting up and maintaining a production network covers how to select routing protocols, configure protocols to handle most common situations, evaluate network equipment and vendors, and setup a help desk. Although it focuses on Cisco routers, and gives examples using Cisco's IOS, the principles discussed are common to all IP networks.

Protecting Networks with SATAN

By Martin Freiss
1st Edition May 1998
128 pages, ISBN 1-56592-425-8

SATAN performs "security audits," scanning host computers for security vulnerabilities. This book describes how to install and use SATAN, and how to adapt it to local requirements and increase its knowledge of specific security vulnerabilities.

Managing Mailing Lists

By Alan Schwartz
1st Edition March 1998
288 pages, ISBN 1-56592-259-X

Mailing lists are an ideal vehicle for creating email-based electronic communities. This book covers four mailing list packages (Majordomo, LISTSERV, ListProcessor, and SmartList) and tells you everything you need to know to set up and run a mailing list, from writing the charter to dealing with bounced messages. It discusses creating moderated lists, controlling who can subscribe to a list, offering digest subscriptions, and archiving list postings.

Managing Usenet

By Henry Spencer & David Lawrence
1st Edition December 1997
512 pages, ISBN 1-56592-198-4

Usenet, also called Netnews, is the world's largest discussion forum, and it is doubling in size every year. This book, written by two of the foremost authorities on Usenet administration, contains everything you need to know to administer a Netnews system. It covers C News and INN, explains the basics of starting a Netnews system, and offers guidelines to help ensure that your system is capable of handling news volume today—and in the future.

System Administration

Volume 8: X Window System Administrator's Guide

By Linda Mui & Eric Pearce
1st Edition October 1992
372 pages, ISBN 0-937175-83-8

This book focuses on issues of system administration for X and X-based networks —not just for UNIX system administrators, but for anyone faced with the job of administering X (including those running X on stand-alone workstations).

System Administration

Essential System Administration

By Æleen Frisch
2nd Edition September 1995
788 pages, ISBN 1-56592-127-5

Thoroughly revised and updated for all major versions of UNIX, this second edition of *Essential System Administration* provides a compact, manageable introduction to the tasks faced by everyone responsible for a UNIX system. Whether you use a stand-alone UNIX system, routinely provide administrative support for a larger shared system, or just want an understanding of basic administrative functions, this book is for you. Offers expanded sections on networking, electronic mail, security, and kernel configuration.

System Performance Tuning

By Mike Loukides
1st Edition November 1990
336 pages, ISBN 0-937175-60-9

System Performance Tuning answers the fundamental question: How can I get my UNIX-based computer to do more work without buying more hardware? Some performance problems do require you to buy a bigger or faster computer, but many can be solved simply by making better use of the resources you already have.

Using Samba

By Peter Kelly, Perry Donham &
David Collier-Brown
1st Edition July 1999 (est.)
300 pages (est.), Includes CD-ROM
ISBN 1-56592-449-5

Samba turns a UNIX or Linux system into a file and print server for Microsoft Windows network clients. This complete guide to Samba administration covers basic 2.0 configuration, security, logging, and troubleshooting. Whether you're playing on one note or a full three-octave range, this book will help you maintain an efficient and secure server. Includes a CD-ROM of sources and ready-to-install binaries.

termcap & terminfo

By John Strang, Linda Mui & Tim O'Reilly
3rd Edition April 1988
270 pages, ISBN 0-937175-22-6

For UNIX system administrators and programmers. This handbook provides information on writing and debugging terminal descriptions, as well as terminal initialization, for the two UNIX terminal databases.

Managing NFS and NIS

By Hal Stern
1st Edition June 1991
436 pages, ISBN 0-937175-75-7

Managing NFS and NIS is for system administrators who need to set up or manage a network filesystem installation. NFS (Network Filesystem) is probably running at any site that has two or more UNIX systems. NIS (Network Information System) is a distributed database used to manage a network of computers. The only practical book devoted entirely to these subjects, this guide is a "must-have" for anyone interested in UNIX networking.

How to stay in touch with O'Reilly

1. Visit Our Award-Winning Web Site

http://www.oreilly.com/

★ "Top 100 Sites on the Web" —*PC Magazine*
★ "Top 5% Web sites" —*Point Communications*
★ "3-Star site" —*The McKinley Group*

Our web site contains a library of comprehensive product information (including book excerpts and tables of contents), downloadable software, background articles, interviews with technology leaders, links to relevant sites, book cover art, and more. File us in your Bookmarks or Hotlist!

2. Join Our Email Mailing Lists

New Product Releases
To receive automatic email with brief descriptions of all new O'Reilly products as they are released, send email to:
listproc@online.oreilly.com
Put the following information in the first line of your message (*not* in the Subject field):
subscribe oreilly-news

O'Reilly Events
If you'd also like us to send information about trade show events, special promotions, and other O'Reilly events, send email to:
listproc@online.oreilly.com
Put the following information in the first line of your message (*not* in the Subject field):
subscribe oreilly-events

3. Get Examples from Our Books via FTP

There are two ways to access an archive of example files from our books:

Regular FTP
- ftp to:
  ftp.oreilly.com
  (login: anonymous
  password: your email address)
- Point your web browser to:
  ftp://ftp.oreilly.com/

FTPMAIL
- Send an email message to:
  ftpmail@online.oreilly.com
  (Write "help" in the message body)

4. Contact Us via Email

order@oreilly.com
To place a book or software order online. Good for North American and international customers.

subscriptions@oreilly.com
To place an order for any of our newsletters or periodicals.

books@oreilly.com
General questions about any of our books.

software@oreilly.com
For general questions and product information about our software. Check out O'Reilly Software Online at **http://software.oreilly.com/** for software and technical support information. Registered O'Reilly software users send your questions to: **website-support@oreilly.com**

cs@oreilly.com
For answers to problems regarding your order or our products.

booktech@oreilly.com
For book content technical questions or corrections.

proposals@oreilly.com
To submit new book or software proposals to our editors and product managers.

international@oreilly.com
For information about our international distributors or translation queries. For a list of our distributors outside of North America check out:
http://www.oreilly.com/www/order/country.html

O'Reilly & Associates, Inc.
101 Morris Street, Sebastopol, CA 95472 USA
TEL   707-829-0515 or 800-998-9938
        (6am to 5pm PST)
FAX   707-829-0104

Titles from O'Reilly

International Distributors

UK, EUROPE, MIDDLE EAST AND AFRICA (EXCEPT FRANCE, GERMANY, AUSTRIA, SWITZERLAND, LUXEMBOURG, LIECHTENSTEIN, AND EASTERN EUROPE)

INQUIRIES
O'Reilly UK Limited
4 Castle Street
Farnham
Surrey, GU9 7HS
United Kingdom
Telephone: 44-1252-711776
Fax: 44-1252-734211
Email: josette@oreilly.com

ORDERS
Wiley Distribution Services Ltd.
1 Oldlands Way
Bognor Regis
West Sussex PO22 9SA
United Kingdom
Telephone: 44-1243-779777
Fax: 44-1243-820250
Email: cs-books@wiley.co.uk

FRANCE

ORDERS
GEODIF
61, Bd Saint-Germain
75240 Paris Cedex 05, France
Tel: 33-1-44-41-46-16 (French books)
Tel: 33-1-44-41-11-87 (English books)
Fax: 33-1-44-41-11-44
Email: distribution@eyrolles.com

INQUIRIES
Éditions O'Reilly
18 rue Séguier
75006 Paris, France
Tel: 33-1-40-51-52-30
Fax: 33-1-40-51-52-31
Email: france@editions-oreilly.fr

GERMANY, SWITZERLAND, AUSTRIA, EASTERN EUROPE, LUXEMBOURG, AND LIECHTENSTEIN

INQUIRIES & ORDERS
O'Reilly Verlag
Balthasarstr. 81
D-50670 Köln
Germany
Telephone: 49-221-973160-91
Fax: 49-221-973160-8
Email: anfragen@oreilly.de (inquiries)
Email: order@oreilly.de (orders)

CANADA (FRENCH LANGUAGE BOOKS)

Les Éditions Flammarion ltée
375, Avenue Laurier Ouest
Montréal (Québec) H2V 2K3
Tel: 00-1-514-277-8807
Fax: 00-1-514-278-2085
Email: info@flammarion.qc.ca

HONG KONG

City Discount Subscription Service, Ltd.
Unit D, 3rd Floor, Yan's Tower
27 Wong Chuk Hang Road
Aberdeen, Hong Kong
Tel: 852-2580-3539
Fax: 852-2580-6463
Email: citydis@ppn.com.hk

KOREA

Hanbit Media, Inc.
Sonyoung Bldg. 202
Yeksam-dong 736-36
Kangnam-ku
Seoul, Korea
Tel: 822-554-9610
Fax: 822-556-0363
Email: hant93@chollian.dacom.co.kr

PHILIPPINES

Mutual Books, Inc.
429-D Shaw Boulevard
Mandaluyong City, Metro
Manila, Philippines
Tel: 632-725-7538
Fax: 632-721-3056
Email: mbikikog@mnl.sequel.net

TAIWAN

O'Reilly Taiwan
No. 3, Lane 131
Hang-Chow South Road
Section 1, Taipei, Taiwan
Tel: 886-2-23968990
Fax: 886-2-23968916
Email: benh@oreilly.com

CHINA

O'Reilly Beijing
Room 2410
160, FuXingMenNeiDaJie
XiCheng District
Beijing, China PR 100031
Tel: 86-10-86631006
Fax: 86-10-86631007
Email: frederic@oreilly.com

INDIA

Computer Bookshop (India) Pvt. Ltd.
190 Dr. D.N. Road, Fort
Bombay 400 001 India
Tel: 91-22-207-0989
Fax: 91-22-262-3551
Email: cbsbom@giasbm01.vsnl.net.in

JAPAN

O'Reilly Japan, Inc.
Kiyoshige Building 2F
12-Bancho, Sanei-cho
Shinjuku-ku
Tokyo 160-0008 Japan
Tel: 81-3-3356-5227
Fax: 81-3-3356-5261
Email: japan@oreilly.com

ALL OTHER ASIAN COUNTRIES

O'Reilly & Associates, Inc.
101 Morris Street
Sebastopol, CA 95472 USA
Tel: 707-829-0515
Fax: 707-829-0104
Email: order@oreilly.com

AUSTRALIA

WoodsLane Pty., Ltd.
7/5 Vuko Place
Warriewood NSW 2102
Australia
Tel: 61-2-9970-5111
Fax: 61-2-9970-5002
Email: info@woodslane.com.au

NEW ZEALAND

Woodslane New Zealand, Ltd.
21 Cooks Street (P.O. Box 575)
Waganui, New Zealand
Tel: 64-6-347-6543
Fax: 64-6-345-4840
Email: info@woodslane.com.au

LATIN AMERICA

McGraw-Hill Interamericana
Editores, S.A. de C.V.
Cedro No. 512
Col. Atlampa
06450, Mexico, D.F.
Tel: 52-5-547-6777
Fax: 52-5-547-3336
Email: mcgraw-hill@infosel.net.mx

O'REILLY™

O'Reilly & Associates, Inc.
101 Morris Street
Sebastopol, CA 95472-9902
1-800-998-9938

Visit us online at:
**http://www.ora.com/
orders@ora.com**

O'REILLY WOULD LIKE TO HEAR FROM YOU

Which book did this card come from?

_____

Where did you buy this book?
- ❏ Bookstore   ❏ Computer Store
- ❏ Direct from O'Reilly   ❏ Class/seminar
- ❏ Bundled with hardware/software
- ❏ Other _____

What operating system do you use?
- ❏ UNIX   ❏ Macintosh
- ❏ Windows NT   ❏ PC(Windows/DOS)
- ❏ Other _____

What is your job description?
- ❏ System Administrator   ❏ Programmer
- ❏ Network Administrator   ❏ Educator/Teacher
- ❏ Web Developer
- ❏ Other _____

❏ Please send me O'Reilly's catalog, containing a complete listing of O'Reilly books and software.

Name _____   Company/Organization _____

Address _____

City _____   State _____   Zip/Postal Code _____   Country _____

Telephone _____   Internet or other email address (specify network) _____

Nineteenth century wood engraving
of a bear from the O'Reilly &
Associates Nutshell Handbook®
Using & Managing UUCP.

BUSINESS REPLY MAIL
FIRST CLASS MAIL   PERMIT NO. 80   SEBASTOPOL, CA

Postage will be paid by addressee

O'Reilly & Associates, Inc.
101 Morris Street
Sebastopol, CA 95472-9902